The Colombian Peace Agreement

A Multidisciplinary Assessment

Edited by Jorge Luis Fabra-Zamora, Andrés Molina-Ochoa, and Nancy C. Doubleday

Routledge
Taylor & Francis Group
LONDON AND NEW YORK

First published 2021
by Routledge
2 Park Square, Milton Park, Abingdon, Oxon OX14 4RN

and by Routledge
605 Third Avenue, New York, NY 10158

Routledge is an imprint of the Taylor & Francis Group, an informa business

British Library Cataloguing-in-Publication Data
A catalogue record for this book is available from the British Library

Library of Congress Cataloging-in-Publication Data
Names: Fabra Zamora, Jorge Luis, editor. | Molina-Ochoa, Andrés, 1974- editor. | Doubleday, Nancy, 1951- editor.
Title: The Colombian Peace Agreement : a multidisciplinary assessment / edited by Jorge Luis Fabra Zamora, Andrés Molina-Ochoa, Nancy C. Doubleday.
Description: Milton Park, Abingdon, Oxon ; New York, NY : Routledge, 2021. | Series: Routledge studies in peace and conflict resolution | Includes bibliographical references and index.
Identifiers: LCCN 2020048696 (print) | LCCN 2020048697 (ebook) | ISBN 9780367528812 (hardback) | ISBN 9781003079743 (ebook)
Subjects: LCSH: Peace-building--Law and legislation--Colombia. | Acuerdo final para la terminación del conflicto y la construcción de una paz estable y duradera (2016 November 24) | Fuerzas Armadas Revolucionarias de Colombia. | Transitional justice--Colombia. | War victims--Legal status, laws, etc.--Colombia. | Insurgency--Colombia--History. | Colombia--Politics and government--1974- Classification: LCC KHH2921 .C6455 2021 (print) | LCC KHH2921 (ebook) | DDC 986.106/35--dc23
LC record available at https://lccn.loc.gov/2020048696
LC ebook record available at https://lccn.loc.gov/2020048697

ISBN: 978-0-367-52881-2 (hbk)
ISBN: 978-0-367-52886-7 (pbk)
ISBN: 978-1-003-07974-3 (ebk)

Typeset in Times New Roman
by MPS Limited, Dehradun

The Colombian Peace Agreement

This book is the first systematic, interdisciplinary examination of the peace agreement signed between the Colombian Government and the Revolutionary Armed Forces of Colombia to end one of the largest and most violent conflicts in the Western Hemisphere. It discusses the achievements, failures, and challenges of this innovative peace agreement and its implications for Colombia's future. Contributors include negotiators of the Agreement, judges of the Special Jurisdiction for Peace, representatives of the civil society, and leading academic experts in peace studies, human rights, international law, criminal law, transitional justice, political science, and philosophy. Based on the premise that peace is a form of transferable social knowledge, and therefore necessitates transformative social learning, the volume also discusses what other countries can learn from the Colombian experience.

This book will be of much interest to students of peace and conflict studies, transitional justice, Latin American politics, human rights, civil wars and International Relations.

Jorge Luis Fabra-Zamora is a Provost's postdoctoral fellow at the Faculty of Law, University of Toronto, Canada.

Andrés Molina-Ochoa is an assistant professor of philosophy at South Texas College, USA.

Nancy C. Doubleday is an associate professor in philosophy and the inaugural holder of the HOPE Chair in Peace and Health at McMaster University, Canada. She is the director of the Water Without Borders Joint Graduate Diploma Program of McMaster University and UNU INWEH.

Routledge Studies in Peace and Conflict Resolution

The field of peace and conflict research has grown enormously as an academic pursuit in recent years, gaining credibility and relevance amongst policy makers and in the international humanitarian and NGO sector. The *Routledge Studies in Peace and Conflict Resolution* series aims to provide an outlet for some of the most significant new work emerging from this academic community, and to establish itself as a leading platform for innovative work at the point where peace and conflict research impacts on International Relations theory and processes.

Series Editors: Tom Woodhouse and Oliver Ramsbotham
University of Bradford

Root Narrative Theory and Conflict Resolution
Power, Justice and Values
Solon Simmons

Healing and Peacebuilding After War
Transforming Trauma in Bosnia and Herzegovina
Edited by Julianne Funk, Nancy Good and Marie E. Berry

Multi-level Reconciliation and Peacebuilding
Stakeholder Perspectives
Edited by Kevin P. Clements and SungYong Lee

Conflict Resolution after the Pandemic
Building Peace, Pursuing Justice
Edited by Richard E. Rubenstein and Solon Simmons

For more information about this series, please visit: https://www.routledge.com/Routledge-Studies-in-Peace-and-Conflict-Resolution/book-series/RSPCR

Contents

Figures

Abbreviations

AFRIDES	The Afro-Colombian National Association for Displaced People
AP	Additional Protocol to the Geneva Conventions
AUC	*Autodefensas Unidas de Colombia*, United Self-Defences of Colombia
BACRIM	*Bandas Criminales*, Criminal Bands
CAJAR	*Corporación Colectivo de Abogados José Alvear Restrepo*, Lawyers Collective Corporation José Alvear Restrepo
CCJ	*Comisión Colombiana de Juristas*, Colombian Commission of Jurists
CODHES	*Consultoría para los derechos humanos y el desplazamiento*, Consultancy for Human Rights and Displacement
Comprehensive System	*Sistema Integral para la Verdad, Justicia y la No Repetición* (SIVJRNR) Comprehensive System for Truth, Justice, Reparations and Non-Recurrence.
DDR	Disarmament, Demobilization and Reintegration
ELN	*Ejército de Liberación Nacional*, National Liberation Army
EPL	*Ejército Popular de Liberación*, Popular Liberation Army
FARC-EP	*Fuerzas Armadas Revolucionarias de Colombia-Ejército del Pueblo*, Armed Revolutionary Forces of Colombia – People's Army
Final Agreement	Final Agreement to End the Armed Conflict and Build a Stable and Lasting Peace
GC	Geneva Convention
HRV	Human Rights Violations
IACHT	Inter-American Commission on Human Rights
IACtHR	Inter-American Court of Human Rights
ICC	International Criminal Court
ICJ	International Court of Justice

ICL	International Criminal Law
ICRC	International Committee of the Red Cross
IHL	International Humanitarian Law
IRR	Integral Rural Reform
JEP	*Jurisdicción Especial para la Paz*, Special Jurisdiction of Peace
LGTBI	Lesbian, Gay, Bisexual, Transgender, and Intersex
M-19	*Movimiento 19 de Abril*, 19th of April Movement
NGO	Non-Governmental Organization
OACP	*Oficina del Alto Comisionado para la Paz*, Office of the High Commissioner for Peace
OAS	Organization of American States
PDET	*Programa de Desarrollo con Enfoque Territorial*, Territorially-focussed rural development program
Search Unit	*Unidad de Búsqueda de Personas dadas por Desaparecidas en el contexto y en razón del conflicto armado* (UBPD) The Special Unit for the Search for Persons deemed as Disappeared the context of and due to the conflict
TJ	Transitional Justice
Truth Commission	*Comisión para el Esclarecimiento de la Verdad, la Convivencia y la No Repetición* (CEVCNR or CEV), Commission for the Clarification of Truth, Co-Existence and Non-Repetition
UN	United Nations
UNHCR	United Nations High Commissioner for Refugees
UNICEF	United Nations International Children's Emergency Fund
UNSC	United Nations Security Council
UP	*Unión Patriótica*, Patriotic Union

Contributors

Javier Aguirre is professor at Universidad Industrial de Santander (UIS) School of Philosophy in Bucaramanga, Colombia. He holds undergraduate degrees in law and philosophy from UIS, and MA and PhD degrees from the State University of New York, United States. He is a Member of Politeia, one of UIS's Research Groups.

Kai Ambos is chair for Criminal Law, Criminal Procedure, Comparative Law, International Criminal Law and International Law at the Faculty of Law of Georg-August-Universität Göttingen, Germany. He is also the director of the *Centro de Estudios de Derecho Penal y Procesal Penal Latinoamericano* (CEDPAL) at the same University. Furthermore, he is a judge at the Kosovo Specialist Chambers in The Hague (Netherlands) and an advisor (*amicus curiae*) of the Colombian Special Jurisdiction for Peace (JEP) in Bogotá. For his research, see https://www.department-ambos.uni-goettingen.de/ and https://www.cedpal.uni-goettingen.de/index.php.

Xiomara Cecilia Balanta-Moreno is Justice and the Vice-President of the Special Jurisdiction for Peace in Colombia. She holds a law degree from Universidad de San Buenaventura, Colombia, a Master of Law from the University of Notre Dame, and a magister on Human Rights and Democracy in Latin America from the Universidad Andina Simón Bolívar in Ecuador. She is currently a PhD candidate in Social and Legal Sciences from Universidad Rey Juan Carlos in Madrid, Spain.

Ryan E. Carlin is professor and director of the Center of Human Rights and Democracy at Georgia State University. His research explores the relationship between political behavior and quality of democracy. Carlin contributes to two global interdisciplinary research collaborations, the Executive Approval Project and Team Populism, and consults regularly for the Latin American Public Opinion Project. Regionally, he serves on the executive boards of the Southeast Latin American Behavior group and the Georgia Area Human Rights Network. He co-edits the *Revista Latinoamericana de Opinión Pública.*

Claudia Milena Díaz-Ríos is an assistant professor at the Ontario Institute for Studies of Education, University of Toronto. She holds a PhD in Political Science from McMaster University. Her research examines the globalization of education policy, education governance, and its effects on social inequality.

Nancy C. Doubleday is an associate professor in philosophy and the inaugural holder of the HOPE Chair in Peace and Health at McMaster University, is currently the director of Water Without Borders Graduate Diploma Program, McMaster University–UNU–INWEH. Specializing in complex social-cultural-ecological systems, she works at the interface of human rights and social justice, resilience, and sustainability to conceptualize policy syntheses and to design legal strategies for realizing peace, health and sustainability, through good governance, and knowledge integration.

Alfredo Duplat is an assistant professor of Spanish at Minnesota State University, Mankato. He holds a PhD in Spanish with a concentration in Latin American literature from the University of Iowa. He is a specialist in modern Latin American literature and culture, with a focus on cultural debates from the Cold War onward. His research focuses on the intersections between history, narrative fiction, and human rights in Latin America during the twentieth century.

Jon Elster is Robert K. Merton professor of the social sciences at Columbia University. His research interests include the theory of rational choice, the theory of distributive justice, and transitional justice.

Jorge Luis Fabra-Zamora is a Provost's postdoctoral fellow at the Faculty of Law, University of Toronto, Canada. He holds a PhD in philosophy from McMaster University and a law degree from Universidad de Cartagena in Cartagena, Colombia. His research focuses on philosophy of law, human rights, and the Colombian peace process.

Gustavo Gallón Giraldo is the founder and director of the Colombian Commission of Jurists, one of the most important institutions in defense of Colombian victims. Mr. Gallón has more than 30 years of experience as a human rights defender and a university professor of Public Law and Human Rights. Previously, Mr. Gallón had been the Special Representative of the United Nations' Commission on Human Rights for Equatorial Guinea (1999–2002) and was fourth Independent Expert of the Human Rights Council on the situation of human rights in Haiti (2013–17).

Roberto Gargarella is professor of Constitutional Theory and Political Philosophy at Universidad de Buenos Aires and a researcher for CONICET in Buenos Aires and the Christian Michelsen Institute in Norway. He received a John Simon Guggenheim grant in 2000 and a

Harry Frank Guggenheim grant in 2002–03 and has published on issues of legal and political philosophy, as well as on US and Latin American constitutionalism.

Juanita Goebertus Estrada is a Colombian congresswoman. Before becoming an elected official, she was the Head of the Transitional Justice Group at the Office of the High Commissioner for Peace of Colombia, during which time she was a member of the Government's Delegation in the Havana peace talks. Previously, she served as an advisor to the National Security Advisor, advisor to the Undersecretary of Defense, and Deputy Director of the Institute for Integrated Transitions.

Óscar Guardiola-Rivera teaches international law and international affairs at Birkbeck College, University of London. He has served as an aide to the Colombian Congress and as a consultant to the United Nations in South America. He has lectured in law, philosophy and politics on three continents, and is the author of *What if Latin America Ruled the World?: How the South Will Take the North into the 22ndCentury.*

Diana Isabel Güiza-Gómez is pursuing a joint PhD in peace studies and political science at the University of Notre Dame, affiliated to the Kroc Institute for International Peace Studies, the Kellogg Institute for International Studies, and the Violence and Transitional Justice Lab. She is a lawyer who holds an LLM from Universidad Nacional de Colombia. Previously, she was a researcher at the Center for the Study of Law, Justice and Society (Dejusticia) and a lecturer at Universidad Nacional de Colombia. Her research agenda relies upon land policies, peacebuilding, constitution-making, and political inclusion.

Sergio Jaramillo Caro is currently a senior advisor of the European Institute of Peace in Brussels. As National Security Advisor (2010–12), he led the secret negotiations with the country's largest guerrilla group, the Revolutionary Armed Forces of Colombia (FARC). He then served for five years as High Commissioner for Peace for Juan Manuel Santos, the 2016 Nobel Peace Prize laureate, between 2012 and 2016. Together with Humberto de la Calle, he led the public negotiations for four years in Havana. As Peace Commissioner, Mr. Jaramillo Caro also had to oversee the disarmament and demobilization process of the FARC, which ended in August 2017 when the UN verification mission extracted the last container with weapons from a FARC cantonment area.

Jennifer L. McCoy is professor of political science at Georgia State University and founder of the Democratic Insecurities Teaching and Research Group at GSU. She is former director of the Carter Center's Americas Program, 1998–2015, where she led projects on international mediation, democratic dialog, election monitoring, and peace negotiations. A specialist on Latin American politics, political polarization, and democratic backsliding, she is co-editor of *Polarizing Polities: A Global Threat to Democracy,* (*AAPSS,* January 2019) and co-author of *International Mediation in Venezuela* (USIP Press, 2011).

Andrés Molina-Ochoa is an Assistant Professor of philosophy at South Texas College. He has a PhD in philosophy from SUNY Binghamton and a law degree from Universidad del Rosario in Bogotá, Colombia. He is a specialist in Philosophy of Law, Human Rights, and Transitional Justice in Latin America.

Colleen Murphy is Roger and Stephany Joslin Professor of Law and Professor of Philosophy and Political Science at the University of Illinois at Urbana-Champaign, where she also serves as Director of the Women and Gender in Global Perspectives Program in the Illinois Global Institute. She holds a PhD in philosophy from the University of North Carolina. Her research and teaching focus on transitional justice, jurisprudence, and the ethics of risk regulation. She is the author of *A Moral Theory of Political Reconciliation* (Cambridge University Press, 2010) and *The Conceptual Foundations of Transitional Justice* (Cambridge University Press, 2017).

Juan Carlos Ospina is a legal advisor of Colombian Commission of Jurist and instructor at the Universidad de los Andes. He is a lawyer, with a specialization in 'Culture of Peace, Intercultural Dialogue and Social Cohesion,' a Master in Human Rights, and currently is a doctoral candidate in law at Universidad de Los Andes, Colombia.

Patricia Pabón is Professor Law at Universidad Autónoma de Bucaramanga, Colombia, Bucaramanga, Colombia and Leader of the Research Group on Legal Theory and Legal Foundations. She is a Doctor in Law, master's in legal Hermeneutics, and holds undergraduate degrees in law and philosophy.

Danilo Rojas Betancourth is Justice and President of the Appeal Section, Tribunal for Peace, Special Jurisdiction for Peace, and Professor of the Universidad Nacional de Colombia. He holds a law degree from Universidad Libre, and master's and doctoral degrees in law from Universidad Nacional de Colombia. He previously was a Justice in the Colombian Council of State. Prior to his judicial appointments, he worked as a consultant in human rights and public policy.

Yuri Alexander Romaña-Rivas works as lawyer at the Chamber for Amnesty and Pardon of the Special Jurisdiction for Peace (JEP) in Colombia. Previously, he worked as a Human Rights Specialist at the Inter-American Commission on Human Rights in Washington. Yuri holds law degrees from the Universidad Tecnológica del Chocó and a Master's in International Law and Legal Studies with emphasis on Human Rights from American University WCL at Washington DC, where he studied with a Fulbright Scholarship.

María Paula Saffon Sanín is a principal researcher from the Institute of Legal Research, Universidad Nacional Autonoma de Mexico. She holds a PhD in political science from Columbia University (2015), a *summa cum laude* law degree and a master's in law from Los Andes University (2005, 2006). Her fields of interest include comparative political history and institutions, social movements, property rights, democracy, violence, and transitions. Her publications include *Participation in Transitional Justice Measures: A Comparative Study* (with Viviana Tacha, Bogotá: Dejusticia, 2019); *Distributive Justice in Transitions* (co-ed. With Morten Bergsmo, César Rodríguez, Pablo Kalmanovitz, Oslo: FICHL, 2010); and "Property and Land," in *The Oxford Handbook of Constitutional Law in Latin America* (Gargarella and Hubner eds, 2020).

Nelson Camilo Sánchez is an assistant professor at the University of Virginia School of Law, where he serves as the director of the International Human Rights Law Clinic and as a co-director of the Center for International and Comparative Law. Before joining UVA in July 2018, he was a research director at the Center for the Study of Law, Justice and Society (Dejusticia), and associate professor of law at Universidad Nacional de Colombia, in Bogota. His research focuses on justice in post-conflict scenarios; land governance and peacebuilding, and the role of international human rights law in the Colombian transitional justice process.

Jelena Subotic is a professor of political science at Georgia State University. She is the author of *Hijacked Justice: Dealing with the Past in the Balkans* (Cornell UP, 2009) and *Yellow Star, Red Star: Holocaust* Remembrance *after Communism* (Cornell UP, 2019) and numerous scholarly articles on international relations theory, memory politics, and transitional justice.

Rodrigo Uprimny-Yepes is professor emeritus of the National University of Colombia, founding partner and senior researcher at Center for the Study of Law, Justice and Society (Dejusticia), and a member of the United Nations Economic, Social, and Cultural Rights Committee (2015–21). He holds a law degree of Universidad Externado, *Diplôme d'études approfondies* in Sociology of Development from Université Paris I (IEDES), Master's (DSU) in Sociology of Law from Université Paris, and PhD in economics from Université Amiens Picardie. His research agenda focuses on ESCR, transitional justice, constitutionalism, and drug policy.

Acknowledgments

Most of the papers in this book were initially discussed at the meeting hosted by the Hope Chair for Peace and Health at McMaster University in May 2017,[1] held under the auspices of the Bertrand Russell Research Centre, with the support of Participedia, and funded by the Social Sciences and Humanities Research Council and the Faculty of Humanities.

We thank his Excellency, Ambassador Nicolás Lloreda, for his participation and his important contributions to this seminal event. In addition to the book contributors, Adebsi Alade, Paul Emiljanowicz, Juan Carlos Forero, Matthew Grellete, Nicholas Griffin, Laura Sofia Guevara-Espitia, Gregory Hooks, Bonny Ibhawoh, Miguel Alberto Londoño-Gómez, Sarah Newell, Nidhi Nagabhatla, Ana María-Rodríguez Alfonso, Jorge Sánchez-Pérez, Vanessa Watts, and Niko Yiannakoulias participated in the meeting and contributed to the discussion of the papers, and we are grateful to all.

Nancy C. Doubleday acknowledges the Hope Chair in Peace and Health endowed by Aventis Pharma Inc., which made possible that initial conference. She also thanks to the Office of the President, the Dean of Humanities, and the Director of the Bertrand Russell Research Centre (BRRC) at McMaster for their active support. A special note of thanks is due to Peter Mascher, Vice-Provost International Affairs, for his active involvement and for hosting the visit of the Ambassador of Colombia to Canada, on the occasion of the conference.

Jorge Luis Fabra-Zamora thanks the support of the University of Toronto Provost's Postdoctoral Fellowship and the University of Toronto Faculty of Law.

Andrés Molina-Ochoa thanks the support of South Texas College.

Finally, we acknowledge the Colombian people for their struggles for peace, and for all that they have achieved.

Note

1 https://brighterworld.mcmaster.ca/articles/conference-explores-what-canada-can-learn-from-the-colombian-peace-process/.

1 Introduction

Jorge Luis Fabra-Zamora, Andrés Molina-Ochoa, and Nancy C. Doubleday

Objective

After a prolonged and intricate process, the Colombian government and the *Fuerzas Armadas Revolucionarias de Colombia—Ejército del Pueblo* (FARC-EP, Revolutionary Armed Forces of Colombia—People's Army) signed a comprehensive Peace Agreement to provide a negotiated solution to a seemingly intractable half-century conflict, one of the largest and most violent in the Western Hemisphere.[1] This agreement was the product of a pioneering negotiation framework aimed at addressing the victims' interests and resolving the conflict's structural causes. Moreover, it creates numerous innovative institutions, particularly a sophisticated system of transitional justice to guarantee the rights to justice, truth, compensation, and nonrepetition of the atrocities committed in the conflict.

This volume is the first systematic, interdisciplinary discussion of the achievements, failures, and challenges of this Peace Agreement and its implications for Colombia's future.[2] Contributors include negotiators of the Agreement, Colombian officials including judges of the Special Jurisdiction for Peace (JEP), representatives of the civil society, and leading academic experts in peace studies, human rights, international law, criminal law, transitional justice, political science, and philosophy. We have made an effort to include a wide range of perspectives from Colombian and international experts.

This work is premised on the assumption that peacebuilding is a form of transferable social learning and that the process itself contains the knowledge of conflict resolution. Despite differences in the context and particularities, every peace initiative needs to address similar questions relating to transitional justice, the possibilities of reconciliation, the role of human rights and international law, and other shared features. In particular, the chapters presented offer an account of the dynamics of conflict and peacebuilding in a situation that is both distinctive and universal in its origins. Hence, this close examination of the successes and struggles to achieve the Colombian Peace Agreement contains important lessons for other peace processes in the world.

This introductory chapter is divided into three sections. The first one provides background on the Colombian conflict, the content of the Final

Agreement, and its implementation challenges. The second section summarizes the content of the chapters and highlights some relationships among them. The brief third section offers some editorial notes.

Background

Colombia's complex conflict

While Colombia has a formally stable democratic political system, a sophisticated legal regime, and a working economic system, it has also experienced one of the most violent, protracted conflicts in the world. The actors of this conflict include the government's armed forces, far-left guerrilla groups, far-right parliamentary groups, and drug trafficking organizations.[3] Although the conflict has affected all the territory, its effects are more seriously felt in rural and remote areas, sometimes called *La Colombia Profunda* (The Deep Colombia), that contrast with the more developed urban areas. It is generally accepted that what we call "the Colombian conflict" started on May 27, 1964, with the founding of FARC.[4] However, this conflict is only part of a more extended history of civil strife that began with independence from Spain in the first two decades of the 1800s. Between 1812 and 1902, Colombia experienced at least ten national civil wars between Liberal and Conservative parties and hundreds of regional revolts.

The most direct antecedent cause of the conflict was *La Violencia* (The Violence), a 10-year undeclared civil war between the Colombian Conservative Party and the Colombian Liberal Party. After an exceptional relative peace between 1903 and 1946, armed confrontations started with the Conservatives' return to power in 1946. Like the Liberals did 16 years before when they regained power from a "Conservative Hegemony" that began in 1902, Conservatives started to take revenge against the "Liberal Republic." At this moment, the Conservative Party encouraged their supporters to seize the agricultural lands of Liberals with the assistance of police, military, and paramilitary forces and the ideological support of the Catholic Church. Liberals organized guerrillas in response. The direct trigger of *La Violencia* was the assassination of Liberal Party presidential candidate Jorge Eliécer Gaitán on April 9, 1948, which was followed by massive riots in Bogotá (known as *El Bogotazo*). Tens of thousands died during this bloody civil war, most of them poor peasants.[5]

Following the short-lived dictatorship of General Gustavo Rojas Pinilla (1953–57), Conservatives and Liberals made a political arrangement known as *Frente Nacional* (National Front). According to this Agreement, the leading parties agreed to alternate in public offices between 1958 and 1974 (four presidential terms), including the presidency, cabinet, and national legislature, departmental assemblies, and municipal councils. While this arrangement successfully ended the Liberal–Conservative war, it did not address the structural causes that led to the violent confrontation, such as land distribution and economic inequality. Nor did it deal with the atrocities committed during the conflict; only a general amnesty was granted to all former combatants. Moreover, the pact excluded outsider political forces, such as the emerging Communist Party, thereby providing an indirect justification for the use of weapons as a means of political action.

Most left-wing guerrillas were created during *Frente National*. The two largest ones, FARC and *Ejército de Liberación Nacional* (ELN, National Liberation Army), were founded in 1964. The origin of FARC lies in a few armed groups formed by peasants and former Liberal guerilla fighters, who endorsed a Marxist–Leninist ideology. These groups successfully established small autonomous enclaves in remote regions of the country for self-defense because many amnestied liberals were killed. However, they also raided cattle ranches and extorted local landowners, which they saw as reparation for the government's unfulfilled promises. Under the pressure of the Conservative lawmakers, the government of Guillermo León Valencia (second of *Frente Nacional*, 1962–66) attacked these so-called "independent republics" to put them into the government's control. The most representative attack was conducted in May and June 1964 over Marquetalia, Tolima, an enclave defended by 40–50 armed fighters led by Pedro Antonio Marín (known as Manuel Marulanda Vélez, *alias* "Tirofijo"). Marulanda and some of the survivors founded the *Bloque Sur* (Southern Bloc), which 2 years later transformed into FARC, which became the largest guerrilla force in Colombia.

Whereas FARC had roots in rural struggles, ELN was a product of university students and Catholic radicals that endorsed Liberation Theology and who hoped to replicate in Colombia Fidel Castro's 1959 communist revolution in Cuba. FARC and ELN collaborated at times, but they also clashed for territorial control in some areas of the country. Also important is the *Ejército Popular de Liberación* (EPL, People's Liberation Army), which was founded in 1967 by dissidents from the Communist Party aligned with Mao Zedong's understanding of Marxism instead of a Soviet conception supported by FARC. In 1974, *Movimiento 19 de Abril* (M-19, April 19 Movement) was founded in response to the allegedly fraudulent presidential elections of April 19, 1970, that elected Misael Pastrana Borrero as the last president of the *Frente Nacional* (1970–74). Other smaller guerrilla groups were created in the 1980s, such as *Movimiento Armado Quintín Lame* (MAQL, Quintin Lame Armed Movement), an indigenous self-defense group turned guerrilla. Other groups were the result of ideological divisions amongst the largest ones.

The conflict started as a proxy of the Cold War. Communist guerrillas supported by the Soviet Union and China opposed a weak state, promising a Communist government that would distribute land and resources equally. In response, the government developed a counter-insurgent strategy with its military and police forces, supported by the United States, interested in preventing the spread of Communism in the Americas. The *foquismo* or *foco theory* of the Cuban revolution, an approach to bring about Marxist revolutions in nonindustrialized countries, profoundly influenced Colombian guerrillas. This approach sees guerrillas as creators of a focus (*foco* in Spanish) of popular discontent against the regime, particularly that of farmers and peasants, which paves the way for a general insurrection.

At their origins, most guerrillas mobilized violent attacks in the rural areas they influenced, often small-scale ambushes against isolated army units or takeovers of towns and only later moved to urban areas.[6] Guerrillas funded themselves through extortion, theft, and kidnappings for ransom. FARC performed the most notorious kidnappings, which included prominent political figures (e.g., presidential candidate Íngrid Betancourt and 12 departmental Assembly Members of the Valle del Cauca) and economic leaders. They also performed "miraculous draughts of fish" (named after a Biblical episode), namely massive road blockades to seek victims for kidnapping. They also held members of the armed forces to gain political leverage, in some cases for years (one police officer, Luis Mendieta, was held for 14 years). Both FARC and ELN performed numerous attacks on the country's energy and transportation infrastructure.

Drug trafficking became a new factor that fueled the conflict and increased the intensity of violence. While marijuana trafficking was common beginning in the 1970s, cocaine became the main product during the late 1970s and early 1980s. By the mid-1980s, there were several organized cartels. The most notable were those of Medellín (led by Pablo Escobar) and Cali (led by the brothers Gilberto and Miguel Rodríguez Orejuela). Though initially tolerated by the government, a confrontation with cartels began after they ordered the assassination of the Minister of Justice Rodrigo Lara Bonilla in 1984.

When the United States declared the "War on Drugs," and extradition to the USA became the Colombian government's most powerful tool, cartels funded terrorist attacks against the government and civilians to gain leverage. Importantly, drug-related activities also became a significant source of funding for FARC and other guerrillas, which began to collect "taxes" for providing security to drug cartels, and later, controlled an important portion of the production and traffic of narcotics directly. Drug money allowed FARC to grow exponentially and change their strategy. At their Seventh Guerrilla Conference in 1982 (in which they added EP, *Ejército del Pueblo*, or People's Army to their name), they proposed to move from small confrontations to stage large-scale attacks on towns and military bases. They also started urban militias that made terrorist attacks on larger cities.

Given the strength of guerrilla actions and the state's inability to protect citizens and their property, right-wing paramilitary forces also grew in influence in the early 1980s, though they existed in Colombia long before.[7] Drug cartels created some of them. For example, *Muerte a Secuestradores* (MAS, Death to Kidnappers) created death squads against guerilla leaders in response to kidnappings. However, most paramilitary forces were created by cattle ranchers, landowners, and corporations who funded, trained, and armed groups for self-protection, while using them to advance their economic and political interests. At several moments, these groups were legally authorized and openly supported by the government's armed forces.

Paramilitaries sought to crush guerrillas by murder and intimidation, both their combatants and anybody how they deemed as supporters, such as left-wing politicians (including elected officials), leaders of labor unions, peasant and human rights organizations, and university professors and students. In 1997, most paramilitary forces in Colombia unified into *Autodefensas Unidas de Colombia* (AUC, United Self-Defenses of Colombia), led by the Castaño Brothers. Like FARC and other guerrillas they fought, AUC also funded their activities with money from their control of a substantial part of Colombia's drug production. Paramilitaries had strong ties with the economic and political elites of some regions, which allowed them to gain significant power in Colombia's formal institutions. By 2014, 60 members of Congress were sentenced for alliances with paramilitary groups, along with numerous regional politicians, in an episode known as "para-politics."

This dangerous mixture generated a deadly tool and devastated the country. Colombia's National Centre for Historical Memory reported that 261,619 people died as a result of the conflict between 1958 and September 15, 2018, the vast majority of them civilians (214,584).[8] Most deaths are attributed to paramilitary forces (94,579), followed by guerrillas (36,682) and state agents (9,837). The conflict left 80,472 disappeared (a number significantly higher than three dictatorships of the Southern Cone together: There were 3,500 documented cases in Chile; around 10,000 in Argentina and 192 in Uruguay)[9]; 15,738 victims of sexual violence (most of them women) and 37,165 people were kidnapped (26,108 of them by guerrillas). According to the National Registry of Victims, 9,031,048 people have been recognized as victims (roughly 19% of Colombians).[10] Among them, more than 8 million people were forced from their homes, most of them poor peasants, creating the second-highest population of internally displaced people in the world (second to Syria), and generating a tremendous transformation in the distribution and possession of land in the country.[11]

Between negotiation and war

Seeking a solution to the problem of guerrillas has been a constant of Colombian recent political history. The first president after the *Frente Nacional,* liberal Alfonso López Michelsen (1974–78), attempted a failed negotiation with FARC. In turn, the next president, fellow liberal Julio César Turbay Ayala (1978–82), implemented a strong security policy against guerrillas during a constant state of siege. Turbay's policies were accused of human rights violations.

In response to the increased intensity of the conflict, Conservative Belisario Betancur was elected as president (1982–86) under a promise of peace. The Betancur government started negotiations with FARC and arranged a truce with M-19. An amnesty was provided for guerrilla groups, and many small groups demobilized. As part of the negotiation with FARC, a new political party was created, *Unión Patriótica* (UP, Patriotic Union), to allow a space in politics for guerrillas and other traditionally excluded unarmed social actors. This party won many elected offices, including 14 seats in Congress.

However, between 2,000 and 3,000 UP members were systematically killed during the 1980s, including their presidential candidates for the 1986 and 1990 elections, by a union of military and paramilitary forces who saw them as FARC's political branch.[12] As a result, the truce ended, and FARC withdrew from mainstream politics. M-19 also ended negotiations with Betancur's government, due to what they regarded as violations to the ceasefire. In 1985, M-19 assaulted the Palace of Justice of the Colombian Supreme Court. Half of the Supreme Court Justices died in the crossfire between guerrillas and military forces.

The end of the 1980s was extremely violent. In 1989, three presidential candidates were killed, and terrorist attacks were frequent. Student movements proposed to tackle violence by replacing the 1886 Constitution, and a Constitutional Assembly was chosen as the mechanism to draft a new constitution. During this time, the new president, Liberal Cesar Gaviria (1990–94), negotiated the demobilization of M-19 and a significant part of EPL, which participated in the Constitutional Assembly. Most importantly, the leader of the political party that arose from the demobilization of M-19 (*Alianza Democrática* M-19) became one of the three presidents of the Constitutional Assembly, along with Liberal and Conservative leaders.

As a result, the Constitution of 1991 was considered, in part, as a pact for peace (in fact, peace was enshrined as a human right and duty in the Constitution). Among other achievements, it radically transformed the structure of the state, created judicial mechanisms to exercise rights, and enshrined social rights and democratic and pluralist principles, which delegitimized the use of violence for political purposes.[13] Regarding security powers, the 1991 Constitution also eliminated the "states of siege" of the 1886 Constitution that granted ample powers to military forces to suppress human rights. However, FARC and ELN were not part of this constitutional process, and hostilities with the government continued. After the enactment of the Constitution, there was a new round of conversations between the Gaviria government and FARC in Mexico during 1992, but these also failed.

The government of Liberal Ernesto Samper (1994–98) also unsuccessfully attempted to negotiate with both major guerrillas. FARC, however, did not regard him as a valid interlocutor, for there were serious allegations that drug cartels funded his campaign. A new failed attempted negotiation occurred during Conservative Andrés Pastrana's administration (1998–2002) in five demilitarized municipalities, including San Vicente del Caguán. However, because the Caguán talks occurred at a time when FARC was at the peak of their military power, they were not fully committed to the process and used the demilitarized area to regroup and strengthen.

AUC was founded in this time, partly in opposition to Pastrana's process. After the kidnapping of the commercial airplane where senator Jorge Eduardo Géchem Turbay was traveling, the government halted the negotiation and ordered a military retake of the Caguán.[14] During this time, Pastrana started the so called "Plan Colombia," a 7.5 USD billion plan to end the conflict and drug trafficking, with significant financial and logistical support of the United States.

The disillusionment created by Pastrana's talk and the violence of FARC generated a strong sentiment against FARC. In 2002, liberal dissident with a conservative agenda Álvaro Uribe was elected with the promise of a hard line against guerrilla. He served for two terms (2002–10) in which he advanced a policy of "democratic security" that strengthened armed forces and created networks of collaborators and monetary rewards to attack guerrillas, particularly high-ranking leaders. The government also actively promoted individual desertion among guerrilla ranks. The strategy was successful on several military aspects: FARC retreated from urban areas and diminished in size (from around 18,000 men and women in 2002 to less than 10,000 by 2010), and many of their actions (e.g., kidnappings, attacks on towns and infrastructure) were reduced. While a complete military victory remained elusive, the sense of security in Colombia increased, and Uribe's popularity with it, allowing him to amend the 1991 Constitution to permit his re-election. However, Uribe's "democratic security" is criticized not only for failing to address the social and economic aspects of the conflict but also for promoting systematic violations of human rights, including the premeditated murders of noncombatant citizens by military forces to falsely present them as guerrilla fighters killed in battle (known as *falsos positivos* or false positives).[15]

During the Uribe government, there was a process to demobilize around 30,000 members of AUC. To facilitate this process, the government promoted the Justice and Peace Law (Law 975 of 2005) that created a procedure for the prosecution and trial of the members of illegal groups and to provide some measures in favor of victims. Critics, however, suggested that penalties were too lenient and failed to provide incentives for truth-telling and reparations. Judgments of the Constitutional Court attempted to remedy these problems and strengthen the legislation.[16]

While it led to the clarification of some of the atrocities of paramilitaries, the legacy of the Justice and Peace Law is far from successful. As of July 2020, after 15 years of operation, there were judgments against fewer than 600 paramilitary combatants (less than 2% of the demobilized forces), and little has advanced truth-telling regarding the contributions of economic and political leaders to the paramilitary project.[17] Moreover, the most prominent AUC commanders were extradited to the United States to face charges of drug trafficking without responding first to the human rights violations committed in Colombia. In addition, middle-ranking commanders reorganized a substantial part of demobilized forces to return to drug trafficking, illegal mining, and other ordinary crimes. The organized new groups, such as "*El Clan del Golfo*" and "*Los Pelusos,*" which are known by the government as *Bandas Criminales* (BACRIM, Criminal Bands) or *Grupos Armados Organizados* (GAO, Armed Organized Groups), lack any sort of political discourse. Their members include both demobilized paramilitary and guerrillas, and they also make alliances with guerrillas to control illegal economies.

The 2012–16 peace process

Juan Manuel Santos, who served as Minister of Defense under Uribe's second term, was elected president from 2010 to 2014 to continue with the "democratic security" project. To the surprise of many, President Santos announced in August 2012 that secret exploratory talks with FARC had been conducted in Havana, Cuba, for one and half years, and a negotiation plan was established. At this moment, some important facts have already taken place. Santos' government had proposed a landmark Victim and Land Restitution to Law (Law 1448 of 2011) to compensate victims and order restitution of land to those forcefully displaced. Furthermore, Congress also approved the *Marco Jurídico Para la Paz* (Legal Framework for Peace), in June 2012, a constitutional amendment that provides avenues to transitional justice in an eventual peace process.

Shortly after the announcement of the talks, the negotiation teams were established. The government's team included Humberto de la Calle, a former vice president (1994–97) as chief negotiator; Sergio Jaramillo Caro, High Commissioner of Peace; and retired army and police officials. In turn, FARC's Leader Rodrigo Londoño Echeverri (alias Timoleón Jiménez or Timochenko) announced that this team was led by Luciano Marín Arango (known as "Iván Márquez"), member of FARC's ruling seven-person secretariat, and Seuxis Paucias Hernández (alias "Jesús Santrich") and Ricardo Tillez (alias "Rodrigo Granda").

Santos pledged that the errors of 30 years of failed negotiations with the guerrilla organization would not be repeated, recognizing that demilitarized zones and ceasefires have strengthened guerrillas and delayed results in the negotiation.[18] Several features of the negotiation framework deserve notice. Unlike previous attempts, the negotiation also had a detailed agenda limited to six points: (i) Rural development and land policy; (ii) FARC's political participation; (iii) the end of armed conflict, including the reintegration into civilian life of FARC forces; (iv) illicit crops and illegal drug trafficking; (v) reparations to victims; and (vi) ratification, implementation and verification of the agreement. This was the first time there was talk of not only "ending the conflict" but also constructing positive peace through addressing the underlying causes and accelerants of conflict, such as rural poverty, inequality, and drug trafficking. The negotiation process was explicitly about the prominent role of victims and preventing impunities for atrocities.

Moreover, for the very first time, women played a central part in the process, both as negotiators and in a special subcommission on gender.

Several instances of public participation were established. The framework also identified clear roles for Cuba and Norway as "guarantors" and Venezuela and Chile as "supporting countries."

The peace talks started in Oslo, Norway, in October 2012, and on November 19, 2012, they moved to Cuba. The negotiation operated under the principle that "nothing is agreed, until everything is agreed"—that is, the negotiation only finished when an agreement was reached on the six points of the agenda.[19] As a result, military confrontation between the government and FARC persisted, which became a source of criticism: Talk about peace in Cuba contrasted with hostilities in Colombia. During the negotiation, the support for the process remained relatively strong despite the opposition to the process. Former President Uribe and the party he created (named *Centro Democrático,* Democratic Center, despite its far-right commitments) became the staunchest critic of the process, which they largely saw as a capitulation to terrorism. Santos was re-elected for a second period (2014–18) with the promise of "finishing the job" of the peace process in a disputed election with *Centro Democrático's* candidate, who campaigned on a hawkish platform of ending the peace process and returning to democratic security policy in Colombia.[20]

The Final Agreement

Negotiations that initially expected to last between four and eight months took 4 years and were only stopped once. The "Final Agreement for Ending the Conflict and Building a Stable and Lasting Peace" (henceforth, the Final Agreement) between the negotiation teams was announced on August 24, 2016. The almost 300-page Final Agreement was composed of six chapters (*puntos*) that corresponded to the six negotiation points of the agenda.

Chapter 1 of the Agreement, about comprehensive rural development seeks to transform access and distribution of law and to reduce rural poverty by 50% in 10 years. Some measures to improve access to and use of law were created (section 1.1). Measures to improve access include a land fund, acquisition subsidies and credits, and a plan for land property formalization. Measures to improve land use include a multi-purpose cadaster, changes in land taxes, and clear borders between agricultural land and ecological reserve lands. A second important measure is the creation programs of territorially focused rural development (PDETs) that seek the structural transformation of 170 selected municipalities harshly affected by the violence, poverty, institutional neglect or presence of illegal crops, and economy (section 1.2). Finally, significant investments in public goods and services—including infrastructure, development, economic stimulus, and right to food—through a national plan were agreed (section 1.3).[21]

Chapter 2 about political participation seeks to promote new voices in the Colombian political systems. The chapter includes the creation of a system of guarantees to exercise political opposition. Other chapters include means of democratic participation, such as guarantees for social movements and peaceful protest, as well as participation in mass media.

Chapter 3 about the end of the conflict lays out rules for the bilateral and definitive termination of the hostilities between FARC and the government, for establishing a ceasefire, the collection and storage of weapons, and the DDR (Demobilization, Disarmament, and Reintegration). According to these rules, former FARC combatants will transition to civilian life in 26 protected encampments, in which they will receive training and economic opportunities. Upon disarmament, FARC will transform into a legal, political party. One of the most controversial measures was that FARC's new political party would have a minimum of five seats in each of the houses of Congress for two periods.

Chapter 4, about the solution to the problem of illicit drugs, promotes rural development as a solution to drug trafficking. Central measures include the creation of a National Program for the Substitution of Illicit Crops (PNIS), based on voluntary substitution, that would generate conditions for the transition from illegal to legal crops (section 4.1). The chapter also promotes a change in the state strategy against drugs, proposing treatment, prevention, healthcare, and social inclusion (section 4.3). More comprehensive policies against the production and commercialization of narcotics were agreed, including prosecution, control of inputs necessary for drug production, and promotion of international dialogues to assess the policies against drugs.

Chapter 5 creates an innovative, comprehensive system to protect the victim's rights to obtain justice and accountability, ensure the elucidation of truth, and obtain reparations and guarantee nonrepetition to promote coexistence and reconciliation.[22] This system provides a mixture of autonomous judicial and nonjudicial institutions that provides alternative criminal treatment and other incentives for agents responsible for serious human rights violations, war crimes and crimes against humanity committed in the armed conflict, war crimes, and crimes against humanity committed in the context of the armed conflict while respecting international standards. The system is composed as follows:

- The JEP is a judicial institution that seeks to investigate, judge, and punish serious human rights violations, war crimes, and crimes against humanity committed in the armed conflict up to December 1, 2016.[23] It will hear cases involving former FARC combatants and members of Colombia's military and police forces for crimes related to the armed conflict. It also investigates nonmilitary state agents and third-party civilians who appear voluntarily. JEPs will last for 15 years, extendable for 5 years more.
- The Commission for the Clarification of Truth, Coexistence, and Nonrepetition (henceforth, Truth Commission) is a nonjudicial institution that seeks to shed light on the violations committed in the conflict and to offer a broad, inclusive, comprehensive explanation of its complexity. After 3 years, the Truth Commission is supposed to provide a final report.[24]

- The Unit for the Search for Persons Presumed Disappeared in the context and by reason of the armed conflict (henceforth, Search Unit) is a nonjudicial, humanitarian entity that seeks the thousands of disappeared persons that have resulted from the armed conflict, and in those cases of death, the recovery, identification, and dignified delivery of the remains. The period of this Search Unit is 10 years.
- There are also several reparative measures, including acknowledgment of collective responsibility, psychosocial rehabilitation, reparations for forcefully displaced people, and land restitution.

Each institution is autonomous, meaning that information given in the Truth Commission and the Search Unit cannot be used in JEP's judicial proceedings, which is expected to facilitate the clarification of truth. Chapter 5 also stipulates that the system is to operate using a territorial, differential, and gender-based approach to address the particularities of victims in different parts of the territory and to provide special protection to women and children who are victims of the armed conflict.

Finally, Chapter 6, about ratification, implementation, and verification, creates a commission to generate a 10-year framework plan and a commission. Many responsibilities of the verification are delegated to the United Nations. Importantly, section 6.2 also creates the "ethnic chapter" of the Agreement to consider the perspective of the ethnic groups, including indigenous and Afro-Colombians, in the decisions that concern them, their land, and resources while preserving their institutions, culture, and traditions in the application of all the chapters.[25] Finally, Colombia and FARC disagreed over the mechanism of ratification: Whereas FARC preferred a Constitutional Assembly, the government supported a plebiscite or referendum, which was ultimately the preferred alternative in the Agreement (section 6.6). A bill enabling the use of a plebiscite for this purpose was previously enacted in December 2015, which included two controversial elements. One was a reduction in the quorum and a vote for the totality of the Final Agreement, not for individual components. The Constitutional Court reviewed this legislation and deemed it constitutional.

A fierce public dispute about the Final Agreement followed its publication. Its defenders presented it as an innovative and fair compromise, a position supported by the international communities as well as international institutions, such as the United Nations (UN) and International Criminal Court (ICC).[26] Opponents, however, deemed that FARC was a terrorist drug-dealing cartel, without a valid political agenda, so they could not hope to transform the Colombian institutions and policies. They also criticized the justice mechanism created by Chapter 5, which they deemed as tailor-made for FARC, for being too lenient with the atrocities, and misrepresented ordinary crimes (e.g., drug trafficking) as conflict-related crimes. Other contested aspects were the rules about FARC's political participation, which allowed former terrorists in the Congress, and some economic incentives (often exaggerated by critics), which were unacceptable in a developing country. Importantly, a great deal of the opposition concentrated on the Agreement's gender-based approach, incorporated in all chapters. While this component aims to address the particular needs of women and Lesbian, Gay, Bisexual, Transgender, and Intersex (LGTBI) communities as victims of the conflict, some influential religious movements depicted it as an attack on the family and traditional values.[27]

The Final Agreement was signed by Juan Manuel Santos and Rodrigo Londoño Echeverri in Cartagena, Colombia, on September 26, 2016. The formal ceremony was attended by the UN Secretary-General Ban Ki-Moon, numerous presidents of Latin America, and delegations of victims. The plebiscite for the Agreement ratification was held on October 2, 2016. A total of 12,808,858 people voted (37.4% of the electorate), and "No" to the Final Agreement won by a short margin: 6,431,376 (50.21%) against and 6,377,482 for (49.78%).[28] Importantly, the regions most impacted by the conflict voted in favor of the Agreement. On October 7, President Santos won the 2016 Nobel Peace Prize.

Following this unexpected result, opponents of the peace process demanded the halt of the negotiation. The Santos government and FARC suggested beginning with a "Great National Dialogue" to revise the Agreement and pave the way for peace, without losing the results of 4 years of negotiations. Seventy meetings were held with politicians, social organizations, victims, youth, unions, and all parties. Both those who supported "Yes" and "No" were invited, but the latter refused to participate actively. From these meetings, almost 60 aspects of the Final Agreement were revised, clarified, adjusted, and changed, particularly the constitutional nature of the Final Agreement, foreign justices, guarantees for justice, and the gender component. However, its core elements remained almost unchanged.

The Revised Final Agreement was signed in *Teatro Colón* in Bogotá on November 25, 2016. Shortly thereafter, the Teatro Colón agreement was approved by both houses of Congress, though *Centro Democrático* boycotted voting. After signing, a fast-track mechanism was created to pass some legislation necessary for the Agreement's implementation.[29]

Achievements and challenges

The Final Agreement's detailed demobilization plan was closely followed and led to clear results. More than 13,000 men and women who were listed as members of FARC demobilized despite numerous logistical difficulties.[30] FARC demobilized forces surrendered their weapons in a one-one-basis, unique in the world. FARC became a political party with the same acronyms, *Fuerza Alternativa Revolucionaria del Común* (Common Alternative Revolutionary Force) and started to participate in mainstream politics. Furthermore, there is also a road map to implement the 16 plans of action for the regional transformation designed in fulfillment of the agreement.[31]

According to the Koch Institute, the Colombian government has developed productive projects with 3,159 former members of FARC.[32]

The signature of the Final Agreement left other undeniable advances at the institutional level. The entities of the Comprehensive System of Truth, Justice, Reparation, and Nonrepetition have been working, and there is a participative process for the victims of the conflict. JEP, for instance, have opened seven cases to judge responsibility of some of the more representative and significant crimes communities through the conflict.

Violence substantially decreased with FARC demobilization. For example, 2017 was the least violent year in the history of Colombia. In turn, the congressional and presidential elections held between March and June 2018—the first held since the Agreement was signed—reported significantly fewer security issues than all previous elections during the conflict. An important section of FARC has been committed to the process, participating legally in politics and activities, appearing before JEP, and collaborating in reparations.

However, there are new political challenges after the 2018 presidential election in Colombia. The overwhelming winner was Iván Duque from *Centro Democrático*, a protégé of Álvaro Uribe who represented the moderate side of his party. Notably, the runner-up was left-wing Gustavo Petro, a former M-19 guerrilla fighter, with significant support. The Duque government has had a mixed attitude towards the Final Agreement. While it defends the Agreement in the international arenas, domestically, it has continued his party's attack against it, particularly against the JEP.

The Final Agreement thus does not have an easy path. Besides the legitimacy deficits and lack of social support, implementation of the Agreement remains unclear.[33] The Colombian state remains slow to transform words into deeds. Economic stressors undermine key principles of the Agreement, and slowly erode trust and hope in the lives of the marginalized. Such feeble implementation efforts endanger the Peace Agreement, and may push members of FARC and other groups toward illegal activities for economic opportunities. The undermining of gender rights provisions by the religious right and other Conservatives threatens the safety and well-being of those affected and the health of the Agreement.

Critics of the Duque government also allege that he has slowed down the implementation and the reduced resources for many of the commitments. According to the Center for Investigation and Popular Education, and the Conflict Analysis Resource Center, the Colombian government has not allocated enough resources to fulfill the obligations derived from the Peace Agreement. It is not even clear whether some of the resources allocated by the government to the national offices are really allocated to fulfill the obligations of the Peace Agreements, or they are derived from other legal obligations. Moreover, there are not important advances in important topics such as the implementation of the agreement in the use of land concerning the gender perspective.[34]

Violence and endemic insecurity remain critical factors. During the Duque government, violence has resurged, particularly in areas formerly controlled by FARC armed forces. A sad illustration of this resurgence of violence is that 970 community leaders and defenders of human rights have been killed since the signing of the Peace Agreement.[35] Dissidents and paramilitary forces have selectively killed former FARC combatants. Moreover, while most former FARC combatants remain committed to the process, there have been some important defections that have given rise to "dissidents" who have returned to weapons and criminality. According to the Ideas for Peace Foundation, there are 28 dissident groups with more than 2,000 members, although not all of them are former members of FARC.[36] Finally, ELN remains an important actor, and all attempts to make peace with them were halted after a terrorist attack on the Colombian School of Police Officials.

One incident that particularly affected the peace process was the defection of *Iván Márquez* and *Jesús Santrich*, two of the most influential FARC participants of the peace process, who decided to leave the process and to continue the conflict with former members of the guerrilla. Santrich's case, in particular, gained significant media attention. He was arrested on April 9, 2018, in Bogotá, accused of drug trafficking by a New York court. Colombian Attorney General argued Santrich's crimes were committed after the signature of the agreement, so he could not accede to the Agreement's benefit for nonextradition. However, the JEP ordered his release, arguing insufficient evidence was provided about the date on which the crimes were committed.[37] On June 30, 2019, after his release, Santrich escaped from the Colombian authorities and joined Iván Márquez in the dissident group he was commanding. This incident prompted a strong reaction against the peace process by the right-wing sectors of society, who used Santrich's liberation to discredit JEP and the process.

The final set of challenges of cultural and symbolic character. Colombia remains a politically polarized country, and decades of conflict have left numerous sequels, including societal mistrust and collective trauma. One key challenge is to rebuild the social fabric and relationships to secure a healthy social, political, and economic reality. Only then, the promises of the Final Agreement of "building a stable and lasting peace" could be realized.

Content

Genesis

The book is organized into six sections. The first section describes the genesis of the peace process in Colombia. In Chapter 2, Sergio Jaramillo Caro, former High Commissioner of Peace, reveals the objective, strategies, and difficulties for a Peace Agreement. Jaramillo Caro lays out the details and connects them to the "big picture" of transferability and strategy. He gives a comprehensive account of the dynamic process of the negotiations and the design elements he identifies as key to success. He provides a substantive guide to the inner workings of the Colombian peace process, especially regarding the four and one-half years in which the negotiations were held in Havana.

In Chapter 3, Jon Elster provides an account of the origins of the peace process in 2014, after a meeting with members of the Transitional Justice Team and an official visit. He also shares what he has learned from these observations in the context of the conflict in Colombia, and its roots, and the successes and challenges of the negotiation of transitional justice. Most importantly, by giving close attention to the dynamics of the processes of conflict and peace within the frame of social justice, Elster gives us insights into some of the broader factors enabling social learning and makes well-informed proposals and suggestions for the future of the process.

Overall assessments

The second section presents various academic and practitioner descriptions of the components of the Agreement, the main difficulties, and future challenges. Chapter 4, by Gustavo Gallón Giraldo and Juan Carlos Ospina from the Colombian Commission of Jurists, one of Colombian's most important human rights organizations, provides three lines of argument for an overall assessment of the Final Agreement. These are, first, the transitional justice regime created by the Final Agreement (discussed in Chapters 6–Chapters 9); second, the problem of land creation and exacerbation of the context of the conflict (see Chapter 13) and, third, the question of political polarization.

Completing this section, Chapter 5, by María Paula Saffon Sanín, provides an analysis of the potentialities and limitations of the peace agreement for achieving social transformations that are needed in the country, such as political and social inclusion, and the strengthening of the rule of law. Saffon Sanín insightfully identifies several forces operating in multiple sectors of Colombian society and the Colombian peace process explicitly. Her views of political economy and the relationship to peace and conflict are clear and intense. She brings an important voice to the analysis of successes and challenges regarding the negotiations and the Agreement, giving a fascinating account of the plebiscite, and the "No" vote in the process.

Transitional justice in theory and practice

The third section focuses on transitional justice (the politico-moral standards to assess the transition from war to peace) and the important, yet contested measures to achieve truth, justice, and reconciliation created by the Final Agreement.

In Chapter 6, Jennifer L. McCoy, Jelena Subotic, and Ryan E. Carlin analyze the Colombian process as the first country to engage in peace negotiations under the umbrella of the full implementation of the Rome Statute of the ICC and in a democratic context, laying out the key legal and philosophical questions and the agreements societal impact. They argue that to meet this complex challenge, the negotiation involved innovative norm-making of transitional justice norms that balance several international and domestic competing demands on disputed issues (victims' rights, accountability, and political participation).

The two following contributions provide different perspectives on the compatibility of the Colombian System with international law and human rights standards. Chapter 7, written by Juanita Goebertus Estrada, Colombian congresswoman, former Head of the Transitional Justice Group at the Office of the Colombian High Commissioner for Peace, makes a thorough analysis of the comprehensive transitional justice embodied in the Peace Agreement in the light of the UN human rights system, international humanitarian law, international criminal law, and the Inter-American System for the protection of human rights. In turn, Chapter 8, written by Kai Ambos, an expert of international criminal law and *amicus curiae* of the Colombian Special Jurisdiction of Peace, argues that the strategy of transitional justice of the peace accord is compatible with international law, particularly concerning international criminal law and the crimes that could be amnestied under the Peace Agreement.

The section ends in Chapter 9 with Colleen Murphy's philosophical assessment of the Colombian Final Agreement in light of her prominent theory of transitional justice. She argues that Colombia satisfies all of the circumstances of justice of transitional societies (i.e., those characterized by existential uncertainty), and, as a result, the Colombian Final Agreement depends on the extent to which the outlined transitional justice processes contribute to societal transformation and treat victims and perpetrators fairly and appropriately. While there are reasons for optimism based on the comprehensiveness of the Agreement and its focus on the structural inequality, Murphy also identifies reasons for caution in assuming that these potential contributions to transitional justice will be realized.

Key components of the Final Agreement

The fourth section provides a detailed study of some of the fundamental components of the Peace Agreement. We have selected some of the most representative and unique components, and with those that have attracted more academic attention.

In Chapter 10, the JEP is discussed by Danilo Rojas Betancourth, one of its justices. After a brief description of the JEP, Rojas discusses the three main legal challenges this jurisdiction faces in the application of its innovative model of transitional, restorative, forward-looking, and reparative justice. Among these challenges is the creation of a *corpus iuris* of human rights and international humanitarian law. Overcoming this challenge, however, provides the key to resolving the other two: Its relationships with permanent justice and the clarification of open-textured provisions. Rojas concludes by highlighting some aspects concerning ongoing debates about JEP and some possible lessons for other peace processes.

In Chapter 11, Alfredo Duplat and Andrés Molina-Ochoa discuss the human right to truth in the Peace Agreement between the Colombian government and FARC-EP in the light of the lessons learned by analyzing the efforts of García Márquez to recover the memory of the Banana Massacres in his novel *One Hundred Years of Solitude*. In the first part of their chapter, they define the concept of the right to the truth and explain some of its key characteristics. Then, they analyze the importance of García Márquez's novel as a milestone in the history of the right to the truth, and the lessons we can learn from the impact of this novel in Colombian history. Finally, they confront the right to the truth in the Peace Agreement with the lessons that we can draw from the history of *One Hundred Years of Solitude*.

Nelson Camilo Sánchez analyzes in the policies of Integral Rural Reform ("IRR") established in the Final Agreement in Chapter 12. Sanchez analyzes the implementation of the Agreement in light of the characteristics of the historical conflicts regarding land in Colombia, and the agreements reached in the peace process. He also provides some suggestions for future regulations on access to land, rural development, and land governance in contemporary Colombia.

In Chapter 13, Patricia Pabón and Javier Aguirre examine the gender component of the Final Agreement. Pabón and Aguirre highlight that the gender component was one of the key factors for the victory of the "No" side in the 2016 plebiscite for peace, which led to a renegotiation of the Agreement, in which the gender components were undermined. They argue that these difficulties reflect the lack of representation and recognition of women and representation and recognition of women and people with diverse sexual orientations in Colombia. They also argue that lack of recognition is intricately connected to the role that religious discourse still plays in the Colombian public sphere.

In Chapter 14, Justice Xiomara Cecilia Balanta-Moreno and Yuri Alexander Romaña-Rivas study the main institutions created by the Final Agreement to address the rights of Afro-Colombian communities, which have been disproportionately affected by the armed conflict. The areas of participation discussed include the appointments of members of Afro-Colombian communities in different positions within the Comprehensive System, the possibility that communities make reports to the System's institutions, and advancing an ethnically differential approach that would promote the participation and engagement of Afro-Colombian communities in the System.

In Chapter 15, the last one of the section, Claudia Milena Díaz-Ríos investigates the politics of education reform in post-conflict conditions. Díaz-Ríos examines the relationships between the state capacity to provide quality education and power dynamics of dominant groups, which might lose political gains as a result of post-conflict transformations, thereby decreasing their political commitment to policy changes and compromising the chances of providing fair, quality, and peacebuilding education.

Legitimacy and democracy

The fifth section studies the constitutional and political questions of the peace accord, recalling that Colombian voters first rejected it in a plebiscite, and Congress approved a modified version.

In Chapter 16, Diana Isabel Güiza-Gómez and Rodrigo Uprimny-Yepes provide theoretical and empirical elements for analyzing the problems of legitimizing and stabilizing peace processes through political inclusion and enshrining legal documents. Güiza-Gómez and Uprimny-Yepes identify a complex tension between the short-term goals of the peace agreement and the long-term purposes of political inclusion and constitution-building. They discuss the complexities of this tension in the Colombian case, and discuss the role that elites have played in the peace process.

In Chapter 17, Roberto Gargarella examines the Colombian peace process from the perspective of democracy as an inclusive and deliberative procedure. His analysis is focused on the contribution that judicial institutions empowered with the review of legislation can make to the collective public debate about disputed politico-moral issues. After introducing some guiding principles for judges in a deliberative democracy, he examines the role of the Colombian Constitutional Court in public debate about the Final Agreement, particularly, the consultation process and the "fast-track" procedures used to enact some legislation necessary for its implementation.

In Chapter 18, Óscar Guardiola-Rivera examines the categories used to describe and analyze the Colombian conflict. It suggests that instead of analyzing the conflict with the common legal redistributive/restorative justice essentialists categories, we use concepts such as higher law, clinical, critique, and hopeful aesthetic justice; peace agreement is thus understood in terms of its symbolic meaning and not merely in terms of its significance. This framework allows the author to answer two questions: "What is the sense of a peace-process such as Colombia's?" and "why today, at every level of our flattened institutional hierarchies, is the place of the ruler [...] the preferred one that enables psychotics to their erroneous wandering [...] by mistreating/sowing hatred of neighbours?"

Finally, in Chapter 19, Nancy C. Doubleday urges a substantive bridging argument for a path to durable peace that engages social learning to consider emergent approaches in law—specifically, the thoughtful consideration of the role of social-cultural-ecological systems, the implementation of indigenous rights within human rights, and the reframing of agency in ecocentric governance under new rules for peaceful coexistence—that call on international actors to respond ethically with responsible measures supportive of Colombian self-governance and democratically driven peace.

Finally, she looks to future peace and the role of education in social learning, and to the necessity of making commitments to enacting peace, by us all.

Editorial notes

To avoid difficulties and confusion, we have decided to use the official translations of the Final Agreement.[38] We are aware, however, that some terms might sound strange for English readers, so some comments are useful. First, there is some dispute in Colombia about the use of "EP"—*Ejército del Pueblo* or People's Army—after FARC. Some people write it in full because this is how the armed group used to identify itself. However, some people do not write EP because doing it could count as legitimization FARC's violent actions. Others would avoid using it because FARC is no longer an army and have chosen the same acronym for their political party. Both options will be accepted as valid in this volume.

In the original Spanish version, the *puntos* (points) of the agenda became the *puntos* of Agreement. The translation refers to the sections of the final agreement as "chapters," and we have preserved this usage. The Final Agreement uses several complex acronyms, such as SIVJRNR (*Sistema Integral de Verdad, Justicia, Reparación y No Repetición,* Comprehensive System for Truth, Justice, Reparation and Non-Repetition); CEV (*Comisión para el Esclarecimiento de la Verdad, la Convivencia y la No Repetición*, Commission for the Clarification of Truth, Coexistence and Non-repetition), UBPD (*Unidad de Búsqueda de Personas dadas por Desaparecidas en el Contexto y en Razón del Conflicto Armado*, the Unit for the Search for Persons Presumed Disappeared in the context and by reason of the armed conflict) and the JEP (*Jurisdicción Especial para la Paz,* Special Jurisdiction for Peace). As they are not self-explanatory in English, we have avoided them in the volume. Instead, we will refer to the Comprehensive System, the Truth Commission, and the Search Unit. For the last institution, following international human rights terminology, we will refer to the *disappeared* (i.e., victims of forced disappearances) and not the "missing" as sometimes translated.

We have, however, maintained JEP, for it is a widely used term. JEP's institutions will also be named using its official translation.[39] Hence, we will refer to its Chambers (*Salas*) and Sections (*Secciones*). *Justice* is the translation we have provided to its "*magistrados*" to signal that they are amongst the highest judicial offices in Colombia, like those of the Supreme and Constitutional Courts. There is one case that might sound particularly strange to English readers, namely Chamber and Section about "*Reconocimiento de Verdad, Responsabilidad y la Determinación de los Hechos y Conductas.*" "*Reconocimiento*" is a term of the Final Agreement, and it means that the party concurring with the JEP can *acknowledge* that certain acts were committed or that certain facts occurred. "Acknowledgement" is the official translation, yet in other places, the reader might find a more direct translation,

"Recognition." In turn, "Determination" has to do with the *judicial ascertainment* of whether certain facts happened or whether certain conduct was committed, when, and by whom. While *ascertainment* seems more fitting, we will follow JEP and use the official translation, "Determination," for "*determinación*."

Notes

1 "Final Agreement to End the Armed Conflict and Build a Stable and Lasting Peace," November 24, 2016 (Bogotá: Office of the High Commissioner for Peace of Colombia), http://www.altocomisionadoparalapaz.gov.co/Prensa/Documentos%20compartidos/Colombian-Peace-AgreementEnglish-Translation.pdf.
According to Paragraph IV of the Agreement, and upon request of the Colombian President, the United Nations annexed the complete text of the Agreement to Resolution by the Security Council (2261/2016). For this version of the text, see UNSC, S/2017/272, available at: https://colombia.unmissions.org/sites/default/files/s-2017-272_e.pdf.

2 Academic discussion on the agreement has been mainly focused on the innovative transitional justice mechanisms. See, for instance, Kai Ambos, *The Colombian Peace Process and the Principle of Complementarity of the International Criminal Court* (Dordrecht: Springer, 2010); Astrid Liliana Sánchez-Mejía, *Victim's Rights in Flux: Criminal Justice Reform in Colombia* (Dordrecht: Springer, 2017); Fabio Andrés Díaz Pabón (ed.) *Truth, Justice and Reconciliation in Colombia* (London: Routledge, 2018); James Meernik, Jacqueline Demerit, and Mauricio Uribe-López (eds.), *As War Ends: What Colombia Can Tell Us About the Sustainability of Peace and Transitional Justice* (Cambridge: Cambridge University Press, 2019). See also, "Symposium on the Colombian Peace Talks and International Law" eds. Alexandra Huneeus and René Urueña, *AJIL Unbound*, vol. 110, 2016–2017, pp. 161–204 and "Land, Justice, and Memory: Challenges for Peace in Colombia," *Special Issue of Canadian Journal of Latin American and Caribbean Studies*. Co-edited by Catherine Le-Grand, Luis van Isschot and Pilar Riano-Alcala, vol. 42 (3), 2017. In Spanish, see Rodrigo Uprimny et al, *Justicia para la Paz* (Bogotá: Dejusticia, 2014); Jaime Bernal Cuellar et al. *Reflexiones Jurídicas sobre el Proceso de Paz* (Bogotá: Externado, 2016); Carlos Bernal Pulido et al. (eds.), *Justicia Transicional,* 4 vols. (Bogotá: Externado, 2016); Camilo Umaña (ed.), *La Justicia al Encuentro de la Paz en Contextos de Transición* (Bogotá: Externado, 2018); Carlos Fernández and Ernesto Rey (eds.) El Acuerdo de Paz Entre el Gobierno de Colombia y las FARC (Bogotá: Universidad Libre, 2018) and Juan Carlos Ospina, *Desafíos y Oportunidades del Sistema Integral de Verdad, Justicia y No Repetición* (Bogotá: CCJ, 2019).

3 For a detailed map, see Javier Osorio, Mohamed Mohamed, Viveca Pavon, and Susan Brewer-Osorio, "Mapping Violent Presence of Armed Actors in Colombia," *Advances of Cartography and GIScience of the International Cartographic Association*, vol. 1, (16), 2019: pp. 1–9, https://www.adv-cartogr-giscience-int-cartogr-assoc.net/1/16/2019/.

4 For official historical reconstructions, see the report Comisión Histórica del Conflicto y sus Víctimas, Contribución al entendimiento del conflicto armado en Colombia, February, 2012 http://www.humanas.unal.edu.co/observapazyconflicto/files/5714/6911/9376/Version_final_informes_CHCV.pdf; Historical Memory Group, Basta Ya!: Colombia – Memories of War and Dignity (Bogota: Grupo de Memoria Histórica, 2016), http://centrodememoriahistorica.gov.co/descargas/informes2016/basta-ya-ingles/BASTA-YA-ingles.pdf. Colombia's political history has received

significant academic attention. For some examples, in English see David Bushnell, *The Making of Modern Colombia: A Nation in Spite of Itself* (Berkeley: University of California, 1993); Robert A. Karl, *Forgotten Peace: Reform, Violence and the Making of Contemporary Colombia* (Oakland: University of California Press, 2013), Ana Arjona, *Rebelocracy: Social order in the Colombian Civil War* (Cambridge: Cambridge University Press, 2016).

5 Older account estimated around 200,000 deaths. See Norman A. Bailey, "La Violencia in Colombia," *Journal of Inter-American Studies,* vol. 9, 1967, pp. 561–75, citing, Germán Guzmán, Orlando Fals Borda and Eduardo Umaña Luna, *La Violencia en Colombia*, 2 vols. (Bogotá: Tercer Mundo, 1962 and 1964), vol. I, ch. IX, and vol. II, part. III, chapter 2. However, recent studies have suggested that the number might be smaller. Julio-Romero Prieto and Adolfo Meisel-Roca, "Análisis Demográfico de la Violencia en Colombia," *Cuadernos de Historia Económica*, vol. 50, 2019, https://repositorio.banrep.gov.co/bitstream/handle/20.500.12134/9597/CHE_50.pdf.

6 On guerrillas terror attacks, see Centro Nacional de Memoria Histórica, *Tomas y Ataques Guerrilleros (1965–2013)* (Bogotá: CNMH, 2015), https://centrodememoriahistorica.gov.co/tomas-y-ataques-guerrilleros-1965–2013/.

7 See Centro Nacional de Memoria Histórica, *Análisis Cuantitativo del Paramilitarismo en Colombia* (Bogotá: CNMH, 2019), https://centrodememoriahistorica.gov.co/wp-content/uploads/2020/02/Libro_Paramilitarismo_baja.pdf. In English, see J. Hristov, *Blood and Capital: The Paramilitarization of Colombia* (Athens: Ohio University Press, 2009).

8 Data from the Observatorio de Memoria y Conflicto [Observatory of Memory and Conflict], http://centrodememoriahistorica.gov.co/observatorio/.

9 See Centro Nacional de Memoria Histórica, *Hasta Encontrarlos: El Drama de la Desaparición Forzada en Colombia* (Bogotá: CNMH, 2016), https://centrodememoriahistorica.gov.co/descargas/informes2016/hasta-encontrarlos/hasta-encontrarlos-drama-de-la-desaparicion-forzada-en-colombia.pdf.

10 See https://www.unidadvictimas.gov.co/es/registro-unico-de-victimas-ruv/37394 (accessed July 31, 2020).

11 See Centro Nacional de Memoria Histórica, *Una Nación Desplazada* (Bogotá: CNMH, 2015), http://www.centrodememoriahistorica.gov.co/descargas/informes2015/nacion-desplazada/una-nacion-desplazada.pdf.

12 This act has been called an act of political genocide. See, Centro Nacional de Memoria Histórica, *Todo Pasó Frente a Nuestros Ojos: El genocidio de la Unión Patriótica* (Bogotá: CNMH, 2018), https://centrodememoriahistorica.gov.co/todo-paso-frente-a-nuestros-ojos-genocidio-de-la-union-patriotica-1984–2002/.

13 On Colombian innovative constitutional system, see Manuel José Cepeda and David Landau, *Colombian Constitutional Law: Leading Cases* (Oxford: Oxford University Press, 2017).

14 On the Pastrana's peace process, see in English, Harvey Cline, *Chronicle of a Failure Foretold: The Peace Process of Colombian President Andrés Pastrana* (Tuscaloosa: University of Alabama Press, 2007).

15 False positives are currently under investigation in the Special Jurisdiction for Peace. https://www.jep.gov.co/Especiales/casos/03.html. While the Colombian attorney general listed more than 2,000 cases, estimates indicate there could be up to 10,000.

16 In particular, Judgment C-370/06.

17 For a general assesment, Comisión Nacional de Memoria Histórica, *Justicia Balance de la CNMH al Esclarecimiento Histórico* (Bogotá: CNMH, 2018), http://www.centrodememoriahistorica.gov.co/micrositios/balances-jep/descargas/balance-justicia.pdf.

18 On the negotiation, see Chapter 2. For the full history of the process leading to the

agreement, see http://www.altocomisionadoparalapaz.gov.co/legalidad-convivencia/pedagogia/difusion-acuerdo-final (last consulted, July 31, 2020). See also, Andrés Bermúdez Liévano, *Los debates de La Habana: una mirada desde adentro* (Barcelona: Instituto para las Transiciones integrales, 2018), https://www.ifit-transitions.org/resources/publications/major-publications-briefings/the-colombian-peace-talks-practical-lessons-for-negotiators-worldwide/los-debates-de-la-habana.pdf/, view and Renata Segura and Delphine Mechoulan, *Made in Havana: How Colombia and FARC Decided to End the War* (New York: International Peace Institute, 2017).

19 See Chapter 2.

20 The prohibition against presidential re-election was reinstated in 2015.

21 On the land component, see Chapter 12.

22 This system is comprehensively discussed in Chapters 6–9.

23 See Chapter 10.

24 See Chapter 11.

25 See Chapter 14.

26 For example, ICC, "Statement of ICC Prosecutor, Fatou Bensouda, on the conclusion of the peace negotiations between the government of Colombia and the Revolutionary Armed Forces of Colombia – People's Army," September 1, 2016, https://www.icc-cpi.int/Pages/item.aspx?name=160901-otp-stat-colombia.

27 See Chapter 13.

28 For official information, see https://www.registraduria.gov.co/?page=plebiscito_2016 (accessed July 31, 2020). For discussions of this result, see Chapters 5, 16, and 17.

29 See Chapters 5, 14, 16, and 17.

30 In the Office of the High Commissioner for Peace, there are 13,511 people accredited as former members of FARC. See Consejería Presidencial para la Estabilización y la Consolidación, Informe de Gestión, August 7, 2018–June 30, 2020.

31 Ibid, p. 12.

32 See Kroc Institute for Peace Studies, Tres años después de la firma del Acuerdo Final de Colombia. Diciembre 2019 a noviembre 2019. Bogotá, 2020, p. 14

33 See Chapters 4 and 5. On the implementation of the Agreement, see https://peaceaccords.nd.edu/barometer/colombia-reports. For the last report, to June 2020, Instituto Kroc de Estudios Internacionales de Paz, "Tres años después de la firma del Acuerdo Final de Colombia: hacia la transformación territorial," June 2020, http://peaceaccords.nd.edu/wp-content/uploads/2020/06/Cuarto-Informe-Final-with-Annex-Link.pdf.

34 See Chapter 13. Also, CINE-CERAC, Sexto informe trimestral de verificación de la implementación del A.F., 20 de junio de 2019, p. 10, https://www.cinep.org.co/Home2/component/k2/704-sexto-informe-de-verificacion-de-la-implementacion-del-acuerdo-final-de-paz-en-colombia-para-los-verificadores-internacionales.html.

35 Data from NGO INDEPAZ, updated on July 15, 2020, http://www.indepaz.org.co/pazparaliderar/.

36 See D.P. Arias Henao, "La Implementación del acuerdo de paz y la transformación del conflicto armado en Colombia," *Revista Científica General José María Córdova,* vol. 18 (31), 2020, p. 577.

37 For a discussion on this case, which led to Santrich's expulsion from the JEP, see Chapter 11.

38 See Note 1.

39 "The JEP in English," at https://www.jep.gov.co/Sala-de-Prensa/Paginas/The-JEP-in-english.aspx.

Part I

Genesis

2 The possibility of peace

Sergio Jaramillo Caro

The Colombian conflict has been the longest in the history of Latin America. So long that it became a way of life. For decades, our officers spent their entire military careers diligently fighting the same enemy, while the guerrilla, though much weakened, roamed around the mountains and jungles. The civilians in conflict regions, for their part, survived as best they could. But for most Colombians in the cities, only the images on their television screens brought home the reality that they were living in a country at war.

When a conflict goes on for half a century, as happened in Colombia, it is also because there are interests and practices which militate against any attempt at resolution. The question I would like to answer is: If there was an "intractable conflict" in Colombia, as experts like to say, why was it possible this time to arrive at an agreement? Or to put the same question differently: How was it possible to transform the logic of confrontation into a logic of cooperation?

Before attempting a response, let me recall two ideas of Thomas Schelling (who had the kindness in 2014 at age 93 years to hop on a train and attend a brainstorming session we organized in New York on the Havana negotiations). The first is the well-known insight that no conflict is pure conflict or confrontation, but rather is the product of a combination of interests which can motivate both confrontation and cooperation. A mix.

The second idea complements the first: For that very reason, there can be win–win solutions based on cooperation, so that "winning" in a conflict does not mean so much defeating your adversary, as—in Schelling's wonderful phrase—"gaining relative to our own value system."[1]

A negotiation, then, can be the best way to "win" in a conflict, insofar as it can align the interests in cooperation of both sides, motivate them to end the war (need there a greater justification for a negotiation than saving lives?), and allow for the creation of a solution in which the whole of society wins, especially the victims of the conflict—past and present. Which is, I believe, what it means to win "relative to our own value system."

In any case, that is what we tried to do in Havana: To reach an agreement that would put an end to the armed conflict and at the same time open the door to a proper transition phase during which the implementation of the agreement would contribute to building "a stable and lasting peace" and benefit all of society.

Let us return to the question: What made it possible to arrive at an agreement this time? There are two complementary ways to look at the problem. The first is: What conditions changed that made the negotiations possible? This is what scholars of peace processes like to call "ripeness."[2] I will leave that for future analysts to comment on, but it is worth mentioning that the most commonly mentioned change, the change in the military balance, was certainly a necessary condition for the negotiations to occur, but not a sufficient condition to reach an agreement. Many stars had to align, as Helmut Kohl said of German reunification. And practically no guerrilla group ever surrenders. The conflict could have lingered on in the Colombian countryside for decades without a problem.

The point is that favorable conditions in no way guarantee a result. History is full of ripe moments which slipped away *because a solution was not forged.*

This is the other way to look at the problem: To understand the peace process as the creation of a space which enables a change in the "mix" of interests, so that cooperation prevails over confrontation. That is the essence, in my view, of peace-making—and perhaps of strategy in general—the creation of spaces which channel reality and get things to flow in a particular direction, so that people start to behave differently and new possibilities open for change and transformation.

It is, if you will, a form of design, which does not differ greatly from building a house: You agree on a plan, you put down the foundations, then the ground floor, then you add some rooms, and so on. Except that it is literally a house in motion with many moving parts that you try to hold together as best you can.

I

I will now try to describe ten steps or measures—Schelling would call them "strategic moves"—which, in my view, enabled us to establish a logic of cooperation and reach an agreement.

The first step was simply to recognize that there was a window of opportunity for peace. That was what President Santos did when he took office in 2010. Without that clarity of vision and the willingness to take all the political risks, there simply would not have been an agreement.

At the same time, after three major failed peace processes with the Revolutionary Armed Forces of Colombia (FARC)—in la Uribe, in Tlaxcala, and in Caguán—we knew that another failure would close the doors to any future attempt at negotiation. So we had to follow what I would call "a strategy of prudence," which simply means doing things incrementally, building step by step on concrete results. It is well known that the best way to secure cooperation between adversaries is to build up results gradually over time, which in turn builds trust, because it shows seriousness.

At the end of 2010, President Santos publicly acknowledged that there was an internal armed conflict in Colombia. He did so by presenting a draft law on victims' reparations, known the Victims' Law, that referred explicitly to the armed conflict. That may seem like stating the obvious (hundreds of our soldiers died year after year in military operations, all conducted under the International Humanitarian Law), but it was not recognized by the previous administration, which always denied its existence. This denial, to this day, constitutes the basis of the ideology of former President Álvaro Uribe Vélez and a major obstacle to peace and reconciliation.

Without that recognition, there is simply no possibility of setting up the necessary framework for peace negotiations, for two reasons. First, because the cornerstone of any negotiation, anywhere in the world, is the disarmament of the guerrilla in exchange for their transition into politics. This transition is justified by the significance of the ending of an armed conflict and the importance of putting an end, finally, to political violence, and the need to stabilize the peace through political inclusion.

Similarly, without the framework of the armed conflict, there is also no basis of dignity for dealing with your adversary. And without dignity, no negotiation is possible.

Secondly, the framework of the armed conflict enables you to determine which behaviors are legitimate and which should be sanctioned because they constitute a violation of the law of war. And, above all, it justifies the setting up of a transitional justice system to respond to victims.

What is at stake, therefore, is the very idea of a transition. Without a recognition of the existence of the conflict, not only is no peace negotiation possible, but neither is a coherent concept of transition, with all the consequences this has for the victims, for peace, for reconciliation, and for the construction of a collective vision of the future of the country. I will return to these points later.

II

The second step was to create an adequate international environment and secure international participation. In 2010, Colombia was thoroughly isolated in the region. So one of President Santos' first acts as president was to sit down with President Chávez as responsible neighbors, to lower tensions. Within a few months, with the help of his Foreign Minister María Ángela Holguín, President Santos succeeded in normalizing relations with all our neighbors and in gaining the support of the whole region.

I remember well a meeting I had with Hugo Chávez which he ended by telling me: "We use to treat each other as enemies, now we shall treat each other as adversaries." That is what dialog achieves. Chávez changed his position on Colombia radically. Instead of supporting the guerrillas, as he had done, he decided to support the peace process.

After the traumatic negotiations in Caguán (1999–2002) during the Pastrana government, in which nearly two dozen countries were invited as friends of the process without knowing very well what for (if you assign someone a role, they will naturally want to play it), we decided to opt this time for a minimalist strategy with the international community. Or rather, a "needs-based" strategy: Securing what international support was strictly necessary for the tasks at hand, and opening bit by bit to other countries—principally other countries in Latin America—according to the needs of the process itself.

The first and principal supporting roles were played by Cuba and Norway, whom we invited to be "guarantors" of the negotiations, with Cuba as host (they came to all the meetings but did not intervene; in moments of crisis they facilitated the finding of solutions away from the negotiating table).

Why Cuba? We made the calculation that Cuba probably had an interest in helping to end the armed conflict, and that is exactly how things played out. Cuba gave the FARC the necessary security guarantees, offered us a place to conduct negotiations far from the media, and provided us with all the resources to make the process a success.

Norway, for its part, brought all its well-known quiet professionalism to bear on the peace process and provided critical help with some of the thorniest issues (for example, by bringing transitional justice experts to talk to the FARC). Both Cuba and Norway put some of their sharpest and most experienced diplomats, Rodolfo Benítez and Dag Nylander, as heads of their teams. With infinite patience they listened to both delegations and were always at hand to help with the many stumbling blocks and crises of the peace process for more than four years.

Equally important was the role played by the International Committee of the Red Cross (ICRC). The negotiations in Havana were possible thanks to the extremely complex operations to extract FARC commanders from the middle of the jungle, which are a good example of the "incremental strategy." We put together a model in the secret phase with the ICRC and the guarantor countries that allayed the FARC's fears and built trust. And then it opened up like a spiral, multiplying exponentially in dozens of operations during the public phase of negotiations.

We also put together a group of international advisers with deep personal experience in peace negotiations: Jonathan Powell, William Ury, Shlomo Ben Ami, Joaquín Villalobos, and Dudley Ankerson. All conflicts are different, and so are therefore all peace negotiations. As Clausewitz would say, the first condition for a negotiation to work is to understand the nature of the conflict one is trying to resolve. But there are also structural elements in negotiations that are necessarily similar—for example, the problem of guarantees for those who give up their weapons—and you can learn a lot from what others have achieved, as well as from their mistakes.

Later on, in the public phase, we invited Chile and Venezuela to "accompany" the process. They visited us regularly in Havana and subsequently reported on the progress of the talks to different countries in the region.

The United States was a special case. President Obama gave the process his full support and discussed it often with President Santos. His government did not interfere in any way and when in late 2014 it became clear that a more active US role was convenient, Secretary of State Kerry—who could not have been more committed to peace in Colombia or more helpful, and took quite a few risks—quickly dispatched a special envoy to Havana at our request: Bernie Aronson, a very savvy and very patient retired diplomat, who helped the FARC to understand Washington's point of view, and vice versa.

Sadly, with the change of government in the United States came a corresponding change in attitude, which shows again that one cannot let windows of opportunity pass by. With the current international context, the negotiation would have been much more difficult, or perhaps even impossible.

The role of the United Nations Security Council was critical. In the midst of great international disagreements and tensions, at Colombia's request, the Council voted unanimously to pass two resolutions to create and implement a special political mission to verify the ceasefire (and it would subsequently pass three further resolutions in support of the process, also unanimously). The Under-Secretary-General for Political Affairs, Jeff Feltman, also played a key role, by designing a tailor-made mission and coaxing the Council along, as did the UK Mission to the United Nations (UN) which acted as "pen holder" of the resolutions.

We must remember that, historically, the FARC had no trust in the UN. The failed peace process in Caguán (1999–2002) had left a bitter taste. If that was overcome it was in large part due to Fabrizio Hochschild, the resident Coordinator in Colombia, who quietly built a relation with the FARC by supporting the participation of civil society and especially of the victims participation in the talks, and later on to Jean Arnault, who headed the verification mission.

The bilateral ceasefire, under the supervision of the Security Council, was a success. There were practically no incidents during the cantonment of the FARC in the 26 concentration zones. Our Military Forces and National Police showed great professionalism, and the FARC did their bit as well. "For me, Commissioner, it is an honor to have been part of the end of the war," one Army Major told me, in an austere camp in the midst of the Chocó jungle, where he spent his days ensuring the protection of the concentration zone. Similarly, the National Police created a special protection unit (UNIPEP), which quickly gained the respect of the FARC commanders.

At the same time, the tripartite verification mechanism that we had agreed, in which the Colombian officers and the FARC guerrillas, along with the UN, would investigate jointly on the ground any reported violation of the cease fire, dressed in the same beige-colored institutional vests, surprised local communities and built trust.

The process of decommissioning of arms was a success. After decades of collecting intelligence, we had very detailed information on the FARC's weapons, and to our surprise it matched the weapons that the FARC handed over. Close to 9,000 firearms, including 274 heavy machine guns and 266 trench mortars, together with 40 tonnes of explosives, were handed over to the UN observers, mostly officers from Latin American Countries.

III

The third step—and perhaps the most crucial—was to insist on holding secret talks and reaching a framework agreement before launching a public peace process. After a year and a half of back-channelling and sending messages to and fro, thanks to the good offices of Henry Acosta, we started secret talks on February 24, 2012 and then sat in a safe house in Havana covered with white-boards for the next six months, hammering away at the framework agreement.

This had three major advantages. First, it allowed both sides to talk seriously and test each other out without the pressure of public opinion, and without the temptation to use the media to pander to its own audience, which is exactly what happened once the public phase of the process was launched in October 2012. The fact that neither side leaked the secret talks in such a media-mad country as Colombia was an early and telling sign that, this time, both sides were both serious.

Second, the framework agreement we signed on August 26, 2012, which we called the General Agreement, set out not just the agenda, but the terms and the whole vision of the peace process. It was a kind of contract, so that the government, the FARC and—especially—the Colombian public knew exactly what we were getting into, and what the negotiation agenda included (and no less important, what it did not include). Above all, it made it very clear, as we shall see, that this time we were going to discuss the end of the armed conflict itself.

And third, the secret talks conferred the necessary dignity on the negotiations and developed the methods which later keep the negotiations on track. We treated each other as interlocutors at the negotiating table and spoke to each other with respect, and generally with cordiality. That is something that to this day some people in Colombia do not accept; they claim that the government consented to make itself the equal of the FARC. They missed the point: In a negotiation, you need to abide by the same rules and procedures, because it is those rules and procedures that allow you to get to agreements, and they confer the necessary dignity on the other side.

IV

The fourth step was to establish a narrative that would give a sense of direction to the peace process, set clear limits to the negotiations, and yet open a space within which both sides could "live."

That new narrative was "the end of the conflict." From the beginning we said that this process, unlike the previous ones with the FARC, was about *ending the armed conflict*. And by that we meant three things. First, that this time the agenda had to include a point on disarmament, something which the FARC had never accepted and which in fact led temporarily to the only real breakdown of the negotiations. Without written assurances that this time the end of the conflict was for real, we were not willing to risk another peace process after so many failures.

The point was not just that we first needed proof of the FARC's commitment to ending the war—though it was certainly that—if we were going to commit ourselves to discussing issues that went beyond disarmament and, especially, if we were to going to pay the price of moving on to the public phase of the talks. The whole conceptual basis of the process was built on breaking the link between arms and politics and avoiding the mistakes of the past.

In the peace process of La Uribe in the 1980s, the FARC founded a political party with the consent of the government, the Unión Patriótica, during a ceasefire. But they kept their weapons and remained mobilized. The result was that thousands of their supporters were brutally killed by a combination of paramilitaries, drug traffickers and state agents. The primary responsibility for this horrific massacre, which would do much to keep the conflict alive over the next decades, certainly lay with that very unholy alliance. But the government and especially the FARC have much to answer for.

"Never again politics with weapons" was therefore our guiding principle. We were not only very firm with the FARC during the secret talks in insisting that there had to be a point on disarmament in the agenda. We also wrote a sequence into the framework agreement: disarmament must begin simultaneously with the signing of the final agreement and proceed apace. As a result, when the agreement was signed four years later, the FARC handed over their weapons to the UN in a record of eight months.

Nobody in Colombia thought that would happen in their lifetimes, much less so that quickly and comprehensively. Perhaps the main practical reason was that the FARC knew they had to disarm swiftly—and have the UN certify that—if they were going to be allowed to campaign for the congressional and presidential elections. And they knew they were running out of time.

Second, the "end of the conflict" meant not only ending armed confrontation, but also, above all, guaranteeing its non-repetition. The Agreement had to contribute to putting a definitive end to the historic cycles of political violence in Colombia and avoid its recurrence or degeneration into other forms of violence, as had happened so often in the past. For this reason, as we said repeatedly, the Agreement was about far more than the decommissioning of the FARC's weapons. Disarming the FARC was a necessary but not sufficient condition to guarantee non-repetition. We had to address the conditions that had fed and kept the conflict going over so many decades.

That is the logic, or logics, of nonrepetition which the agenda of the General Agreement sought to promote:

- A logic of territorial integration, in order to integrate into the country, over a fifteen-year transition period, the peripheral regions, and populations which have suffered the conflict most, as well as to guarantee minimal conditions of well-being for them—point 1 of the agenda, comprehensive rural reform.
- A logic of activation of political rights of all Colombian citizens, in order for the term "democracy" to have meaning across the whole of the national territory, as communities actively participate in public life in their regions and violence is rooted out from our political culture—point 2 of the agenda, political participation.
- A logic of transformation of those territories ridden with coca crops, by promoting legal sources of income that flush out the illegal economies, along with firm judicial action against local organized crime—point 4 of the agenda, drugs.
- And finally, a logic of acknowledgement of, and response to, the victims, in order to guarantee their rights, soothe the resentment which consumes people and society, and promote conditions of coexistence and reconciliation—point 5 of the agenda, victims' rights.

The narrative about ending the armed conflict also helped us to keep out of the negotiation the dozens and dozens of proposals which the FARC made which had little or nothing to do with the end of the conflict and its nonrepetition, such as their opposition to free trade agreements or the management of the economy. The narrative defined the agenda.

At the same time—this is very important—each side could give its own justification for the points on the agenda. For example, the government believed, as I have said, that the agenda included those points which in our view were enabling conditions which kept the conflict alive, while the FARC saw them the justification for their struggle—something which the government strongly disagreed with. But in practice these conceptual differences did not matter. We could each live with our own interpretation, so long as we were talking about the same concrete things. That is what the narrative of the framework General Agreement achieved: The opening of a space within which both sides could breathe and develop a negotiation.

Most importantly, the narrative of the end of the conflict recognized the enormous window of opportunity for structural change that a peace agreement could mean for Colombia. Our 1991 Constitution is a prime example of contemporary constitutionalism and contains an extensive bill of rights. The peace process offers the opportunity to move from aspirations and promises to concrete actions in those territories and among those populations that were hardest hit by the armed conflict and are most vulnerable, in order to lay the foundations of a lasting peace.

Our critics sometimes asked why these reforms had to be the product of an agreement with the FARC, when they are—they claim—what any government should do. To which I always reply: If it's all so obvious, why has nobody done it? There is clearly a problem with the incentives of the political economy of Colombia that has left large swathes of the country outside of the radar of politicians, and in general of the economy. In my view, only a peace agreement can motivate with sufficient force a process of institutionalization and democratization of those vast regions—what I have called elsewhere "territorial peace," and a more inclusive democracy.[3] I will return to this point later.

Lastly, the narrative of "the end of the conflict" also allowed us to distinguish between the negotiations that were taking place in Havana to put an end to the armed confrontation, on the one hand, and the subsequent peace-building phase, on the other, that requires the participation of all citizens. That difference was both conceptual and practical, and we wrote it from the start into the framework agreement. It was a way of signaling that peace building was something that had to be undertaken by all Colombians on the ground and of recognizing the years of grassroots peace-building work that local organizations and communities have done for decades.

All the above was based on a very simple but very effective principle of the General Agreement: "Nothing is agreed until everything is agreed." In other words, the government was not going to commit to doing anything to end military actions, until the ending of the armed conflict was agreed.

V

The fifth step was to put together a strong methodology that could "carry" the process. Unusually, the negotiations in Havana had no mediation; there was no UN diplomat writing perfect UN language into the agreement. We fought over almost every word that was agreed with the FARC, and yet we managed to write the 300 pages of the agreement together. It has to be said that the FARC really raised their game and were a worthy counterpart. As the government, we naturally had all the advantages.

But the main reason it worked is because of the working method we established in the secret phase of negotiations (to work on a "single text"), which we continued developing in the public phase, and thanks to the various "spaces" and commissions we created:

- The negotiating table with all the plenipotentiaries, where we exchanged visions and made proposals to each other.
- The drafting commission, where we exchanged concrete proposals and agreed on the actual text of the Agreement.
- The gender commission, where the text was revised and proposals were made in order to ensure that the Agreement had a gender focus throughout.

- The commission to work on the point about "Ending of the Conflict," where the terms of the bilateral and definitive ceasefire were agreed, with the participation of active duty officers from the military and the police.
- A group of jurists who worked on the point on criminal justice.

The formal procedures of the negotiations were also important. The fact that we worked for three straight days, stopped for one, and then started again for another three, regardless of what day of the week it was, gave a strange sense of structure to the negotiation. In contrast to all that formality, we also set up informal meetings between the heads of the delegations known as the 3 + 3, where we tried out ideas on each other and got a better sense of what was going on.

But perhaps most important was the incremental manner in which the negotiations proceeded. The whole thing took a long time—I myself was based in Havana for four and a half years—and we paid a huge political price for it. But I wonder if it could have been otherwise. There was hardly a day when we did not work intensely. And our counterpart knew very well how to put the brakes on when they were unwilling to discuss a difficult issue, or to accept a particular proposal. In that situation, we had no other option than arm ourselves with patience and not accept the unacceptable.

Above all, I believe that this incremental and gradual approach was the key to building trust, both in Havana and in Colombia. Every time we reached an agreement on a point of the agenda we made it public. After we had reached one or two of these agreements, it was difficult to imagine either side giving up easily. It had been too much hard work, even if there was more to come.

That, in my view, is what trust in a peace process is about: You trust the results of the process itself. The more you achieve, the more irreversible it seems and, therefore, actually becomes.

VI

The sixth step was to put together a negotiating team that the Colombian public recognized as credible and fully empowered to negotiate. When the public phase of the negotiation started, President Santos brought in Humberto de la Calle, a former Vice-President, who played an extraordinarily important role as head of the delegation and kept the process afloat; the most respected former Commander of the Armed Forces, General Jorge Enrique Mora; the most respected former Director of the Police, General Óscar Naranjo; and finally, myself as the High Commissioner for Peace.

Others came and went at different moments of the negotiation, including Frank Pearl, former Councillor for Reintegration and former High Commissioner for Peace, Luis Carlos Villegas, former President of the ANDI (National Colombian Business Association), Nigeria Rentería, María Paulina Riveros, Gonzalo Restrepo, the senator Roy Barreras, and Foreign Minister María Ángela Holguín.

As so often happens in negotiations, our discussions within the government's team were frequently tough and no less intense than those with the FARC, often more so. But owing to the fact that all proposals which we took to the negotiating table had to pass first through the filter of heated debate between people from very different backgrounds and with very opinions, the proposals the government presented were always solid. At the table we spoke with a single voice.

FARC's Commander, Timochenko, very intelligently made sure that more and more members of the Secretariat, the FARC's directorate, were present in Havana, and especially the key field commanders, who usually make or break a peace process. Most would eventually rotate through Havana, with the help of the ICRC and the guarantor countries. Few measures were more important, because the organization's unity was maintained throughout the negotiation. A rare achievement.

Helicopters with ICRC logos were constantly taking off to pick up members of the FARC from the depths of the jungle or from mountain tops. In the final year of negotiations, the direction was reversed: Those who were in Havana returned to Colombia in order to do pedagogy with the different fronts and explain the agreements to them. This was key if we were to guarantee compliance from those on the ground. For the majority of the FARC, these visits represented the palpable reality of peace. Commanders often had not seen each other for a decade.

Another very important innovation was the decision by President Santos to send officers from the Armed Forces and the National Police in active service to Havana to negotiate the ceasefire. Five generals in active service and one admiral not only helped to hammer out the details of the ceasefire but in effect became a channel through which the negotiations flowed to the Armed Forces and the Police. That helped build trust.

I cannot fail to say a word as well about the many men and women of the Office of the High Commissioner for Peace (my office), in particular Elena Ambrosi, Mónica Cifuentes, Marcela Durán, and Gerson Arias, who were the base of the iceberg. They did most of the hard work, whether it was putting together or reviewing proposals till late at night every day, sorting out all the legal problems or managing the tricky communications. They all made it happen.

VII

The seventh step was to put the victims of the conflict at the center of the process. The Colombian conflict has been by far the most violent in Latin America. Virtually every Colombian knows someone who suffered, and that is no surprise as the conflict left hundreds of thousands dead, close to a hundred thousand missing and many millions internally displaced. No other conflict in our region has produced so many victims, or such horrific acts of violence (on the latest count, about 2,000 massacres occurred).

That is what the conflict represents to most Colombians and what has kept it going as much as anything: The fact of victimhood. If you speak to a young member of the FARC or his equivalent in the former paramilitary militias, more often than not you will find that they joined because their family had been a victim of one group or the other. So if you want to break the cycles of violence and do justice to so many who were wronged, you need to bring the victims' rights and needs to the fore.

For that reason we insisted from the very beginning of the secret talks that no agreement would be possible without a point about victims on the agenda. That is probably the major innovation of the Colombian peace process. It has never happened before in any previous negotiation.

Taking the perspective of the victims had three major advantages. First, it gave us an adequate measure of what it means to combat impunity in a transition to peace —the degree of satisfaction of victims' rights— and guaranteed a response more in line with the expectations of the victims themselves. It is not the same thing to deliver justice in ordinary conditions as after 50 years of war, or at least not entirely the same, because criminal justice alone cannot deliver fully the rights to truth, justice, and reparations and nonrepetition to which the victims are entitled. And in any case, no guerrilla would agree to an ordinary legal process in a peace negotiation.

Second, the focus on victims, rather than on the perpetrators, made it possible to have a reasonable discussion at the negotiating table, without ever losing sight of the obligation to investigate the gravest crimes (and therefore their perpetrators). In fact, as various experts have noted, this was the first peace negotiation anywhere which was done under the framework of the Rome Statute, and we were committed to honoring the international obligations of the Colombian state.

In my view, the thousands of transitional justice experts that write about such things have not faced squarely and honestly the fact that the tension between peace and justice in a negotiation is real. The people sitting across the table with whom you are negotiating are also those who, according to contemporary theories of criminal responsibility, are most responsible for the crimes committed by their group. How do you square that circle and guarantee twenty-first century standards of accountability? Again, by putting the victims at the center. And the victims themselves were among those most supportive of the peace process, because they had suffered most.

Third, the focus on all the victims of the conflict, not just on victims of the FARC, made it possible for the guerrilla to accept things no other guerrilla has accepted in a negotiation, precisely because we agreed that, in order to close the historic conflict and guarantee equal conditions to all victims, we had to address the rights of all victims, not just of the victims of the FARC (something that our own institutions to this day have not understood well).

This was also the most difficult point to negotiate in Havana. It took us about a year and a half, and required the support of many experts, especially of some who—with Norway's support— talked to and advised the FARC.

First, we needed to make sure there was adequate participation of the victims themselves in the process—that they were heard. For previous points on the agenda, every time we started the discussion in Havana, the UN and the National University would invite over a thousand people and organizations from around the country to gather in a meeting in Bogota with clear rules in order to make proposals for the discussion in Havana; it was a huge amount of work, but it guaranteed the participation of civil society in the process. But when we got to the point on victims, we decided to organize four forums in different regions of Colombia.

Afterward we got an enormous pile of books delivered to us in Havana, no less than 12 volumes full of comments and suggestions that gave us a good feeling of what victims thought and felt. Other victims sent us proposals via a "virtual post-box" on the negotiation table's webpage.

But this was not enough. We felt we had to listen to the victims directly. So we invited 60 victims to Havana, who came in five separate delegations composed of 12 members each. They were selected by the Church, the UN, and the National University. The fact that both the government and the FARC were often unhappy with the choice was probably a sign that they were doing a good job.

We heard, one after another and during entire mornings, testimonies of atrocities and examples of extraordinary courage, which reminded all of us why we were sitting at a negotiating table. It was not unlike a truth commission, but instead of commissioners it was the members of the negotiating teams that sat before the victims, some of whom were confronting their own victims for the first time. Several members of the FARC cried in the corridors.

At the same time, if combatting impunity and guaranteeing nonrepetition in a transition to peace means addressing a broad range of victims' rights, we had to think up a system which, with a combination of judicial and extra-judicial mechanisms, could satisfy these rights. We called it the "Comprehensive System of Truth, Justice Reparations and Non-Repetition." It is true that this was not new in terms of transitional justice doctrine (it is not much different from what Kofi Annan—who came to visit us in Havana in 2015 and played a quiet but important role in the process—proposed as UN Secretary General in the standard transitional justice document of 2004). Still, such a system had never been created in one go, much less in a negotiation with a guerrilla group.

We created a whole range of institutions to meet that challenge: The Tribunal and the Special Jurisdiction for Peace, the Commission for the Clarification of Truth, Coexistence and Non-Repetition, and the Special Unit for the Search for Disappeared Persons. We also agreed to put in motion a whole series of reparation measures to complement the existing mechanisms of individual compensation, especially measures that supported the return of the millions of forcibly displaced persons to their land and measures that took greater account of the collective impact of the armed conflict in the regions of

Colombia. In a long and bitter war, it is not only the direct victims of violence that suffer.

The point of the comprehensive system was not just to guarantee accountability and truth for past crimes, but to help build a basis of trust in the state institutions and between individuals in violence-ridden territories, in order to promote reconciliation and build peace. In my view, justice and peace measures should feed off each other. And reconciliation, or at least coexistence, should be promoted from the outset and not be seen simply as a distant end goal.

In regions with decades-long histories of violence, such as Urabá or Magdalena Medio, where everyone knows who did what, it does not seem possible to undertake ambitious collective rural development projects without first, at least in parallel, opening a space in which the victims can receive the recognition that is their due and those responsible can take a step forward.

That is why the point on victims in the Agreement begins with a commitment to acknowledge responsibility for the damage done in the regions, as the FARC started to do in Bojayá in December 2015 and have done subsequently in other places—in order to release the tension of decades-long resentment, to create trust, and to build a joint vision of the future of a region. We now need others to do the same.

The idea of promoting a self-reinforcing relation between justice and peace is in fact an instance of a broader logic that permeates the agenda of the General Agreement of 2012, which is a territorial logic. From the start, we thought if we really wanted to transform the conflict-afflicted regions we needed to implement the various points of the Agreement in a coordinated and mutually reinforcing way, to achieve critical mass for change.

For example, just as the recognition of victims builds trust for development, so the 16 programs of territorially focused rural development (known as "PDETs") which we agreed on are also a form of collective reparation and of social inclusion. Similarly, the transitory political circumscriptions that should have given special representation in Congress for two terms to 16 civil society representatives from the conflict-afflicted regions (and which were blocked by some parties) were understood to be a form of collective political reparations as well.

Also, by embedding the justice measures in the development measures we could achieve the right balance between the demands of corrective justice and the demands of social justice, between the past and the future. That is why I have always insisted that the Agreement is rights-based and aims at delivering justice in the broadest sense.

Finally, in order for the Comprehensive System to work, we needed those most responsible to take part and fully respond. That is, it needed a system of incentives and conditionalities.

The incentives are simple: If you tell the Special Jurisdiction the whole truth in detail about the crimes committed and contribute to the different components of the System from the start—you go to the Truth Commission, you respond to the requests for information from the Special Search Unit, you make the corresponding recognitions of responsibility, etc.—then you receive a special sentence, which supposes a time period of maximum eight years in conditions of "effective restriction of freedom" in some location, but not prison (though these conditions must be verifiable by a UN monitoring system), during which time you must carry out various kinds of reparatory and restorative actions, including such things as demining or contributing to reconstruction projects.

And if you do not tell the truth, you can face up to 20 years in prison.

The other side of the coin—the conditionalities—is that you must fulfill the conditions of the whole system, in order to guarantee a broad response to victims' rights in the transition. If you do not contribute fully to the System, you lose your right to the special sentence.

No guerrilla has ever accepted in a negotiation what the FARC have accepted: That international crimes—war crimes, crimes against humanity—cannot be amnestied; that they had to be accountable before a tribunal for those crimes; and that they had to serve sentences and make reparations to their victims with their own assets.

Why would a guerrilla group agree to *that*? Because it is a system for *all* the victims of the conflict. They would not stand alone on the stage of justice.

VIII

The eighth step was to create a new model of implementation based on citizen participation. The whole of the Agreement is shot through with measures to mobilize citizens around the implementation of every point, whether it be rural development, or political participation itself, or alternative development programs or indeed the justice mechanisms of the Comprehensive System.

The model puts into practice the principle that it is one thing to end the armed conflict, and another to build peace on the ground with the whole of society. At the same time, it ensures that many measures must pass through the filter of citizen deliberation and debate, in order to guarantee that things are implemented in accordance with local needs and preferences, and that they build on the many peace-building efforts of the last decades.

But it goes beyond that. In the end, the only guarantee of a stable and lasting peace is the ability of institutions on the ground to channel conflicts and protect citizens' rights. But how do you do that? Institutions don't fall out of the sky. And the Colombian state has often failed in its many efforts to integrate the vast peripheral regions where the conflict has raged and the coca economy has dominated people's lives.

The point is that we cannot keep on doing more of the same. Instead of creating trust, the lack of results of many of these efforts has increased what John Paul Lederach calls the problem of "distance" between the people in conflict-afflicted regions, who have heard too many promises in the past, and the state. The solution is to open a space where citizens play a central role in the development of the programs and work hand in hand with the national government and the local authorities. That is the key to institutional strengthening.

Why? Because it is only when people have a voice in their own affairs and see that their proposals are taken seriously and meet with an adequate response that they begin to breach their historic lack of trust in the Colombian state. This creates a virtuous cycle in state building: The more they see there are responses, the more they demand. And the more demands they make and the more institutions respond, the more you actually build something that resembles credible and efficient government in those regions where for so long it was every man for himself.

This is what I have called territorial peace. The pacification of the regions of Colombia based on citizens' participation at all levels, from the communities in rural hamlets to the universities and businesses in the departmental capitals, hand in hand with their authorities.

This is a huge challenge, but already tens of thousands of people have participated in the participatory planning processes in the PDETs. It is, again, the great opportunity—and the challenge—that is afforded us by peace: To integrate the conflict-afflicted regions, to deepen and give full meaning to our democracy, and to structure the relation between state and society in those regions anew.

IX

The ninth step was to give the FARC enough guarantees and assurances so as to enable them to move forward quickly with disarmament, as the Agreement specified, and—critically—to bring their organization along. Remember that a cardinal principle of the process was that there would be no transition to politics while still under arms. In order to form a political party and participate in the elections, the FARC first had to hand over all their weapons to the UN and to demobilize before the Office of the High Commissioner for Peace (OACP). I personally had to certify every single member of the FARC as a bona fide member after thorough background checks.

We did not want to repeat the mistakes that were made in the past (2003–06) with the demobilization of the paramilitary militias, when thousands and thousands of "false" combatants (as many as a third of the total, according to their own commanders today) and more than a few drug traffickers sneaked their way into the demobilization lists. Each FARC combatant also had to sign a written pledge to the OACP not to take up arms again. That's what we called in the Agreement "transiting to legality."

There were many and different kinds of guarantees. First, there were guarantees for the political transition: five seats in the Senate and five in the

Chamber (out of a total of 280 seats in Congress), in case they did not reach in the congressional elections the threshold of votes required to get a seat, as they in fact did not. The Minister of the Interior had to work extremely hard in order to get the constitutional amendment that created the seats through Congress, in the face of bitter opposition from the hard right. We also committed to giving special support for the new political party.

Second, security guarantees. Hundreds of members of the FARC have been trained by the National Protection Unit to be part of the security details of their own political leaders, and hundreds of details have been put at their disposal. The situation of the ex-combatants in the most remote regions is a different story, as the government's capacity to provide security in deep rural areas is limited. In fact, the security situation in those areas is proving to be the greatest challenge of the transition. Far too many local leaders and human rights activists have been killed, and the government's response has not been effective enough.

Third, legal guarantees. We created a "fast-track" mechanism in order to pass those laws and reforms that were most important for implementation (essentially, it reduced the number of debates by half), in particular the reform that gave the Comprehensive System of Truth, Justice and Reparations a constitutional footing, and the amnesty law for political crimes. All the legislation that came out of that mechanism immediately went for review by the Constitutional Court.

Fourth, socioeconomic guarantees for the FARC's reincorporation into society. The government agreed to give the men and women of the FARC a support package of two years (which they are receiving), and an additional lump sum for an economic project, which could be individual or collective.

Colombia has long and deep experience in reintegration, but mostly in urban contexts and mostly of individuals. FARC's reintegration will require a more collective approach, as it will often take place in deep rural regions. It is urgent therefore to get more associative projects going that guarantee them an income and that promote reconciliation through joint work with the local communities, which should benefit as well. The European Union announced a big support package for those projects.

X

The tenth step was to put the Agreement to a vote. On October 2 of last year, Colombians voted on a plebiscite which, as is well known, we lost (by a margin of 0.4%: 60,000 "no" votes out of 13.5 million made the difference).

Many people asked us, quite rightly, why we decided to submit the Agreement to a vote. The truth is that there was an inherent tension between the point on ending the armed conflict, which clearly did not require a vote, and other parts of the Agreement, such as comprehensive rural reform, which we thought required democratic legitimacy. And they could not be disentangled: The FARC were prepared to disarm *because* we had agreed to the other points.

We also had the problem of physical distance from Colombia and of the necessarily closed nature of the negotiations, which added more distance between the Colombian public and us, despite the extraordinary efforts of Humberto de la Calle to explain what was being done in Havana. A vote, we thought, would get all Colombians to participate directly in the peace process.

In any case, instead of uniting the country around peace, the plebiscite divided it into two camps, quite artificially in my view.[4] The No campaigners in Colombia always insisted that they were not against peace, not even against all of the agreement. They simply wanted changes made, they claimed. That is what former President Uribe, who led the No campaign and was obsessively opposed to the peace process, said in the months prior to the plebiscite: "If the No side wins, we ask that the negotiating table not break up, just to 'redirect' the dialogue."

President Santos' response was what you would expect in any serious democracy. The very night of the plebiscite he spoke to the country and acknowledged the result. And the next day he sent Humberto de la Calle and myself to sit down with the FARC in Havana and tell them that we would have to make modifications to the Agreement, as the No side demanded. In a remarkable show of maturity, the FARC agreed.

We then flew back to Colombia to hear out the No side for over a month. The whole thing culminated with an entire week of discussions day and night at the Ministry of the Interior. From that meeting we emerged with a document with 60 modifications proposed by the No campaigners. And with that document under our arms we flew back to Havana.

Finally, after two more weeks of negotiating day and night without a break with the FARC, they accepted 58 of the 60 proposed changes. Many more in fact than we ever imagined. The two points we could not change were those that constituted structural pillars of the Agreement—or of any of any peace agreement with a guerrilla force for that matter.

First, the possibility to participate in politics, which from the FARC's point of view was the justification for giving up their weapons, and from the government's was the justification for engaging in negotiations in the first place: To put an end once and for all to political violence in Colombia and to show that the only way forward was democratic politics. Besides, all studies show that, more than any other measure, it is political inclusion that guarantees the stability of peace.

And second, the FARC's refusal to serve sentences in prison-like conditions. A Secretariat member said to me: "We are not going to be the first guerrilla force ever to sign a peace agreement and then go to prison. Even if I accepted that, my own people on the ground would not."

Ultimately, the evident ambition of former President Uribe to use the plebiscite as a platform for the 2018 presidential campaign (his appointed candidate in fact won, so the strategy worked), and his insistent denial of the existence of an armed conflict in Colombia, and therefore of the basic conditions of a peace negotiation, made consensus with the No side impossible.

This leads me to a final reflection on the extraordinary difficulty, paradoxically, of reaching a peace agreement and building peace in a democracy. Certainly we put our faith in democracy as the best system of conflict resolution. And that is what the Agreement in the end is about: To broaden and deepen democracy, especially among the millions in the periphery of Colombia that for so long have not got much out of it.

But it is also true that contemporary democracies have become increasingly often spaces of competition for parties or movements that seem dedicated solely to the achievement of power, without any consideration other than their own interest. And that hunger for power trumps by far the interest in peace, certainly in Colombia, and probably in many other democracies with internal conflicts. In fact, the very positions on peace held by different political sectors define the identities and loyalties of their constituencies, and the politicians themselves therefore end up trapped in what is in effect a vicious circle of intransigence and radicalism. Those conditions do not favor the creation of consensuses and close the doors to the opportunities for transformation and reconciliation which a peace process permits and requires.

*

The new Final Agreement was signed on November 24, 2016, and ratified by Congress a few days later. By January the FARC began to move their combatants into 26 cantonment zones to begin the process of disarmament under UN monitoring. Colombians saw striking images of the FARC's men and women sailing down rivers in wooden boats—some carried parrots on their shoulders, a last reminder of life in the jungle—or marching in rows down small country roads on their way to the zones, while the campesinos cheered them on either side with whistles and shouts. Nobody could believe this was happening. It was the end of the war. There was now the possibility of peace.

Author's note

This is a revised version of the inaugural lecture at the Pearson Institute of the University of Chicago, which was held on April 24, 2017. The lecture was dedicated to the memory of Tom Schelling. My thanks to Jim Robinson for the invitation, and to Malcolm Deas of the University of Oxford and Gwen Burnyeat of University College-London, for their comments.

Notes

1 Thomas C. Schelling, *The Strategy of Conflict* (Cambridge: Harvard University Press, 1960) 4.

2 See, for example, William Zartman, “Ripeness: The Hurting Stalemate and Beyond” in Daniel Druckman and Paul Stern (eds.) *Conflict Resolution After the Cold War* (Washington: National Academy Press, 2000) 225–250.
3 See “La Paz Territorial,” Lecture presented at Carr Center for Human Rights Policy, Harvard University, on March 13, 2013, available at https://interaktive-demokratie.org/files/downloads/La-Paz-Territorial.pdf.
4 The campaign itself had striking parallels to Brexit—both in the tone and in the cavalier attitude to the truth—which had taken place only 3 months before. But with one critical difference: Brexit was a binary choice and could only deliver one result, remain or leave.

3 Notes on transitional justice in Colombia

A view from 2014

Jon Elster

On December 12, 2013, I met with members of the transitional justice (TJ) team of the Presidency of Colombia. In this note, I report what I learned, comment on some of the proposals, and make some proposals and suggestions of my own. I do not name any members of the team as I do not want them to be held responsible for possible misunderstandings.

The process of TJ in Colombia is embedded in the ongoing negotiations between the Colombian government and Colombia's Revolutionary Armed Forces (FARC). A few remarks on the actors are in order.

The current president, Juan Manuel Santos, is strongly committed to peace and justice, whether he views the latter mainly as a means to the former or as a goal to be valued in its own right. In this project, he was dealt a strong hand by his predecessor, President Uribe, who pursued a consistent military repression of the FARC. Hence, government negotiators were in a strong position to impose the procedural conditions described below.

Although originally inspired by the goals of social justice and aiming at gaining political power in the country, both the aim and the ambitions of the FARC have changed over time. On the one hand, the increasing use of narcotrafficking to fund its political activities tends to give FARC a mafia-like profile. On the other hand, the decisive military actions of the Uribe government have killed any hope of taking national power through revolutionary action. At the same time, if negotiations with the government broke down, FARC would probably be able to survive, even without drug money since it has many alternative sources of income: Smuggling, kidnappings for ransom, siphoning oil from pipelines, etc. Hence, a definitive military victory *over the FARC* is as unfeasible as a political victory *by the FARC*.

The issue has an important generational dimension. Although the inner workings of the FARC leadership are shrouded in uncertainty, it seems probable that, on the continuum from social movement to mafia, the second- and third-generation leaders are closer to the latter end. Leaders motivated by social justice may be motivated to accept a deal that implements this goal even if it involves renouncing the vans stacked with hundred-dollar bills, whereas their younger comrades are likely to approach the matter differently. Thus, the current negotiations might be the last chance before the Mafiosi take control of the organization. This aspect of the situation lends an *urgency* to the negotiations that may favor agreement. Nonetheless, even if an agreement were to be reached within this arguably narrow window of opportunity, the ability of the leaders to commit the organization as a whole to respect it may of course be open to question.

In August 2012, representatives of the government and FARC reached agreement on a six-point agenda for peace negotiations, covering (1) comprehensive agrarian development policy; (2) political participation; (3) end of armed conflict; (4) solution to the problem of illicit drugs; (5) victims; and (6) implementation, verification, and endorsement. On May 26, 2013, the two parties announced that they had reached agreement on the first point and on November 6, 2013 that they had reached agreement on the second point.

The agreement also specifies that "Within the framework of point (5) […] the truth about the phenomenon of paramilitarism, among others, shall be sought." The agreement does not explicitly refer to crimes committed by FARC members and to ways of dealing with them. (Implicitly, however, Article 3.3. of the agreement, discussed below, refers to this issue.) The process is, however, constrained by Legislative Act No. 1 of 2012, "By means of which legal transitional justice instruments are established in the framework of Article 22 of the Constitution of Colombia and other provisions are dictated." The law decrees the adoption of two transitory articles to the constitution. The first and most important article opens with procedures to establish (a) criteria of selection and prioritization of cases for criminal prosecution, (b) the conditions for suspension of criminal sentences, and (c) extrajudicial sanctions and alternative sentencing mechanisms. I assume that these criteria, conditions, and mechanisms will be spelled out in the final agreement, under the heading either of point (3) or of point (5).

The process is unprecedented both in its scope and its procedure.

Regarding scope, the agenda addresses both *the injustices that caused the conflict and the injustices caused by the conflict.* A process of "pure transitional justice" that neglects the root causes of the conflict is unlikely to lead to a stable peace. The first issue is central in point (1) of the agenda. The agreement reached in May 2012 details a very ambitious program of rural development which includes giving landless peasantry access to land, mainly by using properties held by others who acquired them by violent or illegal means. The report of the agreement also states that the government will support "zones of peasant reservation" in which former guerillas may receive land and go back to being peasants. (To prevent conflict between former wrongdoers and their victims, they should not be assigned to areas in which they operated.) The second issue, which remains to be settled, will be discussed further below. Note that the granting of lands to landless peasants is a form of distributive (needs-based) justice rather than of transitional (entitlement-based) justice. In recent years, Pablo Kalmanovitz and María Paula Saffon Sanín have done pioneering work in developing this distinction, which has been ignored in most earlier work on TJ.

Point (2) of the agenda, ensuring rights and guarantees for the political opposition, also addresses some of the issues that caused the conflict. One of the guerrillas' main, and original, grievances was the exclusion from political competition of all groups that were not the two main parties (Liberal and Conservative) and the severe repression of the left. The origins of the exclusion of political groups other than Liberals and Conservatives can be found in the National Front, an institutional arrangement which was created in 1958 to put an end to the period of partisan violence of the 1950s and which established a formal alternation in power of the two parties. In later years of the Front, when it was dominated by the Conservatives, the political exclusion of other groups also implied a bi-partisan agreement to stop all efforts of agrarian reform for good, and the severe repression of peasant movements claiming autonomy. This is when and why the first guerrillas were created.

Regarding procedure, the process was innovative in several respects. First, the leaders of the two parties involved (the government and FARC) agreed that the negotiations should be kept confidential. (The choice of Cuba for the site of the negotiations rather than a Colombian venue was motivated by the desire for confidentiality.) In the past, negotiations have been undermined by the leaders of the delegations stating their "non-negotiable demands" in public. Remarkably, the agreement on confidentiality seems, with minor exceptions, to have been respected. Second, the government firmly refused to follow precedent when it declined to declare a ceasefire for the duration of the negotiations or to create a demilitarized zone. In past peace processes, these measures have been exploited by the guerrilla forces—driven to the negotiation table by weakness—to rebuild their strength. Also, there may have been a recognition that a ceasefire would trigger mutual accusations of violating it. Third, the parties agreed that a final agreement should be subject to popular approval. There would be no agreement reached only by private bargaining in the proverbial "smoke-filled back rooms." Later, I discuss possible mechanisms for popular approval. Here I only want to observe that the combination of confidentiality and approval seems to have had a beneficial effect on the negotiations—*both liberating and constraining*. On the one hand, participants were free to make radical or unconventional proposals without risking public outcry as a result of leaks. On the other hand, the need for downstream approval creates an incentive to reach an agreement that will lead to a durable peace and not simply satisfy the short-term interests of the parties. While the actual approval offers to put a stamp of legitimacy on the agreement, *the anticipated need for approval* shapes the agreement itself. This factor may explain, for instance, why FARC renounced radical proposals of land redistribution, such as expropriation of latifundia.

Before I address the core issue of transitional justice with regard to victims and perpetrators of human rights violations (HRV), I shall adopt two comparative perspectives on the current peace process. First, it is natural to consider differences and similarities with the demobilization of the paramilitaries, as initiated in the Justice and Peace Law (JPL). The law, which was adopted in July 2005 after extended negotiations between the paramilitary "United Self-Defense Forces of Colombia" (AUC, *Autodefensas Unidas de Colombia*) and the government, provided a framework for the demobilization and reinsertion of members of "illegal armed groups." In principle, it applied to guerrillas as well as to paramilitaries. Some 2,000 of the former deserted individually and submitted themselves to the JPL procedure. Only paramilitaries, however, chose the option of collective demobilization. Members of illegal armed groups who might choose to demobilize under the JPL were those who hoped to avoid ordinary criminal prosecution, prosecution before the International Criminal Court, and extradition to the United States. In exchange for receiving shorter prison sentences than any of these options would involve, they must render full confessions, hand over illegal assets, cooperate in the dismantling of the armed group, and cease all illicit activities. Victims of crimes committed by the beneficiaries of the law could claim reparations funded by the assets that are handed over. Although other victims did not receive reparation under the law, they can now, at least in theory, obtain compensation under the highly ambitious Law 1448 of 2011 (Victim's Law).

The JPL opened the possibility that drug lords could go free or receive reduced sentences, and at any rate escape extradition to the United States, by virtue of the clause that granted amnesty for crimes with an "indirect" political purpose, the drug trafficking being a "means" to finance political ends. This clause, which may have been crucial in obtaining the agreement, was later struck down by the courts. Several other clauses benefiting the paramilitaries have also been struck down. The fact that these clauses were struck down points to an intrinsic problem in the negotiated settlement of conflict in a democracy. When the government negotiates with insurgents or paramilitaries, the latter know—or should know—that the government is constrained by parliament and the courts. It is in fact a defining characteristic of democracy based on the separation of powers that the executive cannot force the legislative and judiciary branches to uphold its promises. In other words, such promises are not credible.

The current peace process contains an implicit promise that may also suffer from lack of credibility. Point (3.3) of the agreement on peace negotiations states that the government "shall coordinate a revision of the situation of persons imprisoned, accused or convicted for belonging to the FARC or for collaborating with them." I understand this clause as an implicit promise that some prisoners will be released and some indicted or convicted members of FARC may go free. The decision to release them or give up on prosecution would presumably have to be made by parliament, in the form of an amnesty law, or by the courts, on the basis of a reconsideration of the evidence. Yet, as I have suggested, the relevant actors *might not deliver*. This possibility might turn out to be a time bomb for the agreement.

The second comparative perspective may seem more farfetched, yet possibly suggests a way past one of the major obstacles to the peace agreement. The current Colombian process resembles the adoption in 1787–89 of the American constitution in two striking respects. First, the debates of the Federal Convention that drafted the document were held behind closed doors, and the injunction to secrecy was scrupulously respected. Second, the debates took place under the shadow of ratification by the individual states. If the framers had been free to adopt the document without downstream approval, they would probably have imposed strict property requirements on suffrage and eligibility, yet the fear that this proposal might endanger ratification in states with liberal voting requirements held them back.

Before suggesting how this process might have some relevance to the Colombian process, I need to explain the main mechanisms of popular approval that have been canvassed in Colombia. FARC has proposed ratification by a constituent assembly. It seems unlikely that the government negotiators will accept this proposal. To quote Humberto de la Calle, the head of the government delegation, "there is some degree of wishful thinking by the FARC in believing that such a constituent assembly will just sit down to ratify the agreements, and then go home; the expansive capacity of constituent assemblies is well-known."[1] Although many people argue that the Colombian constitution is in acute need of reform, an attempt to combine constitution making with approval of a peace agreement would be highly risky.

The Colombian constitution offers two other paths. (The following comments also apply to the constitutional changes that might be required by other parts of the agreement.) On the one hand lies the option of a referendum, which requires a quorum of 25% and a simple majority of the voters. On the other hand is an ill-defined mechanism of a "popular consultation" that would have to be proposed by the President and approved by the Senate.[2] In either case, the historical record suggests that the necessary quorum might not be attained. A nightmare scenario is one in which the government and FARC manage to agree on a proposal, but the voter turnout is too low for approval. Although it is possible that ratification could piggyback on ordinary elections, where turnout is usually around 35–50%, it is not clear whether the Constitutional Court would approve this scheme.

Against this background one might turn to the American ratification process for inspiration. One might, for instance, stipulate that the agreement would have to be approved by specially elected assemblies of ratification in each of the 32 provinces, and that ratification would require approval in a majority of provinces having between them a majority of the population or of the electorate. This scheme would also allow for a focused *deliberation* that might be more difficult to sustain on a national scale.

I now turn to the crucial and perhaps decisive issue of punishment of FARC wrongdoers. Their massive human rights violations include terrorizing the peasantry in the regions they occupy, extensive use of land mines, kidnappings of political opponents for political concessions or of wealthy individuals for ransom, and, most strikingly, forcible abduction of young people to fill the ranks of the FARC. It is estimated that some 40% of FARC forces have been recruited in this way. Although the heavy involvement of FARC in drug-trafficking and other illegal money-generating activities might also constitute grounds for criminal prosecution, I shall leave this issue to one side, if only for the reason that these crimes do not constitute international crimes for which there exists a duty to prosecute and punish.

Main issues include the justification for punishment, the severity of punishment, and the forms of punishment. I shall first discuss severity of sentencing in the abstract, and then consider what the agreement refers to as "extra-judicial sanctions and alternative sentencing mechanisms." With regard to the severity of sentencing, the negotiators face a problem that may turn out to be insoluble. On the one hand, three sets of actors, the International Criminal Court (ICC), Colombian national courts, and public opinion, may insist on a high minimum level and degree of punishment. On the other hand, FARC may insist on the opposite. It is an entirely open question whether there is a "window" of degree and extent of punishment that is acceptable to both sides,

The peace agreement process takes place "in the shadow of the ICC." As Colombia is a signatory to the ICC, that court can, in principle, intervene if it finds that there are no *genuine* domestic proceedings to address HRV. This appreciation is obviously a matter of judgment, and is also affected by Article 53 in the ICC Charter, which affirms that the Court may abstain from opening an investigation if abstention appears to be in "the interests of justice." It is unclear to me, and, I believe, to the Colombian actors, whether there is a realistic scenario under which the ICC would intervene. In a situation characterized by this kind of uncertainty, some actors may ignore the risk, and others take it seriously. To the extent that it is taken seriously, the fear of ICC intervention could be destabilizing. The jurisprudence (personally I think the term "ideology" may be more appropriate) of the ICC rests on the premise that severe punishment of individuals guilty of HRV is necessary to "send a signal to the future." I shall not repeat the objections I have developed elsewhere to this principle, except to say that it rests on highly implausible assumptions about motivations and causality. If this rigorous standard is imposed on Colombia, there may be no window for agreement. According to some observers, the probability of intervention is enhanced by the "desperate need" of the ICC for a non-African case.

Colombian courts might also, as in the case of the paramilitaries, strike down an agreement that provides a level of sentencing that they consider to be excessively lenient. I know too little about the current thinking of the Constitutional Court and the Supreme Court to assess this possibility. (Nor, as an outsider, do I understand the relation between these two bodies.) Instead, I shall speculate about the impact of the constraint on popular approval. The Colombian case is unique in that this approval is *formalized.* In other transitions, political leaders have no doubt asked themselves: "What is the minimum level and extent of punishment we must impose in order to prevent popular unrest, bad morale among the citizens, and loss of legitimacy of the regime?" These dangers and their impact are obviously diffuse and hard to assess with precision, leaving considerable scope for wishful thinking. In the current Colombian process, there are two *sharp* dangers: A failure to obtain a majority vote for the agreement and a failure to attain a quorum. Although opinion polls are imperfect gauges it should be possible to form an approximate idea of the severity of sentencing that would be needed for the agreement to gain approval. Some notorious HRV are so egregious, notably the abduction of children, that it is hard to imagine popular approval of an agreement that did not impose a severe punishment on the perpetrators.

Yet as Sergio Jaramillo Caro, the High Commissioner for Peace, observed in a speech in May 2013, the motives of those insisting on severe punishment may be somewhat murky: "The discussion around impunity is a performance—in some cases by those acting in good faith, but in others by a series of people whom I would call 'eleventh hour punitivists', who 10 years ago supported amnesties for paramilitary groups and today want to act like the Inquisition." In the TJ process in German-occupied countries after 1945, there was also a tendency for those who had done nothing to oppose the Germans during the occupation to be especially insistent on severe punishment of collaborators. In Colombia, this psychological mechanism might, to an incalculable degree, affect the outcome of a referendum or a consultation.

The maximum level and extent of punishment acceptable to the FARC are shrouded in strategic uncertainty. Whereas the constraints of ICC, national courts, and public opinion may serve to justify *warnings* by the government, FARC may *threaten* to break off negotiations unless it is offered something close to immunity or amnesty. The warnings issued by the government have a basis in fact, the threats issued by FARC do not. Rather, the question is whether they are *credible*: If the FARC threaten to withdraw from the negotiations unless their demands are met, and the demands are not met, will it be in their interest to withdraw? As noted, they could probably survive as a criminal organization. Senior leaders may not, however, be willing to go down this road.

One of my interlocutors affirmed without reservations that FARC would *never* accept any agreement that would include some of them serving prison sentences. Another hesitated to accept this strong conclusion. Be this as it may, what might the "extra-judicial sanctions and alternative sentencing mechanisms" be? One option would be to establish the equivalent of a *penal colony*: Some perpetrators of HRV would be confined to a restricted territory where they could live as ordinary citizens, except for a ban on outside travel. This proposal might not, however, be acceptable to public opinion, which might demand something more akin to forced labor. Another option could be some form of *public humiliation*, through the creation of a truth commission with the power that most truth commissions have lacked to *identify and name wrongdoers*. Social ostracism can be as effective as prison. To respect the principle of the rule of law, the determination of the identity of wrongdoers would have to be a quasi-legal process with adversarial witnesses and hearings.

Point (5) on the peace negotiation agenda, on victims, is remarkably brief. It contains two subheadings: "1. Victims' human rights. 2. Truth," with no further specifications. This brevity contrasts with official statements to the effect that the current process is mainly victim oriented. In the Colombian context, we may, generally speaking, distinguish among several categories of victims. (1) Victims of HRV not related to land dispossessions. (2) Victims dispossessed of lands to which they were legally entitled. (3) Victims of displacement caused by the political violence. Whereas (1) and (2) define victims through the framework of *legal* rights, (3) also includes victims defined by the framework of *human* rights. Some of my interlocutors included the punishment of wrongdoers among the human rights of the victims. A potentially important question, which does not seem to figure prominently in the public debates, is whether the level and extent of compensation, reparation, or symbolic satisfaction to the victims will be an important constraint on popular approval.

In addition to criminal prosecution, reparation, and truth commissions, the arsenal of TJ includes *purges* in the civil and military administration, with no other punishment than dismissal from office. Finally, one can apply the TJ tool of *lustration*, which prevents individuals with a blemished past from acceding to high elected or appointed office, especially if they have lied about their past. The Colombian agreement does not explicitly mention these options, but the language (notably Article 3.5) is sufficiently open ended to allow for both purges and lustration. These measures aim at building a public administration that is committed to the values of peace and democracy, a goal that cannot be realized by criminal prosecution, reparation, and truth commissions alone.

Author's note

This chapter, written on January 6, 2014, has been much improved by comments and suggestions from Pablo Kalmanovitz and María Paula Saffon Sanín. They are not to be held responsible for shortcomings that remain.

Notes

1 Editor Note: De la Calle refers to possibility that Constitutional Assemblies further modify other constitutional aspects, or even issue a new Constitution, since they are constituted as supreme constitutional authorities whose powers are not easily limited.

2 In a talk on September 2, 2013, Humberto de la Calle asserted that a public consultation "demands a higher threshold, and that threshold is set forth in the Constitution: a 33% participation would be required." The constitution does not, however, set any threshold. If it is determined by statute, it could presumably be changed.

Part II

Overall assessments

4 Essential elements and implementation challenges of the Final Agreement

Gustavo Gallón Giraldo and Juan Carlos Ospina

Introduction

This chapter discusses some fundamental aspects of the process of implementation of the "Final Agreement to End the Conflict and to Construct a Stable and Lasting Peace" (henceforth, Final Agreement) that should be considered in the assessment of its ultimate success or failure. We believe that these aspects should be supported to address the challenges that arise with regards to the termination of armed conflict with FARC-EP and the construction of a peaceful co-existence in a society historically and profoundly affected by violence.

The chapter is divided into three parts. The first introduces the fundamental aspects of the Final Agreement with regards to transitional justice. The second underscores the importance of measures taken with regards to land issues and in support of the rural population, as they address the main axis of the armed conflict. Here, we will also explore some difficulties in their implementation. In the third part, we will briefly expose the polarization of Colombian society with regards to the Final Agreement, by which, despite meeting the standards and principles of international law, it is rejected by a significant proportion of Colombian society. Finally, we will present some conclusions drawn from our analysis.

Fundamental aspects of the transitional justice mechanism incorporated in the Final Agreement

Colombia's recent peace process has evidenced the significance of tensions that may exist between the search for peace and the protection of the rights to truth, justice, and the compensation of victims. It is particularly exacerbating the tension between punishing those criminally responsible for violations of Human Rights and infractions of International Humanitarian Law (IHL) in armed conflicts (as defined by international instruments), while also allowing for the possibility of negotiated termination of armed conflicts.

The negotiation process that took place between the Colombian government and FARC was unpredecedent. Previous agreements to end other conflicts have accepted (or imposed) as a necessary condition for their success legal mechanisms to grant generalized amnesties and pardons for all the involved parties, without inquiring into the responsibility of perpetrators, the seriousness of actions committed during the conflict, or the rights of victims. In practice, these agreements amounted to impunity pacts. For example, the several peace processes with guerrillas that took place during the 1980s and 1990s ended with legislation that granted generalized amnesties and pardons,[1] based on a belief in the priority of the need for reconciliation over the rights of victims to truth and justice.

Neither is there precedent at the international level that can be made applicable to the complexity of the Colombian conflict, which is distinctive for its length, the multiplicity of implied actors, the number of victims, the diversity of criminal infractions committed as part of the conflict, among other factors. Nor was there an antecedent system that comprehensively and integrally regulated all aspects incorporated in the Colombian System of Truth, Justice, Compensation and Non-Repetition (*Sistema Integral de Verdad, Justicia, Reparación y No Repetición,* henceforth, the Comprehensive System). Further, it is also novel that all parties of the Final Agreement agreed to appear before the same tribunal and under the same rules, and thus to acknowledge the commission of acts against human rights and IHL so serious that they cannot be the object of amnesties, pardons, or dismissal of charges.

Thus, Chapter 5 of Final Agreement established the creation of the Comprehensive System, which is constituted by three "mechanisms" and two "measures." The mechanisms are the Commission for the Clarification of Truth, Co-Existence and Non-Repetition (henceforth, Truth Commission); the Unit for the Search of Persons Taken as Disappeared (henceforth, Search Unit); and the Special Jurisdiction for Peace (*Jurisdiction Especial para la Paz*, henceforth, JEP). The main functions of these mechanisms are to judicially and extrajudicially address the demands of victims, to provide conditions of stability and legal security to the processes of reincorporation, and to sanction agents responsible for violations of human rights and of IHL. The measures are remedies to victims that continue initiatives of Laws 1448 and 2001 (Victims' and Land Restitution Act), and guarantees of nonrepetition that, per the Agreement's text, are the result of the coordinated implementation of the System's mechanisms and measures (and any other points agreed upon) to enact the termination of the conflict.[2]

These mechanisms and measures were thought to adequately address victims' rights according to international standards. However, they required a complex process of normative implementation to allow their incorporation into Colombia's legal system, as well as review by the Constitutional Court, before they could begin to function according to the Agreement's text and to prevent future modifications that might alter its operation. Such a process was advanced through special powers granted by the Colombian Congress to the President, via a constitutional amendment and through the establishment of a fast-track legislative process to enact provisions necessary for the termination of the conflict.

A constitutional amendment codified the three mechanisms of the Comprehensive System and enshrined them in the Constitution. Through legislative decrees, the functioning of the Truth Commission[3] and the Search Unit was regulated. A different congressional act was required to regulate the JEP, as it involved rights such as due process and access to justice, which demand a statutory regulation per the Colombian Constitution. The process of normative creation ended in the first semester of 2018, with the enactment of JEP's procedural rules. At this time, the Constitutional Court also ruled as constitutional the key provisions that structured all three mechanisms.

In these judgments, the Court also deemed them to be measures that properly address Colombia's international obligations to fight impunity and guarantee victims' rights to truth, justice, compensation, and nonrepetition, though with some exceptions. With regards to the Truth Commission and the Search Unit, it was claimed that their extrajudicial character was an adequate response to victims' demands for truth and recognition, both in general and in specific cases, that might not be addressed adequately through criminal proceedings. Furthermore, the Truth Commission was considered to be a mechanism capable of establishing the foundations for peace building: By promoting co-existence, and establishing guidelines for nonrepetition; by strengthening mutual respect, tolerance, and citizenship trust; and by committing to the protection of human rights. Likewise, the Search Unit's humanitarian approach was also a necessary innovation: Without the operative and procedural difficulties of the criminal proceedings, the Search Unity could promptly search for, locate, recuperate, and return disappeared persons—according to official statistics, more than 80,000 people were disappeared since 1970.[4]

The JEP is a judicial institution with a complex structure that seeks to address the different demands for justice by victims of violations of human rights and infractions of IHL. It has the particular challenge of adjudicating the disputed borders between political and criminal crimes, as well as those actions that cannot be granted amnesty or held exempt from criminal prosecution as they violated human rights or IHL protection, such as forced disappearances, sexual violence, and the recruitment of minors. In this aspect, to satisfy victims' rights, the Peace Agreement establishes an array of mechanisms that incentivize the recognition of responsibility and truth by those involved in any conduct against human rights and IHL. As a result, the Comprehensive System can impose lesser sanction than those typical of the Colombian legal system. Three circumstances are to be distinguished: (1) Special consideration for those who fully acknowledge their responsibility from the outset, in the form of sanctions between five and eight years of effective restriction of liberty, with no prison time; (2) alternative sanctions of between five and eight years in prison for those who recognize their responsibility before trial; and (3) ordinary criminal punishment between

15 and 20 years in prison for those who fail to provide the truth or to recognize responsibility. There are also sanctions between two and five years in prison to those who did not have a determining participation in the punished conduct.

To fulfill its function, the JEP is divided into a Tribunal for Peace as well as several divisions (*Salas*). The most important of these divisions is arguably the Division for "Acknowledgement of Truth and Responsibility and the Determination of Facts and Conduct"—this is the entrance door to this judicial mechanism. This division receives reports from a variety of official institutions, including ordinary criminal institutions, as well as from social organizations, including victims' associations and human rights organizations. From these reports, this division initiates proceedings to bring alleged perpetrators before the Court. At that moment, the alleged perpetrator has the opportunity to acknowledge the facts and/or their responsibilities (and thus to accept lesser punishments), or to start an adversarial trial in which the State would be required to present evidence to refute the presumption of innocence. As of July 2020, this division has opened seven macro cases.

The Tribunal for Peace itself is also divided into several sections that resolve specific matters. These include a section for the acknowledgment of truth and responsibility, a section for when truth and responsibility are not recognized, a section to review decisions issued by ordinary criminal justice prior to the establishment of the JEP, and an appeals section. This complex structure of sections and divisions seeks to guarantee the security and legal stability to the processes of reintegration of former combatants and to protect the victims' right to participation, to the truth of what occurred during the conflict, and the application of restorative justice focused on the elimination of conflict's structural causes.

In conclusion, this complex infrastructure of mechanisms of transitional justice, unique to national and international contexts, seeks to achieve the recognition of responsibilities of actors in armed conflicts, to facilitate the reintegration of former combatants (even allowing their political participation in Congress and public institutions as officials or contractors), and to satisfy the rights of victims. These are goals that the Comprehensive System as a whole, and the JEP in particular, need to achieve; otherwise, new violations of victims' rights could result, as well as the possibility of new conflicts, derived from perceptions of impunity should past atrocities be ignored.

Measures on the land issue and protection for historically excluded population

The problems of distribution, access, and exploitation of land are widely considered to be the main structural cause of the Colombian conflict.[5] For this reason, the first chapter (*punto*) of the Final Agreement was the incorporation of "Integral Rural Reform" as a set of programs, plans, and measures intended to contribute to the structural transformation of Colombia's rural areas and to create conditions that protect historically excluded rural populations against poverty, inequality, and exclusion. These measures are also important because the armed conflict with FARC-EP was more intense in rural areas that were often rich in natural resources and land productivity, but in which the State had greater difficulty protecting citizens and solving the problems of possession and distribution of land.

Colombia is not only of the most unequal countries in the world. It also has the largest inequality in Latin America in terms of the distribution of land. According to a 2017 Oxfam study, 81% of the land is held by the largest 1% of exploitation units (i.e., more than 500 ha); only 19% of the land is distributed among the other 99%.[6] That is, social and economic inequality is graphically evidenced by the extreme concentration of land resources (as well as by unequal access to equipment, financial and technical assistance, etc.). This alone creates a recipe for conflict, as do the effects of conflict as they worsen conditions for the rural population. For example, according to the administrative unit to serve and integrally repair the victims of the Colombian conflict, of the 9.04 million victims, 81% (7.3 million) were affected by forced displacement.[7]

The Colombian Commission of Jurists has documented the extended processes of land spoliation and abandonment that have resulted from the conflict. We wrote in one report:

> The cycle of violence, forced displacement and land spoliation has haunted the Colombian rural population for decades (…) Within the armed conflict, spoliation and usurpation of lands has been one of the strategic objectives of several actors—both armed as well as economic and political—of the Colombian tragedy. (…) The accumulation of land by paramilitary forces and economic actors, both legal—such as national and international agricultural, agro-industrial and extractive—and illegal—such as drug dealers—it is a central component of the Colombian conflict.[8]

Despite the impact of forced displacement on Colombian society, the State did not take adequate measures to stop it or to address the needs of its victims. Furthermore, different mechanisms of so called "rural reform" (i.e., attempts to improve structural deficiencies with regards to land access and distribution) have failed.

As a result, the Constitutional Court declared in 2004 the existence of an Unconstitutional State of Affairs with regards to victims of forced displacement, given the "discrepancy between the severity of the violations of constitutionally and statutorily recognized rights, on the one hand, and the volume of resources effectively destined to protect such rights and the institutional capacity to perform their constitutional and statutory duties, on the other."[9] Although some normative and policy reforms have been advanced, the Unconstitutional State of Affairs remains until today (July 2020).[10]

One significant development was the enactment of the above-mentioned Victims' and Land Restitution Act,[11] which contain provisions to guarantee restitution to victims of spoliation and forced abandonment, and to legalize the land possession of victims who lack property titles to the lands they occupied before the forced displacement. The fundamental rights of victims of forced displacement to restitution have been recognized by numerous international instruments, in acknowledgment of a causal relationship between the victimization of the individual and the spoliation, abandonment, loss and impairment of land, territory, and housing. In this regard, and per the United Nations High Commissioner for Refugees (UNHCR) Guiding Principles on Internal Displacement, property and possessions of internally displaced persons shall be protected in all circumstances (Principle 21), and if necessary, competent authorities have the primary duty to establish conditions and means that allow victims to return or resettle voluntarily, in safety, and with dignity (Principle 28.1).[12]

In the same vein, the UN Principles on Housing and Property Restitution for Refugees and Displaced persons have established the right to restitution as the preferred remedy for displacement, as it exists as a distinct right, and is not prejudiced by either the actual return or the nonreturn of refugees and displaced persons who are entitled to housing, land, and property restitution (Principle 2.2.).[13] Colombia's Constitutional Court has also recognized the right to restitution as a fundamental right in several judgments,[14] and has even declared reinforced character to the rights of property, possession, and occupancy that have generated remedies to victims and the development of public land policies.

Under these considerations, the process of land restitution that began in 2011 has generated great expectations on the part of victims, and despite its challenges has benefitted a significant number of them.[15] However, the process has been neither simple nor expeditious: It suffers several administrative barriers,[16] so the apparent success of this process has been challenged by civil society.[17]

In this context, the inclusion in the Final Agreement of a specific chapter on rural issues gains more relevance, as it incorporates measures to address the effects of armed conflict, to end structural causes and facilitating conditions, and to correct elements that preclude the success of rural reform: The concentration of law, exclusion of the rural population, lack of access to resources, and so on. For this purpose, a group of measures on the formalization, restitution, and distribution of law were included in the Agreement. These are, first, measures for improvement of land access and use (including unproductive use or nonformalized access); second, programs of development with a territorial approach; and, third, national plans for integral rural reform.

In the first of these aspects, the Agreement creates a land fund and mechanisms that promote access to land in conditions that permit exploitation by farmers, such as legalization of ownership and restitution. In the second, a national plan with the territorial approach is formulated in order to diagnose conditions for rural transformation of the country, and to articulate further local and regional planning mechanisms in which community participation is essential. Finally, there is an ambitious plan to improve access of the rural population to health, education, housing, work and income, as well as supports such as infrastructure, economic stimulus, subsidies, and work assistance in areas historically affected by the conflict.

These are important measures that genuinely albeit theoretically seek to remedy the structural situations of exclusion, poverty, and inequality in Colombia's rural areas, and to attend to the demands of numerous bodies from civil society, victims and human rights organizations, as well as to orders of the Constitutional Court, to address conditions that dramatically affect victims' rights.

Despite these efforts, there persist several barriers to bringing to reality the provisions of chapter 1 of the Final Agreement and the desired fundamental rural reform. Three considerations are especially noteworthy: the weakness of the Colombian State, the continuation of the Colombian armed conflict, and the lack of political will to achieve these transformations.

First, Colombia remains a weak state: Namely one that does not perform its necessary functions such as guaranteeing the rights of its citizens, including the provision of basic goods, services, and opportunities.[18] This weakness remains despite a degree of financial and operational government efforts, as well as the technical and financial support of international cooperation.

Second, although the end of the armed conflict with FARC-EP creates a scenario in which the State has a greater financial capacity to address social needs, it still has to address armed conflicts with other actors. These include another large guerilla group, the Army of National Liberation (*Ejército de Liberación Nacional,* ELN), dissident groups of FARC-EP, and the violence of paramilitary groups and other armed actors associated with drug dealing.

These new strands of conflict have generated a substantial impact on local leaders, defenders of human rights, as well as former combatants. According to the CCJ, between January 1, 2016 and June 30, 2020, 812 such leaders were killed.[19] This situation has worsened in areas abandoned by the former FARC and then taken by new armed actors fighting for power, control of the illegal drug trade, and other illegal economies. As a result, these conflicts interfere with rural transformation by eliminating leaders who promote change and by perpetuating the territorial domination of armed actors that preclude social transformation.

Finally, previous conditions are worsened by the lack of will necessary to enact fundamental change, especially on the part of hegemonic political and economic actors who have opposed both land restitution and distribution. Here it is important to mention that the Final Agreement has been enshrined in the Constitution; its text and implementation norms are protected with special stability. Moreover, the Constitutional Court defined the Agreement as state policy and established that all legitimate authorities and institutions are obligated to make their best effort to comply with it.[20] However, in the current context of armed confrontation, land remains a structural cause of conflict, and the land's destiny is predominantly guided by economic, military, and political interests that have generated deep social inequality and generalized violence. In this context, the government must actively advance the reforms incorporated in the Final Agreement in order to achieve the necessary transformation of rural areas of Colombia.

The radicalization against peace and political polarization

While there is no doubt that negotiation is the best solution to the armed conflict, according to the Colombian Constitution and legislation, the legal framework with regards to the implementation of the Peace Agreements in Colombia remains a work in progress. Like all peace processes, the Colombian one involves immense political, legal, and social challenges that must overcome several uncertainty factors.

As part of the process, it was determined that the Final Agreement needed to be formally approved by the Colombian public to grant it the legitimacy and popular support necessary for it to succeed as a public security policy. For the first time in Colombian history, the President decided to submit the Agreement decision to a democratic approval process, despite voices suggesting that it was both unnecessary and risky to subject a fundamental right, such as peace, to majority vote.[21]

Thus, based on democratic principles of the Colombian Constitution,[22] the citizenry was given the opportunity to decide on the acceptance of the content of the Final Agreement, and thereby to control the activity of public officials during the negotiation. However, such an attempt did not take into account that peace processes, as they involve matters of national security (*orden público*), have a different relationship with democratic principles. According to the Colombian constitutional framework, national security is directed by the President: An elected official who serves as head of state, head of government, and as supreme executive authority.

This consultation of the public regarding their support of the Final Agreement took place on October 2, 2016. The result: 50.2% voted "No," rejecting the Agreement. The difference with the "Yes" position was 53,894 votes—that is, 0.4% of those who voted.[23] Such a result further polarized the Colombian population. The sectors opposed to the negotiation with FARC did not seek to modify the Agreement but rejected instead all attempts to implement it. They attempted to justify their position based on the democratic nature of the consultation, which as defined by the Constitutional Court as follows:

> A plebiscite is an expression of participatory democracy (*democracia participativa*), for through such a mechanism the will of the citizenry is

> expressed, which as sovereign power must influence the State's decisions and demand that representative authorities act in conformity with, and give efficacy to, the citizens' political commands. Otherwise, it would imply that the people's command with regards to its collective decisions lack any content and would have merely a symbolic character. In this sense, to ignore the binding nature of the political command would imply the elimination of one of the founding axiological principles of the Colombian constitutional, democratic State.[24]

Following this rationale, the democratic principles that justified a plebiscite in the first place justify in turn the impossibility of renegotiating and implementing a new agreement. For this position, all post-plebiscite activities performed by the government to end the conflict would be both illegal and illegitimate.[25]

However, there are arguments against such a position. For example, influential Italian political and legal philosopher Luigi Ferrajoli claimed: "Certainty, consensus is the main source of democratic legitimacy of government political functions. But it is not the only source of legitimacy of all the legislative and executive decisions, nor is it the source of all other public functions."[26] From this perspective, democratic consensus and majority vote could be used to support the "most disastrous totalitarian involutions."[27]

Per this view, in a constitutional democracy, no majoritarian decision can legitimize decisions against the Constitution. In this sense, the key debate is whether the end of an armed conflict and the conditions for peace building are within the "sphere of what is decidable" by majorities, or, on the contrary, if such is a decision is constitutionally delegated to executive representatives authorities that, while controlled by the Constitutional Tribunal, can balance the constitutional rights, ends, and goals related to the achievement of peace and victim's rights.

As a result of the political decision to subject the first version of the Agreement to a popular vote and obtaining a negative result, it was necessary to renegotiate some aspects of the Agreement objected to by "No" promoters and then to seek the approval of a new Agreement by the Colombian Congress, as representative of the people.[28]

The Constitutional Court endorsed this formulation to give viability to the peace process and its Final Agreement with the following words:

> According to the precedent of this Court, the validation of the Final Agreement took place in a democratic process, participative and representative, whose most important events were (i) the call for a special plebiscite for pace, whose result was the absence of majoritarian political support for the initially agreed text, and (ii) a renegotiation process with different social sectors, in particular, those critics of the first version of the Agreement, and (iii) the renegotiation of several components in La Habana negotiation table, and (iv) the approval by the two Houses of the Congress of the Republic.[29]

The Congress approved the re-negotiated agreement with 205 positive votes and none against. Despite the Court decision and statements by legislative and executive authorities, the political debate continued. Many sectors insisted on the lack of democratic legitimacy of the agreement based on the results of the previous plebiscite.

It is evident that such claims have a political, not legal, foundation. Nevertheless, as a result, the process of implementation and verification of the Final Agreement is situated in a complex scenario involving suspicions about its legitimacy and open debate about tensions between respect for democratic decisions and the constitutional duty to seek peace. As a consequence of these substantive debates, political polarization increased, which in turn affects the possibility to comply with the Agreement and its long-term sustainability.

This situation is especially complex if we consider that the Final Agreement enjoys considerable international support. It has been supported by the United Nations, foreign guarantor countries, and supporting countries.[30] Furthermore, it has been recognized as an ambitious agreement that addresses all the essential and structural elements of the violence in Colombia, as stated above. Finally, this Agreement aligns with international standards for the recognition of the status of victims and efforts to respect and protect their rights, specifically in the form of the fifth component of the Agreement, along with the Comprehensive System of Truth, Justice, Reparation and Non-repetition.

This last point—normative implementation, especially of the Comprehensive System, in order to satisfy victims' rights—is the main challenge of the Final Agreement. The phrase "victims are at the core of the agreement" was one of the mottos of the negotiation. Such a principle summarizes the rationale of the mechanisms of measures of the System,[31] and largely responds to victims' expectations regarding the social transformation entailed by compliance. However, the process still suffers from legal uncertainty, and it remains unclear whether authorities and institutions will in fact comply with its content. Both topics should be items of significant attention by the international community, as well as global mechanisms for universal human rights.

Conclusions

Colombia is currently under a *sui generis* transitional justice process, which, if successful, would provide a learning experience for other armed conflicts in the world. Some noteworthy features of this process are its approach to protecting the rights of victims to truth, justice, reparation, and nonrepetition. However, implementation is particularly challenging, given the particular conditions of the Colombian armed conflicts and impacts on more than 9 million victims.

It is a duty of the State to guarantee the rights of victims as a necessary condition for sustainable peace and the promise of nonrepetition. Such a duty has two main dimensions. On the one hand, the State must provide mechanisms for victims to demand their rights. On the other hand, it must also adopt public policy decisions that remedy their current situations and make said rights effective.[32]

In line with articles 1 and 2 of the Colombian Constitution that command all public authorities to secure social justice and human dignity, counter all existing social inequalities, and offer citizens opportunities to develop their aptitudes and overcome material needs, the measures to promote integral rural reform are critical components of the Final Agreement.[33] These measures, while they are now part of several plans, policies, and programs, still must overcome several obstacles to appropriate implementation that are related to the weaknesses of the Colombian State, the continuation of the armed conflict with other actors, and the frail political will to transform conditions that both originated and maintain conflicts. With regard to this last obstacle, the radicalization of discourse against peace and political polarization in general severely impacts the democratic spirit promoted and enshrined in the Final Agreement and aids those positions that call for noncompliance.

The obligation to respect and guarantee human rights entails a duty of the whole state infrastructure to adopt measures necessary to secure the legal and free exercise and efficacy of their rights.[34] In a similar vein, the Final Agreement entails the State's obligation to comply with its content, implement its measures, and strengthen the instituted mechanisms in order to guarantee the rights of victims. As a result, the main challenge is to generate the conditions of stability and a sustainable peace, to consolidate efforts to end armed conflicts, and to promote the necessary transformations so that violations of human rights and IHL never occur again.

Authors' note

Translated by Jorge Luis Fabra-Zamora.

Notes

1 Colombia, Laws 37 of 198, 35 of 1982, 39 of 1985 and 77 of 1989, as well as Decrees 473 of 1982, 206 of 1990, 213 of 1991 and 1943 of 1991.
2 Final Agreement, 5.1.4.
3 Decree-Law 588 de 2017.
4 According to the National Center for Historical Memory, this describes almost 83,000 people between 1958 and November 15, 2017. The Information System of Disappeared and Corpses (SIRDEC) of the Institute of Forensic Medicine System reports 22,261 to March of 2016. In turn, the National Registry of Victims reports 38,400 direct victims of forced disappearance between 1985 and 2016, and 10,051 before 1985. Furthermore, the Institute of Forensic Medicine estimates 200,000 possible victims, due to the lack of notice and registry. See Claudia Delgado Aguacia, *Desaparecidos, deuda histórica con las víctimas* (Bogotá: Universidad de Los Andes, 2018) and Juan Ospina and Cielo Linares, *La búsqueda humanitaria de los desaparecidos en Colombia* (Bogotá: CCJ, 2018).

5 One of the common elements highlighted by the 12 essays of the Historic Commission on the Conflict and its Victims as the origin of the conflict was the control over land. See Comisión Histórica del Conflicto y sus Víctimas, *Contribución al entendimiento del conflicto armado en Colombia,* February 2015, http://www.humanas.unal.edu.co/observapazyconflicto/files/5714/6911/9376/Version_final_informes_CHCV.pdf.
6 Oxfam, *Radiografía de la desigualdad: lo que nos dice el último censo agropecuario sobre la distribución de la tierra en Colombia* (Oxfam, 2017) https://www.oxfam.org/es/informes/radiografia-de-la-desigualdad.
7 From, www.unidadvictimas.gov.co as of July 2020.
8 CCJ, *Despojo de Tierras Campesinas y vulnernación de los territorios ancestrales* (Bogotá, CCJ, 2001).
9 Constitutional Court, Judgement T-025 de 2004.
10 See https://www.corteconstitucional.gov.co/T-025-04/.
11 Law 1448 of 2011.
12 UNHCR, *Guiding Principles on Internal Displacement,* https://www.unhcr.org/protection/idps/43ce1cff2/guiding-principles-internal-displacement.html.
13 UN, *Principles on Housing and Property Restitution for Refugees and Displaced Persons* ("Pinheiro Principles"), https://www.un.org/unispal/document/auto-insert-182804/.
14 For example, Sentence T-821/07, T-159/11 and C-820/12.
15 Garmenting to the Administrative Unit of Restitution of Land, to 30 of June 2020, judges have decided the restitution of 381.880 ha that has benefited 32.273 people. Information available at: https://www.restituciondetierras.gov.co/estadisticas-de-restitucion-de-tierras (accessed July 2020).
16 As recognized by the Constitutional Court in Order 373 of 2016.
17 For example, Juan Francisco Soto Hoyos, *Cumplir Metas, Negar Derechos: Balance de la Implementación de Tierras en su Fase Administrativa 2012–2017* (Bogotá, CCJ, 2018) 16.
18 Patricia Moncada Roa, *Los Estados Fallidos o Fracasados: Un debate inconcluso y sospechoso* (Bogotá, Siglo del Hombre, 2007), 302.
19 CCJ, *Base de Violencia Sociopolítica* (Bogotá, CCJ, 2020). See, for a previous análisis, CCJ, *¿Cuáles son los Patrones? Asesinatos de Líderes Sociales en el Post Acuerdo* (Bogotá, CCJ, 2018), https://www.coljuristas.org/documentos/libros_e_informes/cuales_son_los_patrones.pdf.
20 Constitutional Court, Judgment C-630/17.
21 In Judgment C-214/93, the Constitutional Court forcefully established that there was a distinction between those preparatory or instrumental agreements of a peace process that can be signed by Government representatives, and those binding agreements that end a conflict, which can only be signed by the President.
22 See, Constitutional Court, Judgment C-245/96.
23 From 34.300.929 people eligible to vote (according to the Electoral Census), 37.29% (12.790.353) voted in the plebiscite: 6.377.482 voted "Yes" (48.8%), while 6.431.376 voted "No."
24 Constitutional Court, Judgment C-379/2016.
25 Members of the Congress that supported "No" insisted on the illegality of further attempts to ratify the Agreement after the plebiscite. See http://www.senado.gov.co/component/k2/item/26366-senador-ramos-denuncia-ilegalidad-de-la-convocatoria-al-fast-track.
26 Luigi Ferrajoli, "Los límites de legitimidad de la jurisdicción," *Reforma Judicial: Revista Mexicana de la Justicia,* vol. 15, 2010, p. 16.
27 Idem.

28 The Constitutional Court, in Judgment C-99/16, stated: "A process of popular validation by previous consultation to the citizenry is real only if the results of such mechanism of popular participation are interpreted, respected and developed in good faith in a scenario that seeks to achieve a greater consensus (…) Therefore, it is necessary not only that there exists a space of deliberation, such as those of the principles of popular validation, but also an authority invited by the Constitution with democratic legitimacy, that embodies or represents the population and guarantees the respect and good faith implementation of its mandates. The Congress of the Republic, for example, harbours the peoples' representatives, with their political and cultural diversity (…)".

29 See, Constitutional Court, C-699/16. Also, C-160/17.

30 See, statement by the ICC (http://www.hchr.org.co/index.php/compilacion-de-noticias/121-proceso-de-paz/8179-acuerdos-de-paz-no-tienen-impunidad-corte-penal-internacional), UN's Verification Commission (https://colombia.unmissions.org/sites/default/files/e-book_brochure_mision_de_verificacion_2.pdf), UNHCR (http://www.hchr.org.co/index.php/informacion-publica/comunicados-de-prensa/ano-2016/8644-el-alto-comisionado-de-las-naciones-unidas-para-los-derechos-humanos-celebra-la-ratificacion-del-nuevo-acuerdo-de-paz-de-colombia, http://www.hchr.org.co/index.php/informacion-publica/comunicados-de-prensa/ano-2016/8640-alto-comisionado-de-las-naciones-unidas-para-los-derechos-humanos-visita-a-colombia-y-acompana-la-firma-de-los-acuerdos-de-paz), and OAS (http://www.oas.org/es/cidh/prensa/comunicados/2016/q178.asp, http://www.oas.org/es/cidh/prensa/comunicados/2016/122.asp), among others.

31 The duty to satisfy the rights of the victims of human rights violations was incorporated in the UN "Basic Principles and Guidelines on the Right to a Remedy and Reparation for Victims of Gross Violations of International Human Rights Law and Serious Violations of International Humanitarian Law," also known as the Van Boven/Bassiouni Principles.

32 See UNSC, The rule of law and transitional justice in conflict and post-conflict societies: Report of the Secretary-General, Doc. S/2004/646.

33 On these constitutional duties, particularly, in the context of conflict, see, Judgments SU-747/1998; C-438/13, C-767/14. Furthermore, the provision creating a "Estado Social de Derecho" demands a factual protection of all constitutional rights, in particular of the material equality and the rights of disadvantaged and persons, as well of those in conditions manifest vulnerability. Likewise, in such type of state in a participative democracy, the rights of victims are also constitutionally protected. See, Constitutional Court, Judgments C-1064/204, T-05/204, C-1033/06, T-328/07, and T-655/15.

34 IACHR, Case of *Velásquez Rodríguez v. Honduras*, Judgment of September 29, 1998, §166.

5 The Colombian peace agreement

A lost opportunity for social transformation?

María Paula Saffon Sanín

Introduction

I think of Colombia as a stubbornly violent country. It has experienced one of the most protracted civil conflicts in the world despite having one of the most durable and competitive electoral systems in the region and exhibiting remarkable levels of legal sophistication and innovation (both in the books and in the work of courts). However, the country has also been in a perennial quest for peace. At multiple times in history, amnesties have been granted and peace processes have been attempted—and in many cases achieved, yet they have never been enough to put a durable end to violence. These processes have tended to be partial—including only some armed actors, not others—and narrow in their goals—focusing on the end of violence but not on the transformation of the factors that made it possible in the first place, or that enabled its continuity. As such, they have allowed for violence to persist or to reemerge soon after.

To a significant extent, the prevalence of violence in Colombian history seems to be the result of it not mattering enough to political and economic elites, and of its sufferers not being sufficiently strong or influential in conquering peace. Perhaps the most intriguing trait of the country is its sharply fragmented political geography and economy. While there are central (mainly urban) areas of the country where state and market institutions generally operate as if violence did not exist at all, there are many peripheral and semi-peripheral areas where several state institutions are not present and the ones that suffer from weakness and lack of autonomy. This has allowed armed, non-state actors to impose their rule, capture state institutions, and align with local elites to protect their wealth, obtain profits from illegal economies, and control from-below mobilization through repression. This differential presence of the state has enabled an enduring (and perverse) equilibrium whereby elites in the periphery profit from violence and state weakness, and the political center allows them to persist at the local level as long as they do not affect its interests or its rule.[1]

Such equilibrium has been stable, to an important extent, because a large proportion of Colombian citizens are not incorporated into politics and do not have equal access to the state. Electoral participation has been—and remains—quite limited in the country. The lack of institutional reach (which includes that of electoral institutions)[2], the voluntary nature of suffrage, and the historical predominance of two center-right parties have all led to quite high levels of electoral abstention (especially marked in rural areas), as well as to a deficit of representation through the marginalization of left-leaning parties (which was formal in periods like the National Front, and ensured through violence in periods of political openings like the one surrounding the 1991 Constitution, and the current one).[3]

The absence of political incorporation has, in turn, engendered structural difficulties for grassroots movements—especially from the periphery—to collectively organize and make influential demands to the state, as well as to avoid violence when they attempt to overcome the obstacles of collective action.[4] This seems to serve the interests of both local and central elites—the former's interests often antagonize explicitly with from-below demands of inclusion and redistribution, and the latter benefit from armed actors' and local elites' capacity to restrict violence to peripheral areas in whatever ways they deem fit, and to thus enable politics to continue as usual.

In such a scenario, the struggle for peace is actually a puzzle, rather than an obvious strategy that state actors should pursue. Generally, peace negotiations have tended to be sought by central elites when the previously described equilibrium has been altered, that is, when regional violence has spilled over to affect central elites—as happened when guerrilla and narco-violence reached the cities in the 1980s and 1990s thus generating the pro-peace environment of the negotiations with M-19, EPL and Quintín Lame, and the 1991 Constitutional Assembly; or when kidnappings and extortions perpetrated by guerrillas against elites became frequent in the late 1990s to early 2000s, thus generating a pro-peace context for the (failed) Caguán negotiations with the Colombian Revolutionary Armed Forces-Popular Army (FARC-EP).[5]

Still, in those circumstances, multiple obstacles stand in the way of reaching a peace agreement, including the seriousness with which armed actors carry out negotiations, the trust built between negotiating parties, and the strength of spoilers. More importantly, it is not nearly enough to forge a peace agreement for peace to be built.[6] Given the structure of incentives that violence has created over the decades, the end of violence requires both the will to transform the conditions that engender such incentives, and the capacity to enforce required transformations. When either of these factors is absent, targeted violence against the potential beneficiaries of peace is likely to ensue after successful peace negotiation and demobilization processes.

As I will argue in the following sections, the peace agreement between FARC-EP and the Colombian government is noteworthy not only because it was reached amid multiple obstacles and in the presence of strong potential spoilers, but also because it clearly identified the conditions that needed to be transformed in order for durable peace to be possible, and even the mechanisms that should be used to ensure enforcement. However, the enforcement of the agreement has been rocky, largely due to its perennial legitimacy deficit, which impeded the consolidation of a strong basis of support for peace, and opened the way for the strengthening of the political standing of its opponents. This exponentially diminished the agreement's potential to achieve social transformation, since it constrained central elites committed to peace, and led most to adopt a rhetorical stance that defends a minimalist version of the agreement (focused on disarmament and punishment of former guerrilla leaders) but does little to ensure the enforcement of its transformational components.[7]

At the same time, the unfulfilled promises of social transformation that the agreement makes have offered grounds for potential beneficiaries to organize, politically participate, and make demands, which significantly threaten the interests of regional elites who have traditionally gained from violence. These two factors combined have reset the "violence equilibrium," and they have even increased the stakes of violence, thus making peace-seekers more vulnerable to it, but also more willing to collectively struggle against it.

The transformative potential of the peace agreement

Against the backdrop set up in the introduction, the 2016 peace agreement between FARC-EP and the Santos government could be considered almost a miracle. For decades, both political elites and guerrilla groups seem to have faced stronger incentives to let violence carry on than to truly vie for peace. Several peace attempts were made but failed because of the lack of commitment of elites to ensure the security of guerrilla members wishing to participate in politics (as happened in the mid-1980s when peace negotiations failed due to the violent persecution of the UP party) or of guerrillas to strive for peace (as happened in the early 2000s when the peace negotiations failed due to FARC-EP's use of the demilitarized zone to strengthen their power).

The balance of power between the state and guerrilla groups changed radically when rightist Uribe took power (in 2002) and—under the lead of later President Santos as Minister of Defense and later High Commissioner for Peace Jaramillo as Vice-Minister—developed an aggressive military strategy against those groups with the support of the US Plan Colombia. The strategy led to the strengthening and professionalization of the Colombian army and to a significant weakening of guerrillas, though not to a full defeat. The change in the balance of power generated strong incentives for FARC-EP to strive for peace, which entailed reaching out for secret negotiations (in 2010). Santos' government initiated them (in early 2012) in a position of strength, which still did not mean that an agreement would be easy to attain, since FARC-EP could threaten to go back to the jungle where it had been for 50 years, and where it had already gone back three times after failed peace attempts.[8]

For an agreement to be forged, two parties which for long had been steadfast enemies and which had quite opposed ideological agendas—FARC-EP still held to be a Marxist-Leninist organization and stood for a radical economic and political transformation, while Santos was elected as the anointed successor to Uribe and generally defended the status quo—had to substitute cooperation for confrontation.[9]

On its own, the public announcement (in September 2012) that peace negotiations would be carried out and an agenda had been agreed upon was a huge achievement. It entailed the government's concession that certain structural economic and political issues would be discussed—rural development, political participation, illicit drugs—but also FARC-EP's concession to put victims' rights at the center of the agenda and its willingness to discuss concrete measures through which violence would end—such as disarmament, something that FARC-EP had never accepted before.[10] The announcement further entailed the parties' realization that the effective enforcement or implementation of the agreement was a crucial issue that had to be negotiated upon—something no prior peace agreement had included.

Still, the path toward a final agreement was slow and bumpy. The agenda was quite ambitious and the initial stances of the parties on each issue very far apart. Moreover, distrust reigned between them. As a result, the announcement of agreements took much longer than what had been initially announced, meaning that national elections for Congress and President were held (in 2014) before most issues in the agenda had been agreed upon. There were several critical moments in which the negotiation was in peril—such as FARC-EP's kidnapping of policemen and Santos' meeting with Venezuela's opposition leader right after Chávez's death (in early 2013); the tight electoral race between Santos and an opponent to the peace process (in 2014); the suspension of FARC-EP's ceasefire in 2015; and the very tense discussion of the most sensitive and still pending issues (in 2016), which made the negotiations carry on months after the final agreement had been anticipated by the President and which allegedly led some negotiators to leave the table in the last few days.[11]

Obstacles notwithstanding, the peace agreement was finally signed in August of 2016. This result was possible due to the gradual increase in the parties' trust toward one another[12] and their willingness to move initial stances away from extremes and toward a middle ground in which they could meet. Indeed, the agreement's text is characterized by compromise on every topic of the agenda.

Thus, for example, on the first topic of rural development, FARC-EP let go of its insistence in radical redistribution through private property expropriation, while the government recognized the need of strongly combatting land inequality and poverty in historically neglected rural areas. The parties hence met midways by agreeing on a program of territorial development that seeks to grant peasants gradual access to public and illegally acquired lands, to protect them against violence and market forces through the formalization of land titles and the establishment of a temporary restriction to land alienation, and to grant technical, financial, and organizational support to small farmers.

In a similar way, topics two to five of the agreement—on political participation, the end of conflict, illicit drugs, and victims' rights—all illustrated each party's willingness to abandon their most extreme stances and make concessions in order to find a middle ground. As compromises, all the agreed upon issues can be considered moderate in the sense that they do not offer grounds for a radical redistribution of resources or power. And yet, because of Colombia's deep deficiencies in economic equality, political incorporation, and state capacity, if effectively enforced, the measures could significantly transform the country's status quo, notably by modernizing the land tenure system and political power, evening out the reach of state institutions and the rule of law, and promoting the participation of citizens in the implementation process.

The parties explicitly committed to that sort of transformation, understanding it as a crucial condition for lasting peace.[13] However, they had divergent interpretations of how the structural conditions in need of transformation had impacted conflict,[14] and hence quite possibly of how deep should such transformations be in practice. For instance, concerning the programs of territorial integration foreseen in chapter one of the agreement, while FARC-EP negotiators bet on their potential to overcome structural violence and offer the grounds for social justice,[15] the government's negotiators interpreted them as being a revised version of consolidation plans—previously established to ensure state (mainly military) presence through US support.[16]

This allowed for tensions not only between parties but also within each party to remain with respect to what had been agreed, which led a minority sector of FARC-EP to withdraw their support to the agreement and become dissidents,[17] and which (as we will see next) also led members of Santos' coalition to grow increasingly shy in the promotion of the agreement's structural reforms. The parties' interpretations of the agreement's transformational potential and the tensions that they entailed further diverged and expanded to other political parties and the general public as the agreement was put to the popular vote, and as the process carried out to "save" it from failure made its legitimacy wane.

The obstacles to implementation and the paradoxes of transformation

One of the most innovative aspects of the Colombian peace agreement is its sixth (and final) topic focusing on implementation. The inclusion of "implementation" illustrated the parties' commitment to the substantive transformations sought by the agreement, since it made explicit their recognition of enforcement as the most serious challenge. The parties identified the lack of state capacity and of adequate political support as the main obstacles to implementation.

To face these obstacles, among other things, the parties agreed on the commitment of state resources for long-term implementation; the establishment of a monitoring and conflict resolution commission in which both parties would have equal participation, and which would be accompanied by representatives of guarantor countries and technically supported by an academic institution; the state's unilateral declaration of the agreement's humanitarian nature under international law and its deposition in Bern; the promotion in Congress of a special legislative procedure for the incorporation of the peace agreement into domestic law and of a transitory article into the Constitution that would give it the status of a constitutional standard of interpretation during the implementation period; and the submission of the final agreement to popular approval,[18] as well as the dissemination and pedagogy of its content.

As it is common knowledge, in the plebiscite held shortly after the signature of the agreement (October 2, 2016), the "No" option against the peace agreement won by a very narrow margin. Since then, a recurring question has been asked about the decision of the parties to submit such a difficult-to-achieve and well-crafted agreement to popular vote when the risk of losing was high and its consequences so devastating. There was no legal reason requiring them to do so, since the government had enough powers to enforce an agreement to end violence and since the negotiated transformations would still require legal (and in several cases constitutional) reform and, hence, democratic (albeit representative) endorsement. Still, the parties found it crucial for the agreement—and especially for the structural transformations it included—to obtain democratic legitimacy.[19]

Indeed, popular endorsement was vital not only for normative reasons—which suggest that the more important the political matter, the more the people should democratically participate in its decision—but also for instrumental ones—which indicate that strong popular support to the peace agreement was necessary for its implementation to be possible. Because of the factors identified in the introduction, the transformations entailed by the agreement were likely to face strong elite resistance precisely in the regions in which they were of the highest priority. The government's political will to strengthen state institutions or to carry out reform therein did not seem enough to overcome such resistance, since local powers were very entrenched and had strong incentives to defend the status quo, and since most central political elites did not care enough for such transformations.

The parties identified local participation as key to transformation, under the rationale that a strong and organized demand-side to peace reforms could push for the successful implementation of each chapter of the agreement.[20] However, that demand-side was at best weak and fragmented, so the plebiscite was seen as a first and crucial step to boost it. The plebiscite was also considered a first and vital step to create a wider front of supporters of the peace agreement, who could make its implementation a matter of national public interest, and hence embrace territorial claims for peace and put pressure on their fulfillment. Such a front was then non-existent, since the peace agreement had been the result of secret and complex negotiations outside the country, which remained distant from the majority of the citizenry.

Consequently, negotiating parties made a bet on popular ratification as the mechanism through which mobilization for peace could begin, and then serve as the basis for the agreement to be implemented on-demand. The bet failed by a small margin, though it is far from clear whether the situation would have been substantially different if the "Yes" option had won by an equally narrow margin. In part, the result was due to the selection of the plebiscite as the approval mechanism—which dramatically polarized the discussion by turning a multifaceted issue into a binary choice[21] and by artificially making that choice one for or against peace, a choice that was not acceptable to many "No" voters.[22] The result was also partly due to the mistakes committed in the "Yes" campaign—which was incapable of creating a united front that could sell a powerful and easy-to-understand message in favor of peace. Instead, the most radical and vocal opponents of the peace agreement—under the leadership of former President, then Senator Uribe—seized the opportunity and promoted a strong and univocal campaign with a very simple, emotional, and often manipulative content, which was able to attract not only core opponents to the agreement, but also peace supporters with caveats, and even indifferent citizens who felt compelled by the "No" message or by the links that campaigners established between it and other politically salient issues like gender equality and same-sex rights.[23]

Be as it may, the plebiscite's result cannot be fully understood if more structural factors (like those discussed in the introduction) are not taken into account. There was a sharp regional divide between richer, more integrated and less-violent departments and municipalities of the country, which tended to vote "No," and poorer, more unequal, peripheral, and violent areas, which tended to vote "Yes,"[24] but which also exhibited high levels of abstention.[25] The plebiscite highlighted the lack of urgency felt in bringing about peace by people in central areas of the country that have not been directly affected by conflict. More importantly, the plebiscite showed that many people in violent areas who are likely to want peace urgently might not have been able to express their preferences.

Indeed, 63% of authorized voters did not participate in the plebiscite—compared to the average abstention rates of 56% in legislative elections and 54% in presidential elections between 1991 and 2014 in the country, and of 30% in Latin America.[26] The relevance of the issue for which the plebiscite was convened did not increase, but rather decreased, the level of political participation. This was likely the result of specific institutional obstacles—such as the fact that the electoral authority did not allow new, previously unregistered voters, to register for this election—but also of historical ones that have traditionally made abstention unusually high in Colombia. Those factors include the small number and large distance of electoral posts from voters in rural areas—who in many cases must travel by bus or boat for several hours to reach them—the lack of state support for voter registration and transportation, and the lack of mandatory voting. Many of these obstacles are quite functional to elites and de facto powers in peripheral areas, who could see in a more active electoral participation a key threat to their interests.

This illustrates the profound paradox inherent to the peace agreement: The transformations that it seeks to bring about require minimal preconditions that do not exist, and whose absence is the precise reason why such transformations are so important. The agreement's ongoing implementation crisis can largely be explained by this paradox, which has been heightened by its persisting deficit of democratic legitimacy. However, also paradoxically, the lacking support for peace was importantly countered by the vigorous mobilization that followed the plebiscite's loss, which demanded an "Agreement Now!", that is, a prompt renegotiation and adoption of an adjusted agreement that would prevent the breakdown of the ceasefire.[27]

In response, the government made serious and speedy efforts to renegotiate the peace agreement, first with leaders of the opposition, and then with FARC-EP's negotiators. In just one month, the government convinced the latter to incorporate the vast majority of objections that the opposition had to the agreement (58 out of the 60 proposed changes, according to the government's commissioner for peace and negotiator, Jaramillo Caro[28]). However, FARC-EP refused a couple of key proposals of the opposition: Their political ineligibility while being criminally prosecuted, and suffering criminal sanctions in jail, instead of in secluded areas. As a result, the opposition refused to acknowledge that the agreement had suffered significant changes, referring to them as merely cosmetic.

Facing a strong urgency to prevent the now groundless ceasefire with FARC-EP from breaking, the government made the difficult decision to sign the new agreement (on November 24th) and submit the agreement to ratification by Congress (on December 1st). The government justified the decision not only on the expediency required by a frail peace, but also on the considerations that it had delivered to the "No" mandate by making substantive changes to the agreement; that it also had a mandate for peace—derived from the close margin of loss of the "Yes" option and from the powerful popular mobilizations for peace after the plebiscite's defeat; that it had legal powers to negotiate a new peace agreement; and that Congress was the democratic forum par excellence, so its ratification of the agreement conferred sufficient legitimacy to the new agreement.[29]

Despite the wide and plural Congressional support for the new agreement and the Constitutional Court's endorsement of its validity,[30] its democratic legitimacy was perceived as severely impaired not only by adamant opponents of the peace process—who strategically seized the opportunity to accuse the government of tricking the people and thus stigmatize the peace agreement as a whole—but also by several supporters of the peace agreement—who thought that the legitimacy deficit produced by the plebiscite's defeat should be cured through more, not less, democracy—that is, through a new plebiscite or through other direct democracy mechanisms enabling greater and more informed popular participation.[31]

The legitimacy deficit allowed the opposition to increase polarization around peace and to garner support to contest power in the 2018 elections. The anti-peace agenda had such strong echoes that it allowed for Duque, an entirely unknown politician sponsored by Uribe, to become one of the youngest and most inexperienced Presidents of the country by a strong majority. But the balance of political power had changed well before then.[32] The plebiscite's debacle made Santos and his coalition calculate that they were better-off (politically, but also possibly ideologically) if they did not actively support the peace agenda, and especially its transformational components.

Thus, throughout 2017, the government and its Congressional coalition subtly turned their backs on peace by not promoting, severely delaying, or plummeting several of the reforms that were necessary for the agreed transformations to take force. This was particularly problematic since the fast-track procedure to enact expeditious reforms through Congress—which had been agreed upon by the negotiating parties and approved by Congress (in December of 2016) would only be valid for a year. When it expired, less than half of the reform bills initially announced by the government had been proposed before Congress,[33] of which a few were approved but only one—the statute of the opposition—concerned the transformational topics of the agreement.[34] The other bills were withdrawn by their proponents, unable to find approval under the required time-period—as happened with those related to rural reform—or did not obtain a majority—as happened with the reforms to the political system and parties, and with the creation of the 16 special electoral circumscriptions for peace, which fell one vote short the very day in which the fast-track ended, and whose failing was considered the most severe blow to the peace agreement.

Even the reforms that passed were so nearly the end of the fast-track and they faced strong obstacles. Perhaps the most illustrative example is the Special Jurisdiction for Peace (JEP). Its creation was considered fundamental to ensure the legal certainty necessary for FARC-EP to begin the demobilization process right after the signature of the agreement—since JEP would be in charge not only of sentencing perpetrators of atrocities but also of approving amnesties for the rest. Yet, the passing of the statutory law containing its substantive rules was sabotaged for weeks by the no-show and foot-dragging of many Congress people, and it was uncertain until the very last day of the fast-track's period whether it would pass. Further, Congress discussed (and eventually approved) important modifications to the bill, which impeded some of the justices (selected in September of 2017) to take office (in January of 2018) and which attempted to change the agreement's conditions but failed to do so due to the Constitutional Court's *ex ante* revision.[35] JEP's procedural rules faced similar difficulties: They were only approved 9 months after the selection of justices and 6 months after they took office (in June of 2018), and the opposition attempted to reform the bill to restrict JEP's jurisdiction to decide on extradition and cases against the armed forces unless a special procedural law was enacted, something that was also declared invalid by the Constitutional Court.[36]

The difficulties for pushing through the reforms necessary to implement the peace process significantly increased in 2018. Not only did they now have to be approved by the longer and more complex ordinary legislative procedure; in the first months of the year, they further faced the utter lack of interest of politicians who were devoting their entire attention to the upcoming Congressional and Presidential elections (held in March and May-June, respectively). This led to the shelving of the multipurpose cadaster bill that was key for rural reform, and of several attempts to bring back to life the 16 peace circumscriptions. It even led the Santos government to propose a bill on lands, without consulting affected peasant or ethnic communities, and which allowed for the allocation of public lands to entrepreneurs and the legalization of ill-acquired ones, hence contradicting central goals of the peace agreement.[37]

The last semester of Santos' period was also characterized by a very slow implementation of the structural components of the peace agreement that could be advanced at the local level. Even though the timetable foresaw that participatory processes related to territorial development programs (PDETs for their Spanish initials) would take place before May 2018, by the end of Santos' period only 33 of the 170 selected municipalities had approved the plans, and only two of the 16 regions had fully finished the process.[38] Overall, more than half of the actions related to rural and political reform had not been initiated on the ground by August of 2018.[39]

Under Duque's government, the obstacles to the implementation of the peace agreement have not only stemmed from the lack of promotion of legal reforms and on the ground programs, but also from overt counter-reform. Since his campaign, Duque dismembered the peace agreement, reducing it to a minimalist core—related to disarmament and the punishment of atrocities committed by FARC-EP (but not by the armed forces or third parties)—while actively attacking its transformational components. To promote this agenda, during his first year of government Duque allocated much fewer resources to institutions in charge of assisting victims; appointed vocal opponents of the peace agreement to crucial peace-building institutions—such as the Land Restitution Unit and the National Center for Historical Memory; publicly criticized JEP for its alleged bias in favor of former FARC-EP combatants, and presented to Congress significant reforms to the peace agreement—such as the denial of a link between drug-trafficking and political crimes so that the former cannot be amnestied in the future; the exclusion of crimes against minors from JEP's jurisdiction; the creation of a special chamber within JEP to judge the armed forces through more lenient rules, and the restriction of access to security information for the purposes of truth-seeking.[40]

Interestingly, however, Duque's attacks on peace have also bolstered the emergence of a political and popular bloc supporting the transformative components of the peace agreement, and thereby a leftist redistributive agenda, which had never been so strong in Colombia. In reaction to Duque's minimalist peace, the left-wing presidential candidate Petro defended a progressive agenda that emphasized the transformative components of the peace agreement and even additional structural reforms that went beyond it, such as the substitution of the extractive economies model. Despite running with the support of an independent party, in the first round Petro overtook the center Green party—supported by the leftist Polo party from which he withdrew—and in the second won 42% of the popular vote, thanks to the strong support of a coalition of small parties, social and grassroots movements, many of which emerged or coalesced around the promises of the peace agreement.[41]

Under Duque's government, Petro's coalition has often defended the peace agreement's implementation by joining forces with the center and left parties (including former FARC-EP's new party, labeled FARC but now standing for "Common Alternative Revolutionary Force"). They thus successfully blocked the appointment of the director of the Center for Historical Memory and forced the withdrawal of the bills limiting access to national security information for truth-seeking purposes and excluding sexual crimes against minors from JEP's jurisdiction.[42]

Beyond Congress, social movements and grassroots organizations have continued and expanded their struggle for the implementation of the transformational components of the peace agreement. Thus, in early 2019, peasant and ethnic organizations of the country's southwestern region promoted one of the largest and longest mobilizations in the last decade, which demanded compliance with the rural and political reforms contained in the peace agreement. Peasant organizations have also made proposals to authorities for their socioeconomic interests to be taken into account in discussions such as the National Development Plan.[43]

The social mobilization for peace is particularly noteworthy, given the high levels of violence to which social and political leaders are subjected. While the total number of murders steeply dropped as a result of the cease fire, leaders and demobilized former combatants—both of whom can be considered key actors for the on-demand implementation of peace at the local level—began to be assassinated and threatened at outrageous rates. Estimates indicate that more than 760 local social and political leaders and 170 demobilized FARC-EP members were assassinated between 2016 and 2019. Targeted assassinations raised significantly between 2016 and 2018. The data for 2019 are still preliminary, but they suggest that like former combatants' assassinations increased, that leaders' assassinations were as high or only slightly lower than in 2018, that murder attempts and especially threats against leaders sharply augmented with respect to prior years, and that all forms of violence against leaders were particularly acute during the regional elections of the second semester of 2019. In turn, early data for 2020 indicate that assassinations and threats in the first month of that year were greater than those for the same month in 2019.[44]

Extant analyses and data suggest that leaders' and former combatants' assassinations are targeting local organizational processes that engage with or promote the transformative components of the peace agreement, such as PDETs, land restitution, and the substitution of illicit crops, especially in areas formerly controlled by FARC-EP and coveted by other armed groups.[45] Even though leaders' assassinations have occurred in the majority of Colombian departments, they have been especially intense in regions like Tumaco, north of Cauca, and the Cauca antioqueño, which have been given priority in the implementation of PDETs. Between October 2018 and February 2019, 73% of registered leaders' assassinations occurred in such territories. Further, registered aggressions against leaders have occurred in 13 out of the 16 PDET territories, and 50% of those registered in January 2020 occurred therein.[46]

Despite the gravity of the situation, state authorities have ostensibly been negligent in preventing the assassination of former combatants and leaders at risk, even though a specific institution—the National Unit of Protection—was created to carry out that task. Moreover, authorities have been almost insulting in their resistance to accept that there is a pattern of assassinations, irresponsible in their distorted reports of the number of cases, and risk-promoting in their stigmatization of social protest.

Reducing the systematic nature of violence to the existence of a centralized extermination policy by an armed organization, top executive officials in the Santos administration denied it; in December of 2017, Santos' Defense Minister went as far as saying that leaders' murders were due to private matters—such as love scandals(!)—and not to a pattern.[47]

In turn, offering untenable interpretations of still preliminary data, Duque's Human Rights Commissioner claimed that violence against leaders declined in 2019 due to his security policy (the *Plan de Acción Oportuna*, PAO), even though the source used tends to underestimate assassinations more than other sources; that using a longer period for such data suggests no evident decline with respect to the prior period; that preliminary data of a subsequent period exhibits increases in assassinations; that even if assassinations slightly dropped in 2019, threats and aggressions exponentially increased,[48] and that it is very difficult to impute causality to Duque's security policy in the alleged reduction of violence, since the PAO restricted leaders' protection to minimal individual security measures without attacking the conditions that generate special risks for social mobilization and political participation—against what the peace agreement foresaw—and that it has been weakly implemented—with notable cases of murdered leaders who demanded protection in multiple occasions to no avail.[49]

Finally, Duque's government has openly stigmatized social protest, to the point of asserting—as the Defense Minister did in 2018—that it was financed by armed actors, something that can justify and hence quite likely increase the risks of violence against social and political leaders.[50]

The systemic nature of violence against ex-combatants and leaders need not only consist in a centralized extermination policy; the fact that there are common characteristics in the profile of victims and common factors at the local label that enable the use of violence against them can also generate patterns of violence.[51] That is why the state's responsibility is not restricted to offering individual protection measures; it must also entail the eradication of the conditions that enable such violence, as the peace agreement foresaw. Even though those conditions are complex and varied, they cannot be reduced to the presence of illegal economies and armed groups, as governmental and press analyses often do.[52]

The endurance of the equilibrium described in the introduction of this essay—on the grounds of which local de facto powers use violence to maintain elites' grip on power and central elites do not care enough to intervene more actively—seems to be an important part of the explanation. As Albarracín et al. show, between 2016 and 2018, the statistical probability of violence against leaders increased in municipalities with lower levels of electoral competition and with greater strength of leftist challenger political movements.[53] This suggests that, in places of strong incumbent control, pro status quo de facto powers are more likely to resort to violence and elites more likely to allow it in the face of challenges to the distribution of power entailed by the leftist agenda, which promotes the transformational components of peace. This indicates that, as has been traditionally the case in Colombia, local powers are using violence to suffocate from-below demands for change and to perpetuate subnational violent political orders, while central elites tolerate them as long as they do not explicitly defy the central state's authority or vulnerate central elites' interests.

Indeed, it has become less and less plausible to argue that the country's problem regarding violence in the periphery is a matter of state capacity and not of political will to make such capacity a reality. Since Uribe's government launched its offensive strategy against guerrilla groups, the Colombian army became one of the most resource-rich and professional in the world, and its strength could well be used to combat the criminal groups—mainly rearmed paramilitaries and drug trafficking groups—whose members have been identified as the main perpetrators of those crimes.[54] Moreover, international resources and technical support have recently poured into the country to contribute to the operation of newly created institutions in charge of enforcing the peace agreement, including those in charge of verification and protection.[55] Yet, authorities seem unwilling to consider the security of rural leaders and demobilized combatants a priority.[56]

In the face of this gruesome picture, it is surprising that most FARC leaders and demobilized troops seem committed to leave violence behind and become political actors. Although a few fronts decided not to demobilize and several combatants and prominent leaders have retaken arms since the peace agreement was signed,[57] overall dissidence is so far a marginal phenomenon, and the most recent rearmament of four chiefs was strongly criticized as shameful by the leader of the FARC party, who insisted in the group's allegiance to peace despite the government's reneging of the agreement.[58]

Demobilized FARC leaders have offered multiple signals of their commitment to peace and institutions, including their acknowledgment of atrocities and public apologies before victimized communities[59]; their disposition to be held accountable before JEP and to collaborate through testimonies and the delivery of a list of assets for reparations[60]; the announcement of their decision to request the intervention of the International Criminal Court—an institution which they should fear—to prevent the impunity derived from the changes to JEP that the government's coalition was promoting in 2018–19[61]; their in-block voting (even with traditional parties, such as Liberals) against counter-reforms to peace (as discussed above); and the disposition to change their party's name to dissociate it from the guerrilla group[62]—an acknowledgment of the popular rejection of its violent past and of the need to transform its political profile.

This, along with the strong social and political mobilization for progressive peace-related changes, seem to be the most important transformations that the peace agreement has achieved. Though they are both being severely threatened by local targeted violence and central elites' ambivalence toward the peace agreement, they are also both resiliently persisting, and the support for the leftist transformational agenda for peace seems to be capable of expansion. This gives us reasons to hope that, despite the enormous difficulties and power asymmetries, the programmatic politics triggered by the peace agreement are here to stay, and that Colombia might be beginning a new period in which the political discussion focuses on redistributive issues where leftist anti-status quo stances have a central role—something unprecedented in the country's history.[63]

Author's note

I thank Diana I. Güiza-Gómez for her very thorough and pertinent comments to both a prior and the current version of this chapter. I also thank an anonymous reviewer and the editors of the book for their very useful suggestions. All mistakes are of course mine.

Notes

1 See Fernán González, "¿Colapso parcial o presencia diferenciada del Estado en Colombia?: una mirada desde la historia," *Colombia Internacional,* vol. 54, 2003, p. 139. https://doi.org/10.7440/colombiaint58.2003.05; James A. Robinson, "Colombia: Another 100 Years of Solitude?" *Current History,* vol. 112, 2013, p. 45.

2 Mauricio García, Miguel García, Juan Carlos Rodríguez, Javier E. Reveló, José R. Espinosa, *Los estados del país. Instituciones municipales y realidades locales*

(Bogotá: Dejusticia, 2011), 38–40, Chapter 2; Fabio Sánchez and Mario Chacón, "Conflicto, Estado y descentralización. Del progreso social a la disputa armada por el control global (1974–2002)," in *Nuestra guerra sin nombre. Transformaciones del conflicto en Colombia*, eds. Francisco Gutiérrez, María Emma Wills, Gonzalo Sánchez, (Bogotá: Norma, 2006) pp. 347–405; Fabio Sánchez, and María del Mar Palau, "Conflict, Decentralisation and Local Governance in Colombia 1974–2004," Documento CEDE 20 (2006); Javier Revelo y Mauricio García, *El Estado en la periferia. Historias locales de debilidad institucional en la periferia* (Bogotá: Dejusticia, 2018).

3 María Paula Saffon Sanín and Diana I. Güiza, "Colombia en 2018: entre el fracaso de la paz y el inicio de la política programática," *Revista de Ciencia Política,* vol. 39 (2), 2019, pp. 222–223. https://doi.org/10.4067/S0718-090X2019000200217.

4 Leah Anne Carroll, *Violent Democratization. Social Movements, Elites, and Politics in Colombia's Rural War Zones, 1984–2008* (Indiana: The University of Notre Dame Press, 2011).

5 This was not the case of the peace process that took place between right-wing paramilitaries and the Uribe government in the early 2000s, which did not consist of a negotiation between contending parties to war, but rather a concerted demobilization of pro-systemic and pro-status quo armed groups. See Leopoldo Múnera, "Proceso de paz con actores armados ilegales y parasistémicos (los paramilitares y las políticas de reconciliación en Colombia)," *Revista Pensamiento Jurídico,* vol. 17, 2006, pp. 68–9; Rodrigo Uprimny and María Paula Saffon, "Uses and Abuses of Transitional Justice in Colombia," in Morten Bergsmo and Pablo Kalmanovitz (eds), *Law in Peace Negotiations* (Oslo: FICHL, 2009) 360. The process does not seem to have been the result of central elites' interest in reducing paramilitary violence—which resumed soon after—but rather of their will to concede beneficial terms for demobilization. When such terms were challenged in court and opened the risk of paramilitary confessions revealing links with political and economic elites, Uribe broke his promises and extradited the main leaders.

6 Thus the distinction between putting an end to conflict and building peace, established by the Colombian Peace Agreement and explained by Sergio Jaramillo Caro, "The Possibility of Peace" (this volume, Chapter 2), Introduction, and Section IV.

7 Saffon Sanín and Güiza, "Colombia en 2018," 225–7.

8 As Jaramillo Caro argues, the change in the balance of military power was necessary for negotiations to begin but not sufficient for a peace agreement to be reached: "History is full of ripe moments which slipped away *because a solution was not forged*" (this volume, Chapter 2), Introduction. In a similar sense see James Head and Ian Shapiro, "The Power of Hope: Strategic Leadership and Democratic Settlements," *American Political Science Review,* vol. 108 (1), 2014, pp. 40–53.

9 Thomas Schelling, *The Strategy of Conflict* (Cambridge MA: Harvard University Press, 1960).

10 Jaramillo Caro (this volume, Chapter 2), Section IV.

11 Personal communications with an actor close to the process.

12 As Jaramillo Caro shows, most of the factors that made this possible were of the parties' own making, including concrete signals of mutual respect and an incremental methodology allowing stalemates to be overcome and making the agreement increasingly irreversible (this volume, Chapter 2), Sections III–V.

13 According to the rationale of the final agreement (stated in the preamble), its central aims and cross-cutting axes were to (i) contribute to the satisfaction of fundamental rights, with special consideration for those of victims and vulnerable populations; (ii) strengthen the presence and effectiveness of the state across the

territory, and especially in regions abandoned by the state or especially affected by violence; and (iii) build a new paradigm of development and welfare, focused on territorial integration and participation in the implementation of the agreement.

14 The Preamble of the Final Agreement states: "(…) in the National Government's opinion, the transformations entailed by the implementation of the present agreement should contribute to reversing the effects of conflict and to change the conditions that have facilitated the persistence of violence in the territory; and in the opinion of the FARC-EP, such transformations should contribute to solve the historical causes of conflict."

15 See *Jesús Santrich*'s interview conducted by Sasha Yumbila, "El acuerdo de paz está vuelto trizas, pero eso va más allá del papel jugado por el uribismo y el centro democrático," *Al Carajo*, July 24, 2020. http://www.alcarajo.org/el-acuerdo-de-paz-esta-vuelto-trizas-pero-eso-va-mas-alla-del-papel-jugado-por-el-uribismo-y-el-centro-democratico-jesus-santrich/?fbclid=IwAR3ShjsWPLNFedQlX8rEen-qYBLKJDFn3WklaTtjJtMQ_VQJzccvURnPLOI.

16 Andrés Bermúdez ed., *Los Debates de La Habana: Una Mirada Desde Adentro* (Barcelona: Institute for Integrated Transitions, 2018) 44. https://www.ifit-transitions.org/resources/publications/major-publications-briefings/the-colombian-peace-talks-practical-lessons-for-negotiators-worldwide/los-debates-de-la-habana.pdf/view.

17 As *Santrich recounts*, the first group of dissidents announced that they would not support the peace agreement after the Tenth FARC-EP conference held in August 2016, in which the agreement was submitted to the group's ratification. The main reason was that they opposed disarmament entailing the unilateral surrender of weapons instead of leaving their use outside of politics. Later, other combatants who were in prison retook arms after having been liberated on the grounds of the peace agreement. In August 2019, several guerrilla chiefs including *Santrich* and *Iván Márquez*, who had participated as negotiators in the peace process and had obtained seats in Congress, returned to the armed struggle arguing that the state had not complied with the agreement. In April 2018, *Santrich* was prosecuted and detained—with the purpose of extradition—for his alleged participation in drug-trafficking after the peace agreement's signature, which impeded him from taking his reserved seat in Congress. To protest this, *Santrich* held a hunger strike and brought a writ before justice, which granted him liberation and the right to take his seat in Congress. In turn, to protest *Santrich's* process and the state's reneging of the peace accord, *Márquez* abstained from taking his reserved seat in Congress but expressed that he would work "day and night" for the consolidation of peace. In August 2019, after *Santrich* was called to appear before justice and he abstained from doing so and from going to Congress, *Santrich, Márquez*, and other two leaders announced their decision to retake arms, alleging it was the only option left due to the state's perfidy. See *Santrich*'s interview, July 24, 2020; and "'Iván Márquez', 'Santrich', 'El Paisa' y 'Romaña' vuelven a la guerra," *El Espectador*, August 29, 2019. https://www.elespectador.com/colombia2020/pais/ivan-marquez-santrich-el-paisa-y-romana-vuelven-la-guerra-articulo-878350/.

18 Because of the parties' disagreement on the precise mechanism for seeking popular approval—FARC-EP defended a Constitutional Assembly while the government proposed a plebiscite—in their implementation agreement of May 2016, they agreed to abide to the Constitutional Court's decision on the constitutionality of the plebiscite that the government had unilaterally advanced in Congress. The Court declared it constitutional under some conditions in Ruling C-379/16.

19 Jaramillo Caro (this volume, Chapter 2), Section X.
20 Idem, Section VIII.
21 Roberto Gargarella, "The Courts' Possible Contribution to a Dialogic Democracy: The Case of The Peace Agreements in Colombia," (this volume, Chapter 19), Section I.
22 Jaramillo Caro (this volume, Chapter 2), Section X.
23 María Paula Saffon Sanín and Viviana Tacha, *Participation in Transitional Justice Measures. A Comparative Study* (Bogotá: Dejusticia, 2019) 51–3; Sandra Botero, "El plebiscito y los desafíos políticos de consolidar la paz negociada en Colombia," *Revista de Ciencia Política*, vol. 37 (2), 2017, pp. 378–80, http://dx.doi.org/10.4067/s0718-090x2017000200369.
24 Leopoldo Fergusson and Carlos Molina, "Un Vistazo a los Resultados del Plebiscito," *La silla vacía*, October 4th, 2016, http://lasillavacia.com/blogs/un-vistazo-los-resultados-del-plebiscito-58200; Juan Sebastián Muñoz and Juan David Herreño, "País(es) Divergentes: radiografía del plebiscito," *El Espectador*, October 13, 2016, http://colombia2020.elespectador.com/pais/paises-divergentes-radiografia-del-plebiscito. The exceptions to this trend were Bogotá and Boyacá where "Yes" won by 50% or more, and several intermediary cities where the margin of victory was tight. Botero, "El plebiscito y los desafíos," pp. 374–6.
25 As Botero notes, the abstention average was ten points higher in departments where "Yes" prevailed than in those where "No" did—69% and 59%, respectively. Botero, "El plebiscito y los desafíos," p. 374.
26 Miguel García, "Sobre la baja participación electoral de Colombia," *Semana,* October 18, 2016, https://www.semana.com/autor/miguel-garcia-sanchez/452; Botero, "El plebiscito y los desafíos," p. 374.
27 Only three days after the plebiscite vote, around 30,000 people mobilized toward Bogotá's Plaza de Bolívar, its central square. In the following month, there were three additional large mobilizations and many smaller demonstrations in different cities and municipalities. There were also two important citizen initiatives: "the camp for peace," which called for people to occupy Plaza de Bolívar until the Final Agreement began being implemented; and "peace to the streets," which convoked citizen assemblies to analyze the juncture and develop proposals. Saffon Sanín and Tacha, *Participation in Transitional Justice Measures*, pp. 32–3.
28 Jaramillo Caro (this volume, Chapter 2), Section X. The changes included, among others, the assurance that rural reform would not threaten private property, fiscal stability, or agro-industrial and tourism development projects; the dropping of the incorporation of the peace agreement into the Constitution and of references to the agreement's gender perspective; FARC-EP's commitment to victims' reparations with their own assets—entailing a deliverance of a detailed inventory; and several changes to JEP—such as the exclusion of foreign judges, the establishment of a fixed period for its operation, and the specification of the places and conditions under which criminal sanctions for atrocities would take place.
29 Rodrigo Uprimny, "No hubo conejo," *El Espectador*, October 17, 2017, https://www.elespectador.com/opinion/no-hubo-conejo-columna-718112/; Diana Güiza and Rodrigo Uprimny, "The Odyssey for Legitimizing and Enshrining Peace Commitments: Inclusivity and Constitution-building in the Colombian Peace Process" (this volume, Chapter 18).
30 The new agreement was ratified by a variety of parties from both the center and the left. Only Uribe's party (Centro Democrático) and the Conservative Party in alliance with it, both in the right, abstained from voting as a signal of protest to the procedure. The Court ruled on its validity in ruling C-699/16.
31 Javier Revelo, "Los riesgos de una paz que ni vence ni convence," *Razón Pública*, December 19, 2016, https://razonpublica.com/los-riesgos-de-una-paz-que-ni-vence-

ni-convence; María Paula Saffon, "Necesitamos más, no menos democracia," *El Espectador*, November 4th, 2016, https://www.elespectador.com/opinion/necesitamos-mas-no-menos-democracia/.

32 Saffon Sanín and Güiza, "Colombia en 2018," 219, pp. 225–6.

33 22 out of 50, according to Michelle Mora, "Un fast track no tan 'fast'," *Congreso visible.org*, July 6, 2018, https://congresovisible.uniandes.edu.co/agora/post/un-fast-track-no-tan-fast/10234/. Important topics like the creation of agrarian judges and the regulation of protest were never presented as bills.

34 Approved bills included amnesties; the creation of FARC's political party and its granting of reserved seats for two electoral periods; the consecration in the constitution of the state's monopoly of weapons and its duty to combat paramilitary groups; the shielding of the peace agreement through a temporary constitutional clause requiring its compliance by the executive for three presidential periods, and the creation and rules of operation of the special jurisdiction for peace.

35 An example of the first problem was the prohibition that human rights defenders became justices, and an example of the second was the declaration that crimes of sexual violence would exempt perpetrators from JEP's sanctions. Both rules were declared invalid by ruling C-080/18.

36 Ruling C-112/19.

37 Saffon Sanín and Güiza, "Colombia en 2018," p. 225.

38 Secretaría Técnica del Componente de Verificación Internacional CINEP/PPP-CERAC, *Tercer informe de verificación de la implementación del Acuerdo Final de Paz en Colombia para los Verificadores Internacionales Felipe González y José Mujica* (Bogotá: CINEP/CERAC, 2018).

39 Kroc Institute for International Peace Studies, *Segundo informe sobre el estado efectivo de la implementación del Acuerdo de Paz en Colombia* (Bogotá: Escuela Keough School of Global Affairs, University of Notre Dame, 2018).

40 Saffon Sanín and Güiza, "Colombia en 2018," p. 227.

41 Saffon Sanín and Güiza, "Colombia en 2018," p. 228.

42 But that has not always been the case. In October of 2018, separating from the Left, the center Green and Liberal parties in the opposition opted for entering a pact with the government to support a reformed version of the bill creating a special chamber to judge the armed forces under the condition that no other reforms would be included in the bill during its approval process. The pact was defended by the opposition as a mechanism to generate a wider political consensus regarding the peace agreement, which could offset its democratic legitimacy deficit and hence "save" it. The problem was that the opposition had little to no leverage to restrain the government from promoting other reforms to the agreement or to ensure that it would not continue to insist on its lack of legitimacy. This explains that, immediately after signing the pact, Uribe announced that his party would strive for widening the number of new justices to obtain "parity"—that is, a number equivalent to the already existing justices—and that the pact in no way implied that they would stop criticizing JEP or promoting further reforms to the peace agreement through other bills. Soon after, the pact was dissolved and the bill shelved, due to Uribistas' increased criticisms of the peace process. Saffon Sanín and Güiza, "Colombia en 2018," 228–9.

43 Saffon Sanín and Güiza, "Colombia en 2018," 229. On the proposal see also Diana Güiza and Natalia Torres, "El campesinado presenta propuestas al Plan Nacional de Desarrollo," *El Espectador*, December 21, 2018, https://www.elespectador.com/economia/el-campesinado-presenta-propues-tas-al-plan-nacional-de-desarrollo-articulo-830482.

44 Diana Güiza, María Paula Saffon, Juan Albarracín, Juan Pablo Milanese and Inge Valencia, "Amicus curiae" presented in the tutela process initiated by ten leaders

and human rights defenders before the Colombian Supreme Court of Justice (Bogotá, February 20, 2020), 11–21. For a summary, see "¿Vuelve a pasar frente a nuestros ojos?", *La Silla Vacía,* March 20, 2020, https://lasillavacia.com/silla-llena/red-rural/vuelve-pasar-frente-nuestros-ojos-72175. For violence against former combatants, we use the data provided by Misión de Verificación de las Naciones Unidas en Colombia, *Informe del Secretario General. S/2019/988* (Bogotá: MVNUC, December 26, 2019), which indicates that 31 were murdered in 2017, 65 in 2018, and 77 in 2019, for a total of 173. The UN mission publicly declared that at least 14 more former combatants had been murdered in the first two months of 2020. Its report also counts 14 forcedly disappeared former combatants and 29 murder attempts. For leaders' assassinations between 2016 and 2018, we draw on Rozo and Ball's study which, using information of six independent datasets collected by governmental and social organizations, applied the multiple estimation technique to infer a universe of cases on the grounds of event concordance across datasets, which throws a higher estimate than that of each dataset (166 for 2016, 185 for 2017, and 284 for 2018). Valentina Rozo and Patrick Ball, *Asesinatos de líderes sociales en Colombia: una estimación del universo—Actualización 2018* (Bogotá: Human Rights Analysis Group, Dejusticia, 2019), https://hrdag.org/wp-content/uploads/2019/12/2019-HRDAG-killings-colombi8a-update-spanish.pdf. Such an exercise is still non-existent for 2019; so, contrary to what the Colombian Presidency's Human Rights Commissioner claimed in October, 2019—that there was a 47% decrease of assassinations between January and October of 2019 with respect to that same period in 2018—it is still not possible to definitively assess what the trend was in 2019. In fact, the periods are not entirely comparable, since national elections took place in the first semester of 2018, but not of 2019. Moreover, the government used the Office of the United Nations High Commissioner for Human Rights (OHCHR)'s data, which tends to register fewer cases than other sources, and which, taken together for the whole of 2019 do not actually exhibit a significant decrease in comparison with 2018, since they total 107 assassinations in comparison with 114 in 2018, but the OHCHR also identifies 13 cases pending confirmation, which would likely make the 2019 data higher. For the Colombian Human Rights Commissioner's declaration, see Presidencia de Colombia, "Hay una reducción del 47% en los homicidios de líderes sociales en Colombia, reveló el Consejero para los Derechos Humanos," October 23, 2019. "https://id.presidencia.gov.co/Paginas/prensa/2019/reduccion-del-47-homicidios-lideres-sociales-Colombia-Consejero-Defensa-Derechos-Humanos.aspx#:~:text=El%20Consejero%20Presidencial%20para%20los,el%20mismo%20periodo%20de%202018, accessed July 24, 2020; and the report on which it was grounded: Consejería Presidencial para los Derechos Humanos y Asuntos Internacionales, *Informe de Homicidios Contra Líderes Sociales y Defensores de Derechos Humanos 2016–2019* (Bogotá: Consejería Presidencial para los Derechos Humanos y Asuntos Internacionales, 2019). For a critique, see Rodrigo Uprimny, "Errores fatales: sobre la supuesta reducción de asesinatos de líderes con Duque," *La Silla Vacía,* August 10, 2019, https://lasillavacia.com/opinion/errores-fatales-sobre-supuesta-reduccion-asesinatos-lideres-duque-72926. For the OHCHR's data, see OHCHR. "Colombia: Human rights activists' killings. Press briefing note on Colombia," January 14, 2020. https://www.ohchr.org/EN/NewsEvents/Pages/DisplayNews.aspx?NewsID=25461&LangID=E, (accessed July 24, 2020).Using preliminary data gathered by the Electoral Observation Mission—which is likely an underestimation, following Rozo and Ball's conclusions—there were at least 126 assassinations in 2019 (compared to 143 in 2018), which added to the 635 of the previous 3 years estimated by Rozo and Ball, total 761. The Mission also calculates 69 murder attempts and 347 threats in 2019, in comparison with 54 and

122 in 2018, respectively. Assassinations, attempts, and threats all exhibit a higher average during the 2019 electoral period (August–October). It further reports 19 assassinations and 32 threats for January of 2020, as compared to 16 and 21, respectively, for the same month in 2019. See Misión de Observación Electoral. *Informe sobre violencia política (1 de enero de 2019 a 30 de enero de 2020)* (Bogotá: MOE, January 30th, 2020); María Camila Pérez Bonilla, Misión de Observación Electoral, *Informe sobre violencia política desde el inicio del calendario electoral* (27 de octubre de 2018 a 25 de febrero de 2019 (Bogotá: MOE, February 25th, 2019).

45 Comisión Colombiana de Juristas, Instituto de Estudios Políticos y Relaciones Internacionales (IEPRI) de la Universidad Nacional de Colombia, Verdad Abierta, Coordinación Colombia, Europa, Estados Unidos, Programa Somos Defensores, CINEP/PPP,... Confederación Acción Comunal, *¿Cuáles son los patrones? Asesinatos de líderes sociales en el posacuerdo* (Bogotá, 2018), http://iepri.unal.edu.co/fileadmin/user_upload/iepri_content/boletin/patrones6.pdf; Procuraduría Delegada para Asuntos Agrarios y de Restitución de Tierras, *Violencia sistemática contra defensores de derechos territoriales en Colombia* (Bogotá, 2018), https://www.procuraduria.gov.co/portal/media/file/180710_Violencia %20sistematica-contra %20defensores-derechos-territoriales.pdf.

46 Güiza, Saffon, Albarracín, Milanese and Valencia, "Amicus curiae," p. 16.

47 See "Asesinatos de líderes son por "líos de faldas": ministro de Defensa," *El Espectador*, December 17, 2017, https://www.elespectador.com/noticias/politica/asesinatos-de-lideres-son-por-lios-de-faldas-ministro-de-defensa/.

48 See supra note 38.

49 Güiza, Saffon, Albarracín, Milanese and Valencia, "Amicus curiae," pp. 22–3.

50 "MinDefensa y líderes sociales: de líos de faldas a 'subvenciones' de narcos," *Verdad Abierta,* September 15, 2018, verdadabierta.com/mindefensa-lideres-sociales-lios-faldas-subvenciones-narcos; Diana Güiza, "De la paz querida a la paz caliente," February 5, 2019, https://www.elespectador.com/colombia2020/opinion/de-la-paz-querida-la-paz-caliente-columna-858948.

51 Francisco Gutiérrez, "Consuelo de pocos," *El Espectador*, January 10, 2020, https://www.elespectador.com/opinion/consuelo-de-pocos-columna-899021.

52 Güiza, Saffon, Albarracín, Milanese and Valencia, "Amicus curiae," pp. 18–9.

53 Juan Albarracín, Juan Pablo Milanese Inge Valencia and Jonas Wolff, "Electoral Competition, Local Political Orders, and Criminal Violence: Analysis of the Assassination of Social and Civic Leaders in Colombia," Paper presented at the First Meeting of the Latin American Peace Science Society (Medellin, January 17–18, 2020). The authors also find a positive association between violence against leaders and prior FARC-EP presence, and a negative one between the former and state capacity at the municipal level.

54 Ariel Ávila, *Detrás de La Guerra En Colombia* (Bogotá: Planeta, 2019).

55 Instituto Kroc de Estudios Internacionales de Paz, "Tres años después de la firma del Acuerdo Final de Colombia: Hacia la transformación territorial. Diciembre 2018 a Noviembre 2019" (Bogotá: Instituto Kroc de Estudios Internacionales de Paz, 2020), http://peaceaccords.nd.edu/wp-content/uploads/2020/06/Cuarto-Informe-Final-with-Annex-Link-1.pdf.

56 Thus the *tutela* judicial decisions requiring the national government to protect the rights of leaders; see Comisión Colombiana de Juristas, "Tutela ordena proteger a líderes y lideresas sociales en Colombia y garantizar el derecho a defender derechos," April 6, 2020, https://www.coljuristas.org/nuestro_quehacer/item.php?id=289; Dejusticia, "Juzgado falla a favor de líderes sociales y ordena que se garantice el derecho a defender derechos humanos," April 3, 2020, https://www.dejusticia.org/juzgado-falla-a-favor-de-lideres-sociales-y-ordena-que-se-garantice-el-derecho-a-defender-derechos-humanos/.

57 See supra note 15.

58 "La vergüenza de Timochenko tras el rearme de Marquez y Santrich," *Las 2 Orillas*, August 29, 2019, https://www.las2orillas.co/la-verguenza-de-timochenko-tras-el-rearme-de-marquez-y-santrich/.

59 See, among others, "'Pedimos que nos perdonen': Farc a víctimas de Bojayá," *El Tiempo*, September 29, 2016, https://www.eltiempo.com/politica/proceso-de-paz/farc-le-pide-perdon-a-victimas-de-bojaya-57359; "Farc pidió perdón a las víctimas del conflicto armado," *El Espectador*, April 10th, 2019, https://www.elespectador.com/noticias/politica/farc-pidio-perdon-a-las-victimas-del-conflicto-armado/.

60 "El Gobierno recibió lista de bienes de las Farc," *El Tiempo*, August 16, 2017, https://www.eltiempo.com/justicia/conflicto-y-narcotrafico/farc-entregan-lista-de-bienes-al-gobierno-nacional-120404; "La JEP llama a 31 líderes de Farc a rendir cuentas por secuestros," *El Espectador*, July 6, 2018, https://www.eltiempo.com/justicia/jep-colombia/jep-llama-a-cupula-de-farc-a-responder-por-secuestros-239982. "Timochenko comparece ante la JEP," *El Espectador*, February 13, 2019, https://www.elespectador.com/colombia2020/justicia/jep/timochenko-comparece-ante-la-jep-articulo-857640/.

61 "'Intervención inmediata'" de la Corte Penal Internacional, pide Farc si se aprueba reforma a la JEP," *Semana*, January 11, 2018, https://www.semana.com/nacion/articulo/partido-farc-rechaza-reforma-a-la-jep-aprobada-en-el-senado/589159.

62 "¿No más Farc? Timochenko plantea cambio de nombre para su partido," *El Espectador*, May 24, 2020, https://www.semana.com/nacion/articulo/timochenko-plantea-cambiar-nombre-de-partido-farc/673747.

63 Saffon Sanín and Güiza, "Colombia en 2018."

Part III

Transitional justice in theory and practice

6 Transforming transitional justice from below

Colombia's pioneering peace proposal

Jennifer L. McCoy, Jelena Subotic, and Ryan E. Carlin

Introduction

Much of contemporary human rights literature builds on models of international norm diffusion and the political effects of domestic norm adoption. In the field of transitional justice, the notion of an international "justice cascade"[1] has guided much research on the domestic implementation of various transitional justice mechanisms. This literature, however, focuses almost exclusively on political elites to explain why some post-conflict governments choose particular justice mechanisms and not others, or why they may reject transitional justice altogether. The penetration of international norms to the mass public has often been less of a concern because official transitional justice decisions are routinely made at the elite level and within non-democratic or weakly institutionalized democracies.

At the same time, scholarship on international norms has primarily focused on the Global South as norm-takers and Western states and international nongovernmental organizations (INGOs) as norm-makers. Amitav Acharya's concepts of norm localization and norm subsidiarity, on the other hand, recognize that any state may adapt norms to its own context, eventually influencing the international norm itself, and that the less powerful may challenge or reject norms proposed by the powerful if they are excluded from their creation or perceive an alternative agenda.[2]

In this chapter, we examine several propositions about the impact of international human rights accountability norms on peace negotiations in a democratic context, where public opinion, Congress, courts, and civil society organizations matter. Colombia's 2012–16 peace talks to end a 50-year-old civil conflict were conducted completely under the 2002 Rome Statute governing accountability for grave human rights crimes. The negotiators set significant international precedents by proposing transitional justice provisions that avoid full amnesty but still allow for peace. The proposals test the International Criminal Court (ICC)'s interpretations of proportional sentencing, as well as the Colombian public's willingness to tolerate alternative sentencing scenarios for human rights perpetrators as a result of peace talks that have put victims' rights front and center for the first time.

We advance two principal arguments. First, the manner of diffusion and internalization of international norms depends on regime type. In authoritarian states, the elite level is most important; in democratic states, mass level is important in two ways. Mass opinion must be considered by elite negotiators who need public support and even explicit endorsement of agreements. It is also independently important as it directly impacts the legitimacy, and therefore the sustainability, of peace agreements. To further complicate things, in Colombia's democracy the negotiators had to consider a strong rule of law with an activist Constitutional Court, and a significant role for Congress in legislating the implementation of an eventual peace agreement.

Secondly, we argue that local elites may attempt not only to adapt international norms to local conditions, but also to influence the international norm itself. Colombian negotiators were clearly responding to their domestic needs to get a peace deal approved in a democracy, but were also betting that the international community (especially the United States and the ICC) would be willing to accept Colombia's interpretation and implementation of the norm for the sake of peace.

We utilize primary interviews we conducted in 2014–16 in Colombia with political and social actors, as well as the negotiating teams in Cuba, and an original survey we conducted in 2015. We also examine other public opinion studies and analyses of the peace process.

The chapter proceeds as follows. We first introduce the case of Colombia as a pathway case for global transitional justice. Next, we briefly review recent scholarship on international norm diffusion and norm localization and add our own theoretical refinement of this body of work. We then analyze Colombia's attempt to change international norms through local normative innovation and negotiators' responses to international and domestic constituencies. We conclude by discussing possible international precedents of Colombia's process and its impact on the continuing legitimacy of the ICC.

Colombia as a pathway case

Over the past two decades, a global transitional justice norm has emerged which presents an expectation that post-conflict states will institutionally address responsibility for grave human rights abuses. This international expectation has been fully institutionalized by the Rome Statute of the ICC in 2002, which places four international crimes—crimes against humanity, genocide, war crimes, and crimes of aggression—under its jurisdiction. Additionally, the increasing visibility of global human rights has heightened public interest in and awareness of transitional justice.

The Colombian case serves as a "pathway case" to test propositions regarding norm evolution and implementation. Specifically, we argue that Colombian negotiators have become norm-makers, not just norm-takers as predicted by the international norms literature, in response to their task of negotiating peace in a democratic regime under the new international context. We hypothesize that in democratic contexts where public approval, judicial review, and Congressional legislation are required to endorse and implement a peace agreement, the negotiators face pressures not only from "above" (international obligations), but also from "below" (responsiveness to public opinion and varied interests). Within this multi-level bargaining game, negotiators strive to construct creative proposals as they face a more complex arena than the traditional "peace vs justice" debate with authoritarian incumbents, often resolved by mutual amnesty. In this way, we argue, they are not only influenced and constrained by the "judicialization of peace,"[3] but they also seek to shape international public opinion and international human rights norms.

Transitional justice mechanisms that are subjects of peace negotiations, rather than created after implementation of peace as in past cases, become vital elements in determining public approval as the new international normative climate helps to generate awareness of and expectations for justice. Thus, measuring and predicting legitimacy of transitional justice options being proposed becomes crucial in predicting the viability of peace.

We further hypothesize that negotiators seeking to end violent conflict within a democratic regime will prioritize, at least initially, the domestic political dynamics and need to legitimize a peace accord above the need to satisfy its international normative obligations for two reasons: (a) The need for approval by domestic institutions, whether it be Congress, courts, or public opinion referenda, is the most immediate need; and (b) the threat of intervention by the ICC is much higher in a state without functioning courts, given the complementarity principle in the Rome Statute.[4]

Our project examines these propositions in the ongoing peace talks in Colombia—a case of a protracted conflict in a democracy with relatively strong rule of law institutions, well-organized civil society and human rights organizations, and a vibrant political dynamic involving both the multiparty Congress and public opinion in the final approval and implementation of the negotiated agreement.

The peace negotiations initiated in 2012 by President Juan Manuel Santos put victims' rights front and center. This dual simultaneous transition—from war to peace, and from a practice of amnesty to increasing pressures for accountability—makes Colombia not only an important case to study for theoretical reasons, but also potentially sets a precedent for ending future civil wars in the new international context.

Global norms of international human rights

While relying on Finnemore and Sikkink's original norm-cycle framework,[5] scholarship has since significantly expanded and nuanced their original model. In particular, scholars have worked on understanding the inherently dynamic and multifaceted nature of norms and specified mechanisms of norm emergence, diffusion, compliance, implementation, institutionalization, and internalization, as well as their change and contestation.

Taking a broader view, the literature on norm diffusion has already produced many explanations for the mechanisms of norm localization, hybridization, and resistance. In one of the first models of norm localization, Acharya demonstrated how local actors reconstruct international norms to ensure the norms fit with the actors' already existing cognitive models and identities.[6] His concept of localization presented a framework for understanding how "active construction [through discourse, framing, grafting, and cultural selection] of foreign ideas by local actors … results in the former developing significant congruence with local beliefs and practices."[7] Norms, in other words, must build on established contextual ideas, be encouraged by locally legitimate actors, and enhance local prestige.[8] Alternatively, norm subsidiarity can be understood as a subaltern phenomenon, when states reject the normative ideas proposed by powerful Western states to guide behavior, either because they resent being excluded from the norm-creation or because they perceive hypocrisy in the lack of universal compliance with or enforcement of the norm by the Western power.[9]

Norm hybridization is a process by which a different norm that is a better local "fit" emerges out of a process of norm adaptation.[10] This leads to less powerful states banding together and redefining the parameters of norm implementation through issue linkage.[11] As the role of civil society in both formulating and implementing human rights norms continues to be acknowledged in this scholarship,[12] recent work has also brought to light the persistent power imbalance between international and local civil society actors which impacts norm enforcement.[13]

Our understanding of norm construction and development has also expanded. Norm creation and evolution are now understood to originate beyond international norm entrepreneurs (such as activists, or INGOs), as the role and agency of less powerful states and local actors are increasingly recognized. Less powerful states can critically shape the way an international norm is disseminated regionally based on their constitutional structures and how they interact with certain normative conceptions, such as those relating to sovereignty.[14]

An additional area of innovation has been further specifying the processes of norm institutionalization and implementation. International institutionalization of norms refers to the process of norm emergence as it becomes reflected in international law and organizations, and is signed, ratified and adopted by particular states. Implementation of norms by a state or organization is visibly manifested by its adoption into formal legal and policy mechanisms.[15]

As empirical gaps between norm acceptance and implementation, or between commitment and compliance, became well documented,[16] scholars began introducing additional factors such as regime type, state capacity, domestic mobilization, centralization of rule implementation, material capability, and social vulnerability to better explain the gaps and understand how, exactly, human rights norms are implemented and complied with in a given state.[17] State capacity, including the ability to control increasingly powerful non-state actors, appears especially important for norm implementation, even where a clear will to comply exists.[18] The role and pliability of elite interests are also significant.[19] These new claims have been further corroborated by work indicating that the implementation of a norm is dependent on additional structural factors including ideational, material, and institutional/ capacity-related features.[20] Finally, the domestic implementation of norms involves political contestation, as state and non-state actors dispute the meaning and interpretation of the norm.[21] This, in turn, provides a continuous feedback loop such that norm interpretation can continue to change.[22]

Negotiating transitional justice in a two-level bargaining game

The literature discussed above emphasizes the importance not only of regime type and state capacity and willingness, but also the role of agency—specifically elite interests, disputes between state and non-state actors over the interpretation of norms—and domestic mobilization to explain variation in implementation among states with a similar level of norm institutionalization or adoption. We start with the basic variable of regime type, asserting that a democratic regime faces greater constraints in interpreting and implementing norms than an autocratic state. In democracies, peace negotiators must deal with an added layer of actors whose legitimacy or endorsement they must win. These include republican institutions of the rule of law and public opinion—which are less important in non-democratic settings. And this informs our understanding of why negotiators become instrumental norm-makers (they are beholden horizontally to other institutions and vertically to the electorate) rather than simply norm-takers (they cannot afford it, politically).

To conceptualize this impact of regime type, we present the negotiation of transitional justice in a democracy as a two-level bargaining game. We draw on the concepts Robert Putnam devised for his classic case of international bargaining between states, in which Level 1 government negotiators at the international bargaining table are constrained by domestic constituents at Level 2, who circumscribe the win-sets of each negotiator.[23]

In the Colombian peace process, we have yet another game: Two domestic actors (the government and the FARC) comprise the negotiations at Level 1, each constrained by constituents from the international and domestic spheres, as shown in the schematic in Figure 6.1. The Colombian government needed to satisfy several domestic constituents ("ratifiers" in the two-level game language): The Congress who approves implementing laws, the Constitutional Court that approves the agreement's compliance with the constitution and international obligations, human rights and victims' advocacy groups who can lend and remove legitimacy, and the public who were asked to endorse the agreement in a referendum. The government must also satisfy its international constituents—namely the ICC and the

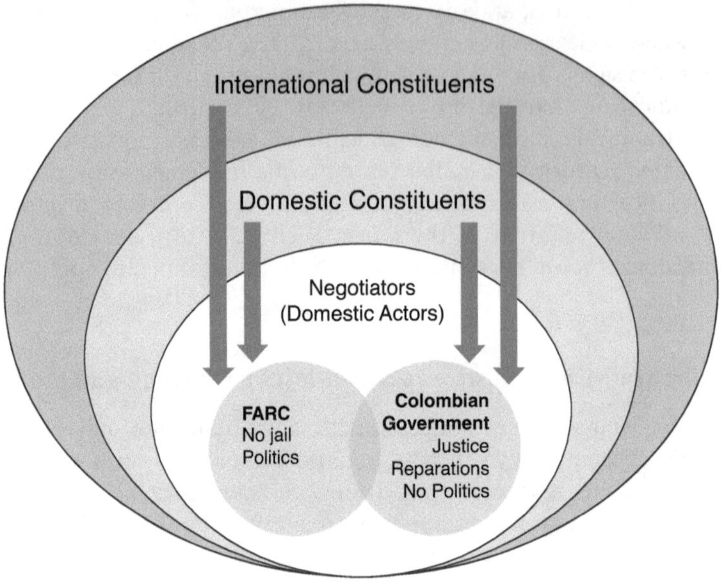

Figure 6.1 Schematic of two-level negotiating game with narrow win-set.

Inter-American Court of Human Rights—due to its legal obligations as signatories to the 2002 Rome Statute and the 1979 American Convention on Human Rights.

Likewise, the FARC needed to satisfy its own internal constituents (ratifiers). It also needed to be concerned about international actors with potential capacity to hold FARC members accountable for grave human rights crimes—the ICC and the US Justice Department through extradition. The international actors are not ratifiers in the sense that they must actively endorse the agreement and engage in its implementation. Unconstrained by the agreement, they are potential saboteurs: Their credible threat to hold accountable FARC members, government security forces, or the state, increases uncertainty. Thus, both sets of negotiators sought to generate *inaction* on the part of their international constituents.

Domestic adaptation of the international norm

The justice agreement signed in 2016 is precedent-setting in several ways. It represents the first negotiated end to a civil conflict in the world under the new international standards of the 2002 Rome Statute to hold accountable armed combatants who committed grave human rights abuses. It is also the first peace process to have included victims at the negotiating table. Finally, it is the first end to a civil war that does not rely primarily on amnesty for all sides to the conflict, but instead provides new forms of restorative justice in the actual peace agreement, in a compromise effort to reach peace while also holding perpetrators of human rights crimes accountable.

The agreement also deals with the future right of the FARC participation in politics by including the right to run for political office, five guaranteed seats in both the Senate and House of Representatives for two election cycles, and amnesty for crimes committed during the course of the conflict that are connected to political rebellion,[24] such as drug crimes. Political participation was, after all, one of their main goals—to transform from an armed rebellion to a peaceful political movement that could affect policy and reform. The accord also established a Commission for the Clarification of Truth, Coexistence, and Non-Repetition for voluntary confessions to uncover the causes of abuses and document atrocities committed.

The innovative nature of this alternative, restorative justice is that it focuses on the victims—those 7.6 million Colombians who were forced from their homes, lost loved ones, or suffered other losses in the course of the long war. At the same time, it seeks to achieve social reintegration of armed combatants and some level of reconciliation, and to avoid the social exclusion observed in many previous cases where former combatants were unable to find new job skills or build homes and returned to organized violence.[25]

Re-interpreting the international norm

The Colombian negotiators were shaping the international norm in two ways: First, by filling in gaps in the norm—namely the definition of "effective sentencing," and second by expanding the actors to be included in the preferential legal treatments. In the path of norm implementation, then, disputation and contestation within Colombia and internationally are becoming a part of the process of norm change described in the literature above.

The legal mechanism to achieve these goals while complying with international norms is alternative sentencing. First, by embracing the concept of restorative justice and "satisfaction of victims," the negotiators asserted that reduced sentences under restricted movement conditioned on acknowledgment of responsibility, reparations, and guarantees of non-repetition should meet the demands for individual criminal accountability. Although questions about the exact nature of the restricted movement—accommodations, size, and potential simultaneous political participation—were not fully answered before the agreement was signed, FARC members would avoid jail while paying reparations such as participating in demining efforts, reconstruction, or financial payments. Negotiators argued that "effective sentencing" under the Rome Statute does not require imprisonment in jails.

Another innovation is the extension of the accord to other sectors of the society beyond the FARC, providing the potential for additional actors in

Colombian society to acknowledge responsibility in the 50-year conflict, while also receiving preferential judicial treatment and juridical security. Security forces were to have access to reduced sentences that may result in some already-convicted soldiers being released from prison earlier than their initial (longer) sentences. The agreement also provided for civilian sponsors (financiers) of paramilitary forces to face the Special Jurisdiction for Peace (JEP).[26] Notably, the accord exempted former presidents of the Republic from the JEP. Any information about criminal activity received by the special tribunals about them would be sent to Congress for action (or inaction).[27]

With these innovations, the Colombian negotiators attempted to identify a narrow overlap of their win-sets to achieve three goals: Accountability for human rights crimes, satisfaction of victims, and the potential for reintegration and political participation of the FARC, as indicated in the overlapping circles in Figure 6.1. In the next sections, we assess the constraints faced by the negotiators from their international and domestic constituents and the prospects that their constituents would indeed ratify the agreement.

International constraints

The international expectation for Colombia was that the most serious human rights violations, such as war crimes or crimes against humanity committed during the prolonged civil conflict should be adjudicated in a court of law, with a proper trial and due process and proportional sentences. Colombia is a signatory to treaties establishing two international courts: The ICC enforces individual criminal accountability for grave human rights crimes; the Inter-American Court of Human Rights ensures that states prosecute, punish, and provide reparations for victims according to the American Convention on Human Rights.

International human rights courts

The Colombian case, with a judicial system affected by the corruption of drug cartels and multiple armed groups but also a strong and independent Constitutional Court, is unusual for the ICC in that it actually has a criminal process to deal with past crimes. Nevertheless, the threat of ICC action hung over the heads of the Colombian government, as reflected in ICC's 2010 assessment of Colombia's "struggles with significant difficulties to comply" and noting only "limited progress."[28]

The ICC opened a Preliminary Examination of Colombia in 2006 and has continued monitoring in that status since.[29] It is interested in two categories of crimes. Under the category of crimes against humanity, it is investigating murder, forcible population transfer, torture, and imprisonment (kidnapping). Under the category of war crimes, it is reviewing crimes against civilians, sexual violence, and the use of child soldiers.[30]

The complementarity principle of the ICC's jurisdiction gives priority to the State to establish accountability for crimes delineated in the Rome Statute, unless the State is unable or unwilling to carry out the investigation or prosecution, the latter evidenced by delays, partiality, or obfuscation. Rulings by the Inter-American Court of Human Rights since 2001 have also declared amnesties and pardons that prevent prosecution of serious human rights violations and international crimes to be unacceptable.[31]

The ICC made it clear early on that it would closely observe any final peace deal to ensure that transitional justice provisions it contains are in accordance with the Rome Treaty.[32] This relates specifically to the final agreement on any prison sentence reduction offered to perpetrators of human rights violations as part of the deal. The ICC has the power to declare Colombia "unwilling" or "non-genuine" in pursuit of proper punishment for human rights abuses and override the complementary principle and take over investigations and prosecutions. This warning is especially relevant for the reduced prison sentences for FARC guerilla members and state security forces deemed most responsible for war crimes and crimes against humanity. The ICC has declared suspended sentences unacceptable, while reduced sentences would only be acceptable under very strict conditions on a case by case basis such as, for example, full acknowledgment of responsibility, demobilization and disarmament, guarantee of non-repetition, assistance in establishing the truth, or a temporary ban from political participation.[33] Reduced sentences also must be proportional to the crime, and this had not been specified by the ICC.[34]

International influence and mixed messages

The robust evolution of international norms and state obligations is clearly evident in Colombia. It includes the threat of the ICC moving to an investigation stage if the government is seen as unwilling to prosecute grave crimes, as well as the possibility of cases taken up by the Inter-American Commission and Court of Human Rights. It also includes the presence of international NGOs as well as strong local NGOs filing constitutional suits to apply international standards to Colombia or filing cases with the Inter-American human rights system. These actions and influences directly contributed to legislative changes and legal procedure changes in the decade leading up to the peace agreement, as well as influenced the government's approach to negotiating with the FARC. The FARC, on the other hand, were much slower to embrace the change in international norms or to recognize the constraints it posed for Colombia, and they pushed hard for alternatives to prison time.[35]

At the same time, Colombians were attempting to influence international opinion and arguing for the importance of peace not only for Colombian security and economic development, but also for the entire hemisphere. In conversations with a broad range of Colombian political actors in 2014–16, we detected a marked tendency to assume that the international community would back the peace accords, and even press the ICC to be flexible in its interpretation. In addition, the former prosecutor indicated that Colombian authorities, unlike other cases under the ICC's investigation, "have committed to genuinely investigating and prosecuting the crimes themselves in order to avoid our intervention."[36]

The new prosecutor, Fatou Bensouda, however, wrote letters to the Colombian Constitutional Court in July and August 2013 advising that suspended sentences and rights to political participation are not envisioned under the Rome Statute for those convicted of grave crimes; reduced sentences could be considered if they were proportional to the crime; and national judiciaries were required to carry out complete, rather than selective, investigations (unlike the ICC).[37]

Rulings of the Inter-American Court of Human Rights also constrained Colombia's options, as noted above. Nevertheless, the International Crisis Group noted an emerging distinction between transitions from armed conflict and transitions from authoritarianism, citing a concurring opinion by the President of the Inter-American Court that in a negotiated end to armed conflict, the state might not be in a "position to implement fully and simultaneously the various international rights and obligations it has assumed" and that the exercise of one right, such as justice, cannot disproportionately affect the exercise of other rights.[38] This ruling was also repeatedly cited by Colombian actors supporting the peace process.

The United States and extradition

Colombia extradited 14 top United Self-Defense Forces of Colombia (AUC) paramilitary commanders to the United States on drug charges before the Colombian process of truth-telling and investigation was completed following the agreement with the paramilitaries in 2005. Victims' groups argued that this affected their rights by curtailing truth and reparations.[39] Many argued that then-President Uribe agreed to the extradition request from the United States to avoid the paramilitaries divulging information affecting political and business allies.[40]

The FARC fears of US extradition were not warrantless, despite reassurances from the Santos government that no ex-combatant would be extradited for crimes committed before the signing of the peace accords. Two former leaders retook up arms in 2019 after being requested for extradition by the United States, followed by charges that they are conspiring with Venezuelan officials to export cocaine to the United States and a US$10 million bounty offered for each of them in 2020.[41]

Domestic constituencies

The Framework for Peace Law stipulated that Congress would have the authority to approve the implementation legislation once a final agreement was reached. But other actors were to play an important role as well: The

Constitutional Court, which has the responsibility to review the legislation (after already changing the Justice and Peace Law (Law 975 of 2005) and associated laws); the Inspector-General who was a critic of the talks; victims' groups and peace and human rights advocacy groups who would sustain or challenge a peace agreement; and the public who could endorse or reject the agreement in a referendum. Thus, their views and proposals are important to understand, and to these we now turn.

The domestic politics of peace

The March 2014 legislative elections provided for a majority coalition to implement legislation on a future peace accord. Nevertheless, the election of former president Álvaro Uribe to the Senate and his new party Centro Democrático becoming the second largest, reduced the number of seats of President Santos' party. The Uribistas opposed the peace talks from the beginning and took a hardline retributive justice stance, arguing the accords allowed for impunity rather than justice. They announced in August 2016 that they would campaign for a No vote in the referendum, and surprised many when voters defeated the agreement by a razor-thin margin on October 2, 2016.

Colombian civil society is very well developed, with many individual and organizational experts in transitional justice, human rights, and peace processes. They engaged in significant debate over the most principled and efficacious ways to achieve peace while protecting victims' rights. Although scholars have noted the change in approach reflected in the Justice and Peace Law (Law 975 of 2005) to include a more expansive view of justice for all armed combatants recognizing victims' rights, truth, and reparations, Colombian human rights NGOs indicated a more critical approach of that law as overly focused on criminal justice and providing legal benefits (and even impunity) to the actors engaging in negotiations at that time—the paramilitary AUC.[42] The 2012 Framework Law, on the other hand, was viewed more positively as providing a variety of transitional justice mechanisms, including truth-seeking and reparations.

Public opinion

One of the central premises of this chapter is that in democratic states, mass level opinion is critically important in two distinct ways. It must be considered by peace deal negotiators who need public support and often explicit endorsement of agreements, such as by public referenda. Public opinion is also important as it directly reflects the legitimacy, and therefore signals the long-term sustainability, of peace agreements in democracies.

According to research based on the Americas Barometer survey in 2014–15 while the talks were ongoing, an appreciable proportion of Colombians believed having the FARC confess their crimes (46%) and pay reparations to victims (58%) would contribute to reconciliation.[43] The public also overwhelmingly wanted the FARC to face justice,[44] although attitudes toward exactly how much jail time would be acceptable were changing. Long sentences (at least 8 years) for FARC members who are guilty of grave crimes remained the most popular form of justice, but Colombians were increasingly willing to accept reduced sentences (5–8 years, similar to those imposed on the AUC paramilitaries). Less amenable to compromise were views of the FARC participating in political life. No more than 20% supported demobilized FARC members forming a party, fielding candidates in local elections, or gaining reserved seats in Congress.[45]

Shortly before the signing of the agreement in September and the referendum on October 2, 2016, polling was trending against the agreement.[46] This shift coincided with a decline in Santos's own popularity. As his approval ratings sagged into the 20–30% range, support for his signature policy followed suit.

The final defeat of the peace agreement was due to a number of factors, including heavy rains, low turnout, and a vociferous No campaign led by the Uribistas and joined by land owners and evangelical churches. But it also comports with another important finding from survey work we conducted in 2014–15 in Colombia,[47] namely the importance of political leaders and negotiators in carefully framing messages to build coalitions of support for peace agreements. For example, our research showed that Colombians who voted against President Santos and his peace platform in the last election, or those who abstained from voting at all, could be persuaded to support not only the peace process in general, but even specific transitional justice proposals to the extent that the government and the FARC can gain these individuals' trust.[48] Therefore, it was crucial that parties to the negotiation carried out trust-building gestures, such as collaborating on the removal of landmines that threaten innocent civilians,[49] or the FARC's announcement that they would no longer recruit children younger than 17.[50] These humanitarian gestures helped build trust from a public that remained very skeptical about the FARC and their commitment to a peace agreement. But the reverse was also true—a decline in trust in the negotiators predicted a decline in support for the peace process.[51] Thus, any posturing against provisions in the accord among the FARC's internal "ratifiers" could be interpreted as signals of bad faith or weak commitment to the peace process.

Outcomes of the peace accord

The peace accords became a focal point in the 2018 legislative and presidential elections, in which the anti-peace Uribista candidate, Iván Duque, won the presidency over the pro-peace, leftist Gustavo Petro, and Santos' own party lost a third of its legislative seats. Unfulfilled promises for land and training in the plans for reincorporation of FARC members contributed to up to 2,000 of the initial 13,000 demobilized combatants turning to armed criminal activity.[52] After 3 years of implementation, protecting the transitional justice mechanisms, including the JEP and the Truth Commission, remained another major challenge.[53] The lack of security guarantees for human rights and community leaders as well as ex-FARC members remained one of the largest threats to the implementation of the final accord and the perceptions of its progress.[54] Nevertheless, given the comprehensive and long-term structural reforms included in the Colombian peace accords, its implementation process is comparable to other such agreements.[55]

Conclusion

Colombia is in the midst of an unprecedented institutional and normative shift. As we demonstrate in this chapter, Colombian policymakers engaged in a series of original and highly innovative transitional justice arrangements. The Colombian experiment may have lasting impact on the sustainability of Colombian peace going forward, but also on other countries thinking about designing a transitional justice system.

Theoretically, our chapter builds on the second-generation normative scholarship that does not assume a top-down international-local normative adoption, but instead appreciates a more complex process of norm localization and, especially in this case, norm hybridization. Our research shows that international norms serve as an important background to local policymaking. They are not ignored and they are not irrelevant. On the ground, however, adoption and implementation are much more of a one step forward, two steps back, process than the traditional norm diffusion models would expect. Norm adoption is, fundamentally, a process of norm-making, norm adjusting, and selective norm activation—with some elements of the norm adapted to the local setting and others cast aside as politically or legally poor fits. This process of modification-through-implementation within a country, if unchallenged internationally, may then constitute part of the cycle of norm change.

We further found that regime type matters. Given the need to secure "ratification" from domestic actors in a democratic context—public approval, Congress, and Constitutional Court, as well as meet international expectations for accountability to avoid the threat of adjudication, negotiators must take into account potential legitimacy deficits of any transitional justice proposals they create. If those deficits become too large, they risk failing to gain the endorsement of their important domestic and international constituents, and thus doom the peace agreement. The result is a creative process of interpretation, modification, and filling in gaps in the international norm to fit in a narrow win-set of acceptable solutions.

Lessons from the Colombian peace process for other contexts include both addressing international and domestic constituencies. We found evidence that Colombian politicians and negotiators assumed that the international community would not jeopardize peace for the sake of justice, despite many formal warnings from the ICC. Instead, Colombian negotiators appealed to international norms and international legal sources that privilege peace (and do not sacrifice it for justice) as justification for their selective application of ICC requirements. For the most part, their gamble succeeded. As of this writing, the ICC has not declared the agreement unacceptable, and Santos won a Nobel peace prize. Colombia's "pick and choose" approach may thus become very appealing to other countries about to embark on a transitional justice project.

While the Colombian model may successfully chart a path toward a successful combination of incomplete justice but sustainable peace, the question is what impact this will have on the institutional legitimacy of the ICC. If countries can selectively choose some criminal justice remedies, and ignore or change others, does this lead to the weakening of the ICC normative power or will the ICC also have to adapt and be less rigid in its recommendations in volatile and unconsolidated political situations? Our research presents the first step in exploring this very dynamic international process.

On the domestic front, the severe political polarization over the peace accords nearly derailed it when the referendum failed. Subsequent approval by Congress of a modified agreement allowed it to go forward, but uneven implementation, particularly of security guarantees and the transitional justice mechanisms, continued to threaten its success. The need for negotiators to give persistent attention to public opinion and legitimacy deficits, such as the lack of support for FARC political participation, are important lessons for future peace processes.

Authors' note

The authors received funding for this project from IIE/USAID Democracy, Human Rights, and Governance Research and Innovation Grant, "Dilemmas of Transitional Justice in the Colombian Peace Process," 2014–2015.

Notes

1 Kathryn Sikkink, *The Justice Cascade: How Human Rights Prosecutions are Changing World Politics* (New York: WW Norton, 2011).
2 Amitav Acharya, "How Ideas Spread: Whose Norms Matter? Norm Localization and Institutional Change in Asian Regionalism," *International Organization,* vol. 58 (2), 2004, pp. 239–75; Amitav Acharya, "Norm Subsidiarity and Regional Orders: Sovereignty, Regionalism, and Rule-Making in the Third World," *International Studies Quarterly,* vol. 55 (1), 2011, pp. 95–123.
3 Scholars have also analyzed the influence of the threat of adjudication by international courts on the peace negotiations, see Courtney Hillebrecht, Alexandra Huneeus, and Sandra Borda, "The Judicialization of Peace," *Harvard International Law Journal,* vol. 59, 2018, pp. 279–330.
4 Under the ICC Statute complementarity principle, as outlined in the Rome Treaty, the ICC has jurisdiction only over cases where the state is either unwilling

or unable to investigate or prosecute alleged crimes. On the other hand, Article 16 of the ICC Statute allows the Security Council to prevent the Court from investigating a particular case, and Article 53 allows the Prosecutor not to investigate a specific case if he/she determines an investigation "would not serve the interest of justice" *Rome Statute of the International Criminal Court.*

5 Martha Finnemore and Kathryn Sikkink, "International Norm Dynamics and Political Change," *International Organization,* vol. 52 (4), 1998, pp. 887–917.

6 Acharya, "How Ideas Spread."

7 Ibid., p. 245.

8 Ibid.

9 Acharya, "Norm Subsidiarity," p. 98.

10 Frances C. Moore, "Negotiating Adaptation: Norm Selection and Hybridization in International Climate Negotiations," *Global Environmental Politics,* vol. 12 (4), 2012, pp. 30–48.

11 Alexander Betts, *Protection by Persuasion: International Cooperation in the Refugee Regime* (Ithaca: Cornell University Press, 2009).

12 Thomas Risse-Kappen, Stephen C. Ropp, and Kathryn Sikkink, *The Persistent Power of Human Rights: From Commitment to Compliance* (Cambridge: Cambridge University Press, 2013); Thomas G. Weiss, *Global Governance: Why? What? Whither?* (Cambridge: Polity Press, 2013); Dongwook Kim, "International Nongovernmental Organizations and the Global Diffusion of National Human Rights Institutions," *International Organization,* vol. 67 (3), 2013, pp. 505–39.

13 Daniela Donno, "Who is Punished? Regional Intergovernmental Organizations and the Enforcement of Democratic Norms," *International Organization,* vol. 64 (4), 2010, pp. 593–625; Susan D Hyde, "Catch Us If You Can: Election Monitoring and International Norm Diffusion," *American Journal of Political Science,* vol. 55 (2), 2011, pp. 356–69.

14 Arturo Santa-Cruz, "Constitutional Structures, Sovereignty, and the Emergence of Norms: The Case of International Election Monitoring," *International Organization,* vol. 59 (3), 2005, pp. 663–93.

15 Alexander Betts and Phil Orchard, *Implementation and World Politics: How International Norms Change Practice* (Oxford: Oxford University Press, 2014), p. 2.

16 Oona A. Hathaway, "Why Do Countries Commit to Human Rights Treaties?," *Journal of Conflict Resolution,* vol. 51 (4), 2007, pp. 588–621; Wade M. Cole, "Human Rights as Myth and Ceremony? Reevaluating the Effectiveness of Human Rights Treaties, 1981–2007," *American Journal of Sociology,* vol. 117 (4), 2012, pp. 1131–71; Emilie Hafner-Burton and Kiyoteru Tsutsui, "Justice Lost! The Failure of International Human Rights Law To Matter Where Needed Most," *Journal of Peace Research,* vol. 44 (7), 2007, pp. 407–25.

17 Risse-Kappen, Ropp, and Sikkink, *The Persistent Power of Human Rights.*

18 Ibid.; Sara Ellen Davies, Adam Kamradt-Scott, and Simon Rushton, *Disease Diplomacy: International Norms and Global Health Security* (Baltimore: Johns Hopkins University Press, 2015).

19 Alexander Betts, *Survival Migration: Failed Governance and the Crisis of Displacement* (Ithaca: Cornell University Press, 2013); Betts and Orchard, *Implementation and World Politics*; Risse-Kappen, Ropp, and Sikkink, *The Persistent Power of Human Rights.*

20 Betts and Orchard, *Implementation and World Politics.*

21 Jelena Subotic, "Truth, Justice, and Reconciliation on the Ground: Normative Divergence in the Western Balkans," *Journal of International Relations and Development,* vol. 18 (3), 2015, pp. 361–82; Betts and Orchard, *Implementation and World Politics*; Wayne Sandholtz and Kendall W. Stiles, *International Norms and Cycles of Change* (Oxford: Oxford University Press, 2009).

22 Betts and Orchard, *Implementation and World Politics.*
23 Robert D. Putnam, "Diplomacy and Domestic Politics: The Logic of Two-Level Games," *International Organization,* vol. 42 (3), 1988, pp. 427–60.
24 Part 3, Points 40 and 41 of the Victims Agreement explain that an amnesty law to be passed by Congress will determine which conducts fall under the grave human rights crimes specified in the Rome Statute and thus not eligible for amnesty, and that common crimes unrelated to rebellion are also not eligible for amnesty. The Constitutional Court would also review the laws for compliance with Colombia's international obligations.
25 For example, the Nicaraguan *contras* negotiated peace with the Sandinistas in 1990 but many returned to violence as the *recontras* when they failed to receive land and services from the government. Many Colombian paramilitaries also returned to violence in the form of organized criminal gangs known as the BACRIM after the 2005 negotiations.
26 The paramilitary organization AUC previously negotiated an agreement with the Colombian government in the Justice and Peace Law (Law 975 of 2005). In the course of those confessions, over 15,000 names were provided of civilians who supported those paramilitary forces in crimes, http://colombiapeace.org/2015/12/23/9-unanswered-questions-about-colombias-victims-and-justice-accord/. While it is unclear that any of these civilians would otherwise face judicial suits, the new accord provides a mechanism to bring them to justice while also providing them preferential treatment (Part 3, Point 32 of the Victim's accord).
27 Part 3, Point 32 of the Victim's accord.
28 Kai Ambos and Florian Huber, "The Colombian Peace Process and the Principle of Complementarity of the International Criminal Court: Is there sufficient willingness and ability on the part of the Colombian authorities or should the Prosecutor open an investigation now?," in *Extended version of the Statement in the "Thematic session: Colombia," ICC OTP – NGO roundtable, 19/20 October 2010, The Hague* (Germany: Göttingen, 2011), p. 12.
29 "The Office of the Prosecutor concludes mission to Colombia," Press Release, January 23, 2020. https://www.icc-cpi.int/Pages/item.aspx?name=pr1510.
30 International Criminal Court, "Report on Preliminary Examination Activities 2014," December 2 (The Hague, Netherlands: ICC, 2014).
31 International Crisis Group, "Transitional Justice and Colombia's Peace Talks," *Latin American Report* #49, August 29, (Brussels: ICG, 2013).
32 International Criminal Court, "Report on Preliminary Examination Activities 2014."
33 International Criminal Court, "Remarks of Mr. James Stewart, Deputy Prosecutor of the International Criminal Court" (Paper presented at the Transitional Justice in Colombia and the Role of the International Criminal Court conference, Bogota, Colombia, May 13, 2015).
34 Private conversation of the author with an ICC representative, Atlanta, 2015.
35 Author's private conversations with both negotiating teams.
36 Luis Moreno-Ocampo, "The International Criminal Court—Some Reflections," *Yearbook of International Humanitarian Law,* vol. 12, 2009, pp. 3–12, cited in Isabella Bueno and Andrea Díaz Rozas, "Which Approach to Justice in Colombia under the Era of the ICC," *International Criminal Law Review,* vol. 13, 2013, pp. 211–47, p. 229.
37 Private letters of the ICC Prosecutor Fatou Bensouda published in *Revista Semana,*http://m.semana.com/nacion/articulo/una-carta-bomba/354430-3.
38 "*Massacres of El Mozote and nearby places v. El Salvador* (Merits, reparations and costs)," October 25, 2012, concurring opinion of Judge Diego Garcia-Sayan, para. 38. Cited in International Crisis Group, "Transitional Justice and Colombia's Peace Talks," n 2 at 8.

39 Interviews with CODHES and CAJAR.
40 CAJAR interview.
41 https://www.reuters.com/article/us-colombia-usa-crime/us-offers-10-million-reward-for-capture-of-former-colombian-rebels-idUSKBN23P2O9. https://www.dea.gov/press-releases/2020/06/18/new-rewards-offered-information-leading-capture-two-farc-leaders.
42 International Center for Transitional Justice (ICTJ) interview, June 24, 2013, Bogota, Colombia.
43 Miguel García Sánchez, Jorge Daniel Montalvo, and Mitchell Seligson, "Cultura política de la democracia en Colombia, 2015. Actitudes democráticas en zonas de consolidación territorial," (Bogotá, DC: Observatorio de la Democracia, Universidad de los Andes, 2015).
44 Ibid.; Miguel García Sánchez, Juan Carlos Rodríguez Raga, Mitchell A. Seligson, and Elizabeth J. Zechmeister, "Cultura política de la democracia en Colombia: Dilemas de la democracia y desconfianza institucional en el marco del proceso de paz" (Bogota: Universidad de los Andes, 2014).
45 García Sánchez, Montalvo, and Seligson, "Cultura política de la democracia en Colombia," 2015, pp. 83–7.
46 Gallup, July 2016, IPSOS, August 2016.
47 With a grant from the USAID Center of Excellence on Democracy, Human Rights, and Governance, Research and Innovation Grant and the Institute for International Education Democracy Fellows and Grants Program, we conducted an on-line panel survey of Colombian citizens in June 2014 (n = 3,400) and again with some of the respondents (n = 1,000) in January 2015. Ryan E. Carlin, Jennifer L. Mccoy, and Jelena Subotic, "Legitimacy Deficits in Colombia's Peace Talks: Elites, Trust, and Support for Transitional Justice," USAID Working Paper (Washington, DC: USAID, 2015).
48 Ibid. Ryan E. Carlin, Jennifer L. McCoy, and Jelena Subotic, "Leading the Public to Peace: Trust in Elites, the Legitimacy of Negotiated Peace, and Support for Transitional Justice," in *After War Ends: What Colombia Can Tell Us about Peace and Transitional Justice*, ed. James Meernik, Mauricio Uribe, and Jacqueline Demeritt (New York: Cambridge University Press, 2019), pp. 282–303.
49 *Al Jazeera*, March 8, 2015.
50 *Independent*, February 13, 2015.
51 Carlin, McCoy, and Subotic, "Leading the Public to Peace."
52 https://www.npr.org/2020/05/19/855567659/many-of-colombias-ex-rebel-fighters-rearm-and-turn-to-illegal-drug-trade
53 "State of Implementation of the Colombian Final Accord, December 2016—April 2019," Kroc Institute, University of Notre Dame, April 2019. https://kroc.nd.edu/assets/333274/executive_summary_colombia_print_single_2.pdf
54 "State of Implementation of the Colombian Final Accord 2018–2019: EXECUTIVE SUMMARY," Kroc Institute, University of Notre Dame, June 2020. http://peaceaccords.nd.edu/wp-content/uploads/2020/06/Executive-Summary_English.pdf
55 Ibid.

7 Compatibility between transitional justice tools in Colombian and international law

Juanita Goebertus Estrada

Introduction

In November 2016 the Colombian Government and the Revolutionary Armed Forces of Colombia (FARC) reached a historic Peace Agreement to end the armed conflict and begin a comprehensive peace-building phase seeking to transform rural areas and satisfy victims' rights. As a result, in 2017 more than 13,000 former FARC combatants demobilized, 92% of which have continued to comply with the terms of the accord.

The peace deal put an end to a 50-year-long armed conflict that left Colombia with approximately 260,000 dead, 8 million internally displaced persons, approximately 47,000 persons deemed disappeared, nearly 2,000 massacres, more than 37,000 kidnapped persons, nearly 12,000 victims of landmines, at least 10,000 victims of torture, 8,000 children recruited, and at least 32,000 victims of sexual violence.[1]

According to the terms of the agreement, those most responsible for the most serious and representative international crimes and human rights violations committed during the armed conflict will be investigated, prosecuted, and sanctioned. Those found guilty by the Special Jurisdiction for Peace (*Jurisdicción Especial para la Paz,* henceforth, JEP) will have to face five- to eight-year sanctions consisting of effective restriction of liberty, as long as they acknowledge responsibility, tell the truth, directly redress victims, and cease all violence.

However, almost four years into the implementation phase, and after the public referendum of October 2016 was won by the No campaign by a margin of 61,000 votes, there remains constant national debate as to whether the Comprehensive System of transitional justice system created by the peace deal complies with international law.

The objective of this article is to demonstrate that it does, for it aims to ensure investigation, prosecution, and sanction of mass atrocities, as well as to ensure that victims' rights are satisfied.

The first section of this article describes Colombia's international human rights obligations and the application of these in the context of a transition from armed conflict to peace. The second part explores the Comprehensive

System of Truth, Justice, Reparation, and Non-Repetition, and analyzes its compatibility with international law.

Colombia's international obligations in the context of the transition from armed conflict to peace

Due to restrictions of space, I will refer to four different sets of international standards in this chapter, namely the Universal Human Rights System, International Humanitarian Law (IHL), International Criminal Law, and the American Human Rights System. In each case, I will refer to existing ordinary obligations of state and non-state parties, and will then analyze the discussions concerning each set of regulations in terms of their application in contexts of transition from armed conflict to peace.

The International Human Rights System

The International Human Rights System generally imposes the obligation of States to provide an effective remedy to those who suffer from human rights violations.[2] In particular, there are conventional obligations related to the duty to investigate enforced disappearances[3] and to punish the crimes of genocide[4] and torture.[5] Additionally, states have the obligation to impose appropriate punishments on those responsible.[6] However, when addressing transitional contexts various United Nations bodies and authorities have developed international soft-law instruments specifying the application of these obligations to such situations.

For example, the first report of the United Nations Secretary-General on the rule of law and transitional justice in societies that suffer or have suffered from conflicts indicated:

In the end, in post-conflict countries, the vast majority of perpetrators of serious violations of human rights and IHL will never be tried, whether internationally or domestically. As such, prosecutorial policy must be strategic, based on clear criteria, and take account of the social context. Public expectations must be informed through an effective communications strategy. Programs must be in place to protect and support victims of gender and sexually based violence and to protect witnesses. And it is essential that, from the moment any future international or hybrid tribunal is established, consideration be given, as a priority, to the ultimate exit strategy and intended legacy in the country concerned.[7]

More recently, Pablo De Greiff, Special Rapporteur for the promotion of justice, truth, reparation, and non-recurrence, has developed a set of resolutions that establish the United Nations' doctrine on the application of transitional justice measures. In this regard, the Rapporteur pointed out that transitional justice measures should be directed toward achieving two long-term objectives (to provide recognition to victims and to foster civic trust) and two final objectives (to contribute to reconciliation and strengthen the

Rule of Law).[8] In this sense, the four components of his mandate, namely the promotion of truth, justice, reparation, and guarantees of non-recurrence, are taken "as a set of measures that are related to, and can reinforce one another, when implemented to redress the legacies of massive human rights violations and abuses."[9]

In particular, with regard to the fulfillment of the duty to investigate, prosecute, and sanction in transitional contexts, the Special Rapporteur indicated:

> In transitional situations [...] not adopting a prioritization strategy may be particularly detrimental. The main risks include: (a) Institutions severely weakened by repression and/or conflict, with low levels of credibility, capacity and resources, may end up dispersing and duplicating investigations and multiplying caseloads; (b) Acting on the implicit promise of addressing cases in the order received may lead to large numbers of poor investigations, weak indictments and, as a result, acquittals and/or low sentences not in line with underlying evidence, further eroding the trustworthiness of the judicial system; (c) Individuals bearing the greatest responsibility may end up being the major beneficiaries of the resulting de facto limited criminal liability, while low-level perpetrators are the focus of whatever investigations are launched; (d) Failing to address cases taking into account the pattern and systemic nature of the violations results in victims testifying in several cases in a unorganized manner, leading to their possible retraumatization, revictimization and even security risks; (e) Specific crimes requiring specialized prosecutorial and investigatory efforts, including sexually-related crimes and the recruitment and use of children in hostilities, are frequently not sufficiently brought to justice.[10]

In addition, the Rapporteur indicated that: "[T]he right to truth should be understood to require States to establish institutions, mechanisms, and procedures that are enabled to lead to the revelation of the truth,"[11] and the implementation of fair, adequate, and effective reparations can best be done through massive administrative programs that are in accordance with international recommendations and adjusted to the needs of the national reality.[12]

International Humanitarian Law

Within the framework of IHL, Colombia has an obligation to bring people who have committed serious violations of IHL before its courts for criminal prosecution or, failing to do so, to extradite them.[13] This conventional obligation has been interpreted by the International Committee of the Red Cross, which has considered that there is a rule of customary law that obliges states to "investigate war crimes allegedly committed by their nationals or armed forces, or on their territory, and, if appropriate, prosecute the suspects. They must also investigate other war crimes over which they have jurisdiction and, if appropriate, prosecute the suspects."[14]

However, Article 6, numeral 5 of Protocol II Additional to the Geneva Conventions establishes that: "At the end of hostilities, the authorities in power shall endeavour to grant the broadest possible amnesty to persons who have participated in the armed conflict, or those deprived of their liberty for reasons related to the armed conflict, whether they are interned or detained."[15]

In this regard, the International Committee of the Red Cross, through the compilation of norms of Customary IHL, has exempted international crimes, particularly war crimes, from such amnesties.[16]

International Criminal Law

The Rome Statute specifies that genocide, crimes against humanity, and war crimes are international crimes. According to this instrument, the International Criminal Court has jurisdiction to investigate and prosecute persons who have committed these types of crimes when the state party is not willing to conduct the investigation or prosecution, or is unable to do so.

In this regard, the Office of the Prosecutor of the International Criminal Court has affirmed that it will assume particular jurisdiction over those who are most responsible for the commission of international crimes. As stated in the Prosecutorial Strategy of the International Criminal Court in 2009, the investigation should focus on those who were "situated at the highest echelons of responsibility."[17]

More recently, in February 2016, the ICC Prosecutor's Office released a draft policy paper on prioritization and selection criteria, in which it stated:

> It is not the responsibility or role of the Office to investigate and prosecute each and every alleged criminal act within a given situation, or every person allegedly responsible for such crimes. This would be practically unfeasible [...]. In relation to cases not selected for investigation or prosecution, it should be recalled that the goal of the Statute, as expressed in its preamble, is to be achieved by combining the activities of the Court and national jurisdictions within a complementarity regime to combat impunity and prevent the recurrence of violence [...]. The Office fully endorses the role that can be played by truth seeking mechanisms, reparations programs, institutional reform and traditional justice mechanisms as part of a broader comprehensive strategy.[18]

In addition, Vice Prosecutor James Stewart referred specifically to the application of International Criminal Law in the Colombian context of transition. He stated:

> With regard to the issue of transitional justice—so important in the ongoing peace talks from the perspective of the victims of the

> conflict—the following question arises: What mechanisms can be established to ensure that those most responsible for the most serious crimes will be held accountable in accordance with Colombia's obligations under the Rome Statute? […] Although the Rome Statute contains provisions related to sanctions in proceedings before the ICC, it does not prescribe a specific type or duration of sentences that States must impose for ICC crimes. Regarding sanctions, States have wide discretion […]. Accordingly, effective criminal sanctions can take different forms. However, they must satisfy adequate goals linked to punishment, such as public condemnation of criminal conduct, recognition of the suffering of victims, and deterrence of subsequent criminal conduct […] Whether a reduction in sentence is compatible with the principles of the Rome Statute will depend on the particular circumstances of the case. These circumstances could include transitional justice measures designed to end the armed conflict, for example, by requiring the convicted person to meet certain conditions, such as: an acknowledgment of his criminal responsibility; demobilization and disarmament; the guarantee of non-repetition of the conduct; full participation in the process of establishing the truth regarding serious crimes; a possible temporary ban on taking part in public affairs; among others. These measures could justify a reduction of the sentence that would otherwise not be proportional to the gravity of the crime and the degree of responsibility of the author.[19]

Inter-American Human Rights System

The Inter-American Human Rights System imposes the obligation to investigate, prosecute, and punish violations of human rights committed in Colombia.[20] However, in the ruling on the *Case of the Massacres of El Mozote and Nearby Places v. El Salvador*, the Court needed to address how to apply this obligation in the context of a transition from armed conflict to peace.

In this regard, it concluded that IHL was applicable, such that it is appropriate to grant the widest possible amnesty at the end of hostilities, while guaranteeing that international crimes are investigated, prosecuted, and punished.[21] This entailed a change in the sub-rule previously reiterated by this Court when encountering transitions from dictatorships to democracies, which stated that all serious violation of human rights must be investigated, prosecuted, and punished.[22]

Although such rule was ignored by the Court in 2014 in *Rochac Hernández v. El Salvador*,[23] it was later confirmed in 2018 in *Herzog v. Brazil* when the Court reiterated the importance of analyzing if there was an armed conflict to establish the scope of amnesties.[24]

However, the Inter-American Commission on Human Rights has not recognized that such decisions involved a change in the case law, and has continued to reiterate that, despite the context of the transition from armed conflict to peace, Colombia must guarantee the investigation of each and all serious violations of human rights and prosecute all those responsible.[25]

In addition, the Inter-American Court has recognized the importance of creating truth commissions and establishing administrative programs for the reparation of victims. In this regard, the Court has indicated that knowledge of the truth, as an end in itself, cannot and should not depend on or be derived exclusively from criminal proceedings.[26] Therefore, adopting criminal proceedings as the only form of satisfaction of these rights could become an obstacle to the comprehensive satisfaction of all the international obligations of the state.

Similarly, the Inter-American Court indicated that

> International law establishes the individual entitlement of the right to reparation. Despite this, the Court indicates that, in scenarios of transitional justice in which States must assume their obligations to make reparation on a massive scale to numerous victims, which significantly exceeds the capacities and possibilities of the domestic courts, administrative programs of reparation constitute one of the legitimate ways of satisfying the right to reparation.[27]

In conclusion, a transition from armed conflict to peace does not give States margin to sidestep their international obligations. But the context of addressing massive atrocities in transitions from armed conflict to peace has opened spaces to interpret that international law demands:

- i The development of comprehensive strategies that include judicial and extrajudicial mechanisms to satisfy the rights of victims.
- ii The creation of administrative victim reparation programs that can reach a broader range of victims in an expeditious manner.
- iii The creation of truth commissions to unveil the context and motivations of what took place.
- iv The possibility of granting the widest possible amnesty, as long as it does not apply to international crimes.
- v The application of prioritization and selection strategies in order to concentrate efforts on the investigation, prosecution, and sanction of those who bear the greatest responsibility for the most serious and representative crimes.
- vi The possibility of imposing alternative or reduced sanctions.

The Havana Peace Talks and the Comprehensive System of Truth, Justice, Reparation, and Non-Recurrence

Considering the rules of international law applicable to transitions from armed conflicts to peace, and based on the lessons learned throughout the process of implementing previous transitional justice measures in Colombia, the Final Peace Agreement created the Comprehensive System of Truth, Justice, Reparation, and Non-Repetition.

This System is composed of the Truth Commission, the Unit to Search for the Missing, the administrative reparations program, and the JEP. The different components of the System must operate in a coordinated and articulated manner and should contribute to non-repetition.

On paper, the System seeks to be universal, comprehensive, impartial, and participatory. Despite the challenges of an early implementation stage, it aims to be universal, as it will address crimes committed by all parties to the armed conflict, including victims of state agents, guerrillas, paramilitary groups, and those who financed and collaborated with armed groups. It seeks to do so by combining judicial and extrajudicial mechanisms and conditioning all alternative sanctions to truth telling, reparations, and non-recurrence. The System is operated by highly qualified officials, the selection of whom was the result of an open process, much more transparent than that of the ordinary criminal justice system. And all mechanisms are open for effective victim participation along the processes.

The Commission for the Clarification of Truth, Coexistence, and Non-Repetition

The Commission is an independent, transitional, and extrajudicial truth-seeking body. Its aims to:

- i Clarify what took place during the armed conflict and offer a comprehensive explanation of its complexity.
- ii Promote the recognition of victims, the responsibility of those who participated directly and indirectly in the armed conflict, and inform the entire society about what happened.
- iii Promote peaceful coexistence.

In addition to producing a final report, the Commission will have to listen to the different voices and promote the participation of different sectors of society, including those who participated directly or indirectly in the armed conflict.

As of February 2020, the Commission had created 20 truth houses throughout the country and had conducted 7,500 interviews.[28]

The Unit for the Search for Persons Presumed Disappeared

In addition, the Agreement created a Unit that conducts humanitarian and extrajudicial actions to search and identify persons deemed disappeared as a result of the armed conflict.

One of the main innovations of this Unit is that the location of the remains does not rely on the progress of criminal proceedings. As of December 2019, the Unit had opened 17 offices throughout the country.[29]

Comprehensive reparation measures for the construction of peace

The Agreement also included measures to strengthen the Comprehensive Victim Reparation Program that the State had been implementing since 2011 when the Victims' Law was enacted. The idea was to promote the acknowledgment of responsibility, assure commitment of those who caused damage to redress (both through restorative actions like building infrastructure or de-mining, and by contributing to the material reparation of victims), and by articulating collective reparations, land restitution, rural development, and community psycho-social care.

So far, however, only 13.8% of victims have received compensation and only 8% of land restitution claims have been solved.[30]

Special jurisdiction for peace

The JEP is the judicial component of the System. It is aimed at satisfying victims' right to justice, fighting against impunity, fulfilling the state's duty to investigate, prosecute, and sanction, and granting legal certainty to those who comply with the conditions of the System.

The Agreement explicitly prohibits granting pardons or amnesties for crimes against humanity, genocide, serious war crimes, hostage-taking, or other serious deprivations of liberty such as the kidnapping of civilians, torture, extrajudicial executions, forced disappearance, sexual violence, forced displacement, and child recruitment.

Those most responsible for the most serious and representative crimes that acknowledge their responsibility and comply with all the conditions of the System will experience effective restriction of their liberty ranging from 5 to 8 years. Those most responsible who fail to comply with the condition will serve ordinary prison sentences of between 15 and 20 years.

Finally, those who did not play a decisive role in the most serious and representative crimes, may have access to measures such as amnesties, pardons, the decision not to prosecute, and alternative sanctions of 2 to 5 years, depending on the seriousness of the crimes and the degree of participation in them. In any case, special criminal treatment will be conditional on the contribution to truth, justice, and non-recurrence.

As of January 2020, the JEP had claimed jurisdiction over 12,422 persons (78.3% former members of the FARC and 20.9% members of the Colombian armed forces). So far it has prioritized seven cases. Four thematic: Kidnapping, extrajudicial executions, the extermination of the UP party, and child recruitment. And three territorial cases: Nariño, Urabá, and Cauca.[31]

Compatibility with international law and the road ahead

Massive and heinous crimes have been committed in Colombia by all parties to the armed conflict. Addressing such a vast and complex universe of victims will not be easy. Colombia's experience of implementing transitional justice mechanisms has allowed the country to forge a significant experience through trial and error. The question that remains is how we can guarantee access to effective judicial remedies, clarify the truth, and assure effective reparations in a context as complex as that of Colombia.

The peace agreement demonstrates a commitment to the implementation of a comprehensive transitional justice strategy that is consistent with the state's national and international obligations. However, for this to be possible, it is necessary for the international system to approach the Colombian case from the perspective of a country that is seeking to end an armed conflict through a political agreement. As evidenced in the first part of the article, there are currently sufficient elements in the different branches of international law to demonstrate that, in transitions from armed conflict to peace, it is necessary and admissible to implement different strategies to comply with international obligations.

In this context, the serious violations of human rights and breaches of IHL committed during the armed conflict must be addressed with a transitional justice strategy of an exceptional nature, in which different elements of a judicial and extrajudicial nature play a determining role in the comprehensive satisfaction of victims' rights. It must be guaranteed that international crimes will not be amnestied, but also that prosecution efforts are focused on the most serious and representative of crimes, and on those who bear the greatest responsibility.

Therefore, this is a comprehensive strategy that does not aim to sacrifice justice to achieve peace, but to achieve peace as a necessary condition to be able to satisfy the victims' rights to truth, justice, and reparation to the highest possible degree. If well implemented, Colombia has the opportunity to demonstrate to the world that it is possible to serve justice and satisfy the rights of victims at the domestic level, even in the context of a negotiated transition from armed conflict to peace.

Author's note

A version of this article was presented as an expert opinion before the Inter-American Court of Human Rights in the *Vereda La Esperanza vs. Colombia* case in June 2016. Translated by Andrés Molina-Ochoa.

Notes

1 Data from the Victims Unit, the Historical Memory Center, and the Directorate for the Comprehensive Action against Anti-Personnel Mines.

2 International Covenant on Civil and Political Rights. "Article 2. […] Each State Party to the present Covenant undertakes: (a) To ensure that any person whose rights or freedoms as herein recognized are violated shall have an effective remedy, notwithstanding that the violation has been committed by persons acting in an official capacity[.]"

3 International Convention for the Protection of All Persons from Enforced Disappearance. Article 7. "1. Each State Party shall make the offence of enforced disappearance punishable by appropriate penalties which take into account its extreme seriousness. 2. Each State Party may establish: (a) Mitigating circumstances, in particular for persons who, having been implicated in the commission of an enforced disappearance, effectively contribute to bringing the disappeared person forward alive or make it possible to clarify cases of enforced disappearance or to identify the perpetrators of an enforced disappearance; (b) Without prejudice to other criminal procedures, aggravating circumstances, in particular in the event of the death of the disappeared person or the commission of an enforced disappearance in respect of pregnant women, minors, persons with disabilities or other particularly vulnerable persons."

4 Convention on the Prevention and Punishment of the Crime of Genocide: Article V. "The Contracting Parties undertake to enact, in accordance with their respective Constitutions, the necessary legislation to give effect to the provisions of the present Convention, and, in particular, to provide effective penalties for persons guilty of genocide or any of the other acts enumerated in article III."

5 Convention against Torture and Other Cruel, Inhuman or Degrading Treatment or Punishment (1984): "Article 4.1. 1. Each State Party shall ensure that all acts of torture are offences under its criminal law. The same shall apply to an attempt to commit torture and to an act by any person which constitutes complicity or participation in torture. 2. Each State Party shall make these offences punishable by appropriate penalties which take into account their grave nature [...] Article 6. 1. Upon being satisfied, after an examination of information available to it, that the circumstances so warrant, any State Party in whose territory a person alleged to have committed any offence referred to in Article 4 is present shall take him into custody or take other legal measures to ensure his presence. The custody and other legal measures shall be as provided in the law of that State but may be continued only for such time as is necessary to enable any criminal or extradition proceedings to be instituted. 2. Such State shall immediately make a preliminary inquiry into the facts."

6 Promotion and Protection of Human Rights, Impunity Report of the independent expert to update the set of principles to combat impunity, Diane Orentlicher. Economic and Social Council, 2005: Principle 1: "Impunity arises from a failure by States to meet their obligations to investigate violations; [including grave breaches of the Geneva Conventions of 12 August 1949, and the Additional Protocol I, and other violations of international humanitarian law that constitute crimes under international law: Genocide, crimes against humanity and other internationally protected human rights, violations that are crimes under international law and/or for which international law requires States that impose penalties for crimes, such as torture, enforced disappearances, extrajudicial execution, and slavery] to take appropriate measures in respect of the perpetrators, particularly in the area of justice, by ensuring that those suspected of criminal responsibility are prosecuted, tried and duly punished; to provide victims with effective remedies and to ensure that they receive reparation for the injuries suffered; to ensure the inalienable right to know the truth about violations; and to take other necessary steps to prevent a recurrence of violations [...] Principle 19: States shall undertake prompt, thorough, independent and impartial investigations of violations of human rights and international humanitarian law and take appropriate measures in respect of the perpetrators, particularly in the area of criminal justice, by ensuring that those responsible for serious crimes under international law are prosecuted, tried and duly punished. Although the decision to prosecute lies primarily within the competence of the State, victims, their families and heirs should be able to institute

proceedings, on either an individual or a collective basis, particularly as *parties civiles* or as persons conducting private prosecutions in States whose law of criminal procedure recognizes these procedures. States should guarantee broad legal standing in the judicial process to any wronged party and to any person or non-governmental organization having a legitimate interest therein."

7 United Nations, Security Council, Report of the Secretary-General, The rule of law and transitional justice in conflict and post-conflict societies.

8 United Nations, General Assembly, Report of the Special Rapporteur on the promotion of truth, justice, reparation and guarantees of non-recurrence, Pablo de Greiff, A/HRC/21/46.

9 Ibid.

10 United Nations, General Assembly, A/HRC/27/56, Report of the Special Rapporteur on the promotion of truth, justice, reparation and guarantees of non-recurrence, Pablo de Greiff, August 27, 2014.

11 United Nations, General Assembly, A/HRC/24/42, Report of the Special Rapporteur on the promotion of truth, justice, reparation and guarantees of non-recurrence, Pablo de Greiff, August 28, 2013.

12 De Greiff, Pablo. "Justicia y Reparaciones," in DÍAZ, Catalina (ed.), *Reparaciones para las Víctimas de la Violencia Política* (ICTJ, 2008) 312.

13 Convention (I) for the Amelioration of the Condition of the Wounded and Sick in Armed Forces in the Field. Geneva, August 12, 1949. Article 49: "The High Contracting Parties undertake to enact any legislation necessary to provide effective penal sanctions for persons committing, or ordering to be committed, any of the grave breaches of the present Convention defined in the following Article. Each High Contracting Party shall be under the obligation to search for persons alleged to have committed, or to have ordered to be committed, such grave breaches, and shall bring such persons, regardless of their nationality, before its own courts. It may also, if it prefers, and in accordance with the provisions of its own legislation, hand such persons over for trial to another High Contracting Party concerned, provided such High Contracting Party has made out a 'prima facie' case […] Article 50: Grave breaches to which the preceding Article [link] relates shall be those involving any of the following acts, if committed against persons or property protected by the Convention: willful killing, torture or inhuman treatment, including biological experiments, willfully causing great suffering or serious injury to body or health, and extensive destruction and appropriation of property, not justified by military necessity and carried out unlawfully and wantonly."

14 Customary IHL, 158. ICRC, 2007.

15 ICRC, Protocol Additional to the Geneva Conventions of 12 August 1949, and Relating to the Protection of Victims of Non-International Armed Conflicts (Protocol II).

16 Customary IHL, ICRC, 2007. "Rule 159. At the end of hostilities, the authorities in power must endeavor to grant the broadest possible amnesty to persons who have participated in a non-international armed conflict, or those deprived of their liberty for reasons related to the armed conflict, with the exception of persons suspected of, accused of or sentenced for war crimes."

17 International Criminal Court, Prosecutorial Strategy 2009–2012, The Office of the Prosecutor, February 2010, http://www.icc-cpi.int/NR/rdonlyres/66A8DCDC-3650-4514-AA62-D229D1128F65/281506/OTPProsecutorialStrategy20092013.pdf.

18 Draft: Policy Paper on Case Selection and Prioritisation, February 29, 2016, OTP-ICC. https://www.icc-cpi.int/iccdocs/otp/29.02.16_Draft_Policy-Paper-on-Case-Selection-and-Prioritisation_ENG.pdf.

19 James Stewart, Deputy Prosecutor of the International Criminal Court, "La justicia transicional en Colombia y el papel de la Corte Penal Internacional," May 13, 2015.

20 Organization of American States, *Inter-American Commission on Human Rights,* 1969, Article 1: "1. The States Parties to this Convention undertake to respect the rights and freedoms recognized herein and to ensure to all persons subject to their jurisdiction the free and full exercise of those rights and freedoms, without any discrimination for reasons of race, color, sex, language, religion, political or other opinion, national or social origin, economic status, birth, or any other social condition." Article 2: "Domestic Legal Effects Where the exercise of any of the rights or freedoms referred to in Article 1 is not already ensured by legislative or other provisions, the States Parties undertake to adopt, in accordance with their constitutional processes and the provisions of this Convention, such legislative or other measures as may be necessary to give effect to those rights or freedoms." Article 8: "Right to a Fair Trial 1. Every person has the right to a hearing, with due guarantees and within a reasonable time, by a competent, independent, and impartial tribunal, previously established by law, in the substantiation of any accusation of a criminal nature made against him or for the determination of his rights and obligations of a civil, labor, fiscal, or any other nature." Article 25: "Right to Judicial Protection 1. Everyone has the right to simple and prompt recourse, or any other effective recourse, to a competent court or tribunal for protection against acts that violate his fundamental rights recognized by the constitution or laws of the state concerned or by this Convention, even though such [a] violation may have been committed by persons acting in the course of their official duties."

21 Inter-American Court of Human Rights, *Case of the Massacres of El Mozote and Nearby Places v. El Salvador,* October 25, 2012. Merits, reparations and costs, para 265–86.

22 Inter-American Court of Human Rights *Case of Barrios Altos v. Peru* Judgment of March 14, 2001; Inter-American Court of Human Rights *Case of Almonacid-Arellano et al v. Chile* Judgment of September 26, 2006 (Preliminary Objections, Merits, Reparations and Costs) para 105–114; Inter-American Court of Human Rights *Case of La Cantuta v. Perú* Judgment of November 29, 2006 (Merits, Reparations and Costs), Serie C, No. 162, para 152 & 168; Inter-American Court Of Human Rights *Case Of Gomes Lund et al.* ("Guerrilha Do Araguaia") *v. Brazil* Judgment of November 24, 2010 (Preliminary Objections, Merits, Reparations, And Costs) para 147; Inter-American Court of Human Rights Case *Gelman v. Uruguay* Judgment of February 24, 2011 (Merits and Reparations), para 195.

23 Acosta-López, Juana Inés y Espitia-Murcia, Cindy, *Pasado, presente y futuro de la justicia transicional en el sistema interamericano de derechos humanos, 30 International Law, Revista Colombiana de Derecho Internacional*, 9–40 (2017). https://doi.org/10.11144/Javeriana.il15-30.ppfj.

24 Juana Inés Acosta-López, *El derecho internacional de las transiciones del conflicto armado a una paz negociada: ¿Un espacio regulatorio interamericano?* Working Paper, 2020.

25 See the Country Report "Truth, Justice and Reparation," *Inter-American Commission Court*, 2013, para 272.

26 Inter-American Court of Human Rights *Case of Zambrano Vélez et al. v. Ecuador* Judgment of July 4, 2007 (Merits, Reparations and Costs), para 128; Inter-American Court Of Human Rights *Case Of Contreras et al. v. El Salvador* Judgment of August 31, 2011 (Merits, Reparations and Costs); para 135.

27 Inter-American Court of Human Rights *Case of the Afro-Descendant Communities Displaced from the Cacarica River Basin (Operation Genesis) v. Colombia* Judgment of November 20, 2013 (Preliminary objections, merits, reparations, and costs), para 470.
28 Informe 03: ¿En qué va la Paz?, Congreso de la República de Colombia. April, 2020.
29 Ídem.
30 Ídem.
31 Ídem.

8 Transitional Justice in Colombia

The Amnesty Law 1820 of 2016 and the international legal framework

Kai Ambos

Preliminary observations: The international legal framework

As analyzed in detail elsewhere,[1] the international law framework has emerged along the lines of a bifurcated focus distinguishing between absolute and conditional amnesties. Absolute (blanket) amnesties, which have the primary goal of concealing past crimes by prohibiting *any* investigation into *any*body, are unequivocally prohibited by international law.[2] Unlike these amnesties, conditional amnesties do not automatically exempt from punishment, but make the benefit of an amnesty conditional on certain concessions or acts by the benefitted person.[3] This is why conditional amnesties may (depending on the concrete conditions and circumstances of the particular case) contribute to true reconciliation.[4] Article 6 (5) of Additional Protocol (AP) II to the Geneva Conventions (GC) makes explicit reference to amnesties after an armed conflict, demanding that they must remain possible as an appropriate and necessary tool to achieve reconciliation if this does not undermine the State's duty to prosecute under international law.[5] Pursuant to this approach, supported by the overwhelming doctrine,[6] conditional amnesties under certain and exceptional circumstances are allowed under current international law.[7]

The Colombian Amnesty Law and the international legal framework

Based on the Final Peace Agreement of 24 November 2016,[8] the Colombian Amnesty Law 1820 of 2016[9] provides, *inter alia*, for several provisions on amnesty, pardon, and special criminal treatment[10] within the framework of the Special Jurisdiction for Peace (JEP). In order to facilitate the termination of the armed conflict and to establish "a stable and lasting peace," Law 1820 regulates amnesties and pardons for political and related offences as a special criminal treatment (hereinafter "Amnesty Law"). It differentiates between the punishable conduct by agents of the State on the one hand and members of armed groups, in particular of the FARC-EP, on the other.[11] Decree 277 of 2017[12] establishes the procedure for the effective implementation of the

Amnesty Law. It has been complemented by Decree 700 of 2017[13] that addresses those cases in which the Amnesty Law cannot be applied in a timely manner, thus unduly prolonging the deprivation of liberty.[14] On March 1, 2018, the Colombian Constitutional Court found that the Amnesty Law is, in general terms, compatible with the constitution. However, the Court set clear conditions on several points and even declared unconstitutional certain aspects of the Law.[15] I will come back to this later.

General considerations

Interestingly, Article 1 of the Amnesty Law explicitly declares the referendum process of the Final Peace Agreement as "an open and democratic process." One possible explanation for that unusual start of the Law may be the Colombian government's serious attempt to meticulously comply with the international law requirements regarding conditional amnesties. As previous cases before the Inter-American Court of Human Rights (IACtHR) have shown, amnesty laws do not meet the standards of the Convention if the issuing government was not elected democratically.[16] Although the IACtHR has not established very clear criteria for conditional amnesties,[17] its rather vague approach can be seen as a deference to domestic amnesty processes which should only be barred if they entail a serious human rights violation. Accordingly, amnesties granted under democratic conditions are permitted, provided that no other requirements are violated.[18]

The second general observation refers to the term *de iure* amnesty (*amnistía de iure)*, employed in Chapter I of the Amnesty Law. According to Article 15, this type of amnesty is granted only for the political crimes enumerated in that provision—such as rebellion, sedition, conspiracy, and seduction—and for related crimes listed in Article 16.[19] The term *de iure* amnesty is misleading because, in fact, there is no administrative amnesty in the sense of an executive act without any type of judicial process. Rather, the "administrative" amnesty must be confirmed in each concrete case either by the respective judicial authorities or—according to Chapter II, Article 21[20]—through a verification of the Amnesty and Pardon Chamber of the JEP.[21] Therefore, the notion *de iure* is confusing. Taking into account the provisions of Decree 1252 of 2017,[22] the matter causes further ambiguity: According to this Decree, the judicial authority will not need a list or certification of accreditation for the granting of *de iure* amnesties or conditional freedom corresponding to Article 17 numbers 1, 3, and 4 of the Amnesty Law (Article 2.2.5.5.1.4.).[23]

Another relevant aspect of the Amnesty Law is the different treatment of the FARC-EP on the one hand and State agents on the other, according to which amnesty is foreseen for the first (Article 17) and renunciation of criminal prosecution for the second (Articles 44 et seq.).[24] This distinction—which has no basis in international law—is complemented by the further divergent treatment of civilian third parties (*terceros civiles*)[25] and members of demobilized paramilitary groups.[26] The Amnesty Law explicitly refers in its first paragraph of Article 21 to—the already mentioned—Article 6 (5) of AP II to the GC, which calls for the widest possible amnesty without distinguishing between State and guerrilla.[27] In fact, the idea of a differential treatment does not exist in International Humanitarian Law (IHL) since from an international law perspective, State and guerrilla are both simply parties to the (non-international armed) conflict.[28] Even though making this distinction does not constitute an IHL violation per se, from a legal point of view it was not necessary to take this option. The reasons are clearly of a political nature, since the Colombian public forces do not want to be treated like the guerrillas, just as the guerrillas do not want to be treated like the paramilitary groups. As a matter of fact, after the presidential elections won by the right-wing candidate Iván Duque, the Congress incorporated a provision in the JEP's procedural norms which excludes members of the armed forces from the JEP unless they want to opt in voluntarily.[29] However, this provision which aimed at the establishment of an additional Chamber with exclusive jurisdiction for the military was declared unconstitutional by the Constitutional Court.[30]

From a theoretical point of view, the question regarding the legitimacy of amnesties provided by the Amnesty Law represents a problem of justice,[31] since such an exemption from punishment displace the ordinary criminal justice system: The interconnection between "justice-injustice-guilt-punishment" is suspended and the community renounces the restorative effect that the penalty entails for the victim and the perpetrator, as well as its effect for the general validity of the legal system. This extraordinary treatment can only be legitimate, if there are exceptional circumstances that justify the rejection of the general validity of the legal system.[32] The Colombian armed conflict could constitute such extraordinary circumstances that justify the use of amnesties in cases of political crimes or those related to them since from the perspective of the Colombian legislator, rebellion is essentially politically motivated and aimed at changing State structures toward a better alternative.[33] In other words: The wrongfulness of the act—of rebellion and related behaviors—does not manifest itself in the interpersonal relationship between perpetrator and victim but is reflected in the structures and institutions of the State as a whole.[34] Although the perpetrator's political motive cannot in itself compensate or diminish the wrongfulness of the act or his/her guilt, the political context can certainly influence his/her conscience or attitude toward the law and create circumstances under which the degree of the guilt is diminished.[35] In addition, the main goal of an amnesty in a context like the Colombian one—that is, establishing a stable and lasting peace—must be taken into account.[36] In that sense, the Amnesty Law contains several criteria that determine which crimes are eligible for amnesty, for example, whether the perpetrator is a State agent or a member of the FARC-EP as well as his/her motivation. I will return to that below.

Crimes eligible for amnesty

As we have seen, a key issue of the Amnesty Law is the distinction between crimes that are eligible for amnesty and those that are not. Its Article 23 is one of the central regulations, perhaps even the most important one with respect to amnesties.[37] It states the following:

Article 23. Nexus criteria. The Amnesty and Pardon Chamber will grant amnesties for political or related offences. In any case, crimes that meet any of the following criteria are considered to be connected to the political offence:

a. Those offences specifically related to the development of the rebellion committed during the armed conflict, such as deaths in combat compatible with IHL and the detention of combatants carried out in military operations, or
b. Those offences in which the passive subject of the conduct is the State and its current constitutional regime, or
c. The conduct directed at facilitating, supporting, financing or concealing the development of the rebellion.

The Amnesty and Pardon Chamber will determine the nexus to the political offence on a case by case basis.

The term "serious war crime" means any infraction of IHL committed systematically.

First of all, in order to apply the quoted provision, the political offence concept must be correctly understood (Article 8 of the Amnesty Law). This is a very important legal concept in Colombia, difficult to understand for foreign observers: While there is a tendency to restrict the effect of political offences at the international level, especially in extradition treaties,[38] in Colombia it operates as a basis for granting benefits. In other words, political offenders enjoy a privileged treatment in Colombia,[39] which is—to make it more complicated—extended to those offences related to political crimes.

The political offence doctrine has a long tradition in Colombia.[40] Based hereon, left-wing guerrilla groups have always been privileged over right-wing paramilitary groups, claiming that only the former want to change the State and the society toward an alternative and better future.[41] The Colombian Constitution of 1991 makes explicit reference to political as opposed to ordinary offences and provides for a differential treatment in terms of amnesties and pardons.[42] The Criminal Cassation Chamber (*Sala de Casación Penal*) of the Colombian Supreme Court ruled in 2007[43] that the mere forming and belonging to a paramilitary group cannot be considered a political offence. The Court argued that these groups act for "selfish" reasons and are supported by important institutional sectors.[44] Thus, according to Articles 7, 8, and 9 of the Amnesty Law and in line with the Colombian tradition, only political and related offences committed by members of guerilla groups may be subject to amnesty within the framework of the JEP. Offences that cannot be qualified as "political" or "related" are not granted this privileged treatment.[45] Accordingly, the question is: What are those related offences? On this I will return later, especially with regard to drug trafficking.

In the above cited Article 23 (paragraph), the Amnesty Law defines precisely which crimes cannot be subject to amnesty. Apart from going beyond the Statute of the International Criminal Court (ICC Statute)[46] this list entails many problems.[47] Articles 5 to 8*bis* ICC Statute define genocide, crimes against humanity, war crimes, and the crime of aggression—the latter not being relevant in the Colombian context. When analyzing in detail Article 23 of the Amnesty Law, it becomes clear that the first part of the list corresponds more or less to the ICC Statute: crimes against humanity, genocide—although in Colombia the latter is defined more broadly because it includes also political groups[48]—and serious war crimes. However, in relation to war crimes there may be difficulties, since the ICC Statute does not include "*serious* war crimes" as the Amnesty Law does, but just "war crimes." Thus, for example, the killing of a protected person—such as a civilian—constitutes a war crime under Article 8 ICC Statute. In Colombia on the other hand the Amnesty Law requires to inquire whether such conduct is "serious" or not. As a consequence, the killing or abduction of a person might not be considered a "serious" case, while the massacre of a population could do. The outcome will depend on interpretation and, thus, may cause a problem with the ICC Statute which does not foresee this limitation. The ICC Statute only establishes a limit in Article 8 (1) by saying "as part of a plan or policy or as part of a large-scale commission," but this limitation is only jurisdictional, not substantial. A further non-substantial limitation—of admissibility as a procedural concept—can be found in the gravity threshold of the complementarity test pursuant to Article 17 ICC Statute.[49]

With that in mind, the ICC Prosecutor could claim that Colombia, by applying a narrower concept of war crimes not consistent with the ICC Statute, does not meet its international obligations. Against that, it could be argued, however, that the adjective "serious" only constitutes a jurisdictional limitation, just like the expression "as part of a plan or policy or as part of a large-scale commission" in Article 8 (1) ICC Statute.[50] At any rate, the Constitutional Court concluded in its judgment of March 1, 2018 that the term "serious," as referring to crimes, is unconstitutional.[51] Accordingly, the qualifier was eliminated from six articles of the Amnesty Law which will lead to greater consistency and clarity in the application of the provision—especially with respect to the paragraph of Article 23 discussed here.

In any case, the list of crimes that cannot be subjected to amnesty in the Amnesty Law includes further crimes that do not necessarily correspond to international crimes. It is important to bear in mind that international crimes in the sense of International Criminal Law (ICL) are not the same as transnational crimes. Examples of the second category are drug trafficking or terrorism. International crimes require a contextual element. This contextual element is a prerequisite for an ordinary crime, such as several murders, to become an international crime. Thus, for example, lit. a) of the paragraph of Article 23 of the Amnesty Law refers to the taking of hostages and as such to an offence that does not constitute an international but rather an ordinary crime. A similar example is the crime of forced disappearance. This crime is based on international conventions, such as the Inter-American Convention on Forced Disappearance of Persons,[52] but only constitutes an international crime when committed as part of a systematic or generalized attack against the civilian population. This means that the conduct must form part of a policy within a "course of conduct" excluding isolated acts.[53]

Enforced disappearance is perhaps the least problematic case since it is obviously a serious crime.[54] An example which is less clear is the case of sexual violence since it is much broader. The Amnesty Law refers in literal a) of the paragraph of Article 23 to "violent sexual intercourse and other forms of sexual violence." This formulation could imply a broad spectrum of crimes, ranging from rape to sexual harassment, depending on how it is being interpreted. Any attack against the sexual autonomy of a person might be qualified as "sexual violence" and yet, certainly not any attack in this regard constitutes an international crime. They are crimes, but not necessarily ones of an international character. Given the vagueness of the concept of "sexual violence," a legality problem could arise.[55] However, in all these cases, the Amnesty Law goes beyond the ICC Statute.

From a normative perspective, taking into account the existing positive law, it is possible to affirm that Colombia has made an attempt to meet ICL-standards and in particular those of the ICC Statute. This represents a substantial difference to other processes of this kind that have taken place in other countries, such as South Africa—often misquoted in Colombia—or in Eastern Europe. Even past processes in Colombia cannot be compared to these foreign examples, since in Colombia the granting of exemptions was always limited; in this regard, the notion of "acts of ferocity and barbarism" can be recalled.[56] The current Colombian legislation is even more progressive in several aspects. In fact, there are not that many problems from a purely normative point of view. The difficulties rather arise in the implementation of this normative framework.

Drug trafficking as an offence connected with a political offence and thus eligible for amnesty?

Another complex and very controversial topic (which I have already discussed previously)[57] refers to drug trafficking as a potential offence connected with a political offence.[58] First of all, it is striking that the term "drug trafficking" has not been included in the text of the Amnesty Law. Hence, Articles 8 and 23 of the Amnesty Law are the starting point to answer the complex question whether drug trafficking constitutes an offence that is eligible for amnesty.[59] As already stated above, these two provisions define the political offence as well as its related offences in accordance with points 38–41 of the JEP chapter of the Final Peace Agreement:

> **38.** [...] political and related offences committed in the development of the rebellion by those persons who are part of the rebel groups with whom a peace agreement is signed, will be amnestied and pardoned. [...] In order to decide on the connection with the political offence of *criminal conduct related to illicit crops*, the criteria manifested by the Colombian domestic jurisprudence will be taken into account with the application of the principle of favorability [...].

> **41.** Nor are common offences eligible for amnesties and pardons that are unrelated to the rebellion, as determined by the Amnesty Law. (emphasis added)

Obviously, drug trafficking itself cannot be qualified as a political offence since it is not directed against "the State and its current constitutional regime" nor is drug trafficking as such executed "without being profit oriented":

> **Article 8 Amnesty Law.** By virtue of the nature and development of political and related offences, differentiated treatment will be granted to common offences for all effects of the application and interpretation of this law. Political crimes are those in which the passive subject of the unlawful conduct is the State and its current constitutional regime, if they are not carried out for personal profit.

But could drug trafficking be considered a related crime when incurred in order to finance the rebellion against the State? The third and fourth paragraph of Article 8 Amnesty Law determine that related offences are both the "conduct specifically related to the development of the rebellion" which must be committed "on the occasion of the armed conflict," "as well as the conduct directed to facilitate, support, finance or hide" the rebellion. In both cases, common offences must be committed "without the intention of *personal* gain, for the own benefit or for the benefit of a third party" (emphasis added). This definition is reiterated in more concrete terms in Article 23 Amnesty Law, excluding certain offences from the category of related offences, thus not being eligible for amnesty. Pursuant to this provision, international offences "in accordance with [...] the Rome Statute" and common offences unrelated to the rebellion or "whose motivation was to obtain personal benefit, for their own or for a third party," that is to say offences committed with the purpose of a *personal* gain, are not being considered related offences. In addition, Article 23 states at the end that "the conduct that has been classified autonomously as a common offence" can be considered a related offence "provided that it has been committed on the grounds of the political offence and the rebellion." In a nutshell, this means that a common offence committed to finance the rebellion, namely with the purpose of profit but not *personal* gain, can be considered an offence related to the underlying political offence. The adjective "personal" is key here because it converts drug trafficking—as a typical (common) offence directed at profit—into a related offence provided that its objective has not been the "personal enrichment of the rebels." In this regard point 38 of the JEP chapter of the Final Peace Agreement stipulates:

> **38.** […] A conduct directed to finance the rebellion shall be understood as all unlawful forms of conduct from which no personal enrichment of the rebels has been derived nor being considered a crime against humanity, a serious war crime or genocide.

Drug trafficking is a common offence since it does not constitute an international but a transnational offence. On the assumption that drug trafficking committed by a rebel group (such as the FARC-EP) is related to the armed conflict that was taking place at the time, it is likely—second assumption—that this conduct was "directed to finance" the rebellion. This is particularly plausible if the respective group had no other sources of funding, such as aid from foreign countries.[60] The question then is whether it can be argued that the offence has been committed without the intention of *personal* gain, taking into account that that this qualifier is decisive for the classification of the offence (as common or politically related offence) and thus whether it is eligible for amnesty (related offence) or not (common offence). The possibility that drug trafficking was not committed with the intention of personal gain cannot be ruled out *a limine* but will depend on each specific case. One can imagine a situation in which the respective group uses the entire earnings of drug trafficking to buy weapons and other equipment for their troops. In this case the group would have engaged in drug trafficking exclusively to finance the rebellion. Bearing in mind that the FARC-EP apparently obtained significant gains as a result of their activities related to drug trafficking, it becomes clear that this activity was a decisive strategy to finance the insurgency of the group.[61] Ultimately, this is a factual and evidentiary issue in which the distribution of the burden of proof can be decisive. Those responsible for the difficult task of determining "the connection with the political offence case by case" are the judges of the Amnesty and Pardon Chamber of the JEP.

The effective implementation of Amnesty Law 1820

The first challenge with regard to the implementation of the Amnesty Law is that the JEP aims to be an integral system. This goal is far from being modest since it implies a "holistic" system where the different components are actually connected.[62] Even though the necessary provisions have been adopted in the meantime and the JEP started functioning in March 2018,[63] its statutory law only entered into force in June 2019.[64] Regardless of this, the Amnesty Law was applied by the ordinary justice system even before the JEP's establishment pursuant to the Amnesty Law and Decree 277.[65] With the functioning of the JEP, its Amnesty and Pardon Chamber has assumed this function.[66] In order to be able to benefit from an amnesty, the person concerned needs to sign a declaration of commitment (*acta de compromiso*).[67] However, the amnesty is conditional upon the said Chamber's verification that the respective person has not committed crimes which are not eligible for amnesty.[68] When signing the declaration the person does not need to "confess" or say anything with regard to possible crimes committed. This is different from the situation under the Justice and Peace Law where the option of a spontaneous declaration (*version libre*) existed.[69] Obviously, such a declaration is not necessarily truthful, but at least the person had to confess something in return for the amnesty.[70]

Interestingly, the procedural Rules of the JEP[71] provide in their Articles 67–69 for a monitoring mechanism according to which the respective Chamber or Section controls the compliance of the requirements and conditions established in its decisions. Furthermore, Article 35 of the Amnesty Law provides for the possibility of revoking parole of those who fail to comply with any of the requirements of the Amnesty and Pardons Chamber and the Tribunal for Peace.[72] However, it will be difficult to implement this mechanism since those granted an amnesty in the first place will be released and surely will not surrender themselves back to the State authorities.[73] Taking into account the position of the Constitutional Court in its ruling of March 1, 2018, this doubt is further aggravated. Here, the Court clarified that those who want to benefit from an amnesty have to be willing to tell the entire truth and to compensate the victims at the JEP. Otherwise, they will have to face criminal proceedings in ordinary courts and lose the benefit of amnesty.[74] That is to say, the Court establishes an indispensable requirement that goes beyond the legal framework of the JEP.

Taking the aforementioned into account and considering the large number of cases that would have to be reviewed, the question arises whether the already granted amnesties will actually be verified by the respective Chamber of the JEP. Probably the objective pursued with this is to grant amnesties to the greatest number of people so that afterwards there is less workload for the JEP. This is reasonable, given that in any case a minimum selection is needed. But the question is whether this is the most transparent way to do it. It would probably have been better to make clear from the beginning that there are thousands of people who will never be prosecuted and that only a reduced number of individuals—for example, 5%—will be tried and selected according to the criteria established in ICL (or in the directive that the then Colombian Attorney General Eduardo Montealegre Lynett issued a few years ago[75] with a view to prioritize the investigation of cases, focusing *inter alia* on representative cases, leaders, etc.). Clearly, accepting openly the limitation of this system would have been difficult, especially taking into account the political impact and the possible reaction of various social sectors, especially victims and NGOs representing them. At any rate, in June 2018 the Chamber of Recognition of the JEP has published a (non-binding) guide to prioritize cases and situations.[76] This is the correct way forward—to be transparent in prioritization and selection by making the criteria public—since the practical limitations of the JEP are already becoming evident. The question is how those individuals who are granted amnesties can be requested to contribute to the truth or to provide reparation for the victims. This issue must be monitored by Colombian civil society and international stakeholders.

Another aspect with regard to the effective implementation of amnesties and pardons in the framework of the JEP concerns the writ of *habeas corpus*.[77] Decree 700 and 277, which implement and regulate the Amnesty Law, establish the possibility to exercise this recourse in cases where the deprivation of liberty is unduly prolonged. Based on Decree 700, the jurisprudence of the Constitutional Court on *habeas corpus* is applicable in case of omission or unreasonable delay in processing requests for conditional release. In particular, this benefit is granted to members of the FARC-EP deprived of liberty to whom either a *de iure* amnesty applies, or to whom it does not apply provided that they have served at least five years of imprisonment. Furthermore, a *de iure* amnesty is granted to persons deprived of liberty for a conduct deployed in contexts related to the exercise of the right to protest or internal disturbances. According to Article 14 of Decree 277, in these three cases conditional release must be granted within a maximum period of ten days, provided that the beneficiaries meet the other requirements. For those who cannot receive a *de iure* amnesty but have been deprived of liberty for more than five years, this procedure involves that the competent prosecutor verifies if there are additional criminal proceedings pending against the person who has requested conditional release. Thus, the prosecutor automatically assumes responsibility for these other proceedings and must schedule a hearing within five days following the request for conditional release, in which a supervisory judge must decide on the connection criteria and the release.[78] If this procedure is not carried out within the time indicated, the writ of *habeas corpus* can then be filed before any ordinary judge.[79]

Although the guarantee "of the right to individual liberty in the event of eventual omissions or unjustified delays" is laudable, there are several doubts regarding its feasibility. Bearing in mind the extent of the disarmament and demobilization process of the FARC-EP as well as the situation of the Colombian justice administration in general—especially the criminal justice system—the limited period of 10 days seems to be too demanding. Thus, Decree 277 establishes a procedure which would be even difficult to meet under normal circumstances and that increases the overload that judges already suffer with respect to the new and complex system of the JEP. In a nutshell, it can be affirmed that despite the notable efforts the Colombian State has made to issue norms which allow the implementation of the Amnesty Law, it is not clear if the provisions pursuant to Decree 700 are an appropriate means to achieve this end.

Conclusion

The Peace Agreement between the Colombian Government and the FARC-EP—together with the Amnesty Law and its two regulatory Decrees 277 and 700—forms a highly, perhaps unique sophisticated normative framework regarding amnesties. In line with ICL, absolute amnesties are prohibited and conditional amnesties allowed under certain conditions. The beneficiaries of conditional amnesties are required particularly to reveal the truth and to contribute to the reparation of the victims in order to contribute to true reconciliation. Crimes against humanity, genocide, and war crimes must not go unpunished and as such shall not be covered by conditional amnesties. The Colombian legal framework even goes beyond these standards and excludes amnesties not only for the most serious international crimes but seeks to ensure an effective investigation of other equally serious crimes.

With regard to those crimes that are eligible for amnesties, the situation is more complex. The Peace Agreement as well as the Amnesty Law foresee a variety of provisions aimed at guaranteeing that the beneficiaries of the amnesty comply with the corresponding conditions. At the normative level, the Colombian legal framework ensures an effective investigation by competent authorities in order to adequately sanction violations of ICL and to guarantee effective remedies to victims. These regulations constitute a sophisticated and novel framework which goes way beyond similar measures implemented in other peace processes. In fact, the Colombian authorities have been particularly diligent in designing a conditional amnesty that largely complies with the normative standards of international (criminal) law. However, some aspects are not consistent with the International Legal Framework. In the first place, the differential treatment between the FARC-EP on the one hand and agents of the State on the other regarding the granting of amnesties does not correspond to IHL. The latter treats all groups involved in an armed conflict equally, regardless of whether a party of the conflict is a state or a non-state actor. Therefore, from the perspective of international law, both parties should be subject to the same legal framework, without a distinction between amnesties for the ones and waiver of criminal prosecution for the others. Although this differential treatment can be explained by the Colombian tradition and, to a certain degree, by the political context in which the Peace Agreement was signed, it should be noted that the Amnesty Law expressly refers to IHL and, therefore, should be analyzed in that context. The (failed) attempt to create a further special jurisdiction for the military within the JEP was difficult to reconcile with the spirit of the peace agreement and the ensuing constitutional amendments.

In addition, the rules pursuant to the Amnesty Law raise doubts as to the effective implementation of the Law—especially those rules that make a distinction between political and related crimes, particularly with regard to the unclear contours of these concepts. The same applies to the tight deadlines set forth in Decree 277 and the provenance of *habeas corpus*. Thus, the normative framework and the reality do not coincide and the value of legal provisions—which may be well made—might lose any practical relevance. Either way, one must wait to see if the competent authorities will be able to apply the intricate legislation established on the basis of the Peace Agreement. Considering the great legal and political impact of this delicate and highly controversial issue, the handling of amnesties and pardons in the framework of the JEP will be a key element for the successful development of the peace process in Colombia.

Author's note

The author would like to thank Susann Aboueldahab, doctoral researcher at the Study Center for Latin American Criminal and Criminal Procedural Law (CEDPAL) at the Georg-August-Universität Göttingen and at the German-Colombian Peace Institute (CAPAZ), Bogotá, for assistance in the preparation of this article. She also translated all Colombian provisions into English (for reasons of space we cannot reproduce the original text). I further thank Dr. Carlos Guillermo Castro (Prof. Universidad del Rosario) and Dr. Gustavo Cote (Prof. Universidad Javeriana) for important suggestions.

Notes

1 Cf. Kai Ambos, *Treatise on International Criminal Law. Volume I: Foundations and General Part* (Oxford: Oxford University Press, 2013), 419 et seq.; Kai Ambos, "The legal framework of Transitional Justice: A Systematic Study with a Special Focus on the Role of the ICC," in *Building a Future on Peace and* Justice. *Studies on Transitional Justice, Peace and Development*, ed. Kai Ambos et al. (Berlin/ Heidelberg: Springer, 2009), 55–62.
2 Ambos, "The legal framework of Transitional Justice," 55–62.
3 *Ibid.*, p. 62. See also Ambos, *Treatise I*, 425.
4 Ambos, *Treatise I*, 425.
5 cf. Ambos, "The legal framework of Transitional Justice," 58–62.
6 Gerhard Werle and Florian Jeßberger, *Principles of International Law*, 4th edition (Oxford: Oxford University Press, 2020), 113 (arguing that "International Criminal Law cannot completely dismiss amnesties, which are sometimes inevitable. A waiver of punishment may be essential in certain situations to restore peace and facilitate national reconciliation"); Louise Mallinder, "Can Amnesties and International Justice be Reconciled?," *International Journal of Transitional Justice* (IJTJ), vol. 1 (2) (August 2007), p. 214; Stefanie Bock, *Das Opfer vor dem Internationalen Strafgerichtshof* (Berlin: Duncker & Humblot, 2010) 302–03. Cf. also Jens David Ohlin, "A Meta-Theory of International

Criminal Procedure: Vindicating the Rule of Law," *UCLA Journal of International Law and Foreign Affairs* vol. 14, 2009, pp. 116–18; Elizabeth B. L. King, "Amnesties in a Time of Transition," *George Washington International Law Review* vol. 41, 2010, 610; Robert Cryer, "Alternatives and Complements to Criminal Prosecution," in *An Introduction to International Criminal Law and Procedure*, Robert Cryer et al., 4th ed 2019 (Cambridge: Cambridge University Press, 2019), 541 ("Still, international law has not yet developed so far as to prohibit all amnesties in all situations"); Gerhard Werle, "Die juristische Aufarbeitung der Vergangenheit," in *Transformation von Diktaturen in Demokratien und Aufarbeitung der Vergangenheit*, eds. Francisco Muñoz Conde and Thomas Vormbaum (Berlin: De Gruyter, 2010) 23.

7 Ambos, *Treatise I*, 426.

8 Final Agreement to End the Armed Conflict and Build a Stable and Lasting Peace, available at: https://www.jep.gov.co/Marco%20Normativo/Normativa_v2/01%20ACUERDOS/N01.pdf; English version available at: http://especiales.presidencia.gov.co/Documents/20170620-dejacion-armas/acuerdos/acuerdo-final-ingles.pdf (accessed June 20, 2020).

9 Colombia. Congreso de la República. Ley 1820 (30 December 2016).

10 This refers to the extinction of responsibilities in criminal and administrative terms and the State's renunciation of criminal prosecution with regard to the State security forces (Article 7 of Law 1820).

11 Cf. Preliminary Considerations of Law 1820; Arts. 1 and 2 ff. (objective and scope of application).

12 Colombia. Presidencia de la República. Decreto 277 (February 17, 2017).

13 Colombia. Presidencia de la República. Decreto 700 (May 02, 2017).

14 Moreover, Decree 1252 of 19 July 2017 and Decree 1269 of July 28, 2017 contain further regulations concerning the implementation of Law 1820.

15 Cf. Colombia. Constitutional Court. Judgment C-007/18 (March 1, 2018, Reporting judge Diana Fajardo Rivera), paras 520, 757.

16 Gustavo Alvira, "Toward a new Amnesty: The Colombian Peace Process and the Inter-American Court of Human Rights," *Tulane Journal of International and Comparative Law* vol. 22 (1), November 2013, pp. 119–36; Cryer, "Alternatives and Complements," 575.

17 IACtHR. Judgment Series C 219. (24 November 2010), 173, 241–242, 253, 253–258; IACtHR. Sentence Series C 221 (February 24, 2011) 239.

18 Cf. IACtHR. *Massacres of El Mozote and nearby places v. El* Salvador. Judgment Series C 252 (October 25, 2012) 286, opening the door to conditional amnesties. For a different perspective, see King, "Amnesties in Times of Transition," 577 et seq., 613 et seq.

19 For further information, see Tarapués Sandino, "Artículo 15. Amnistía 'de iure'," in Kai Ambos and Gustavo Cote Barco (eds), *Ley de Amnistía. Comentario completo y sistemático* (Bogotá: Temis, 2019) 169 et seq.

20 See, for further information Gustavo Cote Barco, "Artículo 21. Sala de Amnistía o Indulto," in *Ley de Amnistía. Comentario completo y sistemático*, 207 et seq.

21 In cases that the benefited persons are not subject to a *de iure* amnesty in accordance with Art. 15 et seq. of Law 1820.

22 Decree 1252 of 2017, available at http://es.presidencia.gov.co/normativa/normativa/DECRETO%201252%20DEL%2019%20DE%20JULIO%20DE%202017.pdf (accessed June 15, 2020).

23 For further information, see Tarapués Sandino, "Artículo 17. Ámbito de aplicación personal," in *Ley de Amnistía. Comentario completo y sistemático*, 183 et seq.

24 See, for example, Arts. 2, 3 and 9. See also Gustavo Cote Barco, "Artículo 44. Sala de Definición de Situaciones Jurídicas," in *Ley de Amnistía. Comentario completo y sistemático*, 423 et seq.

25 Colombia. Constitutional Court. Judgment C-674 (November 14, 2017). Reporting judge Luis Guillermo Guerrero Pérez. In its decision on the Law establishing the JEP (*Acto Legislativo* 1/2017) the Court declared unconstitutional the compulsory subjection of these third parties to the JEP, cf. paras. 5.5.2.6. et seq. and para 5.5.2.14. of the judgment.

26 Supreme Court of Justice, Radicado (Rad.) 36487 of August 18, 2017, presiding magistrate Eugenio Fernandez Carlier.

27 See Gustavo Cote Barco, "Artículo 21," 211.

28 Kai Ambos, *Treatise on International Criminal Law. Volume II: The Crimes and Sentencing* (Oxford: Oxford University Press, 2014), 124 et seq.

29 Art. 75 Reglas de Procedimiento para la Jurisdicción Especial para la Paz, cf. Gaceta del Congreso 480 (27 June 2018), Informe de Conciliación al Proyecto de Ley 225 de 2018 Senado, 239 de 2018 Cámara. For further information, see Kai Ambos, "Another Challenge for Colombia's Transitional Justice Process: Aggravated Differential Treatment between Armed Forces and FARC," EJIL: Talk!, 19 October 2018, available at: https://www.ejiltalk.org/another-challenge-for-colombias-transitional-justice-process-aggravated-differential-treatment-between-armed-forces-and-farc/ (accessed June 20, 2020); Kai Ambos and Susann Aboueldahab, "The Colombian Peace Process and the Special Jurisdiction for Peace," *Diritto Penale Contemporaneo,* no. 4/18 (December 2018): 261 et seq.

30 The Colombian Constitutional Court reviewed the provision's constitutionality in its Judgment C-112/19 of 13 March 2019 ("Demandas de inconstitucionalidad contra los artículos […] y 75 de la Ley 1922 de 2018"), see mn. 37 (ii), available at: https://www.corteconstitucional.gov.co/relatoria/2019/C-112-19.htm (accessed June 20, 2020). The Rules of Procedure and Evidence are available at: https://www.jep.gov.co/Marco%20Normativo/Normativa_v2/04%20DECRETOS%20Y%20LEYES/7.%20Ley%201922%20reglas%20procedimiento%20JEP.pdf (accessed June 20, 2020).

31 Thereto Katrin Gierhake, "Strafe und Amnestie in Zeiten fragiler Staatlichkeit. Die Bedeutung des freiheitlichen Rechtsbegriffs für die Übergangsjustiz am Beispiel des kolumbianischen Friedensprozesses," *Zeitschrift für Internationale Strafrechtsdogmatik,* vol. 12, 2017, pp. 391–409.

32 Katrin Gierhake, "Strafe und Amnestie," 405.

33 *Ibid.*, 405 et seq.

34 *Ibid.,* 407 et seq.

35 *Ibid.*, 406.

36 *Ibid.*, 408 et seq.

37 See generally Tarapués Sandino, "Artículo 23. Criterios de conexidad," in *Ley de Amnistía. Comentario completo y sistemático*, 219 et seq.

38 As noted in the European Convention for the Suppression of Terrorism of 27 January 1977 and the European Convention on Extradition of 13 December 1957. See the explanatory report of the Council of the European Union, No C 191/03 of 23 June 1997, p. 13 regarding Art. 5 of the Convention relating to extradition between the Member States of the European Union; cf. Joachim Vogel, "Abschaffung der Auslieferung? Kritische Anmerkung zur Reform des Auslieferungsrechts der Europäischen Union," *JuristenZeitung,* vol. 56 (19), October 2001, pp. 937–38; Zsuszanna Deen-Racsmány and Rob Blekxtoon, "The Decline of the Nationality Exception in European Extradition? The Impact of the Regulation of (non)-Surrender of Nationals and Dual Criminality under the European Arrest Warrant," *European Journal of Crime, Criminal Law and Criminal Justice,* vol. 13 (3), August 2005, 317 et seq. and 352 et seq.

39 Breanne Hataway, "The FARC's Trafficking as Political Crime: Determining the Success of Colombia's Peace Talks," *North Carolina Journal of International Law,* vol. 41 (01), Fall 2015, 163-et seq. and 177 et seq.

40 Iván Orozco Abad, Combatientes, rebeldes y terroristas. Guerra y Derecho en Colombia (Bogotá, D. C.: Temis, 2006), 55-et seq.; Alejandro Aponte Cardona, El proceso penal especial de justicia y paz. Alcances y límites de un proceso penal concebido en clave transicional (Madrid: CITpax, 2011), 29 et seq.; Ricardo Posada Maya (coord.), Delito Político, Terrorismo y Temas de Derecho Penal (Bogotá, D. C.: Uniandes, 2010), 75 et seq.; Ana María Gutiérrez Urresty, "Las amnistías e indultos, un hábito social en Colombia," in Justicia Transicional: Teoría y Praxis, ed. Camila De Gamboa Tapias (Bogotá, D. C.: Universidad del Rosario, 2006) 388 et seq. See also Colombia. Constitutional Court. Judgment C-007/18 (1 March 2018, Reporting Judge Diana Fajardo Rivera), para. 146, 154.

41 Luis Carlos Pérez, *Tratado de Derecho Penal. Tomo 3* (Bogotá, D. C.: Temis, 1978), 111 et seq. and 135 et seq.

42 Cf. Arts. 150 and 201, available at: Colombian Constitutional Court. *Constitución Política de Colombia. Actualizada con los Actos Legislativos a 2015* (Bogotá, D. C.: Imprenta Nacional, 2015), 42–3, 57. http://www.corteconstitucional.gov.co/inicio/Constitucion%20politica%20de%20Colombia%20-%202015.pdf (accessed June 20, 2020).

43 Colombia. Supreme Court of Justice. Criminal Cassation Chamber. Judgment No. C-26945 (July 11, 2007).

44 Kai Ambos, *El marco jurídico de la justicia de transición* (Bogotá, D. C.: Temis, 2008) 193, 195 et seq.

45 See in this respect Colombian Supreme Court of Justice, Rad. 46334 of 13.09.2017; Rad. 47636 of 13.09.2017; Rad. 50628 of 06.09.2017; Rad. 49647 of 11.07.2017; Rad. 50220 of 28.06.2017; Rad. 49895 of 28.06.2017: Rad. 49647 of 07.06.2017; Rad. 50402 of 05.06.2017; Rad. 50325 of 23.05.2017; Rad. 49253 of 10.05.2017; Rad. 49134 of 10.05.2017. See also Tarapués Sandino, "Artículo 23. Criterios de conexidad," 221 et seq.

46 Of course, there are other relevant sources apart from and prior to the ICC Statute. For example, positive and customary law based on IHL in relation to the issue of command responsibility. But in any case, the ICC Statute codifies what can be considered as the current state of ICL. In that sense—and since Colombia is a State party—it is a good starting point.

47 See generally in this regard Tarapués Sandino, "Artículo 23. Criterios de conexidad," 222 et seq.

48 Cf. Art. 101 of Law 599 of 2000.

49 Cf. Art. 17 RS. See also in that regard Kai Ambos, *Treatise on International Criminal Law. Volume III: International Criminal Procedure* (Oxford: Oxford University Press, 2016), 271 et seq.

50 Ambos, *Treatise II*, 118 et seq.

51 Cf. Colombia. Constitutional Court. Judgment C-007/18 (March 1, 2018, Reporting Judge Diana Fajardo Rivera), paras. 512 et seq., 520, 521; *Ámbito Jurídico.* "Conozca las principales decisiones de la Corte sobre la Ley de Indulto y Amnistía," March 2, 2018, https://www.ambitojuridico.com/noticias/general/constitucional-y-derechos-humanos/conozca-las-principales-decisiones-de-la-corte (accessed June 16, 2020); *El Espectador.* "Corte Constitucional da luz verde a la Ley de Amnistía," March 1, 2018, https://www.elespectador.com/noticias/judicial/corte-constitucional-da-luz-verde-la-ley-de-amnistia-articulo-740607 (accessed June 16, 2020).

52 Inter-American Convention on Forced Disappearance of Persons, adopted 9 June 1994, Organization of American States Doc. OEA/Ser.P/AG/Doc.3114/94 (1994).

53 Cf. Kai Ambos, "Art. 7," in *Rome Statute of the ICC*, ed. Kai Ambos (München et al.: Beck/Hart/Nomos, 4th ed. 2021), mn. 15 et seq., 200 et seq.

54 Kai Ambos and María Laura Böhm. "La desaparición forzada de personas como tipo penal autónomo," in Kai Ambos (ed.), *Desaparición forzada de personas. Análisis comparado e internacional* (Bogotá, D.C.: GTZ-ProFis, 2009), 195 et seq.

55 See in this regard Gustavo Cote Barco, "Artículo 46. De la renuncia a la persecución penal," in *Ley de Amnistía. Comentario completo y sistemático*, 464-5. saa.

56 Kai Ambos, *Impunidad y derecho penal internacional* (Buenos Aires: Ad Hoc, 1999), 53 et seq.; Edulfo Peña, "Caso M-19: solución política o jurídica," *El Tiempo*, June 2, 1992, http://www.eltiempo.com/archivo/documento/MAM-128046 (accessed June 16, 2020); Kai Ambos, "¿Revisión de indultos para M-19?," *El Espectador,* November 14, 2015, http://www.elespectador.com/opinion/opinion/revision-de-indultos-para-el-m-19-columna-599308 (accessed June 16, 2020).

57 Kai Ambos, "Amnistía y narcotráfico," *El Espectador*, January 21, 2017, http://www.elespectador.com/opinion/opinion/amnistia-y-narcotrafico-columna-675841 (accessed June 16, 2020).

58 Diego Tarapués Sandino, "El narcotráfico como delito político: ¿desatino o condición para el posconflicto?" *Razon Pública*, 25 September 2017, https://razonpublica.com/index.php/econom-y-sociedad-temas-29/10554-el-narcotráfico-como-delito-pol%C3%ADtico-desatino-o-condición-para-el-posconflicto.html (accessed June 17, 2020).

59 See in this regard also Colombia. Constitutional Court. Judgment C-007/18 (1 March 2018, Reporting judge Diana Fajardo Rivera), paras. 587 et seq. and 757 et seq.

60 This was for example the case during the Cold War when the United States on the one hand and the Soviet Union on the other financed such groups.

61 Hataway, "The FARC's Trafficking": 163 et seq. and 174 et seq.; John Otis, "The FARC and Colombia's Illegal Drug Trade," *Woodrow Wilson Latin American Program* (2014), https://www.wilsoncenter.org/sites/default/files/media/documents/publication/Otis_FARCDrugTrade2014.pdf (accessed June 16, 2020); Alberto Lozano Vila, "Los ingresos de las FARC," *El Espectador*, March 12, 2017, http://colombia2020.elespectador.com/opinion/los-ingresos-de-las-farc (accessed June 16, 2020); *Semana.* "FARC obtuvo US$ 22,5 millones por narcotráfico entre 1995 y 2014," September 6, 2016, http://www.semana.com/nacion/articulo/fiscalia-habla-sobre-ingresos-de-las-farc-por-narcotrafico/477020 (accessed June 16, 2020); Yagoub, Mimi. "Las elusivas finanzas de las FARC y sus implicaciones para la paz," *InSight Crime*, April 21, 2016, http://es.insightcrime.org/analisis/las-elusivas-finanzas-de-las-farc-y-sus-implicaciones-para-la-paz (accessed June 16, 2020).

62 See Kai Ambos and Susann Aboueldahab, "The Colombian Peace Process," 256.

63 Cf. "La JEP abre sus puertas al público," JEP, https://www.jep.gov.co/Sala-de-Prensa/Paginas/¡La-JEP-abre-sus-puertas-al-público!.aspx (accessed June 16, 2020).

64 Cf. Law 1957 of 6 June 2019. Estatutaria de la Administración de Justicia en la Jurisdicción Especial para la Paz, available at: https://www.jep.gov.co/Marco%20Normativo/LEY%201957%20DEL%2006%20DE%20JUNIO%20DE%202019.pdf, last accessed June 18, 2020. This delay can be explained in particular by the objections raised by President Duque which lead to another review by the Constitutional Court, see https://id.presidencia.gov.co/Paginas/prensa/2019/190310-Alocucion-del-Presidente-Ivan-Duque-Marquez-sobre-la-Ley-Estatutaria-de-la-Justicia-Especial-Para-La-Paz-JEP.aspx (accessed June 18, 2020); critically Kai Ambos and Susann Aboueldahab, "Colombia: Time for the ICC Prosecutor to

Act?," *EJIL: Talk!*, April 2, 2019), https://www.ejiltalk.org/colombia-time-for-the-icc-prosecutor-to-act/ (accessed June 18, 2020). However, the Constitutional Court declared the objections unconstitutional due to procedural flaws, see Auto 123 of 20 March 2019, http://www.corteconstitucional.gov.co/relatoria/autos/2019/A123-19.htm, (accessed June 18, 2020).

65 Cf. Ar. 37(2) Amnesty Law. At the beginning of May 2017, judges had already taken 291 guerillas out of jail, of whom 179 gained de iure amnesty, 40 gained conditioned liberties and 72 were transferred to rural areas, cf. *El Tiempo,* "Corte Constitucional inicia estudio de la ley de amnistía," May 10, 2017, http://m.eltiempo.com/justicia/cortes/corte-constitucional-estudia-la-ley-de-amnistia-86562 (accessed 16 June 2020); *El Tiempo,* "Corte Constitucional suspende estudio de la ley de amnistía," May 11, 2017, http://m.eltiempo.com/justicia/cortes/corte-constitucional-suspende-el-estudio-de-la-ley-de-amnistia-87032 (accessed June 16, 2020). In December 2017, already 2972 guerillas were released, cf. *Colombia Informa*, "Ley de Amnistía e Indulto: retos y adversidades," December 2, 2017, http://www.colombiainforma.info/ley-de-amnistia-e-indulto-retos-y-adversidades/ (accessed June 16, 2020).

66 Cf. Cote Barco, "Artículo 21," 209 et seq. For a record of the JEP's activities as of June 2020, see "JEP en cifras," JEP, https://www.jep.gov.co/Infografas/cifras-junio-12.pdf (accessed June 16, 2020).

67 Colombia. Presidencia de la República. Decreto 277 (17 February 2017), Annex I and II, Acts of Commitment *–de iure* Amnesty– Law 1820 of 2016. By June 2020, 9742 ex-guerrillas had signed the act of submission; likewise, 2686 members of the public force subscribed to them, cf. https://www.jep.gov.co/Infografas/cifras-junio-12.pdf (accessed June 16, 2020).

68 Cf. Artículo 16 (2), Artículo 23 (Paragraph) of the Amnesty Law, for further information, see Tarapués Sandino, "Artículo 16," in *Ley de Amnistía. Comentario completo y sistemático*, 177 and "Artículo 23. Criterios de conexidad," 221 et seq.; as well as Arts. 46 (2), 7 (4) of the Amnesty Law, detailed Cote Barco, "Artículo 46. De la renuncia a la persecución penal," 444 et seq.

69 Colombia. Congreso de la República. Ley 975 "Ley de Justicia y Paz" (July 25, 2005).

70 Kai Ambos et al., Procedimiento de la ley de justicia y paz (ley 975 de 2005) y derecho penal internacional. Estudio sobre la facultad de intervención complementaria de la Corte Penal Internacional a la luz del denominado proceso de "justicia y paz" en Colombia (Bogotá: GTZ/ Embajada de la República Federal Alemana en Bogotá/ Georg-August-Universität Göttingen, 2010), http://www.corteidh.or.cr/tablas/26869.pdf (accessed June 20, 2020), 9 et seq. and 81 et seq.

71 Supra note 30.

72 For example, regarding the reparation of victims or because they do not appear before the Truth Commission. For further information, see Óscar Guerrero Peralta, "Artículo 35. Libertad condicionada," in *Ley de Amnistía. Comentario completo y sistemático*, 366 et seq.

73 On 26 April 2019, the JEP for the first time issued a revocation of release in the case of the leading FARC member Velásquez Saldarriaga ("El Paisa") on the ground that he had failed to comply with his obligations, cf. JEP, Chamber for the Recognition of Truth, Auto 061 of 2019, mn. 80 et seq. Despite having ordered Velásquez arrest, he remains at large until today, see "'El Paisa' ahora integra cartel de los más buscados en Colombia," pulzo, https://www.pulzo.com/nacion/cartel-buscados-colombia-paisa-PP919430 (accessed June 20, 2020).

74 Colombia. Constitutional Court. Judgment C-007/18 (1 March 2018), para. 165, 684; *El Espectador,* "Corte Constitucional da luz verde"; *Semana,* "La Ley Amnistía pasó el filtro de la Corte Constitucional," March 1, 2018, https://www.semana.com/Item/ArticleAsync/558629?nextId=558630&nextId=558638 (accessed June 16, 2020).

75 Colombia. Fiscalía General de la Nación. Directiva de priorización No. 001 (October 4, 2012).

76 JEP. Criterios y Metodología de priorización de casos y situaciones en la Sala de Reconocimiento de Verdad, de Responsabilidad y de Determinación de los Hechos y Conductas (June 28, 2018), https://www.jep.gov.co/Documents/CriteriosYMetodologiaDePriorizacion.pdf#search=priorización%20de%20casos (accessed June 20, 2020). See in this regard also Olga Patricia Rendón, "No tenemos capacidad para investigarlo todo," *El Colombiano*, July 20, 2018, http://www.elcolombiano.com/colombia/no-tenemos-capacidad-para-investigarlo-todo-NI9028924 (accessed June 16, 2020).

77 Colombia. Fiscalía General de la Nación. Directiva de priorización No. 001 (October 4, 2012).

78 JEP. Criterios y Metodología de priorización de casos y situaciones en la Sala de Reconocimiento de Verdad, de Responsabilidad y de Determinación de los Hechos y Conductas (June 28, 2018), https://www.jep.gov.co/Documents/CriteriosYMetodologiaDePriorizacion.pdf#search=priorización%20de%20casos (accessed June 20, 2020). See in this regard also Olga Patricia Rendón, "No tenemos capacidad para investigarlo todo," El Colombiano, July 20, 2018, http://www.elcolombiano.com/colombia/no-tenemos-capacidad-para-investigarlo-todo-NI9028924 (accessed June 16, 2020).

79 Colombian Constitutional Court. Constitución Política de Colombia, Article 30, p. 16–7. See also Colombia. Congress of the Republic. Law 1095. (2 November 2006). By means of which Article 30 of the Political Constitution is regulated, June 30, 2018, http://www.secretariasenado.gov.co/senado/basedoc/ley_1095_2006.html (accessed June 16, 2020).

9 Judging the justice of the Colombian Final Agreement

Colleen Murphy

Introduction

After 52 years of conflict, the Final Agreement to End the Armed Conflict and Build a Stable and Lasting Peace (hereafter, Final Agreement) between the Colombian Government and the Revolutionary Armed Forces of Colombia (hereafter FARC) is now being implemented. However, divisions within Colombian society are real, and opposition to the Final Agreement on the part of some remains deep. Thus, the pursuit of peace is a fragile enterprise.

One cause of the fragility of the Colombian peace process is moral in nature. An important source of opposition to the Final Agreement concerns whether justice is achieved in the treatment of past wrongs. In this chapter, I take up this concern and focus on the question: by what standards should we evaluate the justice of transitional justice processes for dealing with past wrongs outlined in the Final Agreement? That is, what are the criteria that must be satisfied for such wrongs to be said to have been dealt with *justly*? It is worth noting the difference between the question I take up and the kinds of questions typically examined in the literature on transitional justice. Studies of transitional justice are characteristically social scientific in orientation and concerned with understanding the choices transitional societies do make, either in terms of the factors that influenced such choices or in terms of the societal impact of processes adopted. My question, by contrast, is a question about how we should think about the choices a given society makes. Should we view the Final Agreement as a success from the perspective of justice?

In the first section, I provide some background to the Colombian case. I focus specifically on the mechanisms of transitional justice outlined in the Final Agreement, and the objections to those processes as articulated in responses to the October 2016 failed plebiscite on the September 2016 version of the Final Agreement. The revisions subsequently made following the failed plebiscite did not substantively alter the form such mechanisms would take and thus the source of moral concern with them. After outlining the processes for dealing with past wrongs and the sources of moral debate about them, I go on in the second section to outline my substantive view of transitional justice developed in my book *The Conceptual Foundations of Transitional Justice.*[1] The third section then applies that framework to the Colombian case, arguing that the processes for dealing with past wrongs outlined in the Final Agreement satisfy criteria of transitional justice, though whether that justice will be realized in fact remains to be seen.

Background to the Final Agreement

The process leading to the formal adoption of the Final Agreement was long and very complex, encompassing negotiations between the FARC and Colombian government begun in 2012.[2] The negotiations focused on six central issues: rural reform; political participation; illicit crops; victims; the termination of conflict; and how to implement and endorse any agreement. These negotiations culminated in a complex and comprehensive agreement comprising over 300 pages, which was formally signed by Colombian President Juan Manuel Santos and FARC leader Rodrigo Londoño, known as Timochenko, on September 26, 2016 in Cartagena, Colombia. Following that signing, there was a public plebiscite on the Final Agreement on October 2, 2016. Part of the impetus for holding the plebiscite was to bolster the legitimacy of the Agreement within Colombian society. In an outcome that shocked the nation and the international community, the plebiscite failed by 0.5%. About 50.2% voted no and 49.7% voted yes, with 60% of the Colombian population abstaining from participating.[3] The failed plebiscite led to a consultation with a large group of stakeholders within Colombian society to seek suggestions for modifications to the agreement. Forty-one days later, a joint communique was issued stating a revised agreement was in place that addressed 56 of the 57 themes for revision that emerged from the process of consultation. On December 1, 2016, the Colombian Congress ratified the Final Agreement.

The necessity of including measures to respond to victims is clear once we consider the numbers of such victims. Colombia's current population is 48 million people. According to the Victims' Unit, more than 8 million have registered as victims since 1985.[4] This includes 7 million individuals forcibly displaced; 260,000 individuals killed; 46,000 enforced disappearances; 30,000 hostage taking; 17,500 rape and other forms of sexual violence; and 10,000 cases of torture. Those directly harmed by the conflict are many; indirectly all Colombians have been affected.

I want to focus in the remainder of this section on the claims of justice that are implicit and explicit in the explanations of why individuals voted as they did in the October plebiscite. But before turning to these views, I want first to summarize the processes for dealing with past wrongs outlined in the Final Agreement. Some details about the structure and functioning of these processes changed between the version of the Final Agreement that was put to the vote in the plebiscite in October and the version that was ratified by the Colombian Congress. However, the changes did not alter substantively the basic structure of the transitional justice processes and, importantly, did not alter the features of those processes that were the source of moral concern.

One component of the Final Agreement is the Special Jurisdiction for Peace (JEP). This consists of a set of judicial bodies that investigate, establish facts and, where applicable, levy penalties for the crimes that fall under its jurisdiction. The JEP is comprised Colombian judges with ten foreign expert observers. It will operate over a ten-year period with the possibility of an extension of an additional five years. Rulings from the JEP can be appealed to the Constitutional Court. Wrongs that fall under its jurisdiction fall into two main groups. In the first group are wrongs committed for political reasons but that do not rise to the level of war crimes or crimes against humanity; an example would be the crime of rebellion. Perpetrators of this category of wrongdoing are eligible for amnesty if they offer a full confession and demonstrate that wrongs committed were not for personal enrichment. Into the second category of crimes are gross human rights violations that are not eligible for amnesty or pardon and that were not committed for personal enrichment. For this set of crimes, there will be three different categories of penalties. For those who fully and immediately confess to wrongs committed, they are eligible to serve 5–8 years in zones of restricted liberty, during which time acts of reparation and restoration will be performed. Such acts could include, for example, clearing land mines, repairing damaged infrastructure, or participating in rural development projects. Individuals who recognize responsibility for wrongdoing later are eligible for prison sentences of 5–8 years. Individuals who do not confess or recognize responsibility for wrongs but are found guilty by the JEP will serve prison sentences of 15–20 years.

In addition to the JEP, the Final Agreement makes provisions for a truth commission. This commission was established on April 5, 2017 and its mandate is to "find out what happened in Colombia that led to the victimization of 8 million."[5] It has three years to function and comprises 11 members, three of whom can be foreigners. The actors of interest in the truth commission are both FARC and state agents. A wide range of wrongs are the subject of its focus, including mass transfers of land. Finally, the Final Agreement makes provisions for a Special Unit for Seeking People Reported Missing and for reparations for victims of the conflict.

There are other features of the Final Agreement worth highlighting for the way they shape moral evaluations of the transitional justice processes. First, the Agreement includes a commitment to political representation for the post-FARC political party. That party will have ten automatic congressional seats between 2018 and 2026. Those eligible to serve in these seats include individuals found guilty of war crimes.[6] There are provisions for rural development programs. There is a scheme for the decommissioning of weapons, a process which has already been completed. There is also a program for the reintegration of FARC members following periods spent in "Temporary Zones for Normalization."[7] Such zones are to be monitored by the United Nations.

In an article published by the British newspaper *The Guardian* shortly after the October 2016 plebiscite, a range of views about the justice of the Final Agreement were expressed.[8] One set of views rested on the claim that justice requires giving perpetrators what they deserve, and what perpetrators deserve is punishment. Therefore, because the JEP does not guarantee punishment, but grants amnesty to non-war criminals, permits time spent in zones of restricted liberty for war criminals, and allows war criminals to serve in political office, the terms for dealing with wrongdoing laid out in the Final Agreement are unjust. Sample quotes reflecting this position include the following: "The agreement gave the wrong message to society as criminals were rewarded with injustice, money, and political representation." Echoing a similar perspective another interviewee stated "Santos was giving more than deserved to the narco-guerrillas. Political liberties shouldn't be granted to terrorists guilty of atrocities." Putting the same point even more directly, another interviewee stated "[I want] a fairer deal that meets the following conditions: That FARC members responsible for war crimes go to jail instead of having a secure place on the senate."

By contrast, another set of views conceptualized transitional justice as a compromise between peace and justice, with differing judgments taken as to whether the balance struck in the Final Agreement was just. For one yes vote, "The peace accord is an imperfect document but I thought the balance between peace for the country and justice for victims was fair." Whereas another individual who voted no claimed, "A little more compromise by the rebels, regarding material reparation for victims and justice."

A third and final set of views appealed to a notion of justice different than that of retribution. Justice requires unity or the overcoming of divisions within Colombian society. Or justice requires participation, where the importance of having a say on policies that will impact one is emphasized. Consider the following yes vote explanations: "[T]he results show a sharp divide[...]The departments in the center[...]voted against the accords while the departments in the rural periphery, including many areas which have been most impacted by the economic and social costs of the conflict, overwhelmingly supported the accords." Similarly emphasizing the importance of unity, another yes vote stated, "The peace agreements are...about unity. We need to unite as a country. The plebiscite showed just how divided we are. Even worse, how indifferent we are."

The various viewpoints expressed above raise questions about what exactly are the criteria we should be using to evaluate the justice of transitional justice processes. Are the salient criteria those articulated by theories of retributive justice? Or is justice rather best conceptualized as a compromise between retributive justice and other moral considerations? Or is justice instead not about retribution, but rather about other kinds of concerns such as societal unity? Each of these views is intuitively plausible as accounts of the justice of transition, and it is not immediately obvious on what basis we should judge a particular view as better or worse than another.

In the next section, I articulate my framework for conceptualizing transitional justice. In brief, transitional justice at its core is about the just pursuit of societal transformation. I explain why this is the core concern of transitional justice and what the just pursuit of societal transformation entails. In the third section, I contrast my view with the three views on justice outlined in this section and evaluate the Final Agreement from within my framework.

Transitional justice

In *The Conceptual Foundations of Transitional Justice*, I approach the question of transitional justice by drawing on the model of justice provided by eighteenth-century philosopher David Hume.[9] Hume famously claimed that a set of circumstances of justice which generate a particular problem of justice becomes necessary for a community to address and possible to resolve. Principles of justice then provide guidance on how a community should resolve a given problem. For Hume, the central problem of justice concerned the stabilization of property. This becomes a problem when specific circumstances exist including, for example, limited scarcity of goods. He illustrates why limited scarcity of goods is salient by considering the contrasting set of circumstances of extreme abundance and extreme scarcity. When goods are abundant, Hume argues, the stabilization of property is not necessary. There is no important purpose served by specifying and articulating who owns which good when the same good can be easily replaced. At the opposite end, in a circumstance of extreme scarcity, stabilization of property is a futile exercise. When faced with the question of survival, property rules will not constrain individuals from taking what they need to survive.

The central insight of Hume is that principles of justice are context-dependent. They become operative or salient in a specific set of circumstances of justice. This is because principles of justice are problem or question-responsive, providing guidance for a concrete question of justice facing a community. Following Hume, then, suggests that before it is possible to adjudicate among competing understandings of the principles that ought to be used to evaluate processes for dealing with past wrongdoing, it is necessary first to articulate the circumstances of justice characterizing transitions. Only then is it possible to identify the central question of justice that is at issue and articulate principles that will provide guidance for dealing with that question.

There are, I argue, four circumstances of justice that characterize paradigmatic transitional societies. I briefly summarize each in turn. I then argue that the salient question of justice is how to justly pursue societal transformation. Finally, I articulate principles for societal transformation and its just pursuit.

Circumstances of transitions

The first circumstance is what I call *pervasive structural inequality.*[10] The subject matter of this circumstance is the basic terms for interaction among citizens and between citizens and officials. "Structural" signals the dominant role of institutions in defining these basic terms. The institutions that shape interaction are many, including legal, political, social, cultural, and economic institutions. They shape interaction by virtue of how their rules and norms govern who is eligible to engage in certain pursuits or actions and who is eligible to shape the rules themselves. Political rules and norms shape the conditions that must be satisfied for someone to be eligible to hold public office, and political and legal rules shape the powers that may be legitimately exercised if one holds such an office. Part of the rules and norms include penalties for their infraction. Such rules and norms can be unequal in two senses. They can be unequal in the sense that different groups enjoy differential freedom to do and become various things of value. For example, the educational opportunities, the prospects for entering politics, and the possibilities for employment vary. Rules can be unequal in a second sense, by virtue of the different ability various individuals or groups of individuals enjoy to shape the institutional rules and norms themselves. When inequality is pervasive, the institutional order is illegitimate in the sense that there exists a right to rebel on the part of citizens. Revolution, and not simply reform, is permissible. A paradigm case of pervasive structural inequality is apartheid South Africa. Inequality can be targeted on the basis of other identities or on the basis of regional location; it can also be pervasive in a less intentionally targeted manner.

The second circumstance of transitions is what I call *normalized collective and political wrongdoing*. By wrongdoing, I mean violations of human rights. Wrongdoing is normalized in an empirical sense; it becomes a basic fact of life around which individuals must orient their conduct. The anticipation of being arrested if speaking out against the government, and the anticipation of being tortured if arrested, irrespective of whether such arrest and torture would be permissible according to declared legal rules, becomes part of what one must take into deliberation when considering whether to speak out. Wrongdoing is collective in the sense that it is characteristically carried out by groups and targets groups. It is political in two ways. First, wrongdoing is done for the sake of furthering political objectives; acquiring control of territory, maintaining a regime, or contesting a regime in power are the reasons for the commission of wrongdoing. Second, wrongdoing is committed by agents of the state or agents acting with the permission of the state or by agents contesting the state. Sexual violence and rape, disappearing of citizens, killing, and torture are some of the many forms such wrongdoing may take. It is common in transitions for categories of perpetrator and victim to overlap in many instances. Such complex victims may be victims of wrongdoing, and then go on to commit wrongdoing themselves.[11]

The third circumstance of transitional justice is what I call *serious existential uncertainty*. The subject matter of this circumstance is the basic trajectory of a political community. When that trajectory is seriously uncertain, it is profoundly unclear in what direction a community is heading. There may have been a truce signed, but it is uncertain whether the terms of the truce will be upheld and, if upheld, whether the truce will be followed by a return to violence or an extended period of calm. It is uncertain whether elections will be held as scheduled and, if held, whether results will be respected. Many attempted transitions to democracy fail; conflict or repression resumes. In the circumstance of serious existential uncertainty, it is thus objectively uncertain whether a transition attempted will ultimately be successful. The aspiration to end conflict or repression does not entail that this will in fact take place. This means subjectively it is very difficult for both members of transitional societies and international observers to know what is the most accurate narrative to tell about unfolding events.

The fourth circumstance of transitions is *fundamental uncertainty about authority*. The state is characteristically implicated in the wrongs which are now the subject of responses such as truth commissions and reparations. The basis of the authority of the state to deal with wrongs in which it is characteristically implicated must be established.

We can contrast the four circumstances of transitions articulated above with what I call the circumstances of stable democracies. These are the circumstances implicitly or explicitly assumed to be present when theorists develop accounts of retributive, corrective, or distributive justice. *Limited structural inequality* is such that while the freedom enjoyed by all individuals to do and become things of value and to shape the institutionally defined terms of interaction are unequal, the inequality does not threaten the legitimacy of the institutional order. Reform, not revolution, is needed. *Deviant individual and personal wrongdoing* is what may be called ordinary criminality. Violations of rules forbidding violations of human rights are the exception, not the rule. They are committed by individuals targeting other individuals for reasons that are personal; greed, jealousy, ambition, fear, or recklessness explain why someone committed this wrong. *Minor existential uncertainty* obtains such that the trajectory of a political community is not seriously in doubt. Where there is *narrow uncertainty about authority*, the authority of a particular individual to hold a specific office may be questioned or there may be narrow debates about which branch should deal with a given question. But the authority of the institutional order itself is not in question.

The question or problem of justice in the circumstances of transitions

Against the background of the four circumstances of transitions (pervasive structural inequality, normalized collective and political wrongdoing, serious existential uncertainty, and uncertainty about authority), I now turn to identifying the salient question or problem of justice in this context. After briefly discussing why retributive justice is not the salient notion of justice, I turn to outlining my understanding of the notion of justice that is.[12]

Using the standards of retribution as the standards by which to assess processes of transitional justice is intuitively plausible. Theories of retributive justice take up the question: what counts as a just response to perpetrators of wrongdoing? Responding to perpetrators of wrongdoing is certainly a prominent issue in contexts of transition. Despite this initial plausibility, however, there are reasons for concern with using retributive theories as guides to what justice requires in transitional contexts. According to the retributivist, perpetrators of wrongdoing deserve to suffer proportional to the culpability of the perpetrator and suffering caused to the victim. In explaining why the retributive answer to the question of the just treatment of perpetrators is the correct answer, accounts of retributive justice aim to respond to two sources of skepticism. The first is skepticism about the moral difference between the suffering wrongdoing inflicts and the suffering constitutive of punishment; here the worry is that instead of meting out justice punishment is instead inflicting an additional wrong. The second is skepticism about the state as an appropriate agent of punishment. Here the worry is that the intentional infliction of suffering by the state is incompatible with its recognition of the moral equality of all citizens; punishment is, in other words, outside the boundaries of the legitimate exercise of authority by the state. In defending the retributive answer to the question of the just treatment of perpetrators, retributivists argue that punishment is different because it has a different moral function: it aims to restore a status quo ante of equality that wrongdoing disrupted.[13] In Herbert Morris's view, punishment restores the distribution of benefits and burdens that punishment upset.[14] In Jean Hampton's view, punishment restores the moral equality between victim and perpetrator which wrongdoing upset by countering the false moral claim about the value of the victim wrongdoing expressed.[15] Implicit in both accounts is the assumption that there is a prior background situation of equality that wrongdoing as an isolated act disrupted. The state, on these views, is the appropriate agent to mete out punishment because it is an impartial agent with respect to the wrongdoing and the central representative of a community and its values.

When we shift to the circumstances of transitions, however, the retributive explanation of the justice of punishment is not compelling. The state's authority to punish cannot be assumed, but needs to be established. Insofar as a state in transition is representative of a community's values, it represents values in need of repudiation. Moreover, punishment cannot be taken to restore a prior situation of equality between perpetrator and victim which wrongdoing disrupted; there was no prior situation of equality that existed given pervasive structural inequality. Insofar as a situation of equality between victim and perpetrator is to be achieved, punishment of an individual perpetrator cannot by itself fulfill this aim, for the threat to that equality is not the function of the isolated act of one individual. Finally, and most fundamentally, responding to perpetrators of wrongdoing is at most part of the problem of justice in the circumstances of transition. Focusing exclusively on perpetrators of wrongdoing misses the broader context which enabled wrongdoing to occur in a characteristically systematic and widespread manner.

A better way of framing the question or problem of justice in the circumstances of transition is: what constitutes the just pursuit of societal transformation?[16] The first two circumstances of transitional justice (pervasive structural inequality as well as normalized collective and political wrongdoing) make transformation necessary. The third circumstance (serious existential uncertainty) makes transformation possible. Absent such serious uncertainty, there is no real prospect for changing the status quo. Serious existential uncertainty creates a situation in which a society may go in a direction different from where it was before. As I explain in greater detail below, the circumstance of normalized collective and political wrongdoing also makes it necessary to evaluate the justness of the pursuit of transformation.

What is the substantive content of the just pursuit of societal transformation? The most salient form of transformation needed is relational transformation. It is the overhauling of the terms for interaction among perpetrators, and between perpetrators and victims, among citizens and between citizens and officials, that is needed. For it is only in so doing and thereby altering how members of a transitional society interact will the aim of preventing a recurrence of conflict and repression and, with it, wrongdoing be achieved.

In my first book, *A Moral Theory of Political Reconciliation*, I develop and defend a substantive account of political reconciliation, which forms the basis of my view of societal transformation in my account of transitional justice.[17] Relational transformation, I argue, has three core components. The first is establishment and/or strengthening of the rule of law, where I follow Lon Fuller in understanding the rule of law to require ongoing cooperative action by and interaction among citizens and officials to ensure there is in fact governance of conduct on the basis of legal rules.[18] Characteristically conflict and repression weaken the rule of law, by, for example, eroding congruence between declared legal rules and their enforcement. The second component of transformation is establishing threshold conditions such that default trust of citizens and officials becomes reasonable. I conceptualize trust as an attitude of optimism about the competence and lack of ill-will of the trusted; competence is defined in a role-specific manner, relative to the duties and responsibilities associated with the role of citizen or of official. The third component is establishing threshold levels of genuine opportunities to be respected; recognized as a member of one's political community; participate in institutions; and avoid poverty.[19] These three components, I argue, articulate the institutional, attitudinal, and interpersonal conditions that must be in place for citizens and officials to interact on the basis of mutual respect for agency and reciprocity.

The question of transitional justice is not limited to societal transformation but also includes its just pursuit.[20] This is because processes of transitional justice pursue transformation via dealing with past wrongs. Those wrongs had particular victims and perpetrators. To simply pursue societal transformation in the most efficient or effective manner risks treating perpetrators and victims of wrongdoing as mere means, thereby failing to recognize the particular moral claims to which being a victim or perpetrator give rise. The "just pursuit" of transformation signals the necessity of treating victims and perpetrators in a fitting and appropriate manner. There are, I argue, a number of factors that inform judgments about whether a response is fitting and appropriate. One factor is whether it contributes to the moral aims associated with responding to victims and perpetrators, which are widely recognized in the literature on moral philosophy and on transitional justice. These aims in the cases of perpetrators include repudiating wrongdoing, holding perpetrators accountable by judging them to have been responsible for the wrong, and contributing to non-recurrence. In the case of victims, these aims include condemning wrongdoing, acknowledging the status of victims as rights bearers and as members of their political community, and providing reparation. Another factor is the relationship between the responder and respondent. Examining reactive attitudes illustrates why. Resentment is taken to be a reactive attitude it is appropriate for victims to have toward perpetrators, but not for third parties or bystanders to wrongdoing. Whereas indignation is an appropriate attitude for such parties. Also informing judgments of appropriateness is the nature of the wrong done. The protests by prisoners in Northern Ireland during the Troubles offers an example of the importance of this condition. In the blanket protest, followed by the dirty protest and hunger strike, prisoners were contesting the change of status that rendered them ordinary criminals. The protest was designed to force the government to re-recognize prisoners as political prisoners of an armed conflict who had committed political, not ordinary criminal, wrongs. Finally, the cultural context in which a response to wrongdoing is adopted is salient. Many of the central moral aims listed above are expressive in nature; acknowledgement, condemnation, and recognition fall into this category. This means it is necessary to consider what kind(s) of processes could plausibly count as expressing, for example, acknowledgement, in a given context. This last factor highlights the fact that it is a mistake to think that any single form of response is required for victims and/or perpetrators to be treated in a fitting and appropriate manner. There may be contextual variability in what responses will be fitting and appropriate, where the limits to this variability will be set by the factors listed above.

For the expressive aims of responses to wrongdoing to be achieved, and indeed for societal transformation itself to be facilitated by transitional justice processes, it is necessary that the design, implementation, and then subsequent evaluation of such processes be holistic.[21] By holistic I mean that processes should be designed and implemented jointly or as a package, rather than approaching the process of dealing with past wrongs in a piecemeal fashion. In transitions, the expressive meaning of a particular response is impacted by what else does or does not occur in a particular transitional context. This is because processes for dealing with past wrongs face risks in transitional contexts that are not present in the same way in the circumstances of stable democracies.[22] Specifically, any process for dealing with past wrongs risks failing to be seen as and thereby serving as an instrument of justice. Trials risk being seen as "victor's justice," reparations as "blood money," and truth commissions as mere words. When seen in these ways, processes not only fail to treat victims and perpetrators appropriately, but they also fail to contribute in any meaningful sense to relational transformation and can serve instead to further entrench extant relational patterns. Countering these risks and establishing that processes are processes of *justice*, requires enacting not a single but a set of processes jointly undertaken to deal with past wrongs. Together, these processes can underscore that the truth is not mere words but words that will be used in ways that will facilitate transformation and will provide the basis for offering reparations to those harmed.[23]

One final comment about my account of transitional justice is worth highlighting before turning to the specific case of Colombia. I conceptualize the relationship between the requirements of societal transformation and the requirements to treat perpetrators and victims of wrongdoing appropriately as structurally analogous to the relationship between the two parts of just war theory. Just war theory is standardly taken to comprise two sets of moral requirements. The first set of requirements, *jus ad bellum*, specifies the conditions that must be satisfied for war to be permissibly undertaken. These conditions include acting for a legitimate reason (e.g., self-defense) and with legitimate authority. The second set of requirements, *jus in bello*, specify the constraints that must be respected during the conduct of war itself. Importantly, noncombatants may not be intentionally targeted in conflict. War can fail to be just in two ways, by being undertaken illegitimately and/or by being conducted in ways that violate the *jus in bello* constraints. Analogously, I see the requirements of societal transformation are the overarching reason for the sake of which transitional justice processes are undertaken. But the demands of fitting and appropriate treatment of perpetrators and victims constrain how that transformation may be permissibly pursued. Thus, just like with war, processes of transitional justice may fail to be just in one of two ways: by failing to contribute to societal transformation or by failing to treat victims and perpetrators in a fitting and appropriate manner.

Application to Colombia

My account of transitional justice aims to provide an articulation of the considerations that are salient from the perspective of justice when evaluating choices about transitional justice processes in a specific context. It also provides the considerations to appeal to when defending or critiquing the justice of choices made. To apply my framework to Colombia, it is first necessary to establish that the circumstances of transitional justice obtain. For it is only with the presence of the four circumstances of transitional justice that the problem of transitional justice, as I articulate it, is salient and the principles of transitional justice provide a normative guide.

The four circumstances of transitional justice are I believe satisfied in the current context of Colombia. There is first pervasive structural inequality. Indeed, one of the sources of the ongoing conflict over the past five decades is the differential life prospects and ability to shape terms of interaction among those who live in rural areas and those who live in the urban centers. This divide can also be seen as tracking racial divisions among more indigenous populations and non-indigenous groups.[24]

Second, Colombia has had normalized collective and political wrongdoing. This is evidenced by the statistics listed in the first part of this chapter on the numbers of individuals displaced, killed, taken as hostage, disappeared, subject to rape or other forms of sexual violence, and/or tortured. The structure of the JEP is predicated on the political nature of at least a significant portion of these cases, and eligibility for participation in the JEP tracks membership as a state actor or as a member of the group contesting the state's authority. A significant portion of the Colombian population was direct victims of the conflict, but all Colombians were indirectly affected by knowing someone who was such a victim. Thus, anticipation of the kinds of wrongs now subject to the transitional justice process became a basic fact of life around which conduct needed to be oriented. Many cases are cases of complex victims.

There is currently significant uncertainty as to the long-term prospects of success for the peace process itself. There is hope and optimism that the Final Agreement is in fact final. There has been progress on the implementation of legislation needed to realize the processes and commitments articulated in the Agreement itself. At the same time, there remains opposition to the Final Agreement both among politicians and among the general public. And acts of violence threaten to undermine the progress made.[25]

Finally, authority comes into question in different ways. One way is in terms of legitimacy of the Colombian government adjudicating wrongs in which agents of the state are implicated in certain cases. Another way is in terms of the legitimacy of members of the post-FARC party who are implicated in wrongdoing serving in official roles, which has also been challenged as at least some of the quotations in the first part of this chapter indicate.

Because the four circumstances of transition are satisfied in the Colombian case, the standards by which we ought to assess the transitional justice processes established are the standards set by the just pursuit of societal transformation. It is thus a mistake to claim, as the first set of claims considered in Part I did, that justice necessarily requires punishment of perpetrators of wrongdoing. It is also a mistake, as some quotes in the second set of views claimed, to conceptualize the Final Agreement as a compromise between peace and justice. Insofar as compromises may be necessary, they will not be compromises between peace and justice. For the societal transformation being sought is itself a form of peace, positive in nature, and by facilitating it processes also facilitate justice. Compromises may be necessary, but such compromises will be between satisfaction of the requirements of societal transformation and the requirements of the fitting and appropriate treatment of perpetrators and victims. Or there may be compromises between transitional justice as an important goal or aim of such processes and other aims that are salient for Colombian society.

How does the Final Agreement fare when evaluated from the perspective of the demands of societal transformation and the demands of fitting and appropriate treatment of both perpetrators and victims? There are reasons to believe it establishes conditions that, if implemented, will meaningfully contribute to the just pursuit of societal transformation. First, the commitment to rural development, to the reintegration of former FARC combatants, and to political participation on the part of the post-FARC party indicate recognition of the necessity of countering the structural inequality that underpinned and was a source of the conflict itself.

Second, these commitments are combined with a comprehensive set of processes for dealing with past wrongdoing. The comprehensiveness of the set (including a truth commission, reparations, criminal trials, and a unit focused on those disappeared) jointly bolster the expressive function each process individually may have. That is, they jointly counter at least in their structure the risk of failing to be and to be seen as instruments of justice. Reparations can less plausibly be claimed as "blood money" to silence victims given that the JEP and the truth commission will be operating as well. In other words, the propensity of such processes to express meaningful acknowledgement of victims, robust condemnation of wrongdoing committed on all sides, and recognition of victims as rights bearers is strengthened by the holistic manner in which wrongdoing is treated. In terms of perpetrators, processes satisfy the constraints of the just pursuit of transformation if they can be said to hold perpetrators accountable, by judging them responsible for wrongdoing and ideally encouraging perpetrators to accept responsibility and make reparations. The JEP is predicated on judging the actions under its mandate as wrong and through the structure of its operation aims to incentivize perpetrators to explicitly acknowledge and accept responsibility for their actions and, in the case of the restricted zones of liberty, engage in acts of reparation. It also includes accountability in the form of criminal punishment for those convicted who confess late in the process or not at all.

Insofar as processes for dealing with past wrongs can express the moral objectives associated with the fitting and appropriate treatment of perpetrators and victims, they are more likely to facilitate broader transformation by underscoring the commitment to non-repetition and by reducing serious existential uncertainty. In contexts of serious uncertainty, processes that may not otherwise have broader significance for the trajectory of a community can come to assume such significance as citizens and observers seek tangible signs of where a community is heading. By underscoring a commitment to deal with past wrongdoing and the underlying sources of the conflict, the components of the Final Agreement, if implemented as envisioned, could meaningfully contribute to broader relational change.

The Final Agreement is a document with a moral vision for transformative change for Colombia. The Constitutional Court unanimously ruled on October 11, 2017 that the Final Agreement has normative force and together with international law will inform interpretations of laws passed to implement the Final Agreement.[26] The process of implementing the Colombian Final Agreement and passing the multiple constitutional amendments needed for this purpose are ongoing.

That there are constitutional implications of transitional justice is not surprising. As the Greek philosopher Aristotle noted more than 2,000 years ago, constitutions reflect the basic conception of justice ordering a political community.[27] Insofar as the ordering of a political community reflects—in part or as a whole—a conception of justice that is indefensible, constitutional change will be necessary. More specifically and drawing on the account in part II, transitional justice requires transformation in the terms structuring interaction among citizens and between citizens and officials. Constitutions articulate the structure of government, the scope of the legitimate exercise of power by government officials, and the basic rights and claims of citizens. Constitutionally recognized rights set basic parameters for the rights and duties of citizens and officials, the process through which a citizen can become a public official in some capacity, and the limits on a government's authority. Thus, transitional justice will have constitutional implications, because constitutions provide a primary architecture of the relationships in need of transformation.

The language of transformation might suggest that following a transition there will be a comprehensive rejection of an old constitution and immediate establishment of a new constitution that creates a fundamentally different framework for governance and for relational possibilities within a political community. However, in fact not every transition leads to a new constitution. Moreover, constitutional changes are often gradual and occur over an extended period of time.[28] What is true in the case of constitutions is true for other dimensions of transformation as well. Transformation of political relationships requires, for example, cultivating the conditions under which trust among citizens who have historically been divided and among citizens and officials when such trust is absent. Such conditions and their influence on the attitudes taken toward fellow members of a political community cannot arise immediately, but attitudes will only change, if they do change, over time. As I wrote in the conclusion of my book on political reconciliation, "Rebuilding political relationships in the aftermath of civil conflict and repressive rule is enormously complicated and difficult, given the comprehensive and often extraordinary changes demanded of political relationships in transitional contexts. Few transitional societies will be able to achieve the required changes in political relationships immediately, or even in a short-term period, following a transition to democratic governance; very likely the process of reconciliation will occur over an extended period of time. In some contexts, the achievement of more than minimal reconciliation may not be possible. Thus, as a corrective to current discussions, my analysis suggests that discourse about political reconciliation be framed more explicitly in terms of degrees of achievement and the promotion of specific kinds of repair, remaining ever mindful of the damage that remains to be addressed and of the long road to rebuilding political relationships that characteristically remains ahead."[29]

The constitutional implications of the pursuit of the transformation of political relationships in Colombia will exist for some time; this is true even if the pace of amendments at the present time is increased through the fast-track option. In recognition of the constitutional implications of the Final Agreement and out of a concern to avoid undue delay in or potentially negatively impact the political will needed for the implementation of the Final Agreement, Congress passed a constitutional amendment, which the Constitutional Court upheld, that establishes a "fast-track" process for the passage of constitutional amendments bound up with the implementation of the Final Agreement. This process reduced the procedural requirements and constrained the parameters of permitted Congressional alteration of proposed amendments, enabling a more rapid implementation of the Final Agreement.[30]

Given the long-term, temporal dimension of transitional justice, there are reasons for caution in any evaluation of the justice of the Final Agreement. One reason is that it is early in the transitional process in Colombia. Whether the processes outlined in the Final Agreement achieve their potential aims will be affected by whether and how the processes are implemented. The full implementation of the Final Agreement in turn requires ongoing political will. At the time of writing, there are reasons to worry as to whether the requisite political will is going to be maintained in the long-term. Failure to contribute to rural reform or failure to offer meaningful reparations can and will in turn negatively impact the justice that the Final Agreement realizes. Current Colombian President Iván Duque, whose campaign platform included opposition to the terms of the Final Agreement especially concerning the JEP, recently defunded the truth commission and is currently seeking other changes to the structure of the JEP.[31] How significant the impact on the implementation of the Final Agreement Duque's efforts and other challenges to the Final Agreement will remain to be seen.

Conclusion

This chapter has evaluated the justice of the Colombian Final Agreement, arguing that its provisions as laid out satisfy the requirements of transitional justice, though for that justice to be realized the terms of the Final Agreement must be implemented. I emphasized the temporal dimension of the pursuit of transitional justice. In the comprehensiveness of its vision, the Final Agreement provides a model for other contexts in which context resolution is being pursued. The Final Agreement demonstrates how it is possible to craft an agreement ending conflict that both addresses the root causes of conflict as well as more specific human rights violations that were committed during the course of conflict. The Colombian experience also illustrates the gap that can develop and often exists between the aspirations of an agreement to end conflict and the reality of what those charged with realizing those aspirations are willing and able to achieve. The signing of an agreement is only the beginning of a very long road to the actual achievement of justice.

Author's note

Earlier versions of this chapter were presented at McMaster University as part of conference on "Global Perspectives on Peace: The Colombian Peace Process with FARC" organized by Jorge Fabra-Zamora, Nancy Doubleday, and Andrés Molina-Ochoa, the Melbourne University Law School Legal Theory Workshop, and the 2019 academic conference of the Colombian Constitutional Court on the "Colombian Constitutional Court in a global perspective." I am grateful for the feedback provided in these venues. I also thank Sebastián Machado, Lulu Weis, and Carlos Bernal-Pulido for their feedback on previous drafts. This chapter draws on Colleen Murphy, "Judging the Justice of the Colombian Final Agreement," in Alejandro Linares-Cantillo, Camilo Valdivieso, and Santiago García Jaramillo (ed.), *Constitutionalism: old dilemmas, new insights* (Oxford University Press, 2021).

Notes

1 Colleen Murphy, *The Conceptual Foundations of Transitional Justice* (New York: Cambridge University Press, 2017).
2 Another related subject for moral evaluation could focus on the process by which the Final Agreement was designed. I restrict my focus here to the evaluation of the terms outlined in the Final Agreement itself.
3 Numerous analyses following the failed plebiscite tried to explain the unanticipated outcome, pointing to factors like the weather that may have influenced turnout as well as lack of information that could have shaped the manner in which individuals voted. However, such explanations are not relevant for my purposes in this chapter.
4 Amnesty International, 2016/2017, Annual Report for Colombia, https://www.amnesty.org/en/countries/americas/colombia/report-colombia/ (accessed August 17, 2017).
5 Ariaan Alsema, "Colombia creates historic Truth Commission," *Colombia Reports*, April 5, 2017, https://colombiareports.com/colombia-creates-historic-truth-commission/.

6 However, it is not clear whether they could serve concurrently with any sentence or only after a sentence is complete.
7 Isabella Flisi, "The Reintegration of Former Combatants in Colombia," *Sustainable Security*, February 13, 2017, https://sustainablesecurity.org/2017/02/13/the-reintegration-of-former-combatants-in-colombia/.
8 "Colombians divided on failed referendum: 'We need to move forward,'" *The Guardian,* October, 4, 2016, https://www.theguardian.com/world/2016/oct/04/colombia-farc-peace-deal-plebicite-readers-reaction.
9 Colleen Murphy, *The Conceptual Foundations of Transitional Justice* (New York: Cambridge University Press, 2017). For discussions of Hume on the circumstances of transitional justice, see David Hume, *A Treatise of Human Nature*, ed. L.A. Selby-Bigge, 2nd. ed. (Oxford: Oxford University Press, 1739/1978); David Hume, *An Enquiry Concerning the Principles of Morals*, ed. Tom L. Beauchamp (Oxford: Oxford University Press, 1751/1998).
10 These four circumstances are discussed at length in Chapter 1 of *The Conceptual Foundations of Transitional Justice.*
11 I take the label of complex victims from Luke Moffett. See his "Reparations for 'Guilty' Victims: Navigating Complex Identities of Victim–Perpetrators in Reparation Mechanisms," *International Journal of Transitional Justice*, https://doi.org/10.1093/ijtj/ijv030.
12 The argument against retributive, corrective, and distributive justice as the salient notion of justice and the argument for my own positive account of the question of transitional justice is in Chapter 2 of *The Conceptual Foundations of Transitional Justice.*
13 Some retributivists, such as Michael Moore, believe the core retributive principle is a bedrock moral intuition not requiring an argument in its defense. However, in the circumstances of transitional justice there is disagreement about whether justice does require punishment, and so an argument in defense of retributivism is necessary. As the quotations from Section 1 highlight, there are conflicting intuitions about what justice requires.
14 Herbert Morris, "Guilt and Suffering," *Philosophy East and West*, vol. 21 (4), 1971, pp. 419–34.
15 Jean Hampton, "Correcting Harms Versus Righting Wrongs: The Goal of Retribution," *UCLA Law Review*, vol. 39, 1992, pp. 1659–1702.
16 The language of transformation is increasingly prominent in the literature on transitional justice.
17 Colleen Murphy, *A Moral Theory of Political Reconciliation* (New York: Cambridge University Press, 2010). Reconciliation is generally understood to be the process of repairing damaged relationships. I discuss transformation specifically in Chapter 3 of *The Conceptual Foundations of Transitional Justice.*
18 See Lon Fuller, *The Morality of Law*, rev. ed. (New Haven, CT: Yale University Press, 1969).
19 I understand "genuine opportunities" in the sense of capability. The presence or absence of such opportunities is a function of what individuals have (e.g., resources, knowledge, skills) and what they can do with what they have (e.g., given the institutional structure).
20 I discuss the just pursuit of transformation in Chapter 4 of *The Conceptual Foundations of Transitional Justice.*
21 I discuss this point in detail in Chapter 4 of *The Conceptual Foundations of Transitional Justice.*
22 On this point see Pablo de Greiff, "Theorizing Transitional Justice," in Melissa S. Williams, Rosemary Nagy, and Jon Elster (eds.), *NOMOS LI: Transitional Justice* (New York: New York University Press, 2012) 31–77.

23 The important work being done by social scientists in understanding the societal impact of different combinations of processes can prove invaluable in understanding what set of mechanisms is likely to contribute to transitional justice. See, for example, Hugo Van der Merwe, Victoria Baxter, and Audrey Chapman, *Assessing the Impact of Transitional Justice: Challenges for Empirical Research* (Washington DC: United States Institute of Peace Press, 2009); Tricia D. Olsen, Leigh A. Payne, and Andrew G. Reiter, *Transitional Justice in Balance: Comparing Processes, Weighing Efficacy* (Washington CD: United States Institute of Peace, 2010).

24 Joel Gillin, "Understanding the causes of Colombia's conflict: Inequality," *Colombia Reports,* January 7, 2015, https://colombiareports.com/understanding-colombias-conflict-inequality/.

25 Cristobal Vásquez, "The Hardest Part is yet to Come for Colombia's Peace Agreement," *World Policy Blog,* March 7, 2017, http://www.worldpolicy.org/blog/2017/03/07/hardest-part-yet-come-colombia's-peace-agreement.

26 Gonzalo Ramírez-Cleves, "The Colombian Constitutional Court Rules that the Peace Agreement is Mandatory for Three Presidential Terms," *I-Connect,* October 27, 2017, http://www.iconnectblog.com/2017/10/the-colombian-constitutional-court-rules-that-the-peace-agreement-is-mandatory-for-three-presidential-terms/.

27 Aristotle, *Nicomachean Ethics,* trans. Terence Irwin, 2nd ed. (Indianapolis: Hackett Publishing, 1999) at V.1.1129b11–19; Aristotle, *The Politics,* trans. T.A. Sinclair, rev. ed. (New York: Penguin Classics, 1981) at III.12.1282b16–17.

28 Ruti Teitel, *Transitional Justice* (New York: Oxford University Press, 2002) 201.

29 Murphy, *A Moral Theory*, p. 192.

30 Gonzalo Ramírez-Cleves, "The Colombian Constitutional Court"; http://es.presidencia.gov.co/normativa/normativa/ACTO%20LEGISLATIVO%2001%20DEL%207%20DE%20JULIO%20DE%202016.pdf.

31 Adriaan Alsema, "Duque defunds Colombia's Truth Commission," *Colombia Reports,* February 20, 2019, https://colombiareports.com/duque-defunds-colombias-truth-commission/; Julia Symmes Cobb and Luis Jaime Acosta, "Colombia court says cannot yet rule on possible changes to peace law," *Reuters,* March 20, 2019, https://www.reuters.com/article/us-colombia-peace/colombia-court-says-cannot-yet-rule-on-possible-changes-to-peace-law-idUSKCN1R12TF.

Part IV

Key components of the Final Agreement

10 The Special Jurisdiction for Peace

Main features and legal challenges

Danilo Rojas Betancourth

Introduction

The fifth chapter of the Final Agreement signed between the Colombian Government and Revolutionary Armed Forces of Colombia (FARC), which concerns the victims of the armed conflict, creates the Comprehensive System of Truth, Justice, Reparation, and Non-Repetition (thereafter, Comprehensive System). A central element of this System is the Special Jurisdiction for Peace (*Jurisdicción Especial para la Paz,* henceforth, JEP) which is in charge of, *inter alia*, judging combatants and non-combatants for conduct that occurred during the conflict through the Tribunal for Peace (*Tribunal para la paz*). This chapter discusses only the legal challenges faced by the JEP in the application of its novel model of transitional, restorative, forward-looking, and reparative justice.

The argument proceeds as follows. The first section describes the main features of the JEP and the second section discusses three main legal challenges faced by it. Among these challenges is the creation of a *Corpus Juris* of Human Rights and International Humanitarian Law (IHL); overcoming this challenge, however, provides the key to resolving the other two. The concluding section highlights some aspects concerning ongoing debates about the JEP and some possible lessons for other peace processes.

The Special Jurisdiction for Peace

This section presents the main features of the JEP, along with its competence, structure, functioning, and sanctions regime. Lastly, I briefly introduce some central elements of its operation.[1]

Central features

The JEP is perhaps the central institution of the Comprehensive System developed by the Final Agreement to address the rights of victims to truth, justice, reparation, and non-repetition. Its structure and functions were incorporated into the Constitution through Legislative Act 1 of 2017.[2]

It was statutorily regulated by Laws 1957 of 2019 and 1922 of 2018. The first of the two pieces of legislation is a "statutory law" (*ley estatutaria*), namely legislation on matters of constitutional rights and thereby of a higher place in the normative hierarchy and subject to special safeguards.

Four institutions compose the Comprehensive System, namely: the JEP; the Commission for the Clarification of Truth, Co-Existence, and Non-Repetition; the Unit of the Search for Persons Presumed Disappeared in the context of and by reason of the Armed Conflict; and the measures for comprehensive reparation and guarantees of non-repetition.[3] While the Truth Commission and the Search Unit are non-judicial institutions, the JEP has a judicial character.

Competence

The JEP was created to administer justice transitorily,[4] autonomously, prevalently, primarily, and exclusively regarding actions committed before December 1, 2016 "caused by, on the occasion of, or in direct relation with the armed conflict,"[5] especially serious IHL infractions and human rights violations.

The JEP shall judge Former FARC-EP combatants who signed the Final Agreement. It shall also judge former combatants who have been investigated, processed, or condemned for belonging to the FARC-EP, before the aforementioned date, even if they are not included in the list of signatories to the Final Agreement.[6]

Similarly, third parties (i.e., persons who were not part of armed organizations but contributed "directly or indirectly" to conflict-related crimes[7]) may likewise have recourse to the JEP, or be called upon by JEP organisms. State agents, including members of the Public Forces,[8] "who may have committed crimes in the context and by reason of the armed conflict," shall also be judged by the JEP. These agents will receive "differential treatment," namely one that is "equitable, balanced, simultaneous, and symmetrical" and acknowledges their status as guarantors of law.[9]

The JEP can also study the situation of people involved in actions committed in the context of social protest and internal disturbances.

Former Presidents of the Republic are excluded from the JEP. Thus, the investigation, judging, and sanctioning of their possible crimes remains ruled by constitutionally granted immunities.

Structure

The JEP has 38 justices divided into three Justice Chambers and the Tribunal for Peace. It also has a Unit for Investigation and Prosecution, and an Executive Secretariat.

The three Chambers, with six justices each, are the activation mechanisms of the Jurisdiction. These are:

1. A Chamber for Acknowledgment of Truth, Responsibility, and Determination of Fact and Conducts (henceforth, Chamber for Acknowledgment). This Chamber decides whether a certain fact of conduct was caused by, on the occasion of, or in direct relation with the armed conflict, and thereby lies within the JEP's competence. It also receives and analyzes reports on conflict-related facts from state institutions, and social and victims' organizations; opens cases on the most serious and representative crimes based on selection and prioritization criteria; receives individual and collective testimonies; convenes hearings for the acknowledgment of responsibility; and submits the resolutions of conclusions to prioritized cases to the Tribunal for Peace.[10]
2. A Chamber for Amnesty or Pardons that, as its name indicates, grants amnesties or pardons for eligible crimes. This Chamber also grants temporary and conditional freedom to former FARC-EP members appearing before the JEP and remits them to the Chamber of Acknowledgment. In turn, it also applies special legal treatment (mentioned below) to those referred by the Chamber of Acknowledgment.[11]
3. A Chamber of Definition of Legal Situations that decides cases of third parties and members of Armed Forces that were not prioritized by the Chamber of Acknowledgment.[12]

The Tribunal for Peace, the JEP's last and supreme instance, is in turn divided into four sections of five justices each, namely:[13]

1. First-Instance Section for the Acknowledgment of Truth and Responsibility of Facts and Conducts that will conduct "dialogical trials," issue judgments, and impose the special sanctions defined below on those defendants who acknowledge responsibility and contribute to truth.
2. First-Instance Section for the Absence of Acknowledgment of Truth and Responsibility of Facts and Conducts that will conduct "adversarial trials" and issue judgments on those defendants who fail to acknowledge responsibility and contribute to truth. When the defendant is guilty, it will impose ordinary or alternative sanctions.
3. Section for Review of Judgments that will exceptionally review, upon request, decisions of the ordinary justice system which are subject to JEP competence. It also decides constitutional writs of protection of constitutional rights (*tutelas*), studies requests for non-extradition guarantees established in the Final Agreement, and resolves conflicts of competence.
4. The Appeal Section is the Final Instance of the Tribunal for Peace. It decides on requests to revoke, confirm, or modify the judgments and decisions of the Judicial Chambers and Sections.
5. When the Tribunal for Peace ceases to function, it will establish a new Section to guarantee the efficacy of, and compliance with, JEP's decisions and judgments.

The Investigation and Prosecution Unit is in charge of investigating and carrying out criminal prosecutions when the alleged individual or collective perpetrator of violations of human rights or breaches of IHL does not acknowledge truth or responsibility. The Unit has the function of judicial police, and is in charge of the prosecution of atrocious crimes advanced in the different Judicial Chambers and Sections of the JEP.[14]

The Executive Secretary manages the administrative, economic, and financial aspects of the JEP. It also has some influence on procedure, for it receives statements from perpetrators who want to appear before the JEP.[15]

Procedure and sanctions regime

There are two main procedures in the JEP, one in the case of acknowledgment of truth and responsibility, and another in cases where this recognition is absent. Both begin in the Chamber for Acknowledgment; the Chamber determines admissibility to the Jurisdiction and determines to which Chamber or Section the case must be referred.

The sanctioning regime imposed by the JEP mirrors this responsibility-driven logical structure and includes three types of sanctions, as follows:

1 *Special Sanctions* (*sanciones propias*) apply to those who fully acknowledge truth and responsibility from the beginning of the proceedings, as verified by the Tribunal for Peace's First-Instance Section for Acknowledgment. They consist of restorative sanctions that aim to redress the harms caused to victims. The special sanctions include effective restrictions on liberty, with no prison time, of between five and eight years for those who directly participated in the crime, and between two and five years for those who participated indirectly in it.
2 *Alternative Sanctions* apply to those who belatedly recognize truth and responsibility, i.e. those who recognize truth before a judgment is issued. They consist of five to eight years of prison time.
3 *Ordinary Sanctions* apply to those who fail to acknowledge truth and responsibility and are found guilty by the Tribunal for Peace's First-Instance Section for the Absence of Acknowledgment of Truth. They consist of sentences between 15 and 20 years in prison.

To maintain their special benefits, any person who submits to the JEP must comply with a "conditionality regime," namely they must contribute to truth and the reparation of victims, they must commit to not repeating their crimes, and to participating in the Comprehensive System when called.

Here, we adumbrate four main features of the sanctions regime.

a Most importantly, sanctions are aimed at restoration and reparation, thereby forward-looking justice (*justice prospectiva*), not at backward-looking retributive considerations. As stated in the constitutional amendment that created JEP, "restorative justice chiefly attends the needs and dignity of victims, and it is applied with a comprehensive approach to guarantee justice, truth, and non-repetition."[16]

b Those who are subject to JEP's special sanctions are not disqualified from participating in elections and holding public offices.

c Former FARC-EP members cannot be extradited for crimes committed before the signature of the Final Agreement (or guarantee of non-extradition).

d State agents that appear before JEP cannot be declared personally liable according to the mechanisms of Article 90 of the Colombian Constitution.

The JEP's operation

Most of the JEP's Justices took oath on January 15, 2018. Of the 38 judges sitting on JEP, 20 are women, four come from indigenous communities, and four are Afro-Colombian. The Jurisdiction started to operate on March 15, 2018. During the first year of operation, the Congress passed the necessary legislation, which was reviewed and approved by the Constitutional Court. During this time, the JEP instituted its internal rules.

The JEP selects and prioritizes cases for investigation, judgment, and sanction based on the severity of the crimes, their representativeness, the differential character of victims, the characteristics of the perpetrators, and the availability of evidence.[17] As of July 2020, the JEP has opened seven macro-cases. Case 001 focuses on wrongful detentions committed by FARC-EP. In Cases 002, 004, and 005, JEP has prioritized the study of the situation of some municipalities severely affected by the conflict. These are Tumaco, Ricaurte y Barbacoas (002), the ten municipalities of the Urabá Region in Antioquia and Chocó (004), and eight municipalities of Northern Cauca (Case 005). Case 003 focuses on the deaths wrongfully presented as killed in combat by state agents, commonly known as "false positives." Case 006 concerns the victimization of the Patriotic Union-UP (Unión Patriótica-UP), a political party formed in 1984 following the agreement between the FARC-EP and the Government of Belisario Betancur, and whose members were systematically persecuted and murdered during the 1980s and 1990s. Case 007 studies the recruitment of boys and girls in the Colombian armed conflict.

By July 2020, 12,554 people have appeared before JEP. These include 9,756 former FARC combatants, 2,686 members of the Public Forces, 1,000 State agents other than Public Forces (including former members of the Colombian Congress), and 12 cases for social protest. At this moment, JEP is studying petitions from 916 third parties and state agents different from the Public Forces who wish to appear before JEP.

The legal challenges

Among the numerous political, social, economic, and administrative challenges faced by the JEP, I shall focus here on the legal ones, namely those that involve the interpretation and application of national and international norms in the adjudication of specific cases. In my view, JEP faces three main challenges: (1) its collaboration and concord with the work of permanent judicial institutions, (2) the clarification of central open-textured provisions, and (3), most importantly, the consolidation and application of a *Corpus Juris* of Human Rights and IHL. With a moderate optimism, I shall argue that many of the JEP's adjudicative challenges can be framed and addressed if it can create, consolidate, interpret, and apply that Corpus.

The relationships between transitional and permanent judicial institutions

Before the establishment of JEP, several permanent national and international institutions had been in charge of the investigation, judgment, and sanctioning of those responsible for human rights violations and infractions of IHL and providing remedies to victims of the Colombian armed conflict. These include, at the national level, the judicial institutions of the criminal, military, disciplinary, and administrative specialties, as well as decisions of some administrative institutions such as the Offices of the Inspector (*Procurador*) General and Comptroller (*Contralor*) General. At the international level, there is also an array of regional and universal bodies in charge of the authoritative application of human rights, IHL and international criminal law. The JEP's first challenge is to articulate its activity as a transitional, temporary judicial institution with the work of national and international permanent institutions.

This co-operative work is evident in some recent interpretative judgments about the norms that regulate the relationships between JEP and judgments of national criminal justice. While it is possible that JEP can review decisions of ordinary criminal justice, this does not mean that JEP are free to ignore them as if they never happened. In the words of the Appeal Section, "JEP are not make a *tabula rasa* from judgments of ordinary criminal justice"; but rather it must analyze if whether those decisions cohere with the criteria that JEP established, or if there are novel facts or legal considerations that are to be taken into account.[18]

There are also other particular exercises of inter-jurisdictional articulation with the indigenous jurisdiction[19] and authorities of ethnic communities, such as Afro-Colombian. In those cases, JEP need to make consultations with the corresponding communities when (i) victims are ethnic collectives such as indigenous or Afro-Colombians, (ii) the defendant or the victim are members of such collectives, or (iii) when the crime has been committed within the territorial jurisdictions of such groups.[20] However, as I argue below, the interaction between transitional and permanent justices is most evident in the creation of the *Corpus Juris of Human Rights and IHL.*

The clarification of open-textured provisions

The correct operation of JEP in accordance with national and international standards demands the clarification of some foundational provisions. These include those related to JEP's competence and some contested foundational terms of the Agreement, such as "effective command and control" and "in direct or indirect relationship" with the conflict. I will briefly sketch these challenges.

According to its *competence* rules, the JEP's special regime applies to those crimes committed *before* December 1, 2016. There are some puzzles about this provision, for example:

a The criminal responsibility for lasting or continued crimes, such as forced displacement or forced disappearance. JEP remains competent for lasting or continued crimes whose effect remains after the signature of the Agreement (November 24, 2016) but it cannot apply special and alternative sanctions if the relevant conditions do not apply.

b The remand of cases involving FARC members who have not signed the Agreement. Two examples illustrate this problem. One is the case of Carlos Carvajal Torres, alias *Alexander Mojoso,* who was not in the list of signatories to the Agreement but surrendered in March 2017 and was recognized by FARC as one of its members. The second corresponds to 117 militia members who claim to be FARC members, but who were not recognized by FARC as their members.

c The assessment of cases of "recurrence" (*reincidencia*) of criminal conduct that lead to exclusion from JEP and its benefits. For example, a group of dissidents who issued a public call to arms—including former negotiator Luciano Marín Arango (alias *Iván Márquez*) and former commanders Henry Castellanos (alias *Romaña*) and José Manuel Sierra Sagobal (alias *Zarco Aldinever)*—were excluded from the JEP.[21]

d Finally, guarantees of non-extradition demand a careful examination of the moment at which the conduct took place, and only those committed before the signature of the Agreement are protected by the guarantee. The most representative example is that of Seuxis Pausias Hernández Solarte, alias *Jesús Santrich*, whose extradition was requested by the US for allegedly helping to smuggle a large quantity of cocaine into the United States. The Section of Review of Judgments initially conceded the guarantee of non-extradition since there was insufficient evidence about the conduct and time it was committed.[22] However, since Hernández Solarte rearmed with *Iván Márquez* and other dissidents, he was subsequently excluded from the JEP's competence and benefits, including those of non-extradition.[23]

A second host of critical puzzles concerns the *determination of a conflict-related conduct.* As stated above, JEP is competent to investigate, and judge conducts "caused by, on the occasion of, or in direct relation with the armed conflict." Despite appearances, it might be challenging to determine whether certain conduct has a *direct* relationship with the conflict in a specific case. In the international experience, for example, the International Criminal Tribunal for the former Yugoslavia had to create standards to distinguish the armed conflict from other acts, such as banditry, unorganized, and short-lived insurrections, or terrorist activities.[24] To do that, the Court evaluated the intensity of the conflict and nature of the organization of the parties involved,[25] emphasizing that the Rome Statute refers to prolonged armed conflicts among armed groups able to plan and carry out military operations that extend throughout time.[26] In Colombia, similar criteria were used by the Decisions of the "Justice and Peace" Tribunals to assess the conduct of former demobilized paramilitary forces in the light of IHL, by acknowledging the existence of an armed conflict in terms of the Additional Protocol II of the Geneva Convention. These disputes have already appeared in the JEP. For example, there was controversy about the competent judge for extrajudicial executions, or "false positives." While some organizations claimed that they were not conflict-related crimes, and thereby should be judged by ordinary justice, many judges declared themselves not competent to decide these cases and submitted them to JEP. The issue was settled when Case 003 was opened, and false positives were categorized as conflict-related conducts.[27]

For related reasons, third, cases that involve *indirect relationships with the conflict* are also controversial. Such an expression appears not only in the definition of the JEP's competence as noted above but also in more specific situations. For example, JEP can revise some administrative decisions of the Inspector General and Comptroller General if they have at "least an indirect relationship" with the conflict. Similarly, third parties can appear before JEP and state agents might get special treatment if their crimes have a direct or indirect relationship with the conflict. In this aspect, little can be learned from the experience of international tribunals, which has been primarily focused on judging direct participants of specific crimes, such as war crimes, genocide, and crimes against humanities. However, in internal protected, violent, multi-causal conflict such as the Colombian, there are numerous ordinary crimes that might have direct or indirect relationships for conflict, and, as a result, the JEP has to create novel constructs to resolve these issues. One notable example concern the case of former Congressman Álvaro Asthon Giraldo, who attempted to bribe Supreme Court justice (i.e., in principle, an ordinary crime) to prevent criminal investigations for conflict-related crimes (Ahston's support and alliances with paramilitary groups, which in return, supported his congressional campaign). The JEP's Appeal Section declared that bribery (cohecho, according to the Colombian criminal code) was an ordinary crime which nonetheless had an indirect relationship to the conflict, for its intention was to cover up criminal alliances between politicians, businessmen, and paramilitaries in the North of the country.[28]

A fourth set of puzzles concerns the clarification of *active or determining involvement* in conflict-related crimes. For example, while third parties can appear voluntarily before JEP, the Jurisdiction remains competent to investigate those who had an "active or determining" involvement in genocide, war crimes, and crimes against humanity. The same provision defines "active or determining" involvement as "effective and decisive actions to the commission of the crime." Similarly, state agents can appear before JEP if they have a "non-determining" involvement of state agents and members of public forces in the commission of some crimes.[29] It remains open how these terms should be precisely understood and applied, particularly the clarification of active involvement in terms of decisive and effective action. Here, it is also worth mentioning the problem created by FARC "supporters" (*colaboradores*), which can also be judged by JEP per the Final Agreement and related norms. However, in practice, it has been proven difficult to determine who can count as support. As a result, the JEP has determined two categories of supporters: subordinates and non-subordinates.[30] The former are those who respond voluntarily, consciously, and frequently to orders of FARC's leaders; whereas the latter do not follow the orders of the armed group's leaders, but they act for their own benefit or those a third party different from the former guerrilla, or because they collaborate with FARC as a result of pressure, coercion, or intimidation. This conceptual distinction has significant practical importance concerning the benefits: subordinate collaborators are treated as combatants, while the non-subordinate ones are considered as third parties.

A final contested point is the application of *command responsibility*, i.e. the attribution of criminal responsibility to higher-ranking members of military forces for crimes and violations of human rights and IHL committed by their subordinates. Legislative Act 1 of 2017 established that command responsibility of members of Public Forces will apply when they have "effective command and control," which is proved through some "concurring conditions" related to competence, rank, knowledge, and available means. Commentators have noticed that there are some differences with the Treaty of Rome, including a higher standard of proof.

In summary, some key provisions of the Final Agreement have what HLA Hart called "open texture," which has generated some controversy about their meaning and application.[31] However, such an open texture is widespread and perhaps inevitable in legislation but does not constitute a defect. For Hart, since the lawmaker cannot foresee all the circumstances of application of norms, the open texture provides both certainty and adaptability: the norms have a stable guiding core, but are also sufficiently flexible to adapt to the circumstances of specific cases. However, judges are not free to remedy the open texture as they wish but must do so in the light of the Comprehensive System's purpose (to satisfy the rights of victims and consolidate a stable and lasting peace) and, as I argue in the next section, through the creation and application of a Corpus of human rights and IHL.

The Corpus Juris of Human Rights Law and International Humanitarian Law

The idea of a *Corpus Juris of Human Rights Law* (henceforth Corpus) was introduced by the Inter American Court of Human Rights. The Court claimed that the American Convention on Human Rights should be applied to specific cases in the light of a set of "international instruments of varied content and judicial effects (treaties, agreements, resolutions, and declarations)" about the applicable human rights norms, both regional and universal.[32] These instruments not only improve our understanding of the Convention, by the Court's lights, but they can also expand the scope of the protection of the rights it enshrines. Daniel O'Donnell clarifies that this Corpus as a tool for legal interpretation comprises three types of materials, namely the 1948 Declarations, universal and regional human rights treaties, and other general and particular instruments about a specific case.[33]

The Corpus then is composed of international and national norms on human rights and IHL, which are authoritatively applied by international and national courts to specific cases which, in turn, refine it, complement it, and clarify it. This collective work, while it has a stable legal core, remains under constant evolution in its interpretation and application. Academic scholars have also made a significant contribution by systematizing and clarifying some of the relevant provisions of the Corpus, and by informing its application. Undoubtedly, the Corpus is the best available material for the correct adjudication of cases about human rights and IHL.

The JEP's constitutive norms have also established that the norms that international tribunals have referred to as "the Corpus" are part of the legal materials the Jurisdiction has to consider. These norms hold that:

> In adopting its orders and judgements, the JEP should judicially assess the conduct subject to it based on the Colombian Criminal Code and/or in the norms of international human rights law, international humanitarian law, and international criminal law, while respecting the principle of favorability.[34]

The Corpus is also explicitly mentioned in the foundational provisions of Law 1957 of 2009 (Articles 2, 5, 6, 8, 13, 23, and 27), and many of its key components, including JEP's definition, competence, and prevalent character (Articles 2, 3 8, and 62 ff), the sanctioning regime, and the regime of responsibility for former FARC-EP combatants (Article 66). Similarly, "differential treatment" for members of the armed forces in Chapter VII of the Legislative Act states that JEP will apply the "Colombian Criminal Code, IHL as a special law and operational rules of the Public Forces regarding IHL when they are not contrary to legal normativity."[35] Victim's rights protected by international human rights standards also have a central role (Articles 1 and 13 of Law 1957, among others). The legislation also states that the internal rules of the JEP, as well as its procedure, should comply with "applicable international standards" with regards to impartiality, independence, and the protection of victims (Articles 3, 75, and 76). As a result, JEP justices are not only bound by the Final Agreement and by Colombian law, but they should also consider the Corpus Juris of human rights law, IHL, and international criminal law in deciding cases before them.

In my view, the Corpus is a central resource to resolve the two aforementioned challenges. On the one hand, transitional judges need to consider the content of the Corpus in adjudicating particular cases and, in particular, by clarifying the open-textured provisions. In other cases, the norms that regulate the transitional process should always be applied in the light of regional and international human rights and IHL standards, whose principles will guide the resolution of difficult cases and help to protect the rights of victims and secure a stable and lasting peace.

On the other hand, the Corpus is the arena of dialogue to articulate the work of transitional judicial institutions with permanent ones, since they all contribute to its creation, consolidation, interpretation, and application through symmetrical, inter-institutional dialogue among permanent and non-permanent institutions. The review of the JEP's constitutive rules by the Constitutional Court in several judgments provides an important example of this inter-institutional dialogue. It is also possible that the Supreme Court engages in the construction of the Corpus in the limited cases when it revises decisions involving non-combatants. Furthermore, JEP's decisions are called to interact with the jurisprudence of international courts, particularly with those that authoritatively apply human rights law, IHL, and international criminal law. It is critical to underscore that this is a *two-way dialogue.* The jurisprudence of universal and regional institutions influences the decisions of Colombian transitional courts. At the same time, however, the developments of Colombian transitional processes (like the similar efforts of other transitional courts around the world), also contribute to the construction of the Corpus Juris.

As a result, the Herculean responsibility of correctly judging those who have caused so much suffering to the victims for so many years demands an effort not just by the transitional judicial institutions, but by all the national and international institutions that collectively contribute to the Corpus Juris of human rights law, IHL, and international criminal law.

Conclusion

The negotiation process with the FARC-EP constitutes a negotiation model that might aid similar processes in other, unrelenting war scenarios. While it has faced difficulties, it has also led to some positive results. These include the bilateral ceasefire between the Government and the FARC-EP, the demobilization and disarmament of about 9,000 former FARC-EP combatants, a substantial reduction of one of the world's highest homicide rates (from 81.1 per 100,000 inhabitants in 1991 to 25.9 in 2017),[36] as well as *bona fide* pacts between the guerrilla groups and their victims (such as the one between the FARC and a group of victims of the attack made at the Nogal club in Bogota).[37] The Peace Process might encourage other guerrilla groups to initiate new dialogues with the national government, as is the case of the National Liberation Army (ELN). But the transition toward a lasting peace still has numerous challenges, many of which are connected with the debts of the social rule of law (*Estado Social de Derecho*), along with the acquired but not yet fulfilled commitments of the United Nations Sustainable Development Goals.

The JEP also has numerous challenges, including its relationship with permanent justice institutions and the clarification of open-textured provisions. Yet these problems can be framed and answered by constituting, interpreting, consolidating, and applying the Corpus Juris of Human Rights and IHL to its cases. The creation, strengthening, and application of this Corpus, through a symmetrical, two-way jurisprudential dialogue, is the major contribution that law can provide to the creation of peace and justice. If this is done correctly, the JEP might not only overcome the aforementioned challenges, thereby strengthening the credibility of Colombian justice, but might also inspire and inform other peace processes around the world.

Author's note

Translated by Jorge Luis Fabra-Zamora.

Notes

1 For more information, see the JEP's website in English: https://www.jep.gov.co/Sala-de-Prensa/Paginas/The-JEP-in-english.aspx.

2 In Colombia, Congressional Constitutional Amendments are called "Legislative Acts" which are different from ordinary legislation.

3 Administrative reparations provided by the Law of Victims and Land Restitution (Law 1448 of 2001) and restorative justice measures taken by the JEP can be included here.

4 The JEP is expected to function for an initial term of 15 years, which can be extended for a further five years. That is, this special justice mechanism will operate for a maximum of 20 years.

5 Legislative Act 1 of 2007, Article 5.
6 Article 62 of Law 1957 of 2019 regulates the “material competence” relating to crimes committed during the disarmament process as well crimes associated with drug trafficking.
7 Legislative Act 1 of 2017, transitory Article 16.
8 Per the Colombian Constitution, “Public Forces” includes the Military and the National Police (Article 216), whereas the Military Forces consists of the Army, Navy, and Air Force (Article 217).
9 Legislative Act 1 of 2017, transitory Article 17.
10 Law 1957 of 2019, Article 79.
11 Law 1957 of 2019, Article 81.
12 Law 1957 of 2019, Article 84.
13 Law 1957 of 2019, Article 90 ff.
14 Law 1957 of 2019, Article 89.
15 Law 1957 of 2019, Article 111.
16 Legislative Act 1 of 2017, transitory Article 1, subsection 4.
17 Law 1957 of 2019, Article 31.
18 See JEP, Tribunal for Peace, Appeal Section, Interpretative Judgement 2 of October 9, 2019, para 137, https://relatoria.jep.gov.co/documentos/providencias/7/2/Sentencia-interpretativa_TP-SA-SENIT-02_09-octubre-2019.docx.
19 According to Article 246 of the Colombian Constitution, the authorities of indigenous communities exercise judicial powers within their territories, according to their own laws and procedure, as long as they are not contrary to the Constitution and laws of the Republic.
20 See JEP, Tribunal for Peace, Appeal Section, Order 556 of April 29, 2020, https://relatoria.jep.gov.co/documentos/providencias/7/1/Auto_TP-SA-556_29-abril-2020.pdf.
21 JEP, Chamber of Acknowledgment, Order 2016, October 4, 2019, https://relatoria.jep.gov.co/documentos/providencias/1/1/Auto_SRVR-216_04-octubre-2019.docx.
22 JEP, Tribunal for Peace, Section for Revision of Judgements, Order 30 of May 15, 2019, https://relatoria.jep.gov.co/documentos/providencias/6/1/Auto_SRT-AE-030_15-mayo-2019.pdf.
23 JEP, Tribunal for Peace, Appeal Section, Order 289 of September 13, 2019, https://relatoria.jep.gov.co/documentos/providencias/7/1/Auto_TP-SA-289_13-septiembre-2019.docx.
24 ICTY, *Prosecutor v. Dusko Tadic*, Case No IT-94-1-AR75, Trial 7/05/1997, par. 563-8; *Prosecutor v Limaj et al*, Case No. IT-03-66-T, 30/11/ 2005, par. 84.
25 IPCY, *Prosecutor v Bokoski and Tarulovski*, IT- 04-82, 10/07/08, para175.
26 ICC, *Prosecutor v Lubanga*, ICC-01/04-01/06, Judgement of July 18, 2016, 234.
27 JEP, Chamber of Acknowledgment, Order 005 of July 17, 2018, https://relatoria.jep.gov.co/documentos/providencias/1/1/Auto_SRVR-005-Caso-003_17-julio-2018.pdf.
28 JEP, Tribunal for Peace, Appeal Section, Order 20 of August 21, 2018, https://relatoria.jep.gov.co/documentos/providencias/7/1/Auto_TP-SA-020_21-agosto-2018.pdf.
29 Legislative Act 1 of 2017, transitory Article 16.
30 JEP, Tribunal for Peace, Appeal Section, Order 362 of August 18, 2019, https://relatoria.jep.gov.co/documentos/providencias/7/1/Auto_TP-SA-362_18-diciembre-2019.pdf.
31 HLA Hart, *The Concept of Law* (Oxford: Oxford University Press, 1961) 121—44.
32 IACtHR, *The Right to Information to Consular Assistance in the Framework of the Guarantees of the Due Process of Law,* Advisory Opinion OC 6/99, Series A No. 16, para 58.

33 Daniel O'Donell, *Derecho International de Los Derechos Humanos: Normativa, Jurisprudencia y Doctrinal de los Sistemas Universal e Interamericano* (Bogotá: ACNUR, 2004).
34 Legislative Act 1 of 2017, Article 5, section 7, and Law 1957 of 2009, Article 23.
35 Legislative Act 1 of 2017, transitory Article 24. Note that "operative rules" refer to the procedures and protocols of the Armed Forces regarding national security. The Legislative Act also states that those operative rules valid at the time of the act will be considered in assessing the alleged perpetrator's conduct as long as they are not against the legal normativity (transitory Article 21).
36 See https://data.worldbank.org/indicator/VC.IHR.PSRC.P5?locations=CO.
37 See "Un abrazo entre excombatientes y víctimas por la verdad detrás del bombazo al club El Nogal," *El Espectador,* April 7, 2020, https://www.elespectador.com/colombia2020/justicia/jep/un-abrazo-entre-excombatientes-y-victimas-por-la-verdad-detras-del-bombazo-al-club-el-nogal-articulo-903556/.

11 The right to the truth in the Colombian conflict

Realities and fiction

Alfredo Duplat and Andrés Molina-Ochoa

Introduction

After decades of internal conflict, most Colombians are left with many questions. What must we remember? Why must we remember? Which institution should be responsible for preserving the memories of crimes committed during the period of internal conflict? These are difficult questions to answer because they involve a wide range of ethical dilemmas and empirical claims. For instance, as Santayana famously claimed, is it true that we need to remember our history in order to not repeat it? Some scholars claim the opposite[1]; they suggest that the histories gathered by truth commissions are irrelevant and harmful, except in a few cases. By the same token, should we remember to honor the dignity of the victims and their relatives, even if it may lead to more crimes? What are the limits of the right to the truth?

We do not have the answers to these questions. However, we believe that in the history of Colombia, there are important milestones in the progress of the right to the truth through which it can be evaluated and its current development assessed. This chapter is about the right to the truth in the Colombian conflict. However, we have chosen an alternative, perhaps an unorthodox route inspired in the law and literature movement. Instead of advancing an arid legal analysis of the agreement, we have decided to use *One Hundred Years of Solitude*, which is considered by many as the most important novel in the history of Colombia, as the way to canvass the right to the truth. This is fitting to our purposes for the right to the truth involves a narrative, and legal narratives are only part of a universe of possibility. In our view, *One Hundred Years of Solitude* is an important victory in the endless struggle for the right to the truth and a legacy that is indispensable to understand the role of the right to the truth in the Colombian post-conflict period.

This chapter is divided in three sections. First, we define the concept of the right to the truth and explain some of its key characteristics. We analyze the importance of *One Hundred Years of Solitude* in the second section, and the lessons we can learn from its impact in Colombian history. The right to the truth played an essential role in the peace dialogues between Revolutionary Armed Forces of Colombia (FARC) and the Colombian government. The final agreement includes a whole chapter on the satisfaction of the rights of victims called: *Comprehensive System of Truth, Justice, Reparation, and Non-Repetition,* whose aim is to satisfy the rights of all the victims, and that is guided by principles that include: "Uncovering the truth about what happened throughout the conflict, including the multiple causes, origins, and effects [...][2] Probably, the most important institution for the right to the truth of this system is *The Truth, Coexistence, and Non-Recurrence Commission* [hereafter, The Commission]." Thus, we are going to analyze in the last section if *The Commission* contradicts or is compatible with the lessons that we can draw from the history of *One Hundred Years of Solitude* and the right to the truth.[3]

The right to the truth

The United Nations (UN) defines the right to the truth, as the right of every person to

> "Know the truth about past events concerning the perpetration of heinous crimes and about the circumstances and reasons that led, through massive or systematic violations, to the perpetration of those crimes. Full and effective exercise of the right to the truth provides a vital safeguard against the recurrence of violations."[4]

As the UN's definition makes clear, the right to the truth is actually a two-fold right that consists of the individual's right to know the whereabouts of relatives and friends after an armed conflict and the collective right of society to know the true causes and circumstances of systematic violations of human rights.[5] The individual component of the right to the truth has its roots in International Humanitarian Law, particularly in those articles that establish the obligation of each party to find and report the whereabouts of those wounded, killed, and disappeared.[6] In Latin America, the collective component of the right to the truth originated in the legal response of the Inter-American Commission of Human Rights (IACHR), and the Inter-American Court of Human Rights (IACtHR) to the social struggles to remember the massive violations of human rights perpetrated during the Cold War throughout the continent. In this chapter, we are only going to analyze the collective component of the right to the truth. Otherwise noted, every time we mention this right, we are referring to its collective component.

One of the first mentions of the Right to the Truth appeared in the 1986 Annual Report of the IACHR, according to which "Every society has the inalienable right to know the truth about past events, as well as the motives and circumstances in which aberrant crimes came to be committed, in order to prevent repetition of such acts in the future."[7] The IACHR established more precisely the collective component in the Ellacuria case, by claiming that, "The right to know the truth is a collective right that ensures society access to information that is essential for the working of democratic systems."[8]

The jurisprudence of the IACtHR and the IACHR, in compliance with the collective element of the right to the truth, demands not only a historiographical reconstruction of crimes committed and their causes but also a disclosure of these findings. This is the reason truth commissions are encouraged to provide an extensive final report of their findings and a summarized version that can be easily accessed by society. According to the UN High Commissioner for Human Rights, this report is the most enduring legacy of truth commissions.[9] Similarly, both IACHR and IACtHR have ordered the publication of reports and the creation of museums to disclose the historic truth of systematic violations of human rights.

One case that illustrates the importance of disclosing the truth to society is the *Río Negro Massacre v. Guatemala*[10] case, in which the IACtHR, following a request from the IACHR, ordered the publication of the historical truth of events surrounding the death and torture of hundreds of Maya Achi to build a dam,[11] in the State's official gazette and in a newspaper with widespread circulation. Among other measures, the Court also ordered the creation of a commemorative museum, "in order to dignify the victims and conserve the historical memory."[12]

To satisfy the right to the truth, thus, it is necessary to disclose and preserve historical memory. The society needs access to an accurate reconstruction of the causes, perpetrators, and main events surrounding the commission of systematic violations of human rights.

There is another element of the right to the truth worth mentioning: Its purpose. Both the UN and the IACHR claim that establishing the truth is necessary to avoid the recurrence of human right violations. The Orentlicher principles, for instance, establishes that, "full and effective exercise of the right to the truth provides a vital safeguard against the recurrence of violations."[13] According to the IACHR, "society's right to know all about its past must be seen not only as a means of ensuring compensation and clarification of the facts, but as a means of preventing future violations."[14] This purpose is expressed in the famous slogan *Never Again,*[15] which was used as a title for the report of National Commission on the Disappearance of Persons (CONADEP), the first successful truth commission.[16]

To sum up, the right to the truth has an individual and a collective component. This last element involves the right of societies to know the truth about the systematic violations of human rights in order to ensure that violations do not recur.

García Márquez and the Banana Massacre

Between December 5 and 6 of 1928, in the small town of Ciénaga, Colombia, an army regiment acting under orders from General Cortés

Vargas massacred between 47 and 3,000 workers of the United Fruit Company and its relatives, including women and children,[17] who were on strike demanding dignified working conditions.

The workers of the United Fruit Company unknowingly fought two different struggles: One for rights such as the abolition of payment through coupons and the right to one paid-day off, weekly and the other for the right to the truth. The first one was lost in the main square of Ciénaga, when soldiers opened fire with machine guns indiscriminately killing innocent and unarmed workers, their wives, and their children. The strikers would win the second battle, thanks to the literary work of Gabriel García Márquez, one of the most influential Colombians and a famous writer.

Just after the occurrence of the massacres, the media controlled by the Conservative Party portrayed the strikes as a dangerous communist conspiracy, and although the victims were unarmed, the Colombian president of the time, Miguel Abadía Méndez, praised General Cortés Vargas for saving the country from anarchy. Few means of communication dared to tell the story of the massacres or even to investigate what happened, and when they did it, it was done very cautiously. The liberal newspaper *El Tiempo,* for instance, while describing some of the events that occurred in Colombia, did not condemn the massacre as a cruel and inhuman act, but as an inefficient military action.[18] After a historical analysis of the way mass media reported the Banana Massacres, the historians Elías Caro and Vidal Ortega concluded that, "the political manipulation of the state of the real information about the events was so obvious that using pressure mechanisms forced the media to misinform and distort reality."[19]

The massacre would have been completely forgotten if not for the efforts of Jorge Eliécer Gaitán, a liberal political leader, whose murder in 1948 led to the ten-year civil war known as *La Violencia* (The Violence). Gaitán, who was a member of the House of Representatives for Cundinamarca, investigated the matter thoroughly. He interviewed more than 100 inhabitants of Ciénaga, took pictures of the victims, and held a debate in the Colombian congress.[20]

Despite Gaitán's efforts and the conclusive evidence he gathered, there were no legal consequences for the Banana Massacres. There were no more investigations, and Carlos Cortés Vargas was promoted to Police Commander in Bogota. Some months later, Colombian President Abadía demanded the resignation of Cortés Vargas, due to the death of Gonzalo Bravo Pérez, the son of a close friend of Abadía. Rightly, Rodrigo Uprimny has pointed out that, "This fact shows the moral asymmetry of Colombian society and the State against its victims. While the massacre of hundreds of humble banana workers did not shake the government of the time, the death of an elite student drove the cabinet down."[21]

Just a few years after the massacre, when García Márquez visited the zone, the massacre had been forgotten.[22] García Márquez denounces this oblivion in *One Hundred Years of Solitude.* When José Arcadio Segundo comes back to Macondo, a woman who confuses him with a ghost, tells him,

"There haven't been any dead here [...] Since the time of your uncle, the colonel, nothing has happened in Macondo."[23]

García Márquez is, thus, facing a situation similar to that faced by those struggling for the recognition of the right to the truth: Heinous and systematic violations of human rights that are not only unpunished but also erased from society's memory. His work, then, seems to address the same problem the right to the truth tries to correct: Oblivion.

García Márquez points out the oblivion in the structure of the narrative he chooses to describe the massacre and in the testimony of the inhabitants of Macondo. The massacre is described in only two or three pages of the book, as if the author was trying to suggest that the murder of thousands of unionists is just a small episode in the tumultuous history of Macondo. It is so insignificant that it is forgotten by all the characters of the novel, apart from José Arcadio Segundo and a child. The oblivion of the massacre is not the fruit of human frailty, but is instead a political oblivion, the final triumph of the historical revisionist efforts of the government: "People did not believe the version of the massacre or the nightmare trip of the train loaded with corpses traveling toward the sea either. [...] The official version, repeated a thousand times and mangled out all over the country by every means of communication the government found at hand, was finally accepted: there were no dead, the satisfied workers had gone back to their families, and the banana company was suspending all activity until the rains stopped."[24]

The hardships and miseries that the inhabitants of Macondo suffered after the massacre are, to a certain degree, the consequence of this crime and its oblivion. García Márquez seems to be reminding Colombians that their history is constructed through the denial and revision of cruel crimes and systematic violations of human rights and that it is necessary to unearth this history to rescue Colombians from the cycle of violence that reigned in the country even before its appearance as an independent state. The writer shares with the defendants of the right to the truth the conviction that keeping the memory is required for enduring peace.

Márquez's intention is more visible if we pay attention to the fact that his description of the massacre is a stylized and exaggerated version of General Cortés Vargas' account.[25] As Robert Lewis Sims explains, "García Márquez even includes, either verbatim or in modified form, certain sentences found in the official account."[26]

Revisionists usually do not deny the existence of heinous crimes but try to justify them by altering the facts. In his description of the massacre, Vargas Cortés only recognizes the death of eight strikers, while the Colombian mass media characterized the strikers as dangerous rebels, influenced by Mexican revolutionaries, trying to change the political regime.[27] In this way, the massacre is silenced, not as an event that did not occur, but an event that had to happen (i.e., the strikers were dangerous subversives that needed to be controlled). The event was positioned as one that was not clearly atrocious: Only eight deaths, a simple crime that can be forgotten in Colombia's tumultuous history.

By altering an official account of the massacre, García Márquez is pointing to the facts that inspired the novel, and on which even the revisionists agree: on December 8, 1928, soldiers under the orders of General Carlos Cortés Vargas shot an indeterminate number of unionists and their relatives. However, in contrast to the revisionists' account, García Márquez exaggerates the number of victims (3,000) and underlines the human dimension of the tragedy. García Márquez describes the indignation of a woman next to José Arcadio Segundo, "Those bastards might just shoot,"[28] as well as the last sigh of one of the victims: "It was as if the machine guns had been loaded with caps, because their panting rattle could be heard and their incandescent spitting could be seen, but not the slightest reaction was perceived, not a cry, not even a sigh among the compact crowd that seemed petrified by an instantaneous invulnerability. Suddenly, on one side of the station, a cry of death tore open the enchantment: *Aaaagh, Mother*."[29]

With this original and creative style, García Márquez not only mixes fiction with history, but brings the massacre out of oblivion. The deaths of the unionists are no longer relegated to the study of scholars and historians but became part of Colombian culture. After *One Hundred Years of Solitude,* singers wrote songs commemorating the massacre,[30] and artists made sculptures depicting the story of the crime.[31] The influence of Márquez's work in the memory of the massacre can be seen in the scholarly articles dedicated to its study. Out of 12 papers that appear on an advanced search with the words "banana massacre" in the popular database JSTOR, all reference *One Hundred Years of Solitude.*[32] It seems that it is impossible to speak about the massacre without speaking about the novel.

Fiction and truth

García Márquez's account of the massacre shares most of the mentioned elements of the right to the truth. First, it is an intervention to remember a heinous crime committed with the complicity or participation of the State, whose memory is untrustworthy due to parties interested in keeping the crimes in oblivion. As we mentioned, the facts that surrounded the massacre were subject to multiple misrepresentations and distortions. The Colombian War Minister, for instance, claimed that, "In Magdalena there was no strike, but a revolution,"[33] and suggested that the soldiers were merely defending themselves against a previous attack committed by strikers.[34]

These circumstances are repeated in almost all cases in which the right to the truth was invoked. In Argentina, for instance, CONADEP was created, among other reasons, to address the efforts of the Military Junta to deny the occurrence of the systematic violations of human rights during their governmental reign. In 1978, the Junta launched the campaign *Somos Derechos y Humanos* (*We are right and humans*) with the aim to: "Neutralize or revert the denunciations made by the survivors of the clandestine centers of concentration, the exiles and relatives of the victims abroad."[35] Years later, in the aftermath of the military regime and the dawn of democracy, the Military Junta launched an offensive to deny the crimes during its government that included *The Final Document,* a text in which it was stated that the disappearance of thousands of people had been the "consequence of the way terrorists operate."[36]

This pattern of the systematic violation of human rights and battles over the truth of the facts is repeated in the most important cases discussed by the IACHR and IACtHR. The first case decided by IACtHR, *Velásquez Rodríguez v. Honduras,*[37] which is also for most scholars the first case in which an international tribunal protected the right to the truth,[38] is a clear example of battles over the truth. *Velásquez* is one of a triad of cases[39] that the IACtHR decided with the intention of stopping the Honduran government practices of forced disappearance. However, even in the twenty-first century, the Honduran government, as Andrea DeGaetani points out, "[has] denied that any wrongdoing took place, and have blamed the Sandinista regime for threatening Honduran stability with propaganda and exaggerated Committee for the Defense of Human Rights reports."[40]

Most importantly, both *One Hundred Years of Solitude* and the Right to the Truth are interventions that in some way altered the traditional narrative of the State. In the case of *One Hundred Years of Solitude,* as has been mentioned, García Márquez uses the official narrative of the massacre told by Cortés Vargas and transforms it to not only denounce the atrocity of the crimes but to unveil the truth behind the lies contained in the official report. García Márquez "[depicts] reality objectively but with a magical dimension."[41] For us the magical dimension is a space free from governmental intervention.[42] The objective reality allows the author to denounce the past crimes; the free dimension is a space where the author has the necessary liberty to describe what the political authority denies. In other words, García Márquez's style aims to "[...] rupture the socio-spatio-temporal membrane of society and, in magic-realistic fiction, operate as traces of subaltern trauma."[43]

The right to the truth also ruptures the political space of the State. The recognition of the collective element of the right to the truth is the outcome of the struggles of human rights organizations and political leaders. As Gloria Park claims, "in contrast to other legal rights that originate from formal legal precedents and binding documents, the right to truth was largely constituted by extralegal, norm-setting channels such as the Aspen Conference."[44] It is not a coincidence, therefore, that the collective element of the right to the truth was recognized by an international institution and by an international tribunal before it appeared in any Latin American Constitution. While the internal law recognized rights such as the freedom of speech or the right to due process even before the twentieth century,[45] the collective element of the right to the truth only recently appears in Latin

America in the Constitutions of Colombia, Ecuador, and Bolivia.[46] All these legal recognitions are from the twenty-first century, decades after *Velásquez Rodríguez v. Honduras.*

For this reason, the right to the truth can be considered paradigmatic of a different understanding of human rights that began after the Second World War with the creation of international tribunals such as the European Court of Human Rights and the IACtHR. In this new version, the ultimate guardian of the protection of human rights is not the State but the international tribunal.[47] A new set of legal concepts that reflects this idea began to appear in Latin American constitutional jurisprudence and legal theory. Theories such as *Constitutional Block*[48] and *Conventional Control*[49] have become popular in recent decades. As we have mentioned, it is not a coincidence, therefore, that the first decision taken by IACtHR was precisely the first jurisprudence that recognized the collective element of the right to the truth.

If the right to the truth pioneers a new understanding of human rights, it is unique in its relationship with the power of the State. In its origins, the constitutionalization of human rights contributed to the legitimacy of political power. The Bill of Rights, for instance, was added to the American Constitution, after the Philadelphia Convention to guarantee the votes required for ratifying the Constitution. The recently independent colonies wished anything but delivery of the newly conquered sovereignty to a government located thousands of miles away with an army of its own. The Bill of Rights was then drafted to calm the anxieties of those who did not want a federal government.[50]

Analogously, the Colombian Constitution of 1991 included a long list of human rights and new protection mechanisms for the time, as well as the limitation of the State of Siege, in order to incorporate into political life several guerrilla groups that were in peace negotiations. The consecration of human rights in modern constitutions, therefore, is a kind of guarantee against the political power that constitutions legitimize. The dissident factions decide to be part of the State because it guarantees a series of rights. The State manages, in this way, to achieve the contest of its former enemies.

The right to the truth, on the other hand, obeys a different logic. Instead of establishing trust in the State, the right to the truth remembers the crimes that the State allowed or of which it was an accomplice. While traditional human rights tell citizens: "Do not worry, under the protection of the State, these guarantees will be protected," the right to the truth asks that they "Remember that the same State that you must obey also murdered, tortured, or disappeared thousands of people."

Of course, it is also true, as some scholars have noted[51] that after a series of systematic violations of human rights, trust begins to be reconstructed when parties acknowledge their participation in the crimes. However, the historic reconstruction of the crimes also keeps alive a healthy distrust in the political institutions. The right to the truth reminds us that, even in democratic societies, atrocities may occur, and, therefore, it is necessary to always be alert.

The goal of the right to the truth

Both the literary reconstruction of the Banana Massacre and the recent recognition of the right to the truth have in common the redefinition of a political space usually controlled by the State. In the case of *One Hundred Years of Solitude,* García Márquez uses and alters the official version of the facts to give an account that captures the seriousness of the crimes and the impunity of the oblivion. In the case of the Right to the Truth, the right is not enshrined to legitimize the power of the State, but to foster a healthy distrust that allows citizens to remain alert to when human rights violations occur.

One Hundred Years of Solitude also shares with the Right to the Truth the goal of socialization: namely, the idea that the truth about human rights violations must not only be known but also disclosed. The narrative of the massacre in Márquez's novel intends to make public what the government wanted to keep secret. Analogously, as we show in the second part of this chapter, the final reports written by the truth commissions, the creation of museums, and the publication of IACtHR's decisions in local and national newspapers, among other measures, seek to socialize facts surrounding human rights violations.

In the post-conflict era, Colombians can learn important lessons from the parallel between the right to the truth and *One Hundred Years of Solitude.* Although an important tool to prevent future atrocities, the right to the truth is not a sufficient condition to guarantee peace and justice. As we have already mentioned, disappearance continued in Honduras after *Velásquez,* and massacres still occur in Colombia, despite the socialization of the facts surrounding the Banana Massacre.

Nevertheless, the right to the truth is an important tool to alert citizens to the possible occurrence of systematic violations of human rights. *Never Again,* the CONADEP report, is probably the most paradigmatic case of a society using the memory of the past to prevent future atrocities. Between 1989 and 1990, *Never Again* was published to defend the social and political demands of the most vulnerable populations and to reject Menem's *Full Stop Law* as well as his economic policies.[52]

Second, the reconstruction of systematic violations of human rights is never a pacific endeavor but an intense battle. Abadía Méndez' government did the impossible to conceal the Banana Massacre and alter the facts. The Argentine Military Junta enacted laws and official documents to prevent investigation of the systematic violations of human rights committed during its government, and the Honduran government still denies responsibility for forced disappearances occurring in the 1980s.

This is precisely the reason writers and social activists who fought for the right to the truth seek a political space that is not controlled by the State.

Only in the fictitious world of *One Hundred Years of Solitude* can García Márquez write a story about the cruelty of the Banana Massacre. Only in the supranational space of the International Tribunals can social activists make national states tell the truth about the systematic atrocities and violations of human rights.

Finally, the right to the truth does not achieve its goal if truth is not disclosure. As IACtHR recognized, for instance, in the decision of Río Negro Massacres, which has already been mentioned, art fulfills a very important function in disseminating the findings of the truth commissions and legal research. The Banana Massacre is probably the most well-known massacre in the history of Colombia, because its history was divulged by García Márquez and other writers and artists.[53]

Final Agreement to end the armed conflict and build a stable and lasting peace

If our analysis of the right to the truth in *One Hundred Years of Solitude* is accurate, to ensure the guarantees of non-recidivism, the right to the truth must work as an alert for future violations, and it must be the outcome of a space that subverts the power of the State, in which different voices take center stage and are listened.

The Final Agreement between FARC and the Colombian government created a *Comprehensive System for Truth, Justice, Reparations, and Non-Recurrence* that is entrusted with the duty of: "Uncovering the truth about what happened throughout the conflict, including the multiple causes, origins, and effects thereof […]"[54] To fulfill this purpose, the *Comprehensive System* counts with three important institutions: the *Truth, Coexistence, and Non-Recurrence Commission, Special Unit for the Search for Persons deemed as Missing in the context of an due to the armed conflict,* and the *Peace Special Jurisdiction* (its Spanish acronym Jurisdicción Especial para la Paz).

The Commission was designed as a space where voices usually silenced by the official narrative could be heard. The president of the Commission is Francisco de Roux, a Jesuit priest who previously was the director of Center for Research and Popular Education (CINEP), a non-governmental organization that, among other activities, documented the human rights violations during the conflict. Indeed, Carlos Guillermo Ospina, a retired major, is the only member of the Commission with strong ties with the Colombian government. Similarly, the agreement establishes as one of the Commission's guiding criteria: "[…] a territorial-based approach in order to achieve a better understanding of the regional dynamics of the conflict and the diversity and particularities of the territories affected."[55] It is worth stating that Colombia is a centralist State in which most of the decisions are taken in its capital without considering the voices from the periphery. The agreement also demands the Commission to take, "[…] into account previous efforts to establish the truth, including as basic input, *inter alias,* the reports of the Historical Commission of the Conflicts and its Victims."[56] In this way, the Commission recovers the extraofficial reconstruction of the internal conflict. Finally, the Commission must "prepare a final report that [...] shall be officially submitted by public act to the public authorities and to Colombian society as a whole."[57] This duty guarantees that there will be disclosure of the historical reconstruction of the events, which, as we noted at the beginning of this article, is essential to use the right to the truth as a political tool to avoid further human rights violations. The publication of the report is complemented with a strategy of dissemination that includes the creation of a National Memory Museum.[58]

The Commission, in conclusion, incorporates the main lessons we have mentioned, at least, as it was designed in the Final Agreement between FARC and the Colombian government. The obligation to disclose the findings of the Commission allows people to get enough information to grow a healthy distrust that allows civil society to be alert for future human rights violations. The participation of silenced voices allows the Commission to write a narrative of the conflict that does not foster a blind trust to the official institutions. However, as Kafka wrote about lawyers: "they're forced to spend all their time, day and night, with their laws, and so they don't have the right feel for human relationships, and that's a serious shortcoming in cases like this."[59]

One of the biggest challenges that the Commission will face is the opposition of the actual government. In 2018, Iván Duque, a candidate from the Centro Democrático party, was elected as president of Colombia. His support came mostly from those Colombians who opposed the Peace Dialogues and who voted No in the 2016 Colombian Peace Agreement referendum. Since he took office, he has tried to modify the Final Agreements and has hindered its implementation. In February 2019, Duque appointed Darío Acevedo as director of the National Center for Historical Memory.[60] His designation was questioned by the Colombian Academy, because Acevedo has denied the existence of an internal conflict in Colombia.[61] Acevedo's decisions in the National Center for Historical Memory led the International Coalition of Sites of Conscience to expel Colombia from this Coalition. Acevedo appointed officials to close the military in key positions, jeopardized the Center's database, and censorship some projects.[62]

Duque's desire to modify and control the historic reconstruction of the internal conflict is one of the biggest challenges of Final Agreement. Instead of creating a healthy distrust toward public institutions, this approach helps to consolidate institutions that have systematically violated human rights in Colombia, and silences extraofficial voices and spaces required for the right to the truth be able to fulfil its purpose.

It is also worthy to ask if the strategy to guarantee the right to the truth in the Final Agreement is effective. Colombian society is different from those societies that inspire the Commission. The final report will face challenges that were unknown when CONADEP, for instance, was formed. The success of the right to the truth is accomplished when the truth is disclosed and socialized. It is the knowledge of the atrocities that raises alarms in society and encourages people to prevent future violations of human rights. However, Colombians have a version of the internal conflict that has been shaped by both parties, by Soap Operas and TV Series[63] that tells the history of the conflict with goals that contradict those pursued by the Commission. Not to mention the flood of fake news about the Commission spread through social media. Nowadays, the problem is not the disclosure of the information but how to protect it from false accusations and procrastination.

Given these problems, it is important to ask: Are there any moral or legal constraints that artists and writers must have when divulging the history of massacres and violations of human rights? Do victims have an epistemic privilege when recounting these crimes? Should people who spread fake news must be criminalized? All these questions deserve an urgent analysis that must consider not only the freedom of speech but also the right to the truth and protection for victims.

Final words

At the end of *One Hundred Years of Solitude,* Aureliano Buendía deciphers the parchments written by Melquíades, the Gipsy, and finds out that Macondo would be

> [...] wiped out by the wind and exiled from the memory of men at the precise moment when Aureliano Babilonia would finish deciphering the parchments, and that everything written on them was unrepeatable since time immemorial and forever more, because races condemned to one hundred years of solitude did not have a second opportunity on earth.[64]

We hope that García Márquez is right and that the massacres and atrocities written in the Colombian books of history and in the truth commission reports will not be repeated and that the peace process brings the reconciliation required for a second chance on earth.

Notes

1 See, for instance, Jack Snyder and Leslie Vinjamuri, "Trials and Errors: Principle and Pragmatism in Strategies of International Justice," *International Security,* vol. 28, 2003–2004, pp. 5–44.

2 Final Agreement to end the Armed Conflict and Build a Stable and Lasting Peace, Article 5.

3 There are two other important institutions in the Comprehensive System. One of the Special Unit goal is to "coordinate and contribute to the implementation of humanitarian actions for searching for and identifying all the people deemed as disappeared due to the conflict who are still alive, and in the cases of those

deceased, whenever possible, for the location and dignified delivery of their remains." See Ibid, 5.1.b. This objective is closer to the individual component of the right to the truth we describe below. For this reason, we are not going to analyze this institution in this chapter. The other institution is the Special Jurisdiction for Peace (JEP for its Spanish Acronym), which is the judicial institution of the System, and it is responsible for prosecuting and punishing "serious human rights violations and serious infringements of international humanitarian law." Ibid. This institution demands a more complex analysis that also discusses the system of amnesties and punishment designed in the Agreement. For this reason, we are only going to focus on the Commission. JEP is essential for the reconstruction of the right to the truth.

4 UN, Commission on Human Rights, E/CN.4/2005/102/Add.1, February 8, 2005, principle 2.

5 The UN *Principles for the Administration of Justice and the Human Rights of Detainees* establishes that "[The Right to Know] is not simply the right of any individual victim or closely related persons to know what happened, a right to the truth. The right to know is also a collective right, drawing upon history to prevent violations from recurring in the future." See UN Commission on Human Rights, E/CN.4/Sub.2/1997/20/Rev.1, October 2, 1997, p. 17. According to Thomas Antkowiak, "The right to the truth actually consists in two fundamental concepts: Both an individual right, applying to the victim and family members, and a general societal right." "Truth as Right and Remedy in International Human Rights Experiences," *Michigan Journal of International Law,* 1, 2002, p. 992.

6 See: International Committee of the Red Cross (ICRC), Geneva Convention Relative to the Protection of Civilian Persons in Time of War (Fourth Geneva Convention), August 12, 1949, 75 UNTS 287, article 16; ICRC, Protocol Additional to the Geneva Conventions of August 12, 1949, and relating to the Protection of Victims of International Armed Conflicts (Protocol I), June 8, 1977, 1,125 UNTS 3, Article 32.

7 Inter-American Commission of Human Rights, *Annual Report of The Inter-American Commission On Human Rights* 1985–, OEA/Ser.L/V/II.68, Doc. 8 rev. 1, September 26, 1986, Chapter V.

8 IACHR, Report No. 136/99. Case 10.488 *Ignacio Ellcauria et al v. El Salvador,* December 22, 1999, p. 224.

9 UN High Commissioner for Human Rights, *Rule-of-Law Tools for Post-Conflict States,* New York, 2006, p. 33. In the same sense, Priscilla Hayner claims that "The report of a truth commission reclaims a country's history and opens it for public review." See: Hayner, Priscilla, *Unspeakable Truths: Transitional Justice and the Challenge of Truth Commissions* (New York, NY: Routledge, 2011), p. 20.

10 IACHR, Case of the *Río Negro Massacres v. Guatemala,* September 4, 2012.

11 Ibid, p. 273.

12 Ibid, p. 279.

13 The UN principles for *The Administration of Justice and the Human Rights of Detainees* establishes that the right to the truth draws in history to, "prevent violations from recurring in the future." UN, Commission on Human Rights, E/CN.4/Sub.2/1997/20/Rev.1, October 2, 1997, p. 17.

14 IACHR, Report No. 136/99, CASE 10.488, *Ignacio Ellacuria et al v. El Salvador,* December 22, 1999.

15 The first edition of the book was published in Spanish by EUDEBA, the editorial of the University of Buenos Aires in 1984, with the title *Nunca Más.* Faber and Faber published the first English titled *Nunca más = Never Again: A report.* See: CONADEP, *Nunca más: Informe de la Comisión sobre la desaparición de*

Personas, Buenos Aires: EUDEBA, 1984; CONADEP, *Nunca más = Never again: a report,* London, Boston: Faber and Faber, 1986.

16 See Haynes, Priscilla, "Fifteen Truth Commissions 1974 to 1994: A Comparative Study," *Human Rights Quarterly,* vol. 16 (4), 2002, pp. 597–655.

17 Although Cortés Vargas only recognized the death of 47 people, scholars claimed that it is possible that 2,000 were massacred by the Colombian army. See Jorge Enrique Elías Caro and Antonio Vidal Ortega, "The worker's massacre of 1928 in the Magdalena Zona Bananera-Colombia. An unfinished story," *Memorias: Revista Digital de Historia y Arqueología desde el Caribe* vol. 18, 2012, pp. 22–54.

18 "Once the violence is unleashed, the need to restore order is not debatable, and the government is mainly called to carry out that task. But it remains to find out if there are no preferable and more effective measures than those of dedicating half of the Republic's army to the killing of Colombian workers." See: Credencial Historia, "La masacre de las Bananeras," *Colombia y el mundo, 1919,* 2005, 190, http://www.banrepcultural.org/biblioteca-virtual/credencial-historia/numero-190/la-masacre-de-las-bananeras (accessed January 29, 2019).

19 Elías Carlo and Vidal Ortega, "The worker's massacre of 1928 in the Magdalena Zona Bananera-Colombia."

20 Credencial Historia, "La massacre de las Bananeras."

21 Rodrigo Uprimny, "La masacre de las bananeras y la desigualdad de las víctimas," *El Espectador,* December 8, 2008.

22 According to Stephen Hart, "10 years after the actual event [...] nobody could remember exactly what happened." "Magic Realism in the Americas: Politicized Ghosts in *One Hundred Years of Solitude, The House of the Spirits*, and *Beloved,*" *Journal of Iberian and Latin American Studies,* vol. 9, 2003, p. 117.

23 Gabriel García Márquez, *One Hundred Years of Solitude,* Gregorio Rabasa (trans) (New York: Avon Books, 1971) 151.

24 Ibid.

25 For a thorough comparison of García Márquez' and Vargas Cortez' accounts. See: Robert Lewis Sims, "The Banana Massacre in Cien Años de Soledad: A Micro-Structural Example of Myth, History and Bricolage," *Chasqui: Revista de literatura latinoamericana,* vol. 8 (3), 1979, p. 6.

26 Lewis points out to the following similarities: "Tienen cinco minutos para retirarse" (Verbatim both accounts); "Pasados los cinco minutos, se dio un toque corto. Un minuto más y se romperá el fuego (Cortés Vargas) "Han pasado cinco minutos, dijo el capitán en el mismo tono, Un minuto más y se hará fuego (*Cien Años de Soledad*). "Le regalamos el minuto que falta, gritó una voz entre el tumulto." (Cortés Vargas) "Cabrones, gritó José Arcadio Segundo. Les regalamos el minuto que falta" (*Cien Años de Soledad*), "Una voz dentro de la multitud gritó al mismo tiempo, Tenderse." (Cortés Vargas). "Varias voces gritaron al mismo tiempo: ¡Tírense al suelo! ¡Tírense al suelo!" (*Cien Años de Soledad).* See: Sims, "The Banana Massacre in Cien Años de Soledad," p. 6 (references omitted).

27 For an account of the different versions, see: Elías Carlo and Vidal Ortega, "The worker's massacre of 1928 in the Magdalena Zona Bananera-Colombia."

28 García Márquez, Gabriel, *One Hundred Years of Solitude,* p. 149

29 Idem.

30 For instance, Santander Duran, *Las Bananeras,* 1974.

31 Rodrigo Arenas Betancourt, one of the most important Colombian artists, in 1978 created the sculpture *Prometeo de la Libertad,* in honor of the victims of the massacre.

32 See Sims, "The Banana Massacre in Cien Años de Soledad;" James C. Jupp "The Necessity of the Literary Tradition: Gabriel García Márquez's 'One-Hundred Years of Solitude,'" *The English Journal,* vol. 89, 2000, pp. 113–115; José David

Saldivar, "Ideology and Deconstruction in Macondo." *Latin American Literary Review,* 13, 1985, pp. 29–43; Tahia Abdel Nasser, "Revolution and Cien Años De Soledad in Naguib Mahfouz's Layālī Alf Laylah." *Comparative Literature Studies*, vol. 52, 2015, pp. 539–561; López, Alfred J. "The Plantation as Archive: Images of 'the South' in the Postcolonial World," *Comparative Literature*, vol. 63 (4), 2011, pp. 402–422; Palencia-Roth, Michael. "The Art of Memory in García Márquez and Vargas Llosa," *MLN,* vol. 105, 1990, pp. 351–366; Stern, Steve J. "The Tricks of Time: Colonial Legacies and Historical Sensibilities in Latin America," *The Princeton University Library Chronicle,* vol. 57, 1996, pp. 371–392; Seymour Menton, "The Last of the Just: Between Borges and García Márquez," *World Literature Today*, vol. 59 (4), 1985, pp. 517–524; Luis B. Eyzaguirre and Carmen Grullón. "Serie Bibliográfica INTI III," *INTI*, vol. 16/17, 1982, pp. 173–193; Zaida Márquez-Farias and Laurent Lapierre, "Company Profile: Gabriel García Márquez and the Foundation for a New Ibero-American Journalism," *International Journal of Arts Management*, vol. 14, 2011, 56–71; Jennifer Harford Vargas, "A Tale of Two Novels from the Global South." *Economic and Political Weekly*, 43, 2008, pp. 52–61.

33 *La Prensa,* Barranquilla, 252, 1928, p. 1.

34 See Jorge Enrique Elías Caro, and Vidal Ortega, Antonio, "The worker's massacre of 1928 in the Magdalena Zona Bananera-Colombia," *An Unfinished Story,* vol. 18, 2012, pp. 22–54.

35 Clarín, "Somos Derechos y Humanos: cómo se armó la campaña," March 23, 2006.

36 Argentina, *Documento Final de la Junta Militar sobre la guerra contra la Subversión y el Terrorismo,* p. 7.

37 IACtHR, Velásquez Rodríguez Case, Judgment of July 29, 1988, (Ser. C) No. 4 (1988).

38 For Priscilla Hayner, "The first clear legal ruling on this way by the Inter-American Court of Human Rights in the *Velásquez Rodríguez* case of 1988, where it was confirmed that the state has a duty to investigate the fate of the disappeared and disclose the information to relatives." *Unspeakable Truths: Transitional Justice and the Challenge of Truth Commissions* (New York, NY: Routledge, 2011) 23. In the same sense, Thomas Antkowiak claims that, "The primary international human rights tribunals have traced the explicit contours of an effective remedy in the wake of gross human rights abuse, starting with the Inter-American Court's seminal *Velásquez Rodríguez* case." Thomas Antkowiak, "Truth as Right and Remedy in International Human Rights Experiences," *Michigan Journal of International Law,* vol. 1, 2002, p. 982.

39 The other cases are IACtHR, Godínez Cruz Case, Judgment of January 20, 1989, (Ser. C) No. 5 (1989); and Case of *Fairén-Garbi and Solís-Corrales v. Honduras Judgment* of March 15, 1989.

40 Andrea DeGaetani, "*Human Rights in Honduras*" *Review Digest: Human Rights in Latin America* (Denver, Colorado: University of Denver, 2006). https://www.du.edu/korbel/hrhw/researchdigest/latinamerica/honduras.pdf, retrieved March 8, 2019.

41 Stephen Hart "Magic Realism in the Americas: Politicized Ghosts in *One Hundred Years of Solitude*, *The House of the Spirits*, and *Beloved*," *Journal of Iberian and Latin American Studies,* vol. 9 (2), 2003, p. 115.

42 While Hart's analysis of the role of popular history in certain Latin American novels is convincing, problems remain with "magical" as a term to describe the narrative structures employed to engage with that popular social perspective. Some of these problems were delineated in Luis Leal's critique of early formulations related to "magical realism." Luis Leal, "El realismo mágico en la literatura latinoamericana," *Cuadernos Americanos,* 15, 1967.

43 Hart "Magic Realism in the Americas," 118

44 Gloria Park, Y.M. "Truth as Justice," *Harvard International Review,* vol. 31 (4), 2010, p. 27

45 The Colombian Constitution of 1886, for instance, recognized the freedom of speech (Article 42), and the right to due process (Articles 20, 23, 25, 26, and 28).

46 In Colombia, the legislative act 01 of 2012 amended the Transitional Article 66 of the Constitution and recognized for the first time in the Constitutional order the right to the truth: "A statute to guarantee the state duties of investigation and punishment will establish transitional justice instruments of a judicial or extra-judicial nature. In any case mechanisms of extrajudicial nature will be applied to clarify the truth and reparations to victims." In Bolivia, the Article 23 of the 2009 Constitution establishes that "every person has the right to freedom and personal security. Personal liberty may only be restricted within the limits set forth by law to assure the discovery of the true facts concerning acts in jurisdictional processes." The Ecuadorian Constitution of 2008 establishes in the Article 78: "The victims of criminal offenses shall benefit from special protection; guarantees shall be provided to them for preventing their revictimization, especially in obtaining and assessing the evidence; and they shall be protected against any threat or other forms of intimidation. Mechanisms shall be adopted for integral reparation, which shall include, without delay, knowledge about the truth of the facts and restitution, compensation, rehabilitation, guarantee of non-repetition, and satisfaction with respect to the infringed right."

47 Samuel Moyn suggests that the concept of Human Rights as an international law tool to domestic violence only appears in the history after 1968. See: Moyn, Samuel, *The Last Utopia: Human Rights in History* (Cambridge: Harvard University Press).

48 Most scholars point out to a 1971 decision of the Constitutional Council that used the Declaration of the Rights of Man of the Citizen to reject a law. See: France, Décision, n° 71-44 DC du 16 juillet 1971. For the history and scope of the Constitutional Block in Latin America, see: Graciela, Rodríguez Manzo, Juan Carlos Arjona Estévez, and Zamir Fajardo Morales, *Bloque de constitucionalidad en México,* CIADH, 2013; Uprimny, Rodrigo, *The block of constitutionality in Colombia: jurisprudential analysis and a trial of the doctrinal systematization,* in *De Justicia,* https://www.dejusticia.org/en/the-block-of-constitutionality-in-colombia-jurisprudential-analysis-and-a-trial-of-the-doctrinal-systematization/ (accessed February 13, 2019).

49 The theory of the Conventional Control was first developed by the IACtHR in the *Almonacid-Arellano v. Chile case.* For the IACtHR, "the Judiciary must exercise a sort of *conventional control* between the domestic legal provisions, which are applied to specific cases, and the American Convention on Human Rights. To perform this task, the Judiciary has to take into account not only the treaty, but also the interpretation thereof made by the Inter-American Court, which is the ultimate interpreter of the American Convention." See: IACtHRm (ser. C) No. 154, para. 124 (Sept. 26, 2006).

50 See: Pauline Maier, *Ratification: The People Debate the Constitution* (New York: Simon & Schuster, 2014).

51 Ruti Teitel, *Transitional Justice* (Oxford: Oxford University Press, 2002) Chapter 1.

52 See specially, Emilio Crenzel, *Memory of the Argentina disappearances: the political history of Nunca más* (London: Routledge, 2017).

53 See supra 29. Before *One Hundred Years of Solitude,* Álvaro Cepeda Samudio also divulged the history of the Banana Massacre in his novel, *La Casa Grande* (Bogota, Mito, 1962).

54 Ibid, Article 5.

55 Ibid, Article 5.1.1.1.1.
56 Ibid, Article 5.1.1.1.4. The Historical Commission of the Conflicts and its Victims was a commission of 12 Colombian historians who presented an account of the causes and consequences of Colombian conflict.
57 Ibid, Article 5.1.1.1.4.
58 Ibid, Article 5.1.1.1.4.
59 Franz, Kafka, *The Trial* (New York: Dover Publications Inc, 2009) 141.
60 The National Center for Historical Memory is a public entity created by the Law 1448/2011, and its goal is to document the historical memory of human rights violations during the Colombian armed conflict.
61 See Andrés Molina Ochoa, "El rifirrafe entre Darío Acevedo y Rodrigo Uprimny", en *Las dos orillas,*https://www.las2orillas.co/el-rifirrafe-entre-dario-acevedo-y-rodrigo-uprimny/.
62 See: Revista Arcadia: "Un director cercano a los militares y un acto de protesta preceden a la instalación de la *primera piedra* del Museo de Memoria, in *Revista Arcadia,* May 2, 2020, https://www.revistaarcadia.com/agenda/articulo/un-director-cercano-a-los-militares-y-un-acto-de-protesta-preceden-la-instalacion-de-la-primera-piedra-del-museo-de-memoria/80371; Revista Arcadia: "Censura en el Centro de Memoria Histórica", in *Revista Arcadia,* October 29, 2019, https://www.revistaarcadia.com/noticias/censura-en-el-centro-nacional-de-memoria-historica/8967.
63 Just to mention a few: About the members of the Cali Cartel and the Norte Valle Cartel: (*El Cartel de los sapos* (The Cartel of Snitches), Caracol Television, 2008; About Pablo Escobar: *Pablo Escobar, El Patrón del mal,* (Pablo Escobar, The drug Lord), Caracol Television, 2012; About the life of the Castaño Brothers: Tres Caínes (Three Cain), RTI, 2013, About the decline of the Cali Cartel: *En la Boca del Lobo* (Into the Lion's Den), Sony Pictures Television, 2014.
64 García Márquez, *One Hundred Years of Solitude,* 201.

12 Land reform and transition in contemporary Colombia

Nelson Camilo Sánchez

Introduction

The Peace Agreement signed between the Colombian government and the *Fuerzas Armadas Revolucionarias de Colombia* (FARC) created high expectations among those who have been long-time defenders of radical change regarding land governance in the country.[1] However, instead of pushing for far-reaching agrarian reform, the negotiating parties settled for a more moderate set of policies in the Integral Rural Reform (IRR) chapter of the agreement. Nonetheless, despite its modest objectives, since day one, this policy has been met with harsh opposition from domestic conservative factions. As a result, there is an open-ended debate about how to overcome the multiple factors that impede the implementation of the IRR policy. This chapter will briefly analyze the content of the Agreement and the current state of affairs regarding implementation, as well as present perspectives for future regulations on access to land, rural development, and land governance in contemporary Colombia.

To this end, this text is divided into four sections. In the first section, I will briefly present the main characteristics of historical conflicts regarding land in Colombia and the repertoire of policy options to confront them. In the second, I will concentrate on the proposals of the peace process negotiators, the agreements reached, and the changes made to the Peace Agreement after the October 2016 failed referendum. In the third section, I will address the implementation of the Agreement under the Santos and Duque administrations. Finally, I will close the chapter with some concluding reflections and perspectives regarding possible future scenarios for the implementation of the Agreement and land policies in the country, in light of the current political and institutional landscape.

A long history of land conflicts

The struggle for land and the social and economic exclusion of peasants were two rallying cries of leftist guerrillas' call to arms during the mid-1960s. Over time, and with the war's persistence, conflicts associated with land and territories increased and diversified. Socio-environmental conflicts regarding land use, such as those derived from the illicit use of crops appeared in addition to historical problems of inequitable access to land tenancy.[2] Additionally, as a result of its own dynamics, the armed conflict produced several waves of forced displacement and uprooting, which were accompanied by processes of abandonment, dispossession, and later, repopulation of territories or processes of land grabbing and accumulation.[3] The situation regarding land was problematic at the beginning of the armed conflict and is even more so at its conclusion.

With this panorama, it is not difficult to explain why rural policies and the regulation of agrarian structures are considered the main priority for a peacebuilding agenda in Colombia. However, the history of implementation of governance strategies to address rural problems demonstrates enormous deficiencies in Colombian institutions. Not only have large-scale attempted reforms failed (including all the "agrarian reforms" attempted in the country), but in recent years, different visions and public policy strategies regarding the issue have been contradictory either on paper or in practice.

In modern Colombia, different government administrations and interest groups related to land and agricultural production have promoted at least three general public policy options to address these problems. The first is a large-scale property redistribution policy based on principles of distributive justice, which privileges access to property for the most vulnerable rural population, generally known as "classic agrarian reform."[4] The second option consists of a policy that focuses on the efficient use of land to produce quick revenue that, in turn, helps cover the costs of the transition, and thus privileges the property or tenancy of rural investors. Finally, in recent years, Colombia has promoted and implemented a policy that is reparative in nature, based on an idea of corrective justice which seeks to restitute land to those who possessed it before they were dispossessed of it through violence.[5]

Elements of these three policies are enshrined in normative instruments that, in many cases, conflict with one another. Although there are social groups who support one or another policy, none has managed to completely impose its vision of land exploitation.

Moreover, the legal framework that regulates land in Colombia is highly complex, not only due to normative dispersion, with different norms applying to different time frames, but also because the Constitution subscribes to five large paradigms regarding the relationship between citizens and the State with respect to land. First, the Constitution recognizes the right to private property, in which the dominant model of justice is the freedom to dispose of land according to the liberal tradition. Second, the Constitution subscribes to the idea of an agrarian property based on social justice. Third, based on a vision of ethno-racial justice, the Constitution protects collective ethnic property. Fourth, in what has been called the Ecological Constitution, the Constitution promotes a model of environmental conservation. Finally, the Constitution permits, based on the idea of general development, a model of administration of public property based on the principle of State eminent domain.

The Constitution recognizes each of these models equally, without granting *prima facie* privilege to any specific model. Thus, in many cases, these models are in conflict with one another. For example, land that peasants claim in order to carry out agrarian reform programs can be the same that indigenous peoples reclaim as collective lands, or that the government reserves for infrastructural development. In the absence of a normative hierarchy, these conflicts tend to become protracted and complicated.

The challenge of negotiating one of the catalysts of the war

At the beginning of this decade, with the representation of agricultural unions and their advisors, the Colombian government began peace dialogues with a Marxist guerrilla group whose main grievance had been the historical inequality in access to land for peasants. The government assured that negotiations regarding the land question were not only a part of the agenda of Havana because they were a vindication of the guerrilla, but also because they were an initiative of the government itself.[6] According to President Juan Manuel Santos, that the government took up the guerrilla's issue regarding land and victims was one of the elements that made the peace process with the FARC possible.

As in all negotiations, the parties came to the table with discussion points. Alejandro Reyes (one of the governmental advisors on the land chapter) provides a good summary of the initial positions of the parties.[7] According to the author, the FARC arrived with the idea of resolving the principal cause of the conflict: The expansion of land concentration (*latifundio*) and the violent exclusion of peasants. The FARC also came to the table to confront new threats to peasant lands: Biofuels, corporate mining, hydrocarbons, extensive land acquisition by foreigners (including multinationals), and the continued dispossession of peasants by criminal and paramilitary groups. Their vision focused on strengthening small and medium family agricultural production and defending against land concentration measures in peasant reserve zones (*zonas de reserva campesina*). The FARC also came to the table opposing the policies of restitution and formalization, which they viewed as "a trap to legalize the transfer of land to large investors and foreigners for mining and agro-business."[8] Also, the FARC did not view themselves as spoilers, and as such, were concerned that restitution would dispossess "peasant possessions," as it would use an information system controlled by the victimizers and rely on judges who ignored the context of the land. In fact, information regarding land relationships was a point of concern for the FARC, who proposed undertaking a social cartography to identify idle, extinguished, and illegally appropriated lands, in order to include this information in a new land registry for restitution, distribution, and formalization policies.[9]

On the other side of the table, the government started from the premise that rural reform that increased the well-being of the rural population and helped close the gap between the urban and rural population was a necessary condition to overcome the conflict. For the government, this gap and violence created a vicious cycle. Thus, although the parties agreed on their objective, they did not necessarily agree on the means to achieve it. The government's proposal was to achieve this objective using three instruments: Restitution, distribution, and formalization. To do so, the government did not view direct intervention in *latifundios*[10] as a priority, but rather viewed the creation of a "land bank" as a more efficient measure. This was because a land bank could be formed through the extinguishment of ownership for illicit enrichment, the clarification and recovery of vacant land, administrative expropriation, and the purchase of land use rights. Like the FARC, the government identified one of the main barriers to carrying out these policies as a lack of information, and therefore, proposed overcoming the lack of cadastral, registration, and tax information regarding property.[11]

After ten cycles of negotiations, on May 26, 2013, the parties signed an agreement regarding the issue of land. The FARC's 110 agrarian proposals were evaluated and determined to be part of its political ideology, which would be presented for democratic debate after they disarmed. The logic of the agreement was that it would later correspond to a democratic process to define the best way to implement the various substantive agreements reached. The parties thus agreed on the following: (1) The creation of a land fund for peasants without land or with insufficient land; (2) comprehensive access that recognizes land as a necessary but insufficient condition to ensure the well-being of the rural population; (3) formalization of small and medium properties, not only by demand, but also by way of voluntary offer, through territorial scanning exercises and social cartographies; (4) the creation of an agrarian jurisdiction responsible for resolving existing and future land controversies; (5) modernization of the rural land registry between national and local governments, with community participation; (6) governmental guidance to local governmental entities to increase property tax collection; (7) productive and environmental land zoning, including measures of productive reconversion, as well as strengthening citizen participation in local planning and zoning; (8) the delimitation of the agricultural borders; (9) support for developmental plans in peasant reserve zones and the creation of new peasant reserve zones; (10) implementation of comprehensive rural reform through national sector plans, in order to reduce rural poverty within 10 years; and (11) development programs with a territorial approach (PDET) that prioritize territories most affected by the conflict, poverty, the presence of illicit crops, and minimal institutional presence.[12]

Thus, the result of the negotiation was not a large-scale reform model of the comprehensive agrarian reform defended during the twentieth century. However, the agreements revive a liberal reformist agenda that could have an enormous impact on the conditions and conflicts described in this chapter. As Mauricio García Villegas expresses, "the agreements contemplate a long list of programs aimed at integrating rural and peripheral areas as part of a Nation-State building project. [...] These are all doubtless, laudable initiatives, well-intentioned, and even necessary, to achieve these goals. Nonetheless, the history of the country is full of this type of proposals. In fact, the problem in Colombia is not the lack of good ideas, but rather the absence of factual and political conditions required to put such ideas into practice."[13]

An important step to begin implementation and fill these agreements with technical content and viable policy options was the establishment of the Mission for Transformation of the Countryside, known as the Rural Mission, led by the economist José Antonio Ocampo.[14] The objective of this mission was to define public policy guidelines, in order to have a portfolio of instruments and policies that could be used to make the best decisions regarding public investment for rural and agricultural development over the next 20 years. The Rural Mission's reports are an important repertoire covering the current problems facing the sector. Additionally, its proposals are crucial for determining strategies that overcome irreconcilable positions on how to confront conflicts regarding land and its use, as well as to propose more conciliatory measures in the quest for rational land management.

One of the Mission's initial recommendations was to reverse the process of dismantling agrarian institutions. The government adopted this recommendation, and at the end of 2015 (prior to signing the Final Peace Agreement), announced a diametrical change in these institutions. This reform included the dissolution of Incoder (the government agency created to implement rural development policies) and the creation of three separate entities: The National Land Agency, the National Agency for Rural Development, and the Agency for Territorial Renovation. Regarding the design of sectoral policies, the government also created the National Council for Land Use and the High Council for Land Restitution. It also created the Directorate for Rural Women in the Ministry of Agriculture and increased sources for the Micro-Financing Fund and the Strengthening of the National Commission for Agricultural Credit.

Despite the apparent moderateness of the proposals and the technical preparation to implement them, those opposed to the Agreement were not satisfied. Conservative sectors (supported by traditional extractive industries, such as the cattle industry) branded the Agreement as an attack against private property and legal security. These sectors were determinative in the Agreement's failure to win approval in the October 2016 national referendum. Thus, in the renegotiation of the Agreement, there were some changes to what had been previously agreed upon. First, a clause was introduced, which clarified that future agrarian legislation would not be included in the Agreement reached in Havana and created an expert commission to review the issue of an agrarian reform. Additionally, the renegotiations determined that new peasant reserve zones, beyond what current legislation permitted, would not be authorized, and that nothing in the Agreement would affect the right to private property. Similarly, the new Agreement clarified that the new land registry would not itself modify land appraisals.

From promises to reality

In this context, Chapter (*Punto*) 1 of the Final Agreement is composed of three main topics: (1) Measures related to land access and use, which include agreements for formalizing rural property, delimiting the agricultural borders, creating a land fund, formalizing and updating land registries, creating mechanisms for the resolution of rural conflicts, and supporting land restitution; (2) PDET;[15] and (3) National Plans for Comprehensive Rural Reform. With regard to the estimated time frame and budget required to implement Chapter 1 of the Peace Agreement, predictions show that significant time and resources will be necessary. In accordance with the "methodology to identify progress," the Kroc Institute (the institute charged with monitoring the implementation of the Peace Agreement) elaborated, in its monitoring of the Agreement, that measures regarding land are catalogued as "issues whose robust implementation may only be achieved over the long-term."[16] This means that at least three successive administrations must implement this agenda, and that the results of these policies will only be noticeable after 7 to 10 years of sustained implementation. For this to be possible, the Kroc Institute recommended implementation efforts to begin as soon as possible, including normative and political modifications necessary to roll out measures at the territorial level. Additionally, the indicated methodology underscored that measures related to commitments regarding land were those that required the most resources for implementation. According to the Peace Implementation Framework Plan, around 110.6 trillion pesos (88,084,216,000,00 GBP) are needed to execute all the commitments contained in this point, which is equivalent to 85% of the total budget required to implement the Peace Agreement.[17]

One of the first steps taken by the Santos administration to start the implementation of Chapter 1 was the issuance of Decree 902. This legal instrument sought to create mechanisms to facilitate access to land and the formalization of rural property as policies derived from the Agreement. To this end, it introduced changes to Law 160 of 1994, created and regulated the Registry of Subjects of Regularization of Rural Property (RESO), instituted the Lands Fund, and designed a unified procedure to resolve claims related to land access and formalization.

The decree had many objectives, all of which it sought to achieve at the same time. On the one hand, the norm attempted to accelerate processes of land formalization in the absence of evident conflict. This refers to cases in which land is occupied by subjects of agrarian reform (e.g., peasant families that use small extensions or measures of land), and in which its use is not disputed. Second, the norm sought to provide legal security to another group of rural residents: Those who have carried out activities on uncultivated land over a long period of time, but who are not subject to agrarian reform (e.g., middle or upper-middle class families who have occupied small parcels of land for many years). For this group, the norm states that they can keep the land by paying a minimum legalization fee. Finally, the decree paved the way to permit larger parcels of land that belong to the State (i.e., unused lands or *baldíos*) to be exploited by investors. To this end, the norm created a pay system based on market prices.

On the other hand, Decree 902 attempted to regularize land and territorial rights in two ways. The first was through simplifying the rights adjudication process, by reducing the more-than-fifteen-existing processes to a single procedure. This new procedure is mixed (administrative and judicial) and seeks to replicate best practices of the land restitution process. It also aims to reduce judicial caseload by resolving cases during the administrative phase, thereby reducing the length of proceedings. The second was through creating the RESO and an associated process, so that stakeholders in the rural areas would be those responsible for coordinating the best uses for land in their territory, thereby avoiding conflicts regarding land use.

The decree was controversial from the beginning. Prior to its promulgation, the government circulated a more comprehensive draft (which included other topics, such as the reversion of illegitimate land transactions). Conservative sectors rejected such a proposal, claiming it affected legal security by promoting expropriation. However, by the time the government had special authority to issue norms with the force of law, some experts considered that on such a controversial topic, in a context of high polarization and fragility of the peace process, it was better to leave major decisions to the Congress,[18] Deferring to these arguments, the Santos administration decided to issue a simplified version of its proposal in Decree 902. Nonetheless, the critiques of the norm did not stop there. Among the citizen interventions presented to the Constitutional Court during its constitutional review of the decree, various stakeholders expressed their disagreement regarding different aspects of the decree. Out of these arguments before the Court, several are worth mentioning. On the one hand, some argued the norm was unconstitutional and inappropriate, as it permitted individuals and companies who did not qualify as subjects of agrarian reform to access property in uncultivated lands. On the other hand, some contended that the procedure to adjudicate rights should be determined through a special law (i.e., a statutory law), and therefore, that the decree, for procedural reasons, was not in accordance with the Constitution. In early July 2018, the Constitutional Court issued a decision approving the majority of the Decree 902's provisions.

However, this legal victory was not enough to bolster the implementation of the overall IRR strategy. The Kroc Institute recognized this challenge in its report from the end of 2017, in which it indicated that Chapter 1 of the Agreement was the point with the least progress made in its implementation. Regarding the first component of this Chapter, access to land, the report found that, of the 23 specific commitments contained in Chapter 1, only one had been completely implemented; this implemented commitment, regarding the creation of a commission of university experts, is equivalent to 4% of the total. The majority of commitments (12), equivalent to 53%, had not been started. With regard to the second component of Chapter 1, PDETs, the Kroc Institute identified five provisions, of which two (60%) had been minimally implemented. Finally, with respect to the third component, National Rural Reform Plans, the Institute identified 65 provisions or commitments, the majority of which (48% or 74%) reported no actions, while several had been minimally implemented (17% or 26%).[19]

By the end of the Santos administration, most of the IRR measures were in the pilot phase. Similarly, the implementation of the PDET policy was to begin with community consultations, starting at the local level, such as *veredas* (an administrative land division used in rural areas, similar to neighborhoods), with later decisions to be taken in municipal fora, and finally, at the departmental level. As in the implementation of the access to land component, the execution of the majority of PDETs was in the initial phase at the close of the Santos administration.

Unfortunately, the pace of the implementation of Chapter 1 of the Peace Agreement did not improve during the first 2 years of the Duque administration. According to the Kroc Institute's 3-year monitoring report, which covers the implementation of the Peace Agreement until December 2019, while there has been some progress regarding planning, "the implementation of the plans... has been incipient."[20] Additionally, the first semester of 2020 has been hampered by further delays, as a result of the impact of the COVID-19 pandemic.

Conclusions

The proposals regarding land in the Peace Agreement are not revolutionary with respect to property and land governance. During peace negotiations, the FARC seems to have abandoned (at least for the short-term) their idea of abolishing private property, their fight against the *latifundio*, and their rallying cry for classic agrarian reform in Colombia. As a result, with respect to land, the Peace Agreement presents a series of social liberalistic proposals that are not only compatible with the Constitution and current laws, but in some cases, merely repeat what Colombian norms already establish. To this end, the Agreement is a roadmap for the implementation of policy measures which, in spite of being state obligations, have been ignored by successive government administrations. Thus, the whole agenda for building infrastructure for rural areas, as well as measures regarding access to health and education services in the countryside, is simply derived from the Constitution's promise of a social welfare state. The measures regarding the formalization of and access to land, production subsidies, etc., merely develop the legal norms in place since the adoption of Law 160 of 1994. Even without radically changing the rules of the game, if the political goals of the Agreement were achieved, the quality of life of rural households could improve substantially.

The key, therefore, seems to be related to how to execute this public policy strategy, without falling into the institutional anomie of previous decades. To do so, the Santos administration, which reached the agreement and committed to the implementation of peace, had two main tasks: (1) To execute, as far as it could, measures within its reach, and (2) to lay the normative groundwork that later would be transformed into state policies (rather than a plan for a specific government) and necessary measures to fulfill the Agreement.

In both instances, and for diverse reasons, the government did not complete these tasks. First, no structural measures were shielded from political changes. In fact, the Congress did not discuss or approve any structural norms regarding land during this period. As a result, the government lost its opportunity to establish the agrarian jurisdiction, which is one of the institutional commitments necessary to guaranteeing a land-dispute system more in line with the needs of peasant populations. The officials responsible for advancing the project floundered in discussions about the jurisdiction's structure, its hierarchy, its relationship with the rest of the judiciary, etc., and the project never made it to congressional debate.

Something similar occurred with the "Comprehensive Land Bill," which the Ministry of Agriculture promised to start drafting at the beginning of the Santos administration in 2010. Initially, different powerful factions within the Ministry could not agree on the approach of the law or the model it should follow (some wanted a law closer to the peasant family model, while others preferred the large-scale exploitation model). Later, the government alleged that the cause of the delay was due to its inability to coordinate with indigenous peoples on the methodology for the prior consultation process. Finally, the Ministry stated that, since the topic was being discussed at the negotiating table with the FARC, the government would wait until it reached agreements to bring the issue to the Congress.[21] But once the Agreement was reached, the government still failed to present its proposal as promised.

In any event, this type of measure must be approved by the Congress, an institution that has not only failed to sufficiently recognize the rights of rural communities, but which also has historically responded more favorably to the interests of business and other powerful groups who seek to maintain the status quo regarding land, in order to maintain or increase their privileges and political influence.[22] Although the Santos administration had a coalition that, in theory, guaranteed a comfortable majority in the Congress, in reality, and particularly in his last year in office, different parties of the coalition did not vote together in favor of projects to implement the Agreement. During the 2018 presidential campaign, the majority of these parties aligned themselves with the party of the current president, Iván Duque, who represents the party that opposed the Agreement, especially Chapter 1.

Thus, it was no surprise that tasks not started by the Santos administration would not be a priority for the new legislative and executive branches.

An influential faction of the current president's political party has vehemently opposed the policy of land restitution for victims of dispossession in the armed conflict. In the past, this party's caucus presented a proposal to reform Law 1448 to modify the burden of proof that the law establishes for those who oppose restitution (a requirement of heighten good faith), which has been fundamental to resolving restitution processes in favor of victims in an expedited fashion.[23] Because this party controls the executive branch and has a majority in the Congress, an attempt by the party to reform this law is expected to begin very quickly.

Additionally, the actions the Santos government undertook in territories to implement measures such as formalization, PDETs, pilot projects of multi-purpose land registries, etc., did not result in a transformative impact. Some of these measures have brought individual material justice to many households and families. Similarly, in some cases, the execution of the policies has surpassed historical rates of implementation. For example, this has occurred with the ANT's formalization policy, which, compared to previous years, has obtained very positive results. However, various factors seem to have played a role, since these policies have not secured a clear social or institutional base that would protect them in changes in administrations.

On the one hand, the Santos government's actions concentrated more on showing that it was implementing the Peace Agreement, instead of creating alliances at the local level that would provide social legitimacy to the programs. Given the short time the Santos administration had, institutions began their work in a race against the clock, which privileged measurable outcomes over social work and community consultations. This also produced coordination problems between entities and a distrust of institutions in territories.[24] On the other hand, institutions at the national level rarely included local authorities in these implementation processes. Such strategy was paradoxical, as the implementation of these measures takes place precisely in the territories where these local authorities have responsibilities. It also eliminated a natural ally who could have vindicated these measures in the absence of the Santos administration.

This unbalanced implementation also created an enormous risk for peasant and ethnic communities with respect to other local players. This is because both Decree 902 and the PDET policy provide for a series of discussion fora regarding land use and distribution, based on the idea that all stakeholders will have a voice, and as a result, this deliberation would produce the best possible outcome among different interests. However, given the power imbalance between these communities and other influential actors in the territories, unless there are specific measures to protect the interests of the weakest players (such as an agrarian law and an agrarian jurisdiction), these settings may lead to a more harmful situation for peasant and ethnic communities.

Under the Duque administration, these problems have only intensified, as the result of a deliberate, three-pronged noncompliance strategy of the Agreement: Rejection, anomie, and co-optation. The first strategy is backed by a sector of the President's party, particularly those who represent an important sector of ranchers and rural businessmen. This strategy seeks to derogate from the normative measures created by the Santos administration, thereby eliminating all the regulations of Chapter 1 of the Agreement. In effect, this would send a clear political message, rejecting these policies for the countryside and supporting the large-scale model of land tenancy and agricultural production. While the Constitutional Court's decisions and the lack of congressional majorities have prevented Duque and his party from normatively dismantling the Agreement, the interest for modifying the land restitution policy is just as strong in 2020 as it was when Law 1448 of 2011 was enacted.[25]

The second strategy is that of anomie. To the extent that the responsibility for the norm's implementation falls on the government, and there are no peremptory norms that require implementing the Agreement within a set time period, a less controversial way to undermine the Agreement is simply to change political priorities and to not continue with the execution of the planned measures, or to execute them at a slower pace, using officials with little knowledge and a small budget. In particular, such a strategy would be less controversial for the international community, which supports the Agreement. This is, perhaps, the most visible strategy. One important example is the current administration's failure to present to the Congress a bill that would create the agrarian jurisdiction, which would not only comply with an important agreement from the negotiation table, but also with recommendations from many experts regarding the matter.

The third strategy is co-optation or appropriating institutional mechanisms which have already been created for implementing the Agreement and using them for purposes other than those for which they were created. For example, co-optation might be used to promote "winners" within the processes of social restructuring of the countryside, thereby creating advantages for the central government's political allies in the territories. The Duque administration has exercised a proactive policy of appointing political allies to positions central to the implementation of the Agreement. These political allies are recognized more for their ideological positions than for their technical competencies related to the offices for which they are appointed. This has taken place in the National Center of Historical Memory, the Ministry of the Interior's Victims Office, and the main institutions in charge of the implementation of land policies, such as the National Land Agency.

In this context, a new wave of disputes has been emerging, both in the territories, as well as in centers of political power, where the country's agrarian model is discussed. Although comprehensive rural reform did not become the dominant discourse in the discussion of rural policy, the revitalization of the idea of an agrarian reform did provide new tools to those who defend a model of rurality with similar postulates. Additionally, the demobilization of the FARC has been a positive step for rural communities to more freely exercise their rights and to more easily mobilize to defend their preferences regarding models of land tenancy and exploitation. However, traditional political power structures have not moved, not even a millimeter. In this peace process, they have demonstrated an enormous capacity to maintain the status quo and have shown that their political agenda is more active than ever. Thus, it is to be expected that disputes regarding land and territory will continue during this new phase in Colombian history.

Notes

1 For the purposes of this chapter, I will be using the terms "Peace Agreement" and "Agreement" interchangeably.

2 Colombian society has faced three historical challenges regarding this issue: (1) Land distribution in rural Colombia has been highly inequitable, and its concentration has tended to increase, especially in recent decades. During the period between 2000 and 2011, the Gini index of land distribution increased from 0.85 to 0.87, while the Gini index of landowners reached 0.896 in 2011 (in 2000 it was 0.977). See Mauricio García Villegas, Juan Carlos Rodríguez Raga, Miguel García Sánchez, Javier Revelo Rebolledo, José Rafael Espinosa Restrepo, *Los Estados del país. Instituciones municipales y realidades locales* (Bogota: Dejusticia, 2011). (2) Informality in land tenancy: According to official data, only 6% of municipalities in the country (71) have a level of land formality greater than 75%, and these are generally the largest parcels. See Misión para la Transformación del Campo Colombiano, *El Campo colombiano: un camino hacia el bienestar y la paz* (Bogotá: DNP, 2015), 15. By contrast, in the remaining 94% of municipalities, 16% of parcels have a level of total or almost total informality. (3) Conflicts regarding land use and tenancy: Unequal distribution of land and lack of expertise regarding its use have led to its underuse and over-exploitation. A 2012 study from the Augustín Codazzi Geographic Institute (IGAC) regarding land conflicts found that 13% of land zoned for agriculture is underused and 15% is overused. See Instituto Geográfico Agustín Codazzi, *Atlas de la distribución de la propiedad rural en Colombia* (Bogotá: Imprenta Nacional de Colombia, 2012). Misión Rural's report found that changes in land use between 2000 and 2009 had led to an increase of 11.8% in agricultural areas and an increase of 2.8% in herbaceous and grass areas used for livestock, while bodies of water had reduced by 8.8% and forests by 3.1%. During the same period, land dedicated to mining increased by 18.8%. As a result, today, out of the land in conservation, 13 million hectares have agricultural uses, and extractive activities are carried out in 935,000 hectares. See Misión para la Transformación, *El Campo Colombiano*, 7–9.

3 According to the Unified Victims Registry (RUV), between 1985 and May 2020, 8,036,014 people were forced to leave their homes, corresponding to approximately 1,200,000 households. This number represents nearly 15.2% of the country's total population. "Single Registry of Victims," Unidad para las Víctimas, last modified May 31, 2020.

4 Michael Lipton uses the term classic land reform (CLR) to refer to legislation that seeks to directly redistribute ownership of land dedicated to agricultural production, such that the poorest people benefit, and their status, power, and income increases as compared to their situation prior to the reform. Thus, in the "simplest" form of CLR, the government creates: (1) A maximum land authority,

(2) a maximum limit for parcels, (3) rules for compensating those who will be expropriated, (4) a minimum limit for parcels, (5) dates in which the authority will expropriate lands that are larger than the maximum allowable size, (6) later distribution of land among those who do not have the minimum parcel size, and (7) rules for land payment or access to credit for beneficiaries. Michael Lipton, *Land Reform in Developing Countries: Property Rights and Property Wrongs* (London: Routledge, 2009), 127.

5 Nelson C. Sánchez, *Tierra en transición. Justicia transicional, restitución de tierras y política agraria en Colombia* (Bogotá: Dejusticia, 2017).

6 Sergio Jaramillo Caro, *La Paz Territorial.* Keynote Speech delivered at Harvard University, March 13, 2013, http://www.eltiempo.com/archivo/documento/ CMS-13791996.

7 Alejandro Reyes Posada, *La reforma rural para la paz* (Bogotá: Editorial Debate, 2016), p. 49.

8 Id. At 50.

9 Id. At 51.

10 Reyes recounts that with respect to land concentration, the government's idea was to focus the discussion on access to land for peasants and to address the problem without limiting "legitimate property rights guaranteed by the Constitution," since the law has not imposed extension limits to land property. Reyes, La reforma rural, p. 53.

11 Id.

12 Mesa de Conversaciones, *Comunicado Conjunto*, La Habana, 26 de mayo de 2013. Recuperado de https://www.Mesadeconversaciones.com.co/comunicados/comunicado-conjunto-la-habana-26-de-mayo-de-2013.

13 Mauricio García Villegas M. "La suerte de los borradores de La Habana," *El Espectador*, October 9, 2014, http://www.elespectador.com/noticias/politica/suerte-de-los-borradores-de-habana-articulo-521475.

14 Misión para la Transformación, *El Campo Colombiano.*

15 One of the pillars of the Integral Rural Reform is the construction of Development Plans with a Territorial Approach (PDET), which seek to accelerate structural transformation of rural areas for inhabitants to live better, to reverse the effects of the conflict, and to contribute to reparation and reconciliation in territories. PDETs include the participatory construction of Action Plans for Regional Transformation (PATR), which will guide public investments in targeted sub-regions for a period of 10 years.

16 The Kroc Institute's report highlights that "the Colombian Agreement is unique in the detailed and profound development of these types of measures focused on Comprehensive Rural Reform, more equitable access to land and the socioeconomic development of the areas most affected by the armed conflict, poverty, or the drug trafficking economy, and the presence of antipersonnel mines," Kroc Institute for International Peace Studies, *Informe sobre el estado efectivo de implementación del acuerdo de paz en Colombia* (Notre Dame: University of Notre Dame, 2017), 18.

17 Gobierno de Colombia, *Plan marco de implementación, Acuerdo final para la terminación del conflicto y la construcción de una paz estable y duradero* (Bogotá: DNP, 2018), 218–19.

18 See Tatiana Alfonso H, Alviar H, Ibáñez AM, y otros AM, *Concepto de la mesa de expertos académicos sobre el proyecto de ley para el ordenamiento social de la propiedad rura* (Bogotá: Universidad de los Andes, Universidad Externado de Colombia, Universidad Eafit, 2017).

19 Kroc Institute, *Informe sobre el estado efectivo.*

20 Kroc Institute for International Peace Studies, *Report Four: State of Implementation of the Colombian Final Accord, December 2016–November 2019* (Notre Dame: University of Notre Dame, 2020), 30.

21 Sánchez, *Tierra en Transicion*.
22 Salomón Kalmanovitz and Enrique López Encizo, *La Agricultura Colombiana en el Siglo XX* (Bogotá: Fondo de Cultura Económica y Banco de la República, 2007).
23 Aura Bolívar A, Gutiérrez L, Sánchez NC, Uprimny CR, *Debates sobre la acción de restitución*. (Bogotá: Dejusticia, 2017).
24 Irina Junieles, "Retos y Oportunidades para la transformación del campo: Programas de Desarrollo con Enfoque Territorial," La Silla Vacia, September 13, 2017, https://lasillavacia.com/silla-llena/red-rural/historia/paz-para-transformacion-del-campo-planes-de-desarrollo-con-enfoque; Kroc Institute, Three Years After the Signing of the Final Agreement in Colombia: Moving Toward Territorial Transformation (Kroc Institute et al., 2020), http://peaceaccords.nd.edu/wp-content/uploads/2020/06/Cuarto-Informe-Final-with-Annex-Link-1.pdf.
25 In June 2020, more than 330 civil society organizations issued a communique expressing their preoccupation regarding the possible "discussion and approval" of Bill 20 of 2019. According to the organizations, the bill represented a grave regression for the reparations for victims or land dispossession and put in risk the formal and material restitution of properties dispossessed during the armed conflict. Comisión Colombiana de Juristas, "*El Proyecto de Ley 20 de 2019 Senado acaba con la Restitución de Tierras a Víctimas de Despojo y Abandono Forzado*," June 22, 2020, https://www.coljuristas.org/nuestro_quehacer/item.php?id=332.

13 The gender component in the Colombian peace process

Obstacles to its inclusion and implementation

Patricia Pabón and Javier Aguirre

Introduction

This chapter explores the path to the inclusion and implementation of the Gender Component of the Peace Agreements in Colombia to understand how historical and structural injustices linked to gender can be addressed. Drawing on the work of Nancy Fraser, we argue that gender justice demands inclusion of the perspectives of women and Lesbian, Gay, Bisexual, Transexual, and Intersex (LGBTI) people in the peace-building process, for they are victims of distinctive conflict-related injustices different from those suffered by other actors. Our working hypothesis is that, despite the participation of women and members of the LGBTI community in the negotiations and the inclusion of the Gender Component in the Final Agreement, these groups still suffer from a lack of representation and recognition in peacebuilding activities. As evidence for this hypothesis we offer the difficulties in the consultations to ratify the Final Agreement, and conclude that inclusion and remedies to gender-related injustices, including those of lack of representation and symbolic and cultural recognition, continue to be unresolved issues in Colombia's peace-building processes.

The argument proceeds as follows. First, we describe the participation of women and the LGBTI community in the negotiation process, the difficulties that the Gender Component faced in the consultation to ratify the 2016 Final Agreement, and the adjustments made after the "No" victory in 2016. Second, drawing from Fraser, we analyze these difficulties using the categories of representation, recognition, and distribution. Third, we discuss the weight of religious arguments in the public sphere. In the concluding section, we highlight some challenges for the implementation of the Agreement's Gender Approach.

The participation of women and members of the LGBTI community in the peace process: The path to inclusion of the Final Agreement's Gender Component

It is a mistake to hold that gender studies only problematize women-related situations. On the contrary, when the category "gender" is used as the fundamental basis of theoretical-practical perspectives, "it is used to describe social identities, roles, expectations, and norms that generally connect with biological sex,"[1] but that do not depend exclusively on biology. Thus, the category "gender" refers to how societies have assigned different roles, behaviors, expectations, and activities to both men and women. Gender studies have made it possible to understand and explain inequalities between women and men as a result of social, cultural, and power interactions that throughout history have marked disadvantages for women and non-hegemonic sexual identities or orientations. In turn, the gender approach as a category of analysis, allows us to show how different phenomena, in all spheres, affect people differently, precisely for their particular location in the gender spectrum. War and armed conflict are emblematic "phenomena" that differentially affect people according to their gender. As María Villellas puts it, "[a]nalyzing armed conflicts without taking into account the gender dimension means carrying out partial and incomplete analyses, leaving causes and consequences on one side and taking the experience of only a part of the population—men—and universalizing it. The gender perspective tries to expose this bias."[2]

Undoubtedly, war has caused severe damage to humanity, but it has caused differential damages to women. In 2000, the United Nations Security Council issued a resolution recognizing the effects of armed conflict on women and girls and indicating guidelines for their protection and full participation in peace processes.[3] Despite these efforts, the UN itself has recognized the difficulties in achieving the required involvement of women in formal peace negotiations. Women represent 8% of those who participate in peace negotiations and less than 3% of those who sign peace agreements,[4] a disproportionately low figure considering that women constitute half of the world population, and that they are profoundly affected by war. This situation parallels the experience of the negotiation process in Havana. While the Havana negotiations are valued as the most advanced peace process in the history of Colombia in terms of incorporating women and members of LGBTI communities, the participation of members of these groups was negligible.

The official start of peace negotiations with FARC-EP was announced in September 2012 by the then President of Colombia, Juan Manuel Santos. Negotiations began; however, without the inclusion of women. In response to this deficit different women's organizations, "in parallel to the Havana dialogues, held meetings to pressure their participation in the process and also to discuss issues related to the armed conflict and women's rights."[5] Consequent to the work carried out by these organizations María Paulina Riveros and Nigeria Rentería were included as plenipotentiaries of the National Government at the negotiating table in November 2013. Their appointments were considered by some analysts as a "milestone in the history of peace in Colombia because, for the first time, we see women in the front line of the discussion."[6]

Despite this step, and the inclusion of women within the inner circles of high decision-making power, some voices questioned whether these women effectively "represent gender interests" because, as Professor Clara Rocío Rodríguez Pico points out, "they are delegates there on behalf of the government or the FARC and have their own legitimate personal or professional interests."[7] This challenge concerning the composition of the table has also been raised on other occasions: "access to power does not guarantee that there is a gender stance that makes women exercise their positions to promote women's rights or necessarily have a disposition toward peacebuilding."[8]

In 2014, a gender subcommittee was created within the negotiation process to build the Agreement's gender approach. In total, 18 women's and LGBTI organizations participated in this process. The subcommittee was composed by María Paulina Riveros, as the delegate of the Government, and Victoria Sandino Palmera, as the delegate of FARC-EP. "This event brought the female presence to 20% in the Government delegation and 15% at the negotiating tables, which were made up of 17 men and three women. (A single woman was included in the FARC-EP delegation.)"[9]

Representatives of female victims and victims in the LGBTI community were also heard at the negotiating tables in March 2015.[10] These actions were carried out to overcome one of the challenges of the peace process in Colombia, namely, to give voice to the direct victims of the conflict. Despite this, several sectors have criticized the lack of recognition and prominence given to the women's groups and movements leading processes of reconciliation and reconstruction in conflict zones.

A peace agreement between the Colombian government and FARC-EP was at last signed in Cartagena, Colombia, on September 26, 2016. In the first version of the Agreement, the expression "gender" was incorporated in a broad sense to include the different situations and realities of "girls, boys, women, and men, including people with diverse sexual orientations and gender identities."[11] On this basis, the differential approach was adopted based on the notion that the Agreement's implementation should take into account "the specific needs and differential conditions of women, according to their life cycle, effects, and needs (gender approach)" and "gender diversity."[12] As a result, a gender component was included in each of the points of Agreement. While it alluded to a plurality of gender identities, it focused on the differential conditions of women. Some of the measures include:

- Chapter 1—Comprehensive rural reform: Access to the right to rural property for women, removing obstacles to obtaining land titles; rural women's right to health at all stages of their lives. Professional training and support in the consolidation of a peasant, familiar, and communal economy as well as labor links of women workers in unconventional areas.

- Chapter 2—Political participation: Security for the exercise of politics, considering a territorial, differential, and gender approach, and an evaluation of the security conditions that might affect the political participation of women. The support and strengthening of organizations and social movements on equal terms, and the strengthening of political training and promotion of democratic values to ensure the participation of women.
- Chapter 3—End of the conflict: Women must participate in the commissions and instruments created to dismantle criminal organizations as well as in the design of criminal policy.
- Chapter 4—Solving the problem of illicit drugs: Promoting job opportunities for women living in territories affected by illicit crops, incorporating a gender approach in addressing the health problems caused by the consumption of illicit drugs, evaluating the impact on women and the LGBTI community.
- Chapter 5—Victims of the conflict: Ensure a gender focus on truth, justice, reparation, and guarantee of non-repetition. Regarding the administration of justice, the incorporation of the gender perspective in courts and truth commissions was taken into account, as well as the impossibility of giving amnesty or pardon to sexual crimes, of which women and the LGBTI community were the primary victims.

The Government, FARC-EP, and many social and academic sectors celebrated the incorporation of the gender perspective in the agreements. However, in August 2016, the month in which the agreements were published and in which a dissemination campaign began prior to the plebiscite of October (the mechanism chosen for its popular ratification), a new type of discourse against the Agreement started: Opponents of the process began to claim that the Agreement incorporated what they called "gender ideology." In different regions, political figures with ties to evangelical organizations promoted voting "No" to the peace agreement, invoking the danger that the incorporation of gender ideology in the text represented for the present and future of Colombia. Two examples can be provided. In the first instance, a Bogotá Municipal Councilor claimed that "the agreement with the FARC will lead us to a dangerous homosexual dictatorship."[13] In the second, at the regional level, several very influential politicians led campaigns for the "protection of the family," connecting opposition to the Peace Agreement with their rejection of the Ministry of Education's human rights training plan for teachers, which include some booklets that introduce a gender-based approach in schools.[14]

The plebiscite of October 2, 2016, resulted in the rejection of the Final Agreement by a small majority (50.2%) before the perplexed gaze of the world. Many analysts held that the "No" vote succeeded due to their campaign against the gender approach and the rights of sexual minorities.[15]

The political solution to this impasse was a renegotiation of some of the components of the Agreement. A new Agreement was signed on

November 24, 2016. What were its consequences? As Olga González points out, while a comparison of the content of the two documents does not show substantial reforms, it is clear that the new Agreement explicitly included references to "religious minorities" and reduced allusions to the "gender approach," sexual minorities and women.[16] How are we to read the rejection of what had been described as a pioneering attempt to include a gender approach in the peace agreement? Why were the mention of a gender perspective, equality for women, and the restoration of rights to victims with diverse sexual orientations publicly perceived as the primary test of the result of 4 years of peace negotiations? In what follows, we will use Fraser's categories to understand the difficulties encountered in the process, the role of religious discourse, and the ongoing challenges to implementing the gender components of the Agreement.

Devalued women and sexualities: Lack of recognition, representation, and redistribution

Equality for women and recognition of the LGBTI community continues to be a deeply divisive issue in Colombian society. To discuss the disadvantages experienced by women and people with non-hegemonic sexual identities, we will draw on Fraser's claim that three fundamental and interrelated dimensions of injustice need to be considered in these situations. These are the absence of representation at the political level, the lack of access and distribution to resources at the economic level, and the absence of recognition (or negative recognition) at the cultural and symbolic levels.[17] Representation, redistribution, and recognition are required to overcome these injustices but these structural measures must be tackled together, since their disarticulation obstructs the attainment of societal equity.

Women and members of the LGBTI community suffer from structural distributive injustices. For example, the transsexual population and women (particularly mothers, even when maternity has been freely chosen) have difficulties in accessing decent and safe jobs. Similarly, feminine and LGBTI identities suffer from a negative social recognition that excludes them from well-paid and stable jobs. At the political level, these groups have been excluded from political participation and decision-making. While they can participate as representative of traditional political perspectives, they seldom can be political actors in terms of their distinctive identities and needs, so they end unrepresented and with little or no involvement in the decisions that affect their lives. These injustices intersect with the fact that the prevailing cultural and social values disparage feminine and non-hegemonic sexual orientations. For this reason they suffer from a lack of recognition or experience a negative recognition that can lead to violent situations and can translate (leads to situations of violence, and that translates) into femicides and hate crimes, some in the context of the conflict, and others in daily life in urban and rural areas.[18]

Overcoming the poverty of women and LGBTI people and the profound difficulties they face in accessing agrarian property or in repairing the damage they have suffered as victims of the conflict cannot be achieved with measures that attack single forms of injustice independently. The moral of Fraser's proposal is that neither recognition theories nor retribution theories alone can adequately understand the injustices in capitalist societies.[19] This is evidenced in the Colombian context when legislation adopts individual legal measures to protect motherhood or to secure quotas for women in public offices or party lists for elections. It is also evident in the attempted laws that punish discrimination: opponents readily reject their approval with arguments based on their constitutional right to freedom of expression.[20] These situations show that in Colombian society there is a deep negative recognition of LGBTI identities and femininity, especially when they attempt to go beyond the roles and spaces traditionally assigned to them.

For Fraser, gender-related injustices characteristically display "androcentrism," namely, "the authoritative construction of norms that privilege traits associated with masculinity. Along with this goes cultural sexism: The pervasive devaluation and disparagement of things coded as 'feminine,' paradigmatically-but not only women."[21] On many occasions, legal, political, and economic systems privilege androcentric values, and these reinforce the stereotypes that already exist in social life. While war affects men and women, the voices of women are systematically excluded in the negotiation of peace agreements. Those who make peace or declare war are men. Negotiations are then reduced to matters of power and victory, and at the table of power, the excluded, when they can achieve a chair (that often is more symbolic than real), are not admitted on an equal footing. Eliminating gender injustices also involves taking cultural measures that seek to transform stereotypes, role expectations, and sexist prejudices. For Fraser, "justice today requires both redistribution and recognition. Neither alone is sufficient."[22] Justice also involves remedying representation deficits, so that women can participate directly and realistically in decision-making that affects them.

Women and groups with diverse sexual orientation and non-hegemonic gender identities should be recognized as discriminated-against minorities. This recognition should lead to the inclusion of their voices in the negotiation of issues that affect them or norms that apply to them. Failure to include them in decisions affecting their interests and rights could be considered as a new act of discrimination, impairing the effect of any measures adopted on their behalf.

All the decisions taken to protect the rights of any minority must be the product of reasoned deliberation and must begin with the minority's active participation. Hence, the perspective of women and LGBTI groups must be incorporated into the structure of the political conception of justice, for they are free and equal people who will be affected by this conception.

The 2016 "No" campaign, that styled itself as being "in favor of peace but against gender ideology," showed that the most traditional and conservative features of a society (private property and reproductive, heterosexual marriage, among others) remain in the social imagination as "universal" values, even if they are not realized in practice. In reality, a large part of the population in Colombia does not own property, lives in free unions and reconstituted families, and does not even want to have children.[23] However, propaganda reproduces other expectations. The religious groups that led the "No" vote as a means to avoid a "homosexual dictatorship" managed to channel the representation of recognized hegemonic values while covering up other interests in the debate. The second version of the Agreement modulated the language and tried to reduce the recognition of women and LGBTI groups, thereby legitimizing the overwhelming conservative machinery of the warlords, the representatives of "Tradition, Family, and Property."[24] On this aspect, the construction of a stable and lasting peace, and the (symbolic) recognition of traditionally excluded groups remain pending debts.

While priests and Catholic communities accompanied the process in the countryside, in the cities, a large number of "Christian" (i.e., evangelical protestant) pastors and preachers led exclusion and discrimination. Their banners were the defense of the role of traditional women, the thesis of homosexuality as a disease from which children must be saved, and the recovery of 'traditional values.'"[25] Catholic leaders, who have generally accompanied efforts to achieve peace in Colombia, made a timid defense of the Agreement (with a few exceptions) and left the plebiscite that sought to endorse it in the hands of the most conservative believers.[26] This showed that, for better or for worse, religion is not a relic of the past. On the contrary, it is a force that still configures the symbolic and the cultural, and on that plane, there are also winners and losers, and dominators and dominated. It is a plane that must be respected, and in which one must also fight.

The role of religious discourse in the construction of "gender ideology" as an enemy

Below the rhetoric of "gender ideology" lies a profoundly negative and reductionist vision of feminine and LGBTI identities. It is necessary to keep our eyes open to this reality since, as Fraser has shown, correcting low economic redistribution and the absence of political representation also requires attacking problems around the lack of recognition. What happened with the Peace Agreement in Colombia is an excruciating lesson that shows the importance of the cultural and symbolic field, which should not be underestimated by supposed perspectives that point to the "truly profound." There can be no redistribution without recognition or recognition without redistribution.

The lack of recognition of the feminine (beyond a particular way of exercising motherhood) and of alternative gender identities facilitates the "moral panic" that was created around the popular ratification of the Agreement, which was were) seen as an attack on the family values, the natural and clear identities of boys and girls, and the stimulation of homosexuality and other "immoral behaviors."[27] In this regard, most religious communities are directly responsible for the lack of recognition. The victory of "No" in the plebiscite was the product of an alliance between evangelical, Catholic, and Protestant groups acting against feminism and gender ideology and accusing them of being a new form of totalitarianism.

A brief note on Catholic doctrine on women is necessary, for Catholicism is still the majority religion in Colombia. This doctrine has shifted from openly upholding the inferiority of women and submission to men, to affirming the so-called "doctrine of complementarity." For the Vatican, as Case explains, "complementarity entails that 'man and woman' have 'equal dignity as persons' but that this equal dignity is premised on and manifested in essential and complementary differences, 'physical, psychological, and ontological' (Ratzinger 2004). The differences the Vatican has in mind as 'essential' include most of what secular law would characterize as sex stereotypes, a term many activist proponents of complementarity embrace rather than repudiate (Kuby 2008)."[28] This doctrine has been strengthened over time and has been maintained in the papacies of John Paul II, Benedict XVI and even Francis II (though in a seemingly relaxed form).[29] However, as Case herself points out, like his predecessors, Francis continues to see "gender theories" as potential threats to human existence comparable to a nuclear war.[30]

The profoundly negative effect that dominant Christian discourses have on gender approaches must be considered in social struggles since, as we indicated, religious lobbies are formidable obstacles to achieving improvements in representation of, and redistribution for, women and LGBTI people. However, we should avoid falling into reductionist characterizations of the social groups and citizens that accept religious views. As Vega points out, "to label them as fundamentalists does not allow us to understand their moral and economic plurality nor the theological and pastoral innovations they introduce."[31] Furthermore, we should value and enhance those religious and theological perspectives that provide inclusive ways of interpreting the dominant Christian heritage in Latin American societies.[32] "The recognition of a plurality of religious positions, favorable to gender, sexual, and reproductive rights, helps the social and political (and analytical) recognition of a plurality of religious meanings, and religious institutions."[33]

Conclusion

The participation of women in the process of building peace agreements has been progressively achieved through three different means: (was progressively achieved and was identified at three levels, namely) "[1] as plenipotentiaries in the delegations; [2] through the counselling mechanisms provided by the Conversation Table, such as the victims' delegations and the thematic forums; and finally [3] from spaces of self-organization, through which participatory networks such as the two Summits of Women and Peace were promoted."[34] Hence, it is safe to state that the Colombian peace process provided some degree of representation for women. In the same sense, there was also the participation of LGBTI through victims' delegations and thematic forums.

The Agreement incorporated measures of redistribution and political representation, such as those stated in the points on agrarian reform and political participation. The widespread use of gender-related language and categories in the first version of the Agreement can be interpreted as a recognition exercise. However, the triumph of the "No" vote and capitulation to the opposition around gender issues brought down the symbolic value of the Agreement and reinforced stereotypes and negative representations about femininity and sexual diversity. The symbolic recognition of the positive perspective on gender in the first Agreement created a new enemy of peace, "gender ideology," which overshadowed the redistribution and representation measures in the renegotiation. Although these measures remained in the final text of the Agreement, some expressions related to gender were reduced, thereby eliminating the symbolic recognition. In the new Agreement, "'the differential, gender, and diversity approach' is replaced by a more general and abstract vision based on a modern universal subject that speaks of 'the inalienable rights of the person,' and sets out a very liberal vision of the gender perspective that reduces it to equal opportunities between men and women."[35] The reengineering of the new Agreement makes people with diverse sexual orientation and gender identities invisible, installing the general category of people belonging to 'vulnerable' groups.

This results in significant new obstacles for the Agreement's implementation. In recent years, with a government openly opposed to equality, contempt for diversity has intensified and the lives of community leaders working for peace, both female and male, have been silenced by bullets. The obstacles are evident in recent reports. For example, a recent report by GPAZ (a consortium of organizations that monitor and demand compliance with the gender component of the Peace Agreement) states that between August 2018 and August 2019, from the 109 measures that remain to be implemented from the Final Agreement, only 19 show satisfactory progress, 50 hardly show partial progress and 40 have no progress at. The report further alarmingly notes that during this time (the 1 year of the Duque Government),

1 The President's political party has led a strong movement of challenges and objections to the Peace Agreement.
2 The new Government has appointed public officials and has made alliances with parties and sectors that promote hate speech against LGBT people or that openly express their rejection."[36]

Similarly, the press has reported that for the Commission to monitor the Agreement, "the implementation of the gender approach has been fragmented and insufficient. They consider that the state has not had a comprehensive or transversal understanding of the subject in public policy."[37]

Women and LGBTI people have been recognized as discriminated-against populations in international instruments such as the Convention for the Elimination of All Forms of Discrimination Against Women (CEDAW). These instruments generally embody a corrective approach based on the "verification that those women live in a situation of discrimination that prevents them from enjoying and exercising their rights in conditions of equality with men."[38] As a result, international institutions such as the CEDAW Committee and UN Human Rights Committee have issued recommendations to states parties to guarantee women the enjoyment of their rights under equal conditions and without any discrimination. Despite these efforts, overcoming the disadvantages experienced by women and the LGBTI community and the elimination of discrimination and inequalities remains a pending task for many states, and Colombia is no exception. While the Peace Agreements were enshrined as constitutional norms, there is an important discrepancy between the law's normative texts and reality.[39] In addition to material conditions that further discrimination, there are formal elements in the legal system that prevent improvements to the situation. In the Colombian context, a traditional and restrictive legal paradigm has prevailed in all domains of law, including human rights, which ignores gender-based perspectives and the particularities of women and LBGTI people.

Multiple reasons can be given for this situation, including the underlying conception of gender roles and stereotypes at the symbolic and cultural level, and the lack of power and representation that women and non-hegemonic sexual orientations have had in politico-legal institutions. As shown by critical legal studies, two strands of feminism have levied two significant criticisms of positive law: First, that law is the product of strongly patriarchal societies and, to that extent, legal institutions are constructed from the male perspective. Second and relatedly, when law tries to protect the interests of women or sexual minorities without considering their perspectives, the remedies continue to embody the dominant patriarchal and heteronormative perspective and thereby do not benefit those they claim to protect.[40]

As a result, it is necessary to incorporate the perspectives of women and sexual minorities in peacemaking processes to address the injustices caused by the armed conflict and create the foundations of a more just society. This involves not only their active participation in decision-making, but also taking a perspective that is aware of the particularities of excluded groups and avoids reproducing the conditions that enable discriminatory acts. Law as a mediation tool should promote more inclusive decision-making. Therefore, the gender approach as a tool for legal analysis allows us "to understand that laws are not neutral and therefore do not have the same effects on men and women, since history has shown us that we are only formally equal before the law."[41]

Women and girls, members of the LGBTI community, and men with non-hegemonic masculinities have been victims of the armed conflict in Colombia. However, their perspective as victims is different from that of men, who have also been victims, and who have also made war, but who have represented the dominant values. The peaceful resolution of the armed conflict and post-conflict peacebuilding must include a gender perspective to recognize the particularities and needs of each of these groups. Peace cannot be reached if all those affected by the conflict are left out, whether they are perpetrators or victims. Thus, the inclusion of the perspectives of women and sexual minorities is a requirement of justice. There is little point in making peace agreements if the views of all those affected by the conflict are not included.

After the disarmament, the next great challenge for Colombia will be (in the words of Vargas and Díaz) to achieve,

> Profound transformations in fundamental areas such as education for peace and coexistence, which allows the reduction of stereotypes and discrimination, the re-signification of traditional gender roles, respect for diversity in all domains, the promotion of autonomy, empowerment and leadership of women, and the re-education and sensitization of men to develop new, more inclusive and less violent masculinities.[42]

It would be a grave historical mistake to set aside women and sexual minorities in the peacemaking processes. These groups have woven new and healthy relationships and challenged old power structures, thereby creating more equitable relations in a society that seeks reconciliation after so many years of violence. One cannot move toward peace and justice if the voices of all involved are not heard in the public sphere. Fraser's proposal offers one further justification, from the theory of justice, for the need to take women and sexual minorities and their perspectives in the Colombian peace process and post-conflict peacebuilding into account.

Authors' note

This text is a product of the research project "The guarantee of social rights and the gender approach in the land restitution policy in Santander" (Code 127) funded by the Universidad Autónoma de Bucaramanga. Translated by Andrés Molina-Ochoa and Jorge Luis Fabra-Zamora.

Notes

1 Rachel Tillman, "Género e interdisciplinariedad: El rol constitutivo del género en la generación del conocimiento," *Revista Temas Socio Jurídicos*, vol. 33, 2014, p. 18.

2 María Villellas, La participación de las mujeres en los procesos de paz. Las otras mesas. Barcelona: Institut Català Internacional per la Pa, 2010, 18, http://www.gencat.cat/icip/eng/icip_wp.html.
3 UNSC, Resolution 1325, October 31, 2000, S/RES/1325.
4 Council on Foreign Relations, Women's Participation in Peace Processes, https://www.cfr.org/womens-participation-in-peace-processes/
5 María Niño, "Aspectos novedosos de la participación política de las mujeres en el proceso de paz con las FARC-EP," *Cuadernos de estrategia*, vol. 189, 2017, 213.
6 Carlos Arturo Velandia, "Las mujeres en la Mesa de diálogos de paz." Revista Semana, November 23, 2013, https://www.semana.com/opinion/articulo/mujeres-en-la-mesa-de-negociacion-proceso-de-paz-opinion-carlos-velandia/366335-3
7 Clara Lucia Rodríguez Pico, "Las mujeres y el proceso de paz," Razón Pública, December 16, 2013: http://www.razonpublica.com/index.php/conflicto-drogas-y-paz-temas-30/7247-las-mujeres-y-el-proceso-de-paz.html
8 Ivonne Wilches, Paz con género femenino. PNUD-UNIFEM, 2010, p. 48
9 Sara Guarracino, La perspectiva de las mujeres en las negociaciones de paz de La Habana y el impacto de la Resolución 1325 del Consejo de Seguridad de las Naciones Unidas en Colombia, Treballs de màster i postgrau. Màster en Relacions Internacionals, Seguretat i desenvolupament (MURISD); Curs 2017/18, p. 13.
10 LGBT rights organizations, Colombia Diversa and the Caribe Afirmativo. The communications and working documents of the organizations regarding their participation in the peace process can be found at https://colombiadiversa.org/ and https://caribeafirmativo.lgbt/
11 Final Agreement, p. 4.
12 Idem.
13 "El acuerdo con las Farc nos lleva de narices a una peligrosa dictadura homosexual," Las Dos Orillas, September 23, 2016, https://www.las2orillas.co/el-acuerdo-con-las-farc-nos-lleva-de-narices-a-una-peligrosa-dictadura-homosexual-concejal-de-la-familia/
14 See "Cartilla sobre discriminación sexual en colegios dividió al país," El Tiempo, August 14, 2016, https://www.eltiempo.com/vida/educacion/cartillas-sobre-diversidad-sexual-en-colegios-genera-debate-en-colombia-39931
15 For example, former President Álvaro Uribe said after the results of the plebiscite: "We reiterate the need to stimulate the values of the family [...] defended by our religious leaders and moral pastors." See "The role of the Christian churches in the victory of 'No' in the plebiscite." Dinero, June 10, 2016, https://www.dinero.com/pais/articulo/que-papel-jugaron-las-iglesias-cristianas-en-la-victoria-del-no-en-plebiscito/234621. Deisy Perilla has suggested that gender ideology was one of the "rhetorical devices" used by opponents to the Agreement. See, Deisy Perilla, "La Plebitusa: movilización política de las emociones posplebiscito por la paz en Colombia, Maguaré, 32 (2018) 153-181.
16 Olga González, "La otra subversión: la emergencia del género," TraHs Números especiales, 1 (2017) 126.
17 Nancy Fraser, "Social Justice in the Age of Identity Politics: Redistribution, Recognition, and Participation" in Nancy Fraser and Axel Honnet, Redistribution or Recognition? A Political-Philosophical Exchange (London: Verso, 2003) 39.
18 For evidence, see Section 4.3 of the report of the National Center for Historical Memory (¡Basta Ya! Memorias de Guerra y Dignidad, Grupo de Memoria Histórica, 2015) and reports from the (on) National Institute of Forensic Medicine. Regarding labor, the ILO reports on women's employment (ILO, Las mujeres en el trabajo. Tendencias de 2016, 2016) and L. Olarte and X. Peña, "El

efecto de la maternidad sobre los ingresos femeninos." Ensayos sobre política económica. 28, 2010, 190–230. In the case of political participation, J. Vargas and A. Díaz (2018) "Enfoque de Género en el acuerdo de paz entre el Gobierno Colombiano y las FARC-EP: transiciones necesarias para su implementación," Araucaria, 20, 389-414, and "Participación de las mujeres en las negociaciones de paz: relaciones entre presencia e influencia" ONU Mujeres, 2010, http://www.unwomen.org/~/media/Headquarters/Media/Publications/es/WPSsourcebook-03A-WomenPeaceNegotiations-es%20pdf.pdf

19 Fraser, "Social Justice in the Age of Identity Politics."

20 This occurred, for example, when former Inspector General Ordoñez (who serves as Ombudsman) rejected the constitutionality of Law 1482 of 2011 that criminalized several forms of discrimination and racism.

21 Justice Interruptus. *Critical Reflections on the "Postsocialist" Condition* (New York: Routledge, 1997), 20.

22 Fraser, "Social Justice in the Age of Identity Politics," 9.

23 See Observatorio de Políticas de las Familias – OPF. Documento de Trabajo No. 2016-1 Departamento Nacional de Planeación, Noviembre de 2015, and Ministerio de Salud y Profamilia. La Encuesta Nacional de Demografía y Salud - ENDS, Tomo 1, 2015. https://profamilia.org.co/wp-content/uploads/2018/12/ENDS-TOMO-I.pdf

24 The leaders of the "No" campaign were the former Inspector General Alejandro Ordoñez; the former Inspector for the Protection of Rights of Children, Adolescents and Family, Ilvia Myriam Hoyos, and Senator Álvaro Uribe Vélez. "They put at the center of the debate the defense of traditional family values and religious principles which, in their opinion, were being threatened by the fact that the gender approach had been included in the final agreement." Eduardo Álvarez, Génica Mazzold and Irina Cuesta, "'Gender ideology': a spoiler for peace?" Open Democracy, October 26, 2016, https://www.opendemocracy.net/en/democraciaabierta/gender-ideology-spoiler-for-pe/

25 In various media, the use of the language used in the protests against the plebiscite and gender ideology was documented as "a strategy to win adherents for the 'No' to the plebiscite." See "Ideología de género: una estrategia para ganar adeptos por el "No" al plebiscito. Semana, August 17, 2016. https://www.semana.com/nacion/articulo/ideologia-de-genero-una-estrategia-para-ganar-adeptos-por-el-no-al-plebiscito/488260

26 The Catholic Church's doctrine on "gender ideology" was initiated by John Paul II in 1995 in his "Letter to Women," from Beijing's Fourth World Conference on Women. http://www.vatican.va/content/john-paul-ii/en/letters/1995/documents/hf_jp-ii_let_29061995_women.html. The criticism was most clearly articulated by the Pontifical Council for the Family: "[t]he most dangerous challenge [to family] comes from gender ideology, born in Anglo-Saxon feminist and homosexual environments and already diffused widely in the world. According to this theory, biological sex is of no importance" ("La familia escuela de humanidad y vida cristiana. Conferencia del Cardenal Ennio Antonelli, Presidente del Consejo Pontificio para la Familia," http://www.vatican.va/roman_curia/pontifical_councils/family/documents/rc_pc_family_doc_20090917_scuola-umanita_sp.html). Similarly, "a cultural challenge of great importance today derives from the 'gender' ideology that denies the difference and the natural reciprocity of men and women. It foresees a society without gender difference and empties the anthropological foundation of the family. This ideology motivates educational projects and legislative guidelines that promote a personal identity and affective intimacy radically disconnected from biological diversity between male and female. Human identity becomes an individualistic option, even modifiable over time. In the perspective of faith, human sexual difference carries

within itself the image and likeness of God." See, Vicente Morro, "La ideología de género en el pensamiento de los dos últimos pontífices: una aproximación" En: Construir la democracia, responsabilidad y bien común: XVII Congreso de Católicos y Vida Pública, Madrid: CEU Ediciones, 2016, 641.

27 Cristina Vega, "¿Quién teme al feminismo? A propósito de la "ideología de género" y otras monstruosidades sexuales en Ecuador y América Latina" Sin Permiso, December 8, 2017, https://www.sinpermiso.info/textos/quien-teme-al-feminismo-a-proposito-de-la-ideologia-de-genero-y-otras-monstruosidades-sexuales-en

28 Mary Anne Case, "The Role of the Popes in the Invention of Complementarity and the Vatican's Anathematization of Gender," Religion and Gender, 6, (2016) 155-172. Case cites Joseph Ratzinger, "Letter from Joseph Cardinal Ratzinger, Perfect, Congregation for the Doctrine of the Faith, to the Bishops of the Catholic Church on the Collaboration of Men and Women in the Church and in the World." Vatican Online Archive, May 31, 2004, http://www.vatican.va/roman_curia/congregatiions/cfaith/documents/rc_con_cfaith_doc_20040731_collaboration_en.html, and, Gabriele Kuby, "Gender Mainstreaming," Vatican Magazine 6 (2008).

29 Pope Francis wrote: "When we speak of complementarity between man and woman in this context, let us not confuse that term with the simplistic idea that all the roles and relations of the two sexes are fixed in a single, static pattern. Complementarity will take many forms as each man and woman brings his or her distinctive contributions to their marriage and to the formation of their children–his or her personal richness, personal charisma." Pope Francis, "'Not Just Good, but Beautiful', Opening Address Humanum Conference," Humanum, November 17, 2014, http://humanum.it/talks/pope-francis-opening-address-humanum-conference/.

30 Case, "The Role of the Popes" 168.

31 Vega, "¿Quién teme al feminismo?"

32 To mention just two examples, see the work of feminist theologian Marcella Althaus-Reid Indecent theology: theological perversions in sex, gender and politics (London; New York: Routledge, 2000) and The Queer God: sexuality and liberation theology (London, New York: Routledge, 2003), as well as papers in the journal Religion and Gender. For example, M. Albarracín and J. Lemaitre, "The Crusade against Same-Sex Marriage in Colombia" Colombia," Religion and Gender, 8 (2018) 32–49 that reflects on the deep religious homophobia that exists in Colombia.

33 M. Pecheny, D. Jones and L. Ariza, "Sexual Politics and Religious Actors in Argentina," *Religion and Gender*, vol. 6, 2016, 221. For a philosophical analysis of the challenges, possibilities, and limitations of the inclusion of religious voices in the democratic public sphere, see Javier Aguirre, Filosofía, religión y democracia: Habermas y el rol de la religión en la esfera pública. Bogotá: Universidad del Rosario, 2018.

34 Guarracino, La perspectiva de las mujeres en las negociaciones de paz de La Habana, 30.

35 Gómez, Diana, "Mujeres, género y el Acuerdo de la Habana." LSA Forum, XVIII (2017) 15

36 Isabelita Mercado & GPAZ, La paz avanza con las mujeres. Observaciones sobre la incorporación del enfoque de género en el Acuerdo de Paz. Bogotá: GPAZ, 2019, p. 7, https://generoypaz.co/informes/gpaz_informe_2019.pdf

37 Andrea Tapia, "Así va el enfoque de género en el Acuerdo de Paz." El Tiempo. April 20, 2020, https://www.eltiempo.com/politica/proceso-de-paz/el-enfoque-de-genero-en-el-acuerdo-de-paz-486600

38 Nicole Lacrampette, *Derechos Humanos y mujeres: teoría y práctica* (Chile: Universidad de Chile y Centro de Derechos Humanos, 2013) 16.
39 See Mauricio García, *La eficacia simbólica del Derecho* (Bogotá: Ediciones Uniandes, 1997) and H. Alviar and I. Jaramillo, *Feminismo y crítica jurídica* (Siglo del Hombre Editores, Universidad de los Andes, 2013) 24.
40 Isabel Jaramillo, *"Estudio preliminar." Robin West, Género y teoría del Derecho* (Bogotá: Ediciones Uniandes, 2004), 51.
41 Mariablanca Staff, "La perspectiva de género desde el Derecho" Legallinfo, Panamá, May 25, 2000, http://www.legalinfo-panama.com/articulos/articulos_21f.htm
42 Vargas & Díaz, Enfoque de Género en el acuerdo de paz entre el Gobierno Colombiano y las FARC-EP, 410.

14 The rights of Afro-Colombian communities in the Final Agreement and its mechanisms of implementation

Xiomara Cecilia Balanta-Moreno and Yuri Alexander Romaña-Rivas

Introduction

The 2016 "Final Agreement to End the Armed Conflict and Build a Stable and Lasting Peace" (henceforth, "the Final Agreement") between the Colombian Government and the Armed Revolutionary Forces of Colombia ("FARC-EP," for its Spanish acronym, or *Fuerzas Armadas Revolucionarias de Colombia-Ejército del Pueblo*) has opened a window of opportunity and hope for ethnic communities to obtain some degree of truth, justice, reparations, and guarantees of non-recurrence.

In the Final Agreement, the signatory parties agreed on six chapters to address some of the structural causes of violence and inequality in Colombia. Briefly, these points can be described as: (1) comprehensive rural reform; (2) guaranteed political participation; (3) measures geared toward a cease-fire and the laying down of arms; (4) measures to address the illicit drugs problem; (5) an agreement regarding the victims of the conflict, the "Comprehensive System for Truth, Justice, Reparations, and Non-Recurrence" ("SIVJRNR" for its Spanish acronym, or the Comprehensive System); and (6) mechanisms to follow-up on the implementation of the Agreement. The Comprehensive System, conceived as a vehicle for the realization of victims' rights, is composed of three institutions. First, the Special Jurisdiction for Peace ("JEP" for its Spanish acronym); second, the Truth, Coexistence, and Non-Recurrence Commission ("CEVCNR" for its Spanish acronym, also called The Truth Commission); and third, the Special Unit for the Search for Persons deemed as Missing in the context of and due to the conflict ("UBPD" for its Spanish acronym or The Search Unit).

For its part, Chapter 6.2 of the Final Agreement contains what is commonly referred to as "the Ethnic Chapter." This chapter of the Agreement seeks to guarantee that an ethnically differentiated approach is taken into consideration in the implementation of the Final Agreement. Likewise, the parties to the Final Agreement agreed on the importance of guaranteeing the participation of Afro-Colombians through the effective implementation of the Comprehensive System.

The purpose of this chapter is to elucidate the legal framework established to guarantee the participation of Afro-Colombians in this system and how that participation has operated in certain instances. To do so, we first discuss the context of structural racism and exclusion of Afro-Colombians that brought about disproportionate impacts of the conflict on their communities. A description of the ethnically differentiated approach and how it operates within the Colombian legal system then follows. Third, the rights of Afro-Colombian communities and their ability to participate in the mechanisms of transitional justice are discussed, with an emphasis on the Ethnic Chapter and the Comprehensive System. In this regard, some examples of how that participation has taken place so far will be provided. Finally, we will offer some concluding thoughts.

A brief context of structural racism and the exclusion of Afro-Colombians

To understand the disproportionate impact of the armed conflict on Afro-Colombians,[1] it is necessary to remember that, since they were brought to this country, Afro-Colombian communities have undergone a history of exclusion, a situation which has been exacerbated by the armed conflict.

In 1510 in the then territory of New Granada (which is now Colombia), the Spanish Crown authorized the institution of enslavement, with the first ship containing Black people brought from Africa or of African descent arriving at Cartagena in 1549.[2] This situation lasted until 1852, when a law abolishing enslavement formally entered into force.[3] It is estimated that by 1778 the enslaved population in the current territory of Colombia numbered 62,547 persons (equivalent to 7.8% of the total population), and by 1851, the date the institution of enslavement was formally abolished, the enslaved population was 15,972 (equivalent to 0.76% of the population).[4] In this respect, it is important to highlight that many Black people in Colombia took different actions to emancipate themselves and obtain their freedom, long before the institution of enslavement was formally abolished.[5] Indeed, because many Black people did not consider the promise of freedom by the authorities as something serious, many enslaved persons decided to run away; to form "*libertos*," gangs that assaulted roads, houses, and estates; or to become "*cimarrones*," enslaved people who escaped to inaccessible areas where they formed communities called *palenques* to live in freedom.[6]

Despite the formal abolition of the institution of enslavement, the conditions of economic, social, and political inequality originated by this institution remain present today.[7] This has led to the establishment of a society where skin color has direct bearings on access to opportunities. This phenomenon, which favors lighter skin shades to darker hues, is known as "pigmentocracy."[8] The term "pigmentocracy" is often used to define Latin American countries that have favored racial mixing or eugenics, as a mechanism to whiten their societies and erase the presence of blackness, over racial segregation, yet which continue to operate based on racial hierarchizations.[9]

Colombia is a pigmentocracy,[10] and as a result, regions, and communities predominantly inhabited by Afro-Colombians have been subjected to structural racism,[11] or what others call *de facto* racism.[12] Indeed, areas with a majority of Afro-Colombian population are among the most impoverished in Colombia.[13] This is evidenced in various indicators. For instance, the illiteracy rate among Afro-Colombians is estimated at 21%, 4.5% above the national average in Colombia.[14] Regarding graduation from higher education, only 3% of Afro-Colombians hold a university diploma[15] as compared to 22% of the national population.[16] The mortality rate among Afro-Colombian children is twice as high as the national average.[17] In this sense, it is important to mention that the most important public hospital (San Francisco de Asís Hospital) in the province of Chocó, a province where 82% of the population are Black,[18] had to wait until 2020, 43 years after it first opened its doors, to receive its first seven intensive care unit beds from the Colombian Government. This only happened because of the dire situation facing the province due to the Covid-19 pandemic.[19] Additionally, many of the municipalities with a significant Black population located in the Colombian pacific region have limited access to the national electricity system or no access at all.[20] A recent case study conducted in certain areas of Bogotá with a significant presence of Afro-Colombians has shown that Afro-Colombians are subjected to racial profiling by the police. Actually, an Afro-Colombian person with darker skin color is "2.67 times more likely to interact with the police and 2.57 times more likely to be arrested, taken to a restricted area, fined, or searched."[21] In addition, studies have shown that Afro-Colombians face obstacles to social mobility from one generation to the next because of their skin color.[22] Therefore, the more than 4.3 million of Afro-Colombians[23] continue to face a serious lack of equal access to opportunities. The armed conflict has aggravated this underlying situation.

Although the territories of Afro-Colombians had traditionally been areas of peace, the armed conflict not only altered the peaceful way of life of Afro-Colombians, but also exacerbated the economic and social hardship of these already impoverished communities.

Colombia is a country of around 48,258,494 million inhabitants,[24] and Afro-Colombians compose 10.6%[25] of the population. It is worth mentioning that there are 1,569 Black Communities in Colombia, organized in 182 legally recognized administrative authorities called "Community Councils."[26] The territories of Black Communities are home to 71,442 families.[27] The disproportionate impact on their territories is due, in part, to the territorial disputes that have arisen in the past twenty years between armed groups fighting for the geostrategic location of these territories and the abundance of their natural resources.[28] Thus, Afro-Colombians, mainly from the provinces of Nariño, Chocó, Valle del Cauca, Antioquia, and Cauca, constitute 11.75% (1,035,068) of the total number of 8,803,836 victims registered in the country.[29] This means that around 23% of the 4.3 million[30] Afro-Colombians are registered victims of the armed conflict, whereas non-Black victims represent around 17.6% (7,768,768) of the total number. The Afro-Colombian population is thus one of the most affected by the last 20 years of the armed conflict.[31] These communities have been victims of attacks by armed groups, murders, and internal forced displacements for the appropriation of their lands, among other acts of victimization.[32] In fact, the massacre of Bojayá, one of the worst massacres in the entire history of the armed conflict in Colombia, took place on the territory of an Afro-Colombian community.[33] During an armed confrontation between paramilitary's armed forces and the FARC-EP, a cylinder bomb was launched and hit a church where civilians had found shelter, resulting in the killing of between 74 and 79 innocent civilians, the injuring of many others, and the internal forced displacement of more than 5,000 people.[34] The Colombian armed conflict has had a disproportionately negative impact on Afro-Colombian communities, and has drastically altered their way of life. Hence, it is legitimate for Afro-Colombians to see in the Final Agreement a source of hope for the restoration of their rights and the guarantee of non-recurrence.

To achieve an effective restoration of rights in favor of Afro-Colombians, their particularities as a social group and their worldview need to be taken into consideration, and for that purpose, the implementation of the ethnically differentiated approach is crucial.

The ethnically differentiated approach in Colombian legislation

In Colombia, the notion of a differentiated approach emanates from the principle of equality and non-discrimination.[35] This notion recognizes that, even though individuals are equal under the law, the law can affect people differently depending on aspects such as class, gender, ethnic group, age, physical or mental health, and sexual orientation.[36] In this sense, State authorities are thus required to adopt positive measures to render equality effective by taking into account such differences.[37]

The notion of an ethnically differentiated approach has emerged from a variety of laws and norms in the Colombian legal system that guarantees rights to ethnic communities. A first piece of legislation that recognized the rights of Black communities as a group is Law 31 of 1967.[38] This Law contains the first legal recognition of the land rights of Afro-Colombian communities in territories they have historically occupied.[39] Subsequently, the Colombian Government incorporated the International Labor Organization's (ILO) Convention 169 of 1989 "concerning Indigenous and Tribal Peoples in Independent Countries" into its domestic legislation through Law 21 of 1991,[40] and the Colombian Constitutional Court has confirmed that the rights contained in this Convention and legislation are also applicable to Afro-Colombian communities.[41]

The ILO Convention 169 of 1989 significantly influenced the adoption of provisions in the 1991 Political Constitution of Colombia that defined and established the scope of the notions of ethnic and cultural diversity in the Colombian constitutional regime.[42] One of the main features of the 1991 Colombian Constitution is that "[t]he State recognizes and protects the ethnic and cultural diversity of the Colombian Nation and recognizes Colombia as a multicultural Nation."[43] In this vein, the Colombian Constitution established transitory Article 55 by which Congress was required, within 2 years following its entry into force, to enact legislation recognizing "the black communities that have come to occupy uncultivated lands in the rural zones adjoining the rivers of the Pacific Basin, in accordance with their traditional cultivation practices, and the right to collective property over the areas which the same law must also demarcate."[44] This Law contains mechanisms for the protection of the rights and cultural identity of these communities, as well as provisions aimed at promoting their economic and social development.[45]

In August 1993, the Colombian Government adopted Law 70 by which it recognized "the Right of Black Colombians to Collectively Own and Occupy their Ancestral Lands" as well as other prerogatives.[46] Importantly, Law 70 concedes that the Community Councils of Black communities are administrative authorities within their territories, whose functions are to facilitate, where possible, friendly dispute resolution within the communities.[47] A Community Council has legal personality and, within a Black community, is the highest administrative authority, which exercises its functions in line with the Constitution, national laws, and the community's own legal framework.[48]

Based on the aforementioned international and national normative instruments, the Constitutional Court of Colombia has understood the ethnically differentiated approach as "the right of Afro-Colombian communities to be considered as 'peoples,' taking into account the social, cultural, and economic conditions that distinguish them from other sectors of the national community, coupled with the fact that they are governed by their customs and traditions, and have their own legislation."[49] This was incorporated into legislation in the following terms:

> [...] measures of help, assistance, reparation and restitution established in this Decree are based on the principle of special and differentiated treatment to which the Communities and their individually considered members have rights. The standards, procedures and mechanisms designed for this purpose, must be interpreted on the basis of ethnic and cultural membership and the collective rights of the communities.[50]

In this spirit, the Constitutional Court has recognized that an ethnically differentiated approach must be taken into account in the adoption and implementation of public policy in favor of victims of the Colombian armed conflict.[51] Government authorities must therefore engage with ethnic communities or their representatives when designing and/or implementing public policies that can affect them and their rights. This may require the use of mechanisms of public participation, such as the exercise of a prior and informed consultation, holding informative meetings, and establishing inter-institutional coordination, to facilitate communication and the process of partnership with Colombian ethnic groups.[52]

Hence, the ethnically differentiated approach is a right in favor of ethnic communities to guarantee their existence as "peoples" according to their traditional worldview and way of life. This right imposes an obligation on State authorities to take into consideration the particular social, cultural, and economic circumstances of ethnic groups when considering the adoption or implementation of measures that can infringe their rights in a particular way. As will be discussed subsequently, the Final Agreement as well as the mechanism for its implementation thus was required to include an ethnically differentiated approach as a recognition of the differentiated impact of the armed conflict on Colombian ethnic groups, particularly on Afro-Colombians.

The rights of Afro-Colombian communities and their participation in the mechanisms of transitional justice

The armed conflict has disproportionately affected the rights of Afro-Colombian communities, and they have a genuine and legitimate interest in participating in the different mechanisms of transitional justice created to satisfy the rights of victims. To gain a better understanding of how Afro-Colombian communities can take part in these mechanisms, it is imperative to discuss the specific rights and mechanisms of participation contained in the Ethnic Chapter of the Final Agreement, and in the institutions that compose the Comprehensive System.

Afro-Colombians and the ethnically differentiated approach in the Ethnic Chapter of the Final Agreement

The first few years of negotiations between the Colombian Government and the Guerrilla of the FARC-EP in Havana (Cuba), were marked by the absence of representatives of the different ethnic communities.[53] This led to intense controversy as, for many sectors of the country, a process to reach a peace agreement without the presence of representatives of ethnic communities was unimaginable. However, over time, and true to their history of resistance and resilience, ethnic communities were successful in obtaining a seat at the negotiating table. This led to the inclusion of the Ethnic Chapter into the Final Agreement, as well as to the creation of the "Ethnic Commission for Peace and Defense of Territorial Rights," whose purpose is to "safeguard the territorial and collective rights of ethnic communities in the process of negotiation and implementation of the peace agreement."[54]

The Ethnic Chapter begins with a recognition by the Colombian State and FARC-EP that ethnic communities have contributed to the construction of a stable and lasting peace in Colombia, as well as to the economic and social development of the country. The Final Agreement acknowledges that ethnic communities have suffered historical and structural conditions of injustice because of colonialism, enslavement, exclusion, and dispossession from their lands, territories, and resources. The Ethnic Chapter also recognizes that ethnic groups have been seriously impaired by the domestic armed conflict. In consequence, the Final Agreement seeks to guarantee Afro-Colombian communities the full exercise of their individual and collective human rights based on their own aspirations, interests, and worldviews.[55]

Furthermore, the Ethnic Chapter contemplates the notion of a transversal interpretation and application of the ethnically differentiated approach throughout the different chapters of the Final Agreement.[56] This means that the ethnically differentiated approach needs to be taken into account in the implementation of all the chapters of the Agreement.

The adoption of the Ethnic Chapter has been fundamental for the implementation of the ethnically differentiated approach in the Comprehensive System, since its inclusion has made the different institutions—the Truth Commission, Search Unit, and JEP—adopt measures and establish commissions, groups or work teams that guarantee the effective incorporation of the ethnically differentiated approach in the exercise of their respective mandates. Consequently, the Final Agreement recognizes the ethnically differentiated approach, and aims at guaranteeing that the particularities and worldviews of the ethnic groups are taken seriously into consideration in its implementation.

The participation of Afro-Colombians in the Comprehensive System of Truth Justice, Reparation, and Non-repetition (SIVJRNR)

In the context of Chapter 5 of the Final Agreement regarding victims of the conflict, the Colombian Government and the Guerrilla of the FARC-EP acknowledged that:

> [m]illions of Colombians have been victims of forced displacement, the dead number in their hundreds of thousands, tens of thousands of people of all kinds have disappeared, and vast numbers of families, groups and communities have been affected throughout the length and breadth of the country, including rural communities, indigenous peoples, the Afro-Colombian, Black, Palenquero, Raizal and Roma communities, persons due to their religious beliefs, political parties, social and trade-union movements, the LGBTI population and economic associations, inter alia.[57]

The most conservative figures indicate that the death toll of the armed conflict may be around 220,000, and 81% of those casualties are estimated to have been non-combatant civilians.[58] In this respect, the parties to the Final Agreement declared that "[r]edress for victims is at the core of the Agreement."[59] To make that declaration a reality, the Colombian Government and the FARC-EP agreed on the establishment of the Comprehensive System,[60] as a way to guarantee the realization of victims' rights to truth, justice, reparations, and non-recurrence.[61] In this line, the parties to the Agreement agreed to the creation of the Truth Commission; the Search Unit; the JEP, and to specific reparation measures.[62] These institutions were officially created through an amendment to the Colombian Constitution via the Legislative Act 01 of 2017.[63] This constitutional amendment indicates that the Comprehensive System will apply a territorial approach, a differentiated approach, and a gendered approach.[64] The implementation of such a victim-centered Final Agreement and an ethnically differentiated approach in the different activities and proceedings of the mechanisms has broken new ground. These mechanisms can be considered as establishing a new reference point for transitional justice processes both in Colombia and around the world.

Chapter 5 of the Final Agreement is the one that has achieved the most progress, and this is in part due to the willingness, autonomy, and independence of the institutions that compose the Comprehensive System.[65] By no means can we overlook the challenges[66] of access to institutions faced by victims who live in rural and isolated areas.[67] However, it is worth highlighting that the institutions of the Comprehensive System have shown their commitment to a fluid dialogue with ethnic communities to incorporate the ethnically differentiated approach into all activities of the Comprehensive System.[68] In the next sections, we will describe how that interaction works.

Participation of Afro-Colombians in the work of the Special Jurisdiction for Peace

The JEP is part of the trend of *sui generis* hybrid tribunals created under domestic law, but which, in the exercise of their jurisdictional competences, can observe and apply both domestic and international law.[69]

The JEP administers justice in a transitory and autonomous way, and exercises preferential jurisdiction over all other jurisdictions to consider cases of crimes (especially with respect to grave breaches of IHL or serious violations of human rights) committed by the parties to the armed conflict before December 1, 2016. Importantly, the JEP's jurisdiction can be exercised with respect to crimes committed in the context and in direct or indirect relationship to the armed conflict.[70] The JEP has, among others, the objectives of satisfying the victim's right to justice; offering truth to Colombian society; and protecting the rights of victims.[71]

As has been discussed in detail in previous chapters of this book, the JEP is composed of three Chambers, a Tribunal with four different sections, an

Investigation and Accusation Unit ("UIA" for its Spanish acronym), and an Executive Secretariat.[72]

For the purpose of this chapter, it is important to highlight that the JEP has created an Ethnic Commission, composed of judges belonging to ethnic communities. The judges of the Ethnic Commission, upon request by organs of the JEP, will seek to guarantee that the ethnically differentiated approach is taken into consideration when deciding cases involving former combatants, victims, or territories involving ethnic communities, or decisions which can conflict with the system of ethnic justices or have an impact on the rights of these communities.[73]

Now, it is relevant to discuss how Afro-Colombians have engaged with the JEP. Afro-Colombians participate in the work of the JEP in three main ways. First, through the appointment of Afro-Colombian judges to the JEP. Second, by the participation of Afro-Colombians in the judicial and quasi-judicial proceedings before the JEP. Third, by the Special Jurisdiction's inclusion of the inputs of Afro-Colombian communities, through consultations on how they think the ethnically differentiated approach should be implemented and how the JEP can carry out its activities on their territories.

With respect to the first point, one of the goals of the parties to the Final Agreement was to guarantee the presence of judges who belong to Colombian ethnic communities in the JEP.[74] In this spirit, it is worth mentioning that of the 38 judges in the JEP there are currently four Afro-Colombian judges.[75] These judges play a fundamental role in ensuring that the ethnically differentiated approach is taken into serious consideration within the work of the JEP. In fact, as members of the JEP's Ethnic Commission, it is a part of their work to draft legal opinions with recommendations to different organs of the JEP about how they should apply or take into consideration the ethnically differentiated approach when dealing with a specific case.[76]

In relation to the second aspect of participation of Afro-Colombians in the work of the JEP, it is important to take into account that one of the features of the JEP is its prevalent and preferential jurisdiction. This means that the JEP has primary jurisdiction to consider cases of crimes committed during and within the context of the armed conflict before December 1, 2016, by former combatants or collaborators.[77] However, legal pluralism[78] or ethnic justices (ethnic judicial authorities) also exist in Colombia, meaning ethnic communities can also exercise judicial authority within their territorial jurisdictions and over members of their own communities.[79] In this respect, to avoid undermining the mechanisms of ethnic judicial authorities (ethnic justices), the JEP is obliged to coordinate with communities that have their own legal system when a community argues it has jurisdiction to try or process a case related to the armed conflict. This coordination can allow for the JEP and ethnic judicial authorities to discuss who should assume jurisdiction over the case under dispute.[80]

If, after the inter-jurisdictional dialogue or coordination has taken place, there is no agreement about who should exercise jurisdiction over a particular matter, the dispute can be sent to the Constitutional Court of Colombia for it to make a final determination.[81] On this point, the Appeal Section of the JEP has indicated that, in proceedings before the JEP involving former combatants who belong to ethnic communities; victims who belong to ethnic communities; and circumstances where a crime was committed in the territory of an ethnic community, the JEP has the constitutional and legal obligation to dialogue and to coordinate its efforts with the respective ethnic justice authorities.[82] Not doing so can result in the violation of due process guarantees.[83]

Afro-Colombians have taken part in different aspects of the work of the JEP. Black communities to which former combatants belong have been allowed to participate in proceedings before the Chamber of Amnesty and Pardon. In fact, Afro-Colombians have been allowed to inform the Chamber of their opinions about the proceedings and how cases should be resolved.[84] Additionally, Afro-Colombian communities have submitted reports of human rights violations and grave breaches of IHL committed in their territories. In June 2019, for example, two Afro-Colombian communities from northern Cauca and Buenaventura submitted reports to the JEP.[85] In these two reports, the communities alleged that crimes against humanity had been committed in their territories. Similarly, in May 2019, Afro-Colombian organizations, such as: the Committee for the Rights of the Victims of Bojayá; La "Comadre," an organization associated to the Afro-Colombian National Association for displaced people ("Afrodes" for its Spanish acronym); and some organizations from Tumaco, provided the JEP with reports about serious human rights violations that occurred in their territories during the armed conflict.[86]

For its part, the JEP has an important responsibility to consult with Afro-Colombian communities on how the ethnically differentiated approach should be implemented, and to provide information to the communities about how they can successfully participate. In this regard, starting in November 2018, the JEP travelled around Colombia carrying out a consultation process on its Rules of Procedures (Law 1922 of 2018), General Regulations adopted by Regulatory Agreement No. 001 of 2018, and the Protocol of Communication with the Victims of the UIA.[87] These instruments are of utmost importance because they contain specific regulations for the participation of ethnic communities in the work of the JEP.[88] The JEP has also created a text with guidelines or instructions for the presentation of reports by organizations of victims from ethnic groups,[89] and has liaison officers in different territories of Afro-Colombian communities.[90] This is a way to bring the JEP closer to the people and to facilitate the participation of more Afro-Colombians in the work of the JEP. The JEP also has a Group of Analysis of Contextual Information ("GRAI" for its Spanish acronym), which is in charge of providing judges with contextual reports related to the armed conflict. This Group also takes into consideration the ethnically differentiated approach,[91] as does the JEP's Executive Secretariat that is undertaking measures to guarantee that Afro-Colombian communities can engage with the JEP by using information technology.[92]

In addition, in the context of the macro-cases[93] opened by the Chamber for Recognition of Truth, Responsibility, and Determination of Facts, three of the territorial cases involved geographic areas of Colombia with a significant presence of Afro-Colombian communities:

- The JEP opened Case 002 on July 10, 2018. This case prioritizes the serious situation of human rights violations and serious breaches of IHL that mainly affect indigenous peoples, Black communities, Afro-Colombians, peasants, women, and LGBTI people in the municipalities of Tumaco, Ricaurte, and Barbacoas in the province of Nariño.[94]
- The JEP opened Case 004 on September 11, 2018. This case prioritizes the territorial situation based on the facts of the conflict that occurred in the Urabá region between 1986 and 2016.[95]
- The JEP opened Case 005 in November 2018. It prioritizes the serious situation of human rights violations in Santander de Quilichao, Suárez, Buenos Aires, Morales, Caloto, Corinto, Toribio, Caldono, Jambaló, Miranda, Padilla, and Puerto Tejada, in Cauca. Likewise, it takes into account the situation of the municipalities of Florida, Pradera, Palmira, Jamundí, and Candelaria, in Valle del Cauca).[96]

Based on internal information of the JEP, 86 Community Councils of Black communities have been recognized as victims in the three territorial cases of the JEP, of which 30 Community Councils have been accredited in Case 002. In total, 67,268 people constitute these Community Councils. In this case, the natural and geographical area that is essential to these Afro-Colombian communities is also recognized as a victim, which is a crucial and groundbreaking finding for Afro-Colombian communities.

Additionally, nine Community Councils have been acknowledged as victims in Case 004. This case relates to the situation of the Urabá region, which involves approximately 22,000 people. A trade union is also recognized as a victim. This trade union is made up of 406 associates with ties to Black ethnicity and nineteen communities, which involve 494 Afro-Colombian people.

Furthermore, 47 Black Community Councils have been recognized as victims in Case 005. These Community Councils are composed of more than 21,000 people and represent more than 110,000 Afro-descendants who can act as special interveners before the JEP.

Thus, in more than 2 years of functioning of the JEP, Afro-Colombians have had the opportunity to engage with the work of the JEP, and the JEP has made genuine efforts to make itself available and accessible to Black communities.

It is important however not to be complacent and to continue working to increase the participation of Afro-Colombians. Particularly, efforts should be made to reach those rural areas historically abandoned and affected by the armed conflict to learn about their version of what happened, what they expect from the JEP, and to learn about specific and collective victims of human rights violations and grave breaches of IHL.

Participation of Afro-Colombians in the work of Colombia's Truth, Coexistence and Non-Recurrence Commission

A truth commission is an institution "designed to collect testimonies of victims from human rights violations or abuses, reveal the suffering by survival victims [,] and facilitate acknowledgement and recognition by society of the suffering of victims.[97]"

The Colombian Truth Commission is a temporary and extrajudicial body tasked with the responsibility of inquiring into the causes and context of the conflict to learn the truth and contribute to the clarification of what happened in the context of the conflict.[98] Additionally, the Commission can provide Colombian society with a comprehensive explanation of the complexity of the armed conflict; contribute to the restoration of victims' rights by promoting their recognition; encourage acknowledgement of individual and collective responsibilities for crimes committed in the context of the armed conflict, and promote peaceful coexistence in those territories impacted by the armed conflict to guarantee non-recurrence.[99] The Commission has a mandate of 3 years starting November 2018 to provide Colombian society with a comprehensive report about the causes and consequences of the Colombian armed conflict.[100]

Afro-Colombians have participated in the work of the Commission in three different ways: (1) by their appointment as members of the Commission; (2) by providing reports on how Afro-Colombians have experienced the armed conflict; and (3) when the Commission has reached out to Afro-Colombians to listen to their version of the root causes of the armed conflict, and by providing these communities with information about how they can interact with the Commission.

Of the 11 Commissioners of the Truth Commission, only one seat has been occupied by Afro-Colombians.[101] The first person to occupy that seat was the late Commissioner Ángela Salazar-Murillo who was succeeded by Commissioner Leyner Palacios.[102] In 2019, [100]Commissioner Ángela Salazar-Murillo stated that "about four million people in Black Communities have been victims of the armed conflict,"[103] and had reaffirmed the Commission's commitment "to make explicit in the final report that we are going to present, the differentiated and disproportionate impact that the armed conflict had on Indigenous Peoples, Black communities, Afro-Colombians, Palenqueros and Raizales communities, and Roma communities."[104] Commissioner Leyner Palacios has also reiterated the Commission's commitment to the victims of the armed conflict.[105] Therefore, the presence of an Afro-Colombian Commissioners such as Ángela Salazar-Murillo or Leyner Palacios can contribute to honoring the Truth Commission's commitment to guaranteeing the ethnically differentiated approach by providing the Colombian nation with a holistic understanding on how the dynamics of the armed conflict have disproportionately affected Afro-Colombians.

The submission of reports by Afro-Colombians to the Truth Commission is another effective vehicle for Afro-Colombians to share with the Commission how they have experienced the armed conflict and how it has affected them. Afro-Colombians expect the Truth Commission to be a space to tell their stories of what they experienced during the armed conflict.[106] In this spirit, on May 28, 2020, "La Comadre," a collective group of Black women associated to Afrodes, submitted to the Truth Commission a report entitled "Report of affectations, damages, resilience, and resistance of Afro-descendant women by the Comadre-Afrodes."[107] With this report, the organization sought to document the harm suffered by Black women in the context of the armed conflict and highlight the need for integral reparation and guarantees of non-repetition.[108] The report was created with the participation of more than 300 women from eleven different territories.[109]

In July 2019, the Association of Afro-descendant Women of the North of Cauca ("Asom" for its Spanish acronym) and the organization Women's Link Worldwide submitted to the Truth Commission a report entitled "Brave Voices" ("Voces Valientes" in Spanish).[110] In this report, six instances of violence and human rights violations against Afro-descendant women in the Northern Cauca Province are documented. On May 21, 2020, these two same organizations presented another report to the Truth Commission entitled "Black women's cries for freedom, reparation and memory."[111] The report shares, in the voices of Afro-descendant women from four municipalities in the North of Cauca, how legal and illegal armed actors have participated in the dispossession of their ancestral lands for development of big economic projects.[112]

These are instances of how Afro-Colombians are engaging with the Commission, and of how this engagement can contribute to guarantee to implement an ethnically differentiated approach in its final report.

For its part, the Truth Commission has played an important role in encouraging the effective participation of Afro-Colombians in its work. In this regard, similar to the JEP, starting November 2018, the Truth Commission travelled around the country to carry out a process of consultation with Afro-Colombian communities on two important documents for its interaction with Afro-Colombians. These documents were (a) the methodology of the ethnically differentiated approach: against racism, racial discrimination, and related forms of intolerance;[113] and (b) the Protocol for relations with authorities and victims from Indigenous, Black, Afro-Colombian, Raizales, and Palenqueras communities, and Roma people.[114] As a result of that process of consultation, in December 2018, the National Space for Afro-Colombian Consultation and the Commission agreed on: A methodology with an ethnic perspective; a protocol for the interaction between the authorities and victims; and mechanisms for participation throughout the Commission's three year mandate.[115] This agreement is an important step in the right direction to ensure there is a formal path for Afro-Colombians to interact with the Commission.

Furthermore, in May 2019, with the participation of 25 Afro-Colombian leaders, the Commission established the Permanent Working Table with authorities from Afro-Colombian, Black, Raizal, and Palenquero communities to seek and establish the truth of the implications of the armed conflict on these communities from a plural and ethnic perspective.[116] The Permanent Working Table will meet every four months. The purpose of this Working Table is to seek the establishment of mechanisms "that allow the contribution of the representatives of Afro-Colombian communities in the dialogue and contrast of the hypotheses, patterns, findings, and milestones that deepen the truth from their perspectives."[117]

Similarly, in December 2019, a Working Table was established with Afro-Colombian, Black, Raizal, and Palenquera women.[118] This is a plural and diverse space that uses the methodology of the Truth Commission to listen to the experiences of Black women and LGBTI Black persons regarding how the armed conflict has particularly affected them.[119] The Truth Commission has also visited territories of Afro-Colombian communities[120] and has held public events to allow for discussion on the lasting impacts of the armed conflict on Afro-Colombians.[121]

Afro-Colombians expect the Truth Commission to be a legitimate vehicle to share with Colombian society how the internal armed conflict has altered their way of life and what it has meant for their individual and collective life plans. To accomplish this, it is necessary that there be a fluid interaction between the Truth Commission and the different Afro-Colombian organizations. This interaction can allow for a comprehensive understanding of the complexity of the armed conflict and how it has altered the way of life of Afro-Colombian communities and individuals. Accordingly, elements such as the presence of an Afro-Colombian Commissioner in the Truth Commission, the submission of reports by organizations from Afro-Colombian communities, and outreach work by the Truth Commission to encourage the participation of Afro-Colombians in its work are all essential for a collective construction of the truth, which includes the differentiated impact of the armed conflict on Afro-Colombians.

Participation of Afro-Colombians in the work of the Special Unit for the Search for Persons deemed as Missing in the context and due to the conflict (Search Unit)

More than 80,000 persons are deemed to have disappeared in Colombia because of the conflict.[122] This led the parties to the Final Agreement to agree to the establishment of the Search Unit.

Pursuant to Legislative Act 01 of 2017, the Search Unit is "humanitarian and extrajudicial in nature and will direct, coordinate, and contribute to the implementation of humanitarian actions aimed at the search and location of persons reported disappeared in the context and by reason of the armed conflict who are alive and in the cases of death, when possible, the identification and dignified delivery of their remains."[123] A General Director leads the Search Unit for a term of 5 years.[124] Although the person currently leading this institution is not Afro-Colombian,[125] we hope that in the future an Afro-Colombian person has the opportunity to be appointed to this position as a measure to promote ethnic presence and participation in the direction of such an important institution.

The domestic legislation (Decree 589 of 2017) establishes that this Special Unit will implement an ethnically differentiated approach in the performance of its functions.[126] As a legal function, the Search Unit has the possibility to request and receive information from social organizations and victims that can contribute to the search, localization, recuperation, and identification of persons deemed disappeared in the context of and due to the conflict.[127] Similarly, the Search Unit can encourage society as a whole to provide information in a confidential way that will contribute to the search for, localization of, recuperation, identification and dignified delivery of the disappeared.[128] Decree 589 of 2017 requires that the delivery of human remains must guarantee, when possible, the observance of the different ethnic and cultural traditions and practices.[129] The Search Unit has indicated that the next of kin of a person deemed disappeared can participate in the search process.[130] Actually, the Search Unit has indicated that the specific knowledge and experiences of Black, Afro-Colombian, Raizal, and Palenquero communities make their participation and support of utmost importance to its work.[131]

Furthermore, when analyzing the constitutionality of Decree 589 of 2017, the Constitutional Court indicated that, when the Search Unit plans to enter the territories of ethnic communities to search for persons deemed disappeared; it must coordinate beforehand with the authorities of such territories.[132] This coordination is necessary to inform the ethnic communities of the work the Search Unit plans to carry out, and provide them with the opportunity to propose measures aimed at preventing any adverse impact on the integrity of their cultural, religious or spiritual values, beliefs, and practices.[133]

Thus, the participation of Afro-Colombians in the work of the Search Unit is designed to take place on a case-by-case basis. The Search Unit is mandated to invite Afro-Colombian communities and/or the next of kin of those deemed to have disappeared from such communities to participate in the search. The communities also have the right to contact the Search Unit to share information about the whereabouts of a person deemed disappeared in the context or due to the armed conflict.

In conclusion, an effective interaction and coordination between the Search Unit and the Afro-Colombian communities can contribute to the localization of the whereabouts of persons deemed disappeared who belong to these communities. As the Search Unit moves forward with its work and undertakes search of disappeared persons, we will learn more about how the interaction and coordination between Afro-Colombian communities and the Search Unit take place.

Final considerations

This chapter has presented the different ways by which Afro-Colombians are participating and interacting with the institutions that compose the Comprehensive System of Truth Justice, Reparation, and Non-repetition (namely the JEP, Truth Commission, and the Search Unit).

An effective interaction between Afro-Colombians and the institutions of the Comprehensive System is necessary to achieve truth and justice, and the restoration of rights for Afro-Colombians. This engagement needs to be guided by the ethnically differentiated approach as a safeguard of the rights of Afro-Colombians. In this sense, the institutions of the Comprehensive System must exercise their constitutional mandate in line with the ethnically differentiated approach.

This is a complex process, but it seems that Afro-Colombians and the different institutions of the Comprehensive System have a genuine commitment to building an effective and lasting peace in Colombia. Accomplishing this goal requires listening to the stories of Afro-Colombians about how they have experienced the armed conflict and the impact it has had on them. Indeed, it is worth highlighting that Afro-Colombian organizations have submitted reports where they document their version of what has happened to them in the context of the armed conflict.

Moreover, the presence of Afro-Colombians in decision-making positions within the institutions that compose the Comprehensive System makes it more plausible that these institutions take into consideration the ethnically differentiated approach in their work.

It seems that the institutions of the Comprehensive System are committed to engaging with Afro-Colombians. The institutions have undertaken measures which include the following: (a) engaging with Afro-Colombian communities and organizations to determine how their participation can be guaranteed; (b) holding information events and distributing guidelines about how to submit reports; (c) exercising presence in territories of Afro-Colombian communities; (d) allowing for the participation of Afro-Colombians as victims in judicial and quasi-judicial proceedings; (e) developing legal standards and practices that guarantee the observance of the ethnically differentiated approach and victims' rights; and (f) granting legal standing for Afro-Colombian communities to participate in the macro-cases.

It remains too early to arrive at definitive conclusions on the effectiveness of the measures aimed at the inclusion and participation of Afro-Colombians within the institutions of the Comprehensive System. As they move forward with their work, we will be able to observe and measure the concrete impacts that their inclusion and participation have achieved in terms of recognition, reparation, restoration, and measures of satisfaction for Afro-Colombian victims. Nonetheless, early measures and attitudes shown by both the Afro-Colombian communities and the institutions of the Comprehensive System inspire hope that the process will allow the restoration of rights in favor of Afro-Colombians.

Finally, it should be noted that putting the rights of victims at the center of a peace negotiation is novel. Moreover, the implementation of an ethnically differentiated approach as a guiding principle to guarantee victims' rights and the taking into consideration of their race, ethnicity, cultural differences, and worldview is a unique feature of the Colombian transitional justice process. Both of these approaches can set an important precedent for the participation of ethnic minorities in future processes of transitional justice. Consequently, this model of transitional justice can be a source of inspiration for other similar processes in Colombia[134] and around the world.

We hope that this collective experiment in Colombia accomplishes positive results not only for the establishment of a successful precedent for the future, but also for achieving the rights to truth, justice, reparation, and guarantee of non-recurrence for millions of victims in Colombia, especially Afro-Colombian communities who have been disproportionately affected by the armed conflict.

Notes

1 Within the Colombian legislation (Decree 4635 of 2011), people of African descent are identified as Afro-Colombians, Blacks, *Palenqueros*, and *Raizales*. For the purpose of this chapter, the term Afro-Colombian refers to a generic denomination to refer to people of African descent living in Colombia. The term Black community will be used to refer to communities who inhabit the rural zones adjoining the rivers of the Pacific Basin and who are organized as Black Councils, according to Law 70 of 1993. The term *Palenqueros* refers to the Black people who inhabit the community of Palenque near the city of Cartagena. San Basilio de Palenque is a community established by runaway enslaved people who have been able to preserve their language of African origin. The term *Raizales* will be used to specifically refer to Black people who inhabit the Island of San Andrés and Providence on the Caribbean Coast of Colombia.

2 David Eltis, "Breve Panorámica del Comercio trasatlántico de esclavos," 2007, https://www.slavevoyages.org/voyage/essays#interpretation/a-brief-overview-of-the-trans-atlantic-slave-trade/early-slaving-voyages/3/es/. Inter-American Commission on Human Rights (IACHR), Third Report on the Human Rights Situation in Colombia (The Rights of Black Communities), February 26, 1999, par. 1.

3 Hermes Tovar Pinzón, "La manumisión de esclavos en Colombia, 1809-1851, Aspectos sociales, económicos y políticos," Red Cultural del Banco de la República en Colombia, https://www.banrepcultural.org/biblioteca-virtual/credencial-historia/numero-59/la-manumision-de-esclavos-en-colombia-1809-185. Ley de 21 de mayo de 1851 "sobre libertad de esclavos," https://www.funcionpublica.gov.co/eva/gestornormativo/norma.php? i=12623. Constitutional Court, Judgement C-931/

2009. IACHR, Third Report on the Human Rights Situation in Colombia (The Rights of Black Communities), par. 2.

4 Tovar Pinzón, "La manumisión de esclavos en Colombia."

5 Ministerio de Cultura de Colombia y Pontificia Universidad Javeriana, "Rutas de Libertad: 500 años de travesía," ed. Roberto Burgos Cantor (Bogotá, Editorial Pontificia Universidad Javeriana, 2010), 16. Sergio Antonio Mosquera, La Trata negrera y la esclavización: Una perspectiva histórico-psicológica (Bogotá: Fundación Social Afrocolombiana Muntú Bantú, 2017), 25.

6 Mosquera, La Trata negrera y la esclavización, 24.

7 IACHR, Third Report on the Human Rights Situation in Colombia (The Rights of Black Communities), par. 3.

8 Edward Telles, *Pigmentocracies: Ethnicity, Race, and Color in Latin America* (Chapel Hill: The University of North Carolina Press, 2014) 81–125.

9 Tanya Katerí Hernández, *Racial Subordination in Latin America: The Role of the State, Customary Law, and the New Civil Rights Response* (Cambridge University Press, 2013) 2–4, 19–26. Telles, Pigmentocracies in Latin America, 81–125.

10 Telles, Pigmentocracies in Latin America, 81–125.

11 Sergio Antonio Mosquera, *Negro ni mi caballo: Historia del racismo en Colombia* (Fundacion Social Afrocolombiana Muntú Bantú, 2020) 235–240.

12 Centro de Estudios de Derecho, Justicia y Sociedad, "Discriminación racial en Colombia: informe alterno ante el Comité para la Eliminación de la Discriminación Racial de la ONU del 15 de mayo de 2009," https://www.dejusticia.org/wp-content/uploads/2017/04/fi_name_recurso_206.pdf.

13 César Rodríguez Garavito, "A propósito de la semana de la afrocolombianadidad, la pregunta es: ¿Colombia es un país racista?," Dejusticia, 25 de mayo de 2007, https://www.dejusticia.org/a-proposito-de-la-semana-de-la-afrocolombianadidad-la-pregunta-es-colombia-es-un-pais-racista/.

14 Ministerio de Cultura de Colombia, "Afrocolombianos, población con huellas de africanía," 2010, 6, https://www.mincultura.gov.co/areas/poblaciones/comunidades-negras-afrocolombianas-raizales-y-palenqueras/Documents/Caracterizaci%C3%B3n%20comunidades%20negras%20y%20afrocolombianas.pdf.

15 Juan Fernando Arenas, "Solo el 3% de los afrocolombianos termina el ciclo universitario," El Mundo.Com, Octubre 12, 2012, https://www.elmundo.com/portal/vida/educacion/solo_el_3_de_los_afrocolombianos_termina_el_ciclo_universitario.php#.XlSQdqgzaUk.

16 "Solo el 22% de los colombianos tiene un título universitario," El Tiempo, September 11, 2018.

17 IACHR, "The Situation of People of African Descent in the Americas," December 5, 2011, par. 18.

18 John Milton Asprilla Echeverría, "CENSO 2005 Jóvenes afrocolombianos: Caracterización Sociodemográfica y Aspectos de la Migración Interna," 24, https://www.dane.gov.co/files/censo2005/etnia/sys/jovenes_afrocolombianos.pdf.

19 "Después de 43 años, llegan las primeras camas de UCI al hospital público de Chocó," El Espectador, June 4, 2020, https://www.elespectador.com/noticias/nacional/coronavirus-en-choco/.

20 Julián Vivas, "El mapa de 1.710 poblados que aún se alumbran con velas en Colombia: El pacífico nariñense y chocoano, zonas del país con más rezago en el servicio de energía eléctrica," El Tiempo, (n.d.), https://www.eltiempo.com/colombia/otras-ciudades/los-lugares-que-aun-viven-sin-energia-electrica-en-colombia-325892.

21 ILEX -Acción Jurídica, Abuso policial y discriminación racial hacia afro-descendientes: Estudio de caso en las localidades de Usme y Kennedy De

Bogotá, D.C. (Bogotá, 2020), 36 y 37, https://www.ilexaccionjuridica.org/wp-content/uploads/2020/06/Abuso-Policial-Final-web.pdf.

22 Carlos Augusto Viáfara López, Movilidad social intergeneracional de acuerdo al color de la piel en Colombia, Revista sociedad y economía n° 33, 2017, 279, http://www.scielo.org.co/pdf/soec/n33/1657-6357-soec-33-00263.pdf.

23 "10,62% de la población del país es afrocolombiana, dice el Dane," El País, May 21, 2015, https://www.elpais.com.co/colombia/el-10-62-de-la-poblacion-del-pais-es-afrona-dice-el-dane.html#:~:text=Seg%C3%BAn%20el%20Dane%2C%20los%20afrocolombianos,son%20las%20islas%20de%20San. The results of a new census in 2018 were questioned by Afro-Colombian organizations for having undercounted the Black population in the country. Therefore, we have deliberately decided not to use the data from this census. "El 'error' del Dane que borró del mapa a 1,3 millones de afros," https://www.eltiempo.com/colombia/otras-ciudades/el-error-del-dane-que-borro-del-mapa-a-1-3-millones-de-afros-436936 ; Caracol Radio, "Admiten acción de tutela contra el Dane instaurada por afrodescendientes," November 20, 2020, https://caracol.com.co/radio/2020/11/20/judicial/1605904714_743843.html.

24 Departamento Administrativo Nacional de Estadísticas (DANE), "Cuantos somos?," https://www.dane.gov.co/index.php/estadisticas-por-tema/demografia-y-poblacion/censo-nacional-de-poblacion-y-vivenda-2018/cuantos-somos.

25 As indicated in footnote 23, we are using the census information of 2005 to establish the percentage and number of Afro-Colombians in Colombia. "El 'error' del Dane que borró del mapa a 1,3 millones de afros," https://www.eltiempo.com/colombia/otras-ciudades/el-error-del-dane-que-borro-del-mapa-a-1-3-millones-de-afros-436936 ; Caracol Radio, "Admiten acción de tutela contra el Dane instaurada por afrodescendientes," November 20, 2020, https://caracol.com.co/radio/2020/11/20/judicial/1605904714_743843.html.

26 According to Law 70 of 1993, Black Communities can collectively own and occupy their ancestral lands, and can organize themselves as Black Community Councils.

27 Yeicy Lorena Echavarria and Lisneider Hinestroza, "The process of redress for the Black Communities in the department of Chocó," *Revista Jurídicas*, 15(2), (2018), 104-130, https://r.search.yahoo.com/_ylt=AwrEeSTc7dJf5QoA2BYXFwx.;_ylu=Y29sbwNiZjEEcG9zAzEEdnRpZAMEc2VjA3Ny/RV=2/RE=1607687773/RO=10/RU=https%3a%2f%2fdialnet.unirioja.es%2fdescarga%2farticulo%2f7537629.pdf/RK=2/RS=4U6ceENZ.rf0_7e9phmXPl_4bN4-.

28 Ibid.

29 Unidad de Víctimas de Colombia, "Más del 10% de las víctimas en el país son afrocolombianos," May 20, 2019, https://www.unidadvictimas.gov.co/es/mes-afro-2019/mas-del-10-de-las-victimas-en-el-pais-son-afrocolombianos/46913.

30 It might seem that there is a discrepancy between the percentage and number of Afro-Colombians when compared to the current data of the nation's population, but this has to do with the fact that we are using the census information of 2005 to establish the percentage and number of Afro-Colombians in Colombia. "El 'error' del Dane que borró del mapa a 1,3 millones de afros," https://www.eltiempo.com/colombia/otras-ciudades/el-error-del-dane-que-borro-del-mapa-a-1-3-millones-de-afros-436936.

31 Truth, Coexistence and Non-Repetition Commission, "Comunidades afro esperan que la Comisión sea la oportunidad para contar su verdad de la guerra," December 20, 2018, https://comisiondelaverdad.co/actualidad/noticias/comunidades-afro-esperan-que-la-comision-sea-la-oportunidad-para-contar-su-verdad-de-la-guerra.

32 Unidad de Victimas de Colombia, "32 de cada 100 personas que fueron víctimas del conflicto por hechos ocurridos en el Valle son afrodescendientes," May 19, 2017, https://www.unidadvictimas.gov.co/es/afrocolombianidad-2017/32-de-cada-100-personas-que-fueron-victimas-del-conflicto-por-hechos.
33 Santiago Pardo-Rodríguez, "A Second Chance on Earth: Understanding the Selection Process of the Judges of the Colombian Special Jurisdiction for Peace," *Notre Dame J. Int'l & Comp. Law*, vol. 10 (2), June 2020, pp. 209–210, https://scholarship.law.nd.edu/cgi/viewcontent.cgi?article=1125&context=ndjicl
34 Informe del Grupo de Memoria Histórica de la Comisión Nacional de Reparación y Reconciliación: Bojayá:La guerra sin límites, 2010, 25–31, http://centrodememoriahistorica.gov.co/wp-content/uploads/2020/01/Bojay%C3%A1-La-guera-sin-l%C3%ADmites.pdf. Steven Grattan & Cady Voge, "Bojaya massacre: After 17 years, victims' remains returned," Aljazeera, November 15, 2019, https://www.aljazeera.com/indepth/features/bojaya-massacre-17-years-victims-remains-returned-191115141000894.html.
35 Ministry of the Interior of the Republic of Colombia, "El enfoque diferencial y étnico en la política pública de víctimas del conflicto armado," (n.d.), 4, https://gapv.mininterior.gov.co/sites/default/files/cartilla_enfoque_diferencial_fin_1.pdf.
36 Ibid.
37 Ibid.
38 This is the text of the legislation by which Colombia incorporated into its domestic legislation the International Labor Organization's (ILO) Convention 107 of 1957 "concerning the Protection and Integration of Indigenous and Other Tribal and Semi-Tribal Populations in Independent Countries."
39 Constitutional Court, Judgment T-955/03, 4.2.1 (a)
40 Ibid; 4.2.1 (a).
41 Constitutional Court, Judgement T-002/17.
42 Constitutional Court, Decision T-955/03, 4.2.1 (a).
43 Colombian Constitution, art. 7.
44 Colombian Constitution, Transitory Article 55.
45 Colombian Constitution, Transitory Article 55.
46 Law 70 of 1993, https://www.wola.org/sites/default/files/downloadable/Andes/Colombia/past/law%2070.pdf.
47 Balanta-Moreno Xiomara Cecilia et al, "El enfoque étnico-racial en la Jurisdicción Especial para la Paz: una mirada desde el estudio de casos de la Sala de Amnistía o Indulto" in La JEP Vsita por sus jueces, ed. Danilo Rojas-Betancourth (Bogotá: Jurisdicción Especial para la Paz, 2020), 526, https://www.jep.gov.co/Documents/LA%20JEP%20VISTA%20POR%20SUS%20JUEVES.pdf. Also, Law 70 of 1993, Article 5.
48 Ibid; 526. Also, Presidency of Colombia, Decree 1745 of 1995, Article 3.
49 Constitutional Court, Judgement T-955 of 2003, 4.1.
50 Presidency of Colombia, Decree 4635 of 2011, Article 18.
51 Ministry of the Interior, "El enfoque diferencial y étnico en la política pública," (n.d.), 10.
52 Ibid; 18–21.
53 Ethnic Commission for Peace and Defense of Territorial Rights in Colombia "Primer Informe de cumplimiento del Capítulo étnico en el marco de la implementación del Acuerdo de Paz en Colombia entre el Gobierno y las FARC-EP," 10 (March, 2019): "During the first three years, the ethnic organizations did not have access to the negotiation table in Havana—Cuba. In light of that, the decision was made to combine the efforts of indigenous peoples, Blacks, Afro-descendants, Palenqueros and Raizales [to achieve the goal of

participation in the negotiation table]." https://www.onic.org.co/images/pdf/1er_informe_cumplimiento_cap_etnico_paz.pdf.
54 Ethnic Commission for Peace and Defense of Territorial Rights, Colombia "Primer Informe de cumplimiento del Capítulo étnico," 10.
55 Final Agreement, 217.
56 Ibid, 217.
57 Ibid, 134.
58 Pardo-Rodríguez, "Understanding the Selection Process of the Judges of the Colombian Special Jurisdiction for Peace," 215.
59 Final Agreement, 132.
60 Ibid; 135.
61 Ibid.
62 Ibid; 134.
63 Legislative Act 01 of 2017, Article 1.
64 Ibid.
65 Instituto Kroc de Estudios Internacionales de Paz, "Tres años después de la firma del Acuerdo Final de Colombia: hacia la transformación territorial," June 2020, 72, http://peaceaccords.nd.edu/wp-content/uploads/2020/06/Cuarto-Informe-Final-with-Annex-Link.pdf, https://www.jep.gov.co/Sala-de-Prensa/Paginas/Instituto-Kroc-destaca-avances-de-la-JEP.aspx.
66 Special Jurisdiction for Peace (JEP), "Organizaciones negras, afrocolombianas, raizales y palenqueras insisten en medidas que promuevan la paz territorial en medio de la emergencia por el Covid-19," June 16, 2020, https://www.jep.gov.co/Sala-de-Prensa/Paginas/Organizaciones-negras,-afrocolombianas,-raizales-y-palenqueras-insisten-en-medidas-que-promuevan-la-paz-territorial.aspx.
67 Libia Rosario Grueso and Juliana Emilia Galindo, Comunidades negras y procesos de Justicia y Paz en el contexto del estado de cosas inconstitucional, (Bogotá: Deutsche Gesellschaft für Internationale Zusammenarbeit (GIZ)), 2011), 129, https://www.jep.gov.co/Sala-de-Prensa/Documents/Enfoque%20diferencial.pdf.
68 Instituto Kroc, "Tres años después de la firma del Acuerdo Final de Colombia."
69 Alexandra Huneeus, "Territory as a Victim of Colombia's War," *Blog of the European Journal of International Law*, May 7, 2020, https://www.ejiltalk.org/territory-as-a-victim-of-colombias-war/.
70 Legislative Act 01 of 2017, Article 5.
71 Ibid, Article 5.
72 Ibid; Article. 7.
73 Balanta-Moreno, "El enfoque étnico-racial en la Jurisdicción Especial para la Paz," 533.
74 Pardo-Rodríguez, "Understanding the Selection Process of the Judges of the Colombian Special Jurisdiction for Peace," 213.
75 Consultoría para los derechos humanos y el desplazamiento (CODHES), "Cartilla étnica del acuerdo de paz el camino: Hacia la implementación efectiva el capítulo étnico," 30, (December, 2017). The four Afro-Colombian judges are: Nadiezhda Natazha Henríquez Chacín; Judge Heidi Patricia Baldosea Perea; Xiomara Cecilia Balanta Moreno; and Adolfo Murillo Granados.
76 General Regulations of the JEP (Regulatory Agreement No. 001 of 2018, and Regulatory Agreement 001 of 2020), Articles 107 and 108.
77 Legislative Act 01 of 2017, Article 6.
78 Margaret Davies, "Legal Pluralism," The Oxford Handbook of Empirical Legal Research (2012): "Legal pluralism refers to the idea that in any one geographical space defined by the conventional boundaries of a nation state, there is more than one law or legal system," https://www.oxfordhandbooks.com/view/10.1093/oxfordhb/9780199542475.001.0001/oxfordhb-9780199542475-e-34.

79 Constitution of Colombia, Article 246. Law 70, Article 5. Decree 1745 of 1995, Article 3. Balanta-Moreno, "El enfoque étnico-racial en la Jurisdicción Especial para la Paz," 526–527.
80 Balanta-Moreno, "El enfoque étnico-racial en la Jurisdicción Especial para la Paz," 520–527.
81 Ibid; 530–532.
82 Appeal Section of the JEP. Auto TP-SA 556 of April 29, 2020 in the matter of Marcos Méndez Becerra, par. 32.
83 Ibid; par. 53.
84 Balanta-Moreno, "El enfoque étnico-racial en la Jurisdicción Especial para la Paz," 541.
85 Special Jurisdiction for Peace (JEP), "Comunidades afrodescendientes del norte del Cauca y de Buenaventura entregan sus informes a la JEP," June 21, 2019, https://www.jep.gov.co/Sala-de-Prensa/Paginas/Comunidades-afrodescendientes-del-Norte-del-Cauca-y-de-Buenaventura-entregan-sus-informes-a-la-JEP.aspx.
86 Special Jurisdiction for Peace (JEP), "Organizaciones afrocolombianas entregan informes a la JEP sobre graves violaciones a los derechos humanos," May 22, 2019, https://www.jep.gov.co/Sala-de-Prensa/Paginas/Organizaciones-afrocolombianas-entregan-informes-a-la-JEP-sobre-graves-violaciones-a-los-Derechos-humanos.aspx.
87 Balanta-Moreno, "El enfoque étnico-racial en la Jurisdicción Especial para la Paz," 534.
88 General Regulations of the JEP (Regulatory Agreement No. 001 of 2018, and Regulatory Agreement 001 of 2020), Articles 107 and 108.
89 Chamber for Recognition of Truth, Responsibility, and Determination of Facts of the JEP, "Documento guía para la presentación de informes elaborados por organizaciones de víctimas, indígenas, negras, afrocolombianas, raizales, palenqueras, Rrom y de derechos humanos colombianas," May 24, 2018, https://www.jep.gov.co/Sala-de-Prensa/Documents/25.05.18%208pm%20SRVR%20GUIA%20para%20la%20elaboracion%20y%20presentacion%20de%20informes%20.pdf.
90 Special Jurisdiction for Peace (JEP), "La JEP fortalece su presencia territorial con una oficina en Corozal, Sucre," August 2, 2091, https://www.jep.gov.co/Sala-de-Prensa/Paginas/La-JEP-fortalece-su-presencia-territorial-con-una-oficina-en-Corozal,-Sucre.aspx.
91 Balanta-Moreno, "El enfoque étnico-racial en la Jurisdicción Especial para la Paz," 536–539.
92 Special Jurisdiction for Peace (JEP), "Organizaciones negras, afrocolombianas, raizales y palenqueras insisten en medidas que promuevan la paz territorial en medio de la emergencia por el Covid-19," June 16, 2020, https://www.jep.gov.co/Sala-de-Prensa/Paginas/Organizaciones-negras,-afrocolombianas,-raizales-y-palenqueras-insisten-en-medidas-que-promuevan-la-paz-territorial.aspx.
93 Law 1957 of 2019, Articles 19, and 79 lit O. JEP, "Criterios y metodología de priorización de casos y situaciones," https://www.jep.gov.co/Documents/CriteriosYMetodologiaDePriorizacion.pdf. "Macro-cases" are those that seek to group the most serious, and representative crimes committed in the context of the armed conflict.
94 Special Jurisdiction for Peace (JEP), "Caso 002. Prioriza la situación territorial de Ricaurte, Tumaco y Barbacoas (Nariño)," https://www.jep.gov.co/Especiales/casos/02.html.
95 Special Jurisdiction for Peace (JEP), "Caso 004. Situación territorial de la región de Urabá," https://www.jep.gov.co/Especiales/casos/04.html.

96 Special Jurisdiction for Peace (JEP), "Caso 005. Prioriza situación territorial en la región del norte del Cauca y el sur del Valle del Cauca," https://www.jep.gov.co/Especiales/casos/05.html.
97 Yuri Alexander Romaña-Rivas, "Advocacy for a US Commission of Inquiry on Torture in the Context of the 'War on Terror' inspired by the Latin America Experience: Chile and El Salvador," Inter-American and European Human Rights Journal, Volume 5—No. 1-2 (March, 2012): 151.
98 Legislative Act 01 of 2017, Article 2.
99 Legislative Act 01 of 2017, Article 2.
100 Presidency of Colombia; Decree 588 of 2017, Article 1.
101 Truth, Coexistence and Non-Repetition Commission, "Los y las Comisionadas," https://comisiondelaverdad.co/la-comision/los-y-las-comisionadas.
102 Truth, Coexistence and Non-Repetition Commission, "Leyner Palacios es el nuevo comisionado de la Comisión de la Verdad," Septembre 29, 2020, https://comisiondelaverdad.co/actualidad/comunicados-y-declaraciones/leyner-palacios-es-el-nuevo-comisionado-de-la-comision-de-la-verdad#:~:text=Leyner%20Palacios%20es%20el%20nuevo,Comisi%C3%B3n%20de%20la%20Verdad%20Colombia.
103 "Conflicto afecta a más de cuatro millones de afrodescendientes," El Heraldo, May 24, 2019, https://www.elheraldo.co/politica/conflicto-afecta-mas-de-cuatro-millones-de-afrodescendientes-635188.
104 Truth, Coexistence and Non-Repetition Commission, "Queremos mostrar el impacto desproporcionado que tuvo el conflicto en los pueblos étnicos,"May 14, 2019, https://comisiondelaverdad.co/actualidad/noticias/queremos-mostrar-el-impacto-desproporcionado-que-tuvo-el-conflicto-en-los-pueblos-etnicos.
105 Revista Semana, "Leyner Palacios: su relato de Bojayá y expectativas por la Comisión de la Verdad," Septembre 30, 2020, https://www.msn.com/es-co/noticias/otras/leyner-palacios-su-relato-de-bojay%C3%A1-y-expectativas-por-la-comisi%C3%B3n-de-la-verdad/ar-BB19A4SU.
106 Truth, Coexistence and Non-Repetition Commission, "Comunidades afro esperan que la Comisión sea la oportunidad para contar su verdad de la guerra," December 20, 2018, https://comisiondelaverdad.co/actualidad/noticias/comunidades-afro-esperan-que-la-comision-sea-la-oportunidad-para-contar-su-verdad-de-la-guerra.
107 Afro-Colombian National Association for Displaced Persons (Afrodes), "Vivencias de mujeres afrocolombianas aportan al esclarecimiento de la verdad del conflicto armado," May 28, 2020, http://www.afrodescolombia.org/verdad-mujeres-afrocolombianas/.
108 Ibid.
109 Ibid.
110 Truth, Coexistence and Non-Repetition Commission, "Sin nuestras voces, la verdad estará incompleta," July 11, 2019, https://comisiondelaverdad.co/actualidad/noticias/sin-nuestras-voces-la-verdad-estara-incompleta#:~:text=La%20Comisi%C3%B3n%20de%20la%20Verdad,afrodescendientes%20del%20Norte%20del%20Cauca.&text=Le%20entregamos%20a%20la%20Comisi%C3%B3n,sido%20silenciadas%E2%80%9D%2 C%20dijo%20Carabal%C3%AD.
111 Women's link Worldwide, "Mujeres afrodescendientes del Cauca presentan ante la Comisión de la Verdad un informe que expone el impacto que han causado sobre sus comunidades la imposición de economías legales e ilegales a través de la violencia," May 21, 2020, https://www.womenslinkworldwide.org/informate/sala-de-prensa/mujeres-afrodescendientes-del-cauca-presentan-ante-la-comision-de-la-verdad-el-informe-que-expone-el-impacto-que-han-causado-sobre-sus-

comunidades-la-imposicion-de-economias-legales-e-ilegales-a-traves-de-la-violencia.

112 Women's link Worldwide, "Mujeres afrodescendientes del Cauca presentan ante la Comisión de la Verdad."

113 Truth, Coexistence and Non-Repetition Commission, "Metodología del enfoque étnico y contra el racismo, la discriminación racial y formas conexas de intolerancia," October 30, 2018, https://www.ohchr.org/Documents/Issues/IPeoples/EMRIP/StudyRRR/Comision_de_la_Verdad_Colombia.pdf.

114 Balanta-Moreno, "El enfoque étnico-racial en la Jurisdicción Especial para la Paz," 535.

115 Truth, Coexistence and Non-Repetition Commission, "Acuerdo para que los pueblos afrodescendientes cuenten su verdad del conflicto armado," December 21, 2018, https://comisiondelaverdad.co/actualidad/noticias/acuerdo-para-que-los-pueblos-afrodescendientes-cuenten-su-verdad.

116 Truth, Coexistence and Non-Repetition Commission, "Sin la voz de los pueblos negros tendríamos una verdad incompleta," May 10, 2019, https://comisiondelaverdad.co/actualidad/noticias/sin-la-voz-de-los-pueblos-negros-tendriamos-una-verdad-incompleta.

117 Ibid.

118 Truth, Coexistence and Non-Repetition Commission, "El diálogo con mujeres y personas LGBTI de las comunidades negras," March 18, 2020, https://comisiondelaverdad.co/actualidad/noticias/el-dialogo-con-mujeres-y-poblacion-lgbti-de-las-comunidades-negras.

119 Truth, Coexistence and Non-Repetition Commission, "El diálogo con mujeres y personas LGBTI de las comunidades negras."

120 "La verdad debe tener el sello de la gente negra del Pacífico," Agencia de Información Laboral – AIL, August 13, 2019, http://ail.ens.org.co/noticias/la-verdad-debe-tener-el-sello-de-la-gente-negra-del-pacifico/.

121 Truth, Coexistence and Non-Repetition Commission, "Causas, dinámicas e impactos del conflicto armado en los territorios étnicos del Caribe,"youtube, May 14, 2020, https://www.youtube.com/watch?v = satSGUib0os.

122 National Center of Historical Memory, "Lo que sabemos de los desaparecidos en Colombia," 2018, http://www.centrodememoriahistorica.gov.co/micrositios/balances-jep/desaparicion.html.

123 Legislative Act 01 of 2017, Article 3.

124 Presidency of the Republic; Decree 589 of 2017, Articles 15, 16, and 17.

125 "Luz Marina Monzón es la directora de la Unidad de Búsqueda de Personas Desaparecidas," El Espectador, September 26, 2017, https://www.elespectador.com/colombia2020/justicia/desaparecidos/luz-marina-monzon-es-la-directora-de-la-unidad-de-busqueda-de-personas-desaparecidas-articulo-855816/.

126 Presidency of the Republic; Decree 589 of 2017, Article 4.

127 Ibid; Article 5.

128 Ibid.

129 Ibid.

130 The Unit for the Search for Persons Deemed Disappeared in the context and by reason of the armed conflict (UBPD), "Respuesta a las preguntas planteadas por la ciudadanía durante la [primer] audiencia de rendición de cuentas de la UBPD," June 19, 2019, https://www.ubpdbusquedadesaparecidos.co/wp-content/uploads/2019/08/Respuestas-Rendici%C3%B3n-de-Cuentas-UBPD-2019.pdf.

131 Ibid.

132 Constitutional Court, Judgement C-067 of 2018: Operative point 4.

133 Ibid.

134 There still are different armed groups operating in the country, which may eventually enter into a peace agreement with the Colombian government. In fact, the International Committee of the Red Cross (ICRC) has indicated that there are five ongoing armed conflicts in Colombia. ICRC, "Colombia: Five armed conflicts—What's happening?," January 30, 2019, https://www.icrc.org/en/document/colombia-five-armed-conflicts-whats-happening. In this respect, it is worth mentioning that peace negotiations between the Colombian Government and the guerilla movement of the National Liberation Army ("ELN" for its Spanish acronym) were suspended in 2019. Jenny Carolina González and Anatoly Kurmanaev, "Colombia Captures Guerrillas Accused in Deadly Car Bombing," *The New York Times*, July 2, 2020, https://www.nytimes.com/2020/07/02/world/americas/colombia-eln-bombing-arrests.html.

15 The politics of education reforms in post-conflict societies

A cautionary tale for the Colombian case

Claudia Milena Díaz-Ríos

Introduction

Education has been typically considered as a key element to rebuilding post-conflict societies and preventing future violence. An equal distribution of quality education and a curriculum oriented toward inclusive citizenship and peacebuilding arguably have a conflict-dampening impact.[1] Yet, recommendations on actions on education that help overcome conflict are typically focused on fixing deficits in resources, skills, technical capacity, and organization of schools, while little attention is paid to the politics associated with policy change.[2] Indeed, institutional and political constraints to educational change are perhaps the most intractable factors of education reforms in conflict-affected and post-conflict societies. However, ignoring them can highly compromise the chances of the school system to contribute to peacebuilding.[3]

This paper analyzes these constraints for the Colombian case. Colombia experienced a very long armed conflict and has recently signed a peace agreement with one of the most standing rebel forces. This agreement acknowledges the role of education in building a durable peace and establishes ambitious and relevant goals focused on rural education.[4] These goals are consistent with international recommendations on education reforms in post-conflict societies, and also reflect laudable commitments with educational and social justice. Nevertheless, a poorly coordinated decentralization model, high levels of clientelism within the school system, and a lip-service to the importance of education in the political agenda may transform such goals into toothless promises. Since this is not the first time that Colombia identifies the main challenges of the education system and implements policies and programs to solve them, it is worth asking what institutional factors may limit the success of this initiative in the post-conflict context.

I start by describing the three-faced role of education in post-conflict countries—as a cause, as a victim, and as a solution—and demonstrate how these three faces entail political and institutional dynamics that limit the contribution of education to building peace. The following section describes these faces in the particular case of Colombia and analyzes the limitations of the Colombian proposals for post-conflict education. The analysis shows how legacies of uncoordinated governance, clientelistic use of the school system, and lack of political will threaten to reduce Colombian education proposals to a well-intentioned plan without concretion. This would ultimately perpetuate inequality and leave the country at risk of repeating violent conflict. Drawing from the Colombian case, my conclusions summarize lessons about the importance of understanding the politics of education reform in order to formulate and implement successful post-conflict education policies.

The relationship between education and violent conflict

Theoretical arguments on the nexus between education and armed conflict point at three facets of this relationship: Education as a cause, as a victim, and as part of the solution to violence. Education has been observed as a cause of violent conflict in cases where the school system is severely biased against a specific group. The segregated or unequal distribution of education that reproduces the privilege of a dominant group at the expense of others has been identified as a factor that increases resentment and hatred.[5] Moreover, denial of education through school closure has been used to weaken civil support for adversary groups.[6] At the same time, limited education opportunities provide youth with insufficient skills to achieve a sustainable life, therefore increasing their chances to be recruited by armed groups.[7] Likewise, a curriculum that legitimates a particular version of history that ignores other narratives, selects content that promotes cultural repression, or under- or misrepresents a specific group can also increase animosities and spur conflict.[8] In short, although it is not the sole cause, the quantity, quality, and content of education may increase the risk of violent conflict, especially in countries with a large school-age population.

Violent conflicts also have devastating effects on education. Wars typically destroy schools and educational infrastructure, either because of unintended effects of military actions, or because schools are directly targeted to intimidate and weaken opponents.[9] Teachers are also usual victims of violent conflicts. They can be threatened as a consequence of what they teach, forced to leave or disappear, or even be killed.[10] Students also experience violence as a consequence of internal conflicts, including, but not limited to, sexual assault, forced recruitment, forced displacement, and torture.[11] Although there is no clear evidence on whether education funds are reallocated to military in times of war, armed conflict often coincides with reduction or stagnation of education expenditure and enrollment.[12] The decline of educational opportunities as a consequence of internal war may even exacerbate conflict, fueling a vicious cycle of violence.

Yet, observers have suggested that education can also dampen conflict. Providing more opportunities of quality, fair, and inclusive education can promote stability and have pacifying effects.[13] Østby and Urdal[14] found that the increase of educational opportunities contributes to peace in at least three ways. First, the rise of public education expenditure reduces animosities, both directly and indirectly, through greater development and equality. Second, more educational opportunities make it less attractive for young people to enlist in armed groups. Finally, higher educational attainment may encourage greater political participation and may act as a democratic way to address conflict through political institutions.

The profound reforms that transform education into a part of the solution to conflict usually require high levels of government leadership, community involvement, and support from international actors.[15] In addition, these reforms usually involve changes in education governance, learning contents, and human and material resources of the school system.[16] Early and consistent educational planning before and during the early stages of the post-conflict context prevents perpetuation or reversal to traditional and inefficient organizational methods that may have previously fueled educational inequality.[17] This type of planning demands long-term steady funding and entails the design and implementation of reliable monitoring and evaluation systems that allow accountability and constant improvement of policies and programs. At the same time, aiming for quality educational services in post-conflict countries usually demands serious, systematic, and innovative investments in the training of teachers and personnel in charge of the education system.[18] Finally, literature on education in conflict situations also points at the importance of community participation. Learning from and promoting successful bottom-up educational initiatives, and engaging communities and civil society in the design of educational policies, programs, and curriculum are crucial actions that have a significant impact on conflict resolution.[19] Participation also makes initiatives accountable to communities and increases the legitimacy and support for reforms.[20]

Literature on education and conflict has also suggested "education for peacebuilding" as a systematic approach that helps students identify differences between and within groups, underlying causes of conflict, and ways to contribute to reconciliation and peace.[21] Similarly, Davies[22] suggests the notion of 'justice-sensitive education' as an approach associated with transitional justice, which aims to minimize the negative impact of education on conflict and maximize its contribution to the transition from oppressive states to more democratic legal and inclusive societies. Justice-sensitive education enables students to identify, understand, and acknowledge human right violations, search the multiple "truths" about the conflict, and use these understandings to nurture a peaceful future.[23]

Unfortunately, the identification of education as part of the solution to violent conflicts often pays little attention to the institutional and political dynamics that may constrain reforms. On the one hand, weak institutions may be unable to lead reforms. Fragile states in post-conflict situations do not have enough legitimacy, often have shortages of skilled personnel, or lack the material resources to formulate, implement, and sustain the required changes to transform education from a cause to a solution to conflict.[24] On the other hand, weak institutions are often intertwined with power-conflict dynamics. Fragile education governance is not just a problem of limited state capacity, but also a reflection of biased institutions (procedures, routines, norms, and conventions) that allow elites and the political establishment to use the education system for their own benefit and at the expense of others.[25] Thus, change not only requires the training or strengthening of state capacity, but also political commitment, which refers to agents who "seek to shape and design political institutions in accordance with particular principles and aims."[26]

Ypi[27] explains that this commitment is shaped by political benefits or the relative advantage that actors can obtain from a position or action. The political benefits of expressing public support to arguably uncontested policy goals, such as closing educational gaps against the poorest, or offering greater educational opportunities for the rural population, may easily fuel commitment. Leaders can also obtain benefits from certain commitment in the form of the production of formal plans, administrative units, commissions, etc., that signal intentions to achieve widely accepted goals. Nevertheless, the actual implementation of policies and programs is less likely to produce clear political benefits, especially if they demand profound policy changes, greater investment, or redistribution of resources or decision-making power. Indeed, such changes may interfere with or harm current political benefits, which can lead to low levels of political commitment and refrain actors from undertaking necessary actions to fulfill policy goals. Ignoring the increasing returns or benefits that existing institutions have for specific actors and the effects of their change on political commitment may transform ambitious proposals into failed or incomplete reforms. Thus, we need to understand the effects on the political commitment of the interaction between weak institutions and the politics of education policy change if we are to design and implement justice-sensitive post-conflict education reforms. The next section analyzes this interaction for the Colombian case and identifies the challenges of the current post-conflict educational plans in the country.

The three faces of education in the Colombian conflict and the Special Plan for Rural Education

As other chapters have already explained, Colombia has experienced five decades of a violent conflict between the rebel group, "Revolutionary Armed Forces of Colombia—People's Army" (FARC-EP), and the state. Although explanations of the conflict have not systematically studied the causal effect of education, and proving the effect of education on Colombian conflict is out of the scope of this work, the Colombian school system shows some of the characteristics that have been identified as catalysts of war.[28] The educational system of the country has been characterized as an educational apartheid in which the wealthy concentrate on elite private schools, while the poor attend underfunded public organizations.[29] This apartheid has perpetuated enormous rural-urban and class-based gaps. By 2017, around 23% of the Colombian population was located in widely dispersed rural areas (11.5 million people), and 35% of this population experienced multidimensional poverty. Although enrolment rates have increased for the entire population, significant gaps persist in secondary education: the net enrolment rate for lower secondary education reached 75% for the urban population, and only 54% for rural dispersed areas; for upper secondary education, urban areas reached 48%, 22% points higher than the rural rate (26%). Similarly, the rural population aged 15–24 have, on average, six years of education compared to ten years for the urban population.[30]

The situation worsens when examined for quality. Specifically, the Colombian performance in PISA is lower than most Latin American countries included in the test.[31] The performance of rural students in the national standardized exams (math and language) for primary school is 7% lower than urban student performance. The gap widens across school levels, reaching 10% in secondary education. There is also a huge performance gap between poor students in public schools and wealthy students in elite private organizations, measured again by the national standardized exams. Unlike enrolment and efficiency, quality gaps do not seem to be decreasing at all in recent years.[32] In addition, rural teachers have fewer training opportunities, and government training plans typically neglect the particular conditions and needs of rural schools.[33] Moreover, national curriculum guidelines tend to stigmatize or neglect particular groups, such as Indigenous peoples and other ethnic minorities, blaming them for the persistence of violence and instability, or dismissing the discussion of the armed conflict and the effects it has on these communities.[34]

While the causal link between education and violent conflict in Colombia has not been studied, the impact of war on Colombian education is better documented. Novelli[35] reports that between 1991 and 2006, 808 teachers were killed, 2015 received death threats, and more than 70 schools were attacked by all armed groups. In 2013, the UN reported 26 education-related attacks that targeted schools, teachers, or students, and 11 schools damaged in crossfire and by explosive devices in 2015. Fewer incidents happened in 2016, with six attacks on schools. Between 2013 and 2017, non-state armed groups killed teachers in at least 16 reported cases.[36] The UN has also verified that the FARC-EP recruited students as soldiers or workers for drug production and traffic.[37] In addition, forcibly displaced children have significant education gaps. Only 51% of them attend secondary education, and the overage of those in primary school is twice as much compared to non-displaced students. While forcibly displaced students are entitled to free education and enrolment without proof of previous schooling, they face enormous difficulties in demonstrating their eligibility status on the one hand, and on the other municipal poor coordination and planning create limitations for effective educational responses.[38] Likewise, the expenditure on education as a percentage of government spending decreased from 18% in 1984 to 16% in 2016. Similarly, the evolution of government education expenditure as a percentage of GDP has been inconsistent with slight increases followed by moderate cuts across the last 20 years.

Acknowledging the effects of the conflict on the school system and the role that education can play as a solution to war, the recently signed peace agreement between FARC-EP and the Colombian state demands the formulation and implementation of a robust rural education plan as part of the first component of the agreement, a comprehensive rural reform. This reform aims at a structural transformation of rural areas of the country closing the urban-rural gap and eradicating rural poverty through the socio-economic development of the rural population, community participation, and promotion of human rights.[39] Within this framework, the agreement states that rural education should.

> [...] provide comprehensive early childhood care, ensure school attendance, education quality and relevance, and eradicate illiteracy in rural areas as well as promote the productive permanence of young people in the countryside, and bring regional academic organizations together to build rural development[40]

To fulfill this purpose, the agreement establishes that the national government should formulate and implement a Special Plan for Rural Education (PREE). Accordingly, the PREE was formulated during 2017 and 2018 based on a fair diagnosis of Colombian rural education. The plan sets relevant policy goals that reflect the agreement's mandate[41]:

- Ensure universal early childcare.
- Implement flexible models for pre-school, primary, and secondary education that acknowledge the diverse needs of the rural population.
- Build and improve education infrastructure and technology, as well as teachers' training.
- Ensure tuition-free early childhood, primary and secondary education, as well as free access to textbooks, school meals, and transportation.
- Implement rural vocational education in upper secondary education.
- Implement forgivable loans for higher education of rural youth.
- Increase higher education supply consistent with rural development needs.

Consistent with international literature on post-conflict education and the Agreement guidelines, the PREE also expresses its commitment with participation of families and communities in education decision-making through school governments and the municipal education assemblies. Finally, the PREE also mentions the importance of rural school curriculum for reconciliation and construction of collective memory on conflict.

In short, the PREE reflects expressed commitments with justice-sensitive education that are hardly contestable.

The PREE, however, is not a structural education reform as suggested by post-conflict education literature, but rather a set of policies focalized on the municipalities most affected by the conflict determined during the Agreement. While targeting these municipalities may ensure that actions will address the most vulnerable population, a significant portion of the dispersed rural population will be left behind, which limits the plan's potential to close the rural-urban gap. Moreover, the plan will be developed in the existing governance institutions of the education system. On the one hand, this situation could favor its short-term implementation because the plan does not demand radical changes that threaten explicitly vested interests on the existing education system. On the other hand, however, existing literature has described how the current country's decentralization model has neglected the needs of the dispersed rural population, has not solved the underfunding of rural schools and their limited autonomy, and has often promoted the misuse, waste, or misappropriation of resources at the subnational level.[42] As this is not the first time that the country engages with similar programs to solve the inequalities of rural education, looking at the achievement and failures of previous experiences, their interaction with the decentralization model of the country, and the political will and constituencies they generated, can illuminate the challenges and the chances of PREE actually achieving its goals.

Weak institutions that perpetuate privilege

The governance of the Colombian education system has been typically weak. By the 1960s, the country implemented fiscal decentralization, but administrative decentralization was truncated because the national education ministry did not have the tools needed to enforce policies and make departments accountable for their actions. Subnational education secretaries became advocates of this arrangement, which favored patronage and political gains.[43] In addition to this semi-anarchic, decentralized educational system, Colombian policy showed a disinterest for rural education as urban primary schools were to provide more years of education compared to rural schools, and rural schools, when available, focused exclusively on practical preparation dismissing intellectual training.[44]

Within this context, three rural education programs, which have likely inspired PREE, exemplified the difficulties created by this institutional setting and lack of political will: Rural Development Concentrations, Escuela Nueva, and the Rural Education Project. Like PREE, the Rural Development Concentrations project in the 1960s aimed to promote a comprehensive development of Colombian dispersed rural areas. This project included a network organization with a central branch that delivered secondary education and concentrated resources for technical education adapted to local needs, healthcare, and community development. This branch was articulated with various smaller branches that delivered primary education in dispersed municipalities nearby.[45] Yet, the implementation of Rural Development Concentrations assumed an institutional design of the school system based on educational planning that did not exist in practice.[46] Consequently, the project experienced a high turnover of the staff in charge of implementing the program, and the distribution of the Concentrations responded to political pressures rather than to the established technical criteria.[47] Lack of coordination and vested interest frustrated the attempt to bring development to rural areas through these Concentrations.

Escuela Nueva is also a national comprehensive rural education project implemented in 1975 that had its boom in the 1980s and 1990s, and is still active in different rural areas of the country. Although funded by USAID, Inter-American Development Bank, and the World Bank,[48] Escuela Nueva emerged from local rural multigrade education experiences that developed a strategy for teacher training and the development of instructional materials and practices relevant for the rural sector.[49] In its formulation, Escuela Nueva has characteristics that are also reflected in the current PREE, including flexible learning modules with strong educational resources, in-service teacher training adapted to school and rural conditions, and community participation as a key to supporting student learning.[50] However, as the Escuela Nueva implementation was mainly in charge of subnational secretaries, program development varied substantially across the country, and schools often did not follow the prescribed principles of self-instruction, in-service training, participation, etc.[51] While evaluations suggest that Escuela Nueva improved student achievement compared to traditional rural schools,[52] McEwan and Benveniste[53] argue that the uncoordinated character of the program permitted some departments to dismiss or substantially alter program implementation compromising its success. While the government originally supported the program because it was seen as a way to pacify peasants after the violence between Liberals and Conservatives, the program lost momentum later as the elites found they could perceive more gains and also pacify peasants by short-term actions, such as building schools rather than long-term investments, such as pedagogical interventions.[54]

Finally, the Rural Education Project (PER), implemented in the 2000s, became the main initiative in the country to improve public education in rural areas. Building on previous experiences, PER aimed at improving the access of quality education in rural areas and promoting peaceful coexistence in the community by upgrading various existing flexible education models and adapting initial and in-service teacher training to the particular needs of rural education.[55] Goal similarity between programs and the participation of PER experts and officials in the formulation of PREE suggest that PER is one of the main sources for the plan that is expected to implement the educational components of the Peace Agreement. The project was developed in two phases: a pilot project implemented between 2000 and 2007, and the scaling-up phase between 2008 and 2016. Unlike Escuela Nueva, during PER-first phase established a clear governance structure that ensured adequate distribution of responsibilities and accountability between jurisdictions. The World Bank provided financial and technical assistance for the implementation and monitoring of the project to the national ministry of education. In turn, the national ministry of education promoted and monitored a structure parallel to the country's decentralization scheme created only for PER management, the "Alianzas." These Alianzas were partnerships between municipalities, departments, regional productive sectors, universities, and other NGOs, created to lead the formulation of municipal education sub-projects, and assist municipalities in the implementation of such projects by providing services or contracting them out.[56] This structure took away some of the authority of local secretaries over the program and established additional local controls to resource management. With this structure, the program showed significant achievements in enrolment, efficiency, and quality in the 6,536 schools of the 537 municipalities included in the pilot project.[57]

However, during the second phase, the project's coordination mechanism changed to adapt to the current decentralization scheme of the country and improve the project's sustainability in the long run. With this change, the national education ministry retained control over PER decisions by giving subnational units authority only on targeting beneficiary schools and monitoring their use of funds. While the ministry expected to isolate the program from political influences and corruption, local communities became disengaged from the process as implementation slowed, did not respond to local needs, and politicians and policymakers did not perceive enough incentives to promote the program.[58] Ultimately, PER's second phase was not able to improve the quality of rural education and close the rural-urban gap as planned.[59] Together, Rural Development Concentrations, Escuela Nueva, and PER show the dilemmas of centralized projects that generate low political commitment due to scarce political gains, and decentralized initiatives that promote commitment, but at the cost of distorting goals on equity and quality to favor personal interests.

Lessons of past experiences for the PREE

Will governance problems and a lack of political commitment affect the implementation of the PREE? While coordination of the Colombian education system has improved in the last decades, subnational jurisdictions still have very dissimilar and heterogeneous capacities to govern education. Corruption and clientelism in the poorest subnational units continue fueling a vicious cycle of limited capacity and weak institutions.[60] The aforementioned experiences dealt with this problem by retaining authority at the central level, leaving subnational units to operate with ample flexibility, or creating parallel informal decentralization structures. Yet, none of these strategies were successful or sustainable in the long run. As these previous experiences, current PREE's formulation suggests that this plan can also become a failed promise that would compromise the commitments established in the peace agreement.

PREE's governance structure establishes roles and responsibilities based on the current decentralization model of the country. The national education ministry is in charge of assisting and monitoring the work of local education secretaries. Secretaries are in charge of assisting municipalities and schools with program implementation. In addition, communities have participation in decision-making through the education municipal assembly, a local body composed of policymakers and municipal educators formally in charge of advising and monitoring the development of national and departmental education plans.[61] With this structure, the PREE attempts to combine bottom-up models used in Escuela Nueva and PER-first phase with the top-up models used in PER-second phase in order to increase the capacity of the subnational jurisdictions and promote accountability at the central level.

Nevertheless, this plan would likely encounter various important problems. First, the plan has not secured funding. While previous programs relied on international aid, for PREE's development the economy ministry did not authorize loan requests to the Inter-American Development Bank and the World Bank,[62] due to the economic recession the country experienced in 2018, and the need to cope with the multiple and competing demands of post-conflict. This decision suggests that current political commitment with rural education does not go beyond formal plans. Without funding or any other mechanism to increase political commitment at the local level, it is very unlikely that PREE's focalized municipalities and local secretaries will develop the capacity to implement the program, as they will not have the incentives and resources to do so. In addition, like in PER-first phase, the national education ministry has not established a unit responsible for the plan, which compromises the monitoring, adjustment and assessment of the program. Moreover, education municipal assemblies have been reported to operate effectively when they communicate well with effective municipal and departmental governments.[63] Yet, as PREE's focalized municipalities have been typically ignored by departmental governments and local government capacity is evenly distributed, the plan implementation may become, at best, as heterogeneous as Escuela Nueva was.

To increase the odds against PREE, the government elected in 2018 was the strongest opponent of the peace agreement and consequently, it diverted attention from the associated initiatives. Even though the education sector did not suffer the cuts of other social policy sectors, resources for investment are still very marginal, reaching only 8% of the total education budget, which is insufficient for PREE's ambitious goals. Moreover, this government did not mention PREE in its current education plan, is revising PREE formulation, and has not started its implementation.[64]

Conclusions

The Colombian challenges of education in the post-conflict context shed light to an important prerequisite that needs to be considered in the analysis of the relationship between education and violent conflict, and the prospects of successful post-conflict education reforms: Political commitment. This country-specific case shows that weak education institutions are often reproduced by vested interests that do not see gains in increasing the opportunities of the most vulnerable population. When reforms threaten these interests, they lose the political commitment of powerful actors. Moreover, when reforms involved change in sectors of public disinterest, such as rural education in Colombia, and such disinterest legitimates a specific social structure, challenges increase while political commitment declines.

Understanding these politics is crucial for post-conflict education reforms. In the Colombian case, the decentralization model and the lack of commitment with rural areas is preventing the success of the peace agreement in relation to education. Previous experiences have shown that these problems will not be fixed through one-time, short-term projects. Changes require strong, sustainable incentives for local actors that gradually break the vicious cycle of clientelistic management of education and weak technical capacity at the subnational level. These incentives can also nurture constituencies that could promote the sustainability of changes. Yet, such a new dynamic requires a national commitment and consensus that goes beyond the formal peace agreement and that has not been achieved in the country.

Notes

1 Kenneth David Bush et al., *Two Faces of Education in Ethnic Conflict: Towards a Peacebuilding Education for Children.* (Florence: International Child Development Centre, 2000); Mario Novelli, "Political Violence against Teacher in Colombia: Opportunities for Change in the Midst of Conflict?," in Susan Nicolai (ed.), *Opportunities for Change: Education Innovation and Reform during and after Conflict* (Paris: IIEP-UNESCO, 2009) 189–200.
2 Derick W Brinkerhoff, "Capacity Development in Fragile States" (Maastricht: ECDPM Working Paper 58D, 2007), https://ecdpm.org/wp-content/uploads/2013/11/DP-58D-Capacity-Development-in-Fragile-States-2007.pdf.
3 Lynn Davies, "Learning for state building: capacity development, education and fragility," *Comparative Education* vol. 47 (2), 2011, pp. 157–80.
4 Final Agreement to End the Armed Conflict and Build a Stable and Lasting Peace (henceforth, Final Agreement).
5 G Østby and H Urdal, "Education and Conflict—What the Evidence Says" (Oslo: PRIO, 2011), https://www.prio.org/Publications/Publication/?x = 7228.
6 Bush et al., Two Faces of Education in Ethnic Conflict.
7 UNESCO, ed., *The Hidden Crisis: Armed Conflict and Education, EFA Global Monitoring Report 2011* (Paris: United Nations Educational, Scientific and Cultural Organization, 2011).
8 Bush et al., Two Faces of Education in Ethnic Conflict; Elisabeth King, "Educating for conflict or peace: challenges and dilemmas in post-conflict

Rwanda," *International Journal* vol. 60 (4), 2005, pp. 904–18, https://doi.org/10.2307/40204090.

9 Ashley Gilbertson, "Education Under Attack 2018," 159; Brian Lai and Clayton Thyne, "The Effect of Civil War on Education, 1980—97," *Journal of Peace Research*, vol. 44 (3), May 2007, pp. 277–92.

10 Novelli, "Political Violence against Teacher in Colombia: Opportunities for Change in the Midst of Conflict?"; Marcela Bautista and Gloria González, Docencia Rural En Colombia: Educar Para La Paz En Medio Del Conflicto Armado (Bogotá: Fundación Compartir, 2019).

11 Gilbertson, "Education Under Attack 2018."

12 Østby and Urdal, "Education and Conflict—What the Evidence Says."

13 Novelli, "Political Violence against Teacher in Colombia: Opportunities for Change in the Midst of Conflict?"; Bush et al., Two Faces of Education in Ethnic Conflict.

14 "Education and Conflict—What the Evidence Says."

15 Novelli, "Political Violence against Teachers in Colombia: Opportunities for Change in the Midst of Conflict?"

16 Bush et al., Two Faces of Education in Ethnic Conflict; Davies, "Learning for State building."

17 Emily Ann Vargas-Barón and Bernardo Bernal Alarcón, From Bullets to Blackboards: Education for Peace in Latin America and Asia (IDB, 2005).

18 Bush et al., Two Faces of Education in Ethnic Conflict.

19 Christopher Blattman, Alexandra Hartman, and Robert Blair, "Can We Teach Peace and Conflict Resolution?: Results from a Randomized Evaluation of the Community Empowerment Program (CEP) in Liberia: A Program to Build Peace, Human Rights, and Civic Participation" (New Jersey: Innovations for Poverty Action, 2011); Mario Novelli and Mieke T.A. Lopes Cardozo, "Conflict, education and the global south: new critical directions," *International Journal of Educational Development* vol. 28 (4), July 2008, pp. 473–88.

20 Vargas-Barón and Bernal Alarcón, From Bullets to Blackboards.

21 UNICEF, *Evaluation of UNICEF's Peacebuilding, Education and Advocacy Programme (PBEA)* (New York: UNICEF, 2015); Bush et al., Two Faces of Education in Ethnic Conflict.

22 Lynn Davies, "Justice-Sensitive Education: The Implications of Transitional Justice Mechanisms for Teaching and Learning," *Comparative Education* 53 (3), 2017, pp. 333–50.

23 Ibid.

24 Alan Smith, "Education in the twenty-first century: conflict, reconstruction and reconciliation," *Compare: A Journal of Comparative and International Education* vol. 35 (4), 2005, pp. 373–91; Novelli, "Political Violence against Teacher in Colombia: Opportunities for Change in the Midst of Conflict?"

25 Smith, "Education in the Twenty-first Century."

26 Lea Ypi, "Political commitment and the value of partisanship," *American Political Science Review* 110 (3), 2016, p. 604.

27 "Political Commitment and the Value of Partisanship."

28 Bautista and González, Docencia Rural En Colombia: Educar Para La Paz En Medio Del Conflicto Armado.

29 Mauricio García et al., *Separados y Desiguales. Educación y Clases Sociales En Colombia* (Bogota: DeJusticia, 2013).

30 Ministerio de Educación Nacional, *Plan Especial de Educación Rural. Hacia El Desarrollo Rural y La Construcción de Paz* (Bogotá: MEN, 2018).

31 Luis Fernando Gamboa and Fábio D. Waltenberg, "Inequality of opportunity for educational achievement in Latin America: Evidence from PISA 2006–2009,"

Economics of Education Review vol. 31 (5), October 1, 2012pp. 694–708, https://doi.org/10.1016/j.econedurev.2012.05.002.

32 García et al., Separados y Desiguales. Educación y Clases Sociales En Colombia.

33 Bautista and González, Docencia Rural En Colombia: Educar Para La Paz En Medio Del Conflicto Armado.

34 Kathy Bickmore, Ahmed Salehin Kaderi, and Ángela Guerra-Sua, "Creating capacities for peacebuilding citizenship: history and social studies curricula in Bangladesh, Canada, Colombia, and México," *Journal of Peace Education* 14 (3), 2017, pp. 282–309.

35 Novelli, "Political Violence against Teachers in Colombia: Opportunities for Change in the Midst of Conflict?"

36 Gilbertson, "Education Under Attack 2018."

37 UNESCO, The Hidden Crisis.

38 UNESCO.

39 Final Agreement.

40 Final Agreement, 26.

41 Ministerio de Educación Nacional, Plan Especial de Educación Rural. Hacia El Desarrollo Rural y La Construcción de Paz.

42 Bautista and González, *Docencia Rural En Colombia: Educar Para La Paz En Medio Del Conflicto Armado; Jesús Duarte and María Cristina Restrepo, Educación pública y clientelismo en Colombia* (Medellín: Editorial Universidad de Antioquia, 2003); Ligia Melo, "Impacto de La Descentralización Fiscal Sobre La Educación Pública Colombiana," *Borradores de Economía*, 350 (2005).

43 Mark Hanson, *Educational Reform and Administrative Development: The Cases of Colombia and Venezuela* (Stanford: Hoover Press, 1986); Jesús Duarte, "State weakness and clientelism in Colombian Education," in Eduardo Posada-Carbó (ed.), *The Politics of Reforming the State* (London: McMillan Press, 1998) 125–53.

44 Hanson, Educational Reform and Administrative Development.

45 Daniel Lozano Flórez, "Contribuciones de la educación rural en Colombia a la construcción social de pequeños municipios y al desarrollo rural," *Revista de la Universidad de la Salle* vol. 57, 2012, pp. 117–36.

46 Claudia Díaz Ríos, "When Global Ideas Collide with Domestic Interests: The Politics of Secondary Education Governance in Argentina, Chile and Colombia" (Ph.D. Thesis, Hamilton (ON), McMaster University, 2016).

47 Abner Prada, "Informe Final: Proyecto Col. 72/033 Concentraciones de Desarrollo Rural" (Bogota, 1976).

48 Noel McGinn, "Resistance to Good Ideas: Escuela Nueva En Colombia," in Education Reform in the South in the 1990s, ed. Lene Buchert (Unesco, 1998), 29–51; Ernesto Schiefelbein, Redefining Basic Education for Latin America: Lessons to Be Learned from the Colombian Escuela Nueva (Paris: UNESCO, International Institute for Educational Planning, 1992).

49 Schiefelbein, Redefining Basic Education for Latin America.

50 Patrick J. McEwan, "The effectiveness of multigrade schools in Colombia," *International Journal of Educational Development* vol. 18 (6), 1998, pp. 435–52.

51 Víctor Manuel Gómez, "Visión crítica sobre la Escuela Nueva en Colombia," *Revista Educación y Pedagogía* vol. 14/15, 1995, pp. 280–306.

52 McEwan, "The Effectiveness of Multigrade Schools in Colombia."

53 Patrick J. McEwan and Luis Benveniste, "The Politics of Rural School Reform: Escuela Nueva in Colombia," *Journal of Education Policy* vol. 16 (6), November 2001, pp. 547–59, https://doi.org/10.1080/02680930110087816.

54 McEwan and Benveniste.

55 "Colombia—Rural Education Project" (Washington D.C.: World Bank Group, 2000), http://documents.worldbank.org/curated/en/611591468770497457/Colombia-Rural-Education-Project.

56 "Colombia—Rural Education Project."

57 Catherine Rodríguez and Fabio Sánchez, "Do interventions at school level improve educational outcomes? Evidence from a Rural Program in Colombia," *World Development* vol. 38 (3), 2010, pp. 415–28, https://doi.org/10.1016/j.worlddev.2009.10.002; World Bank, "Rural Education Project. Implementation and Completion Report" (Washington D.C.: World Bank, 2007), https://documents.worldbank.org/en/publication/documents-reports/documentdetail/472651468020683834/colombia-rural-education-project.

58 Econometría Consultores and Sistemas especializados de información, "Evaluación de Los Resultados de La Implementación Del Programa de Fortalecimiento de La Cobertura Con Calidad Para El Sector Educativo Rural PER Fase II" (Bogotá: Ministerio de Educación Nacional, 2015).

59 World Bank, "Rural Education Project Phase II. Implementation and Completion Report" (Washington DC: World Bank, 2016); Econometría Consultores and Sistemas especializados de información, "Evaluación de Los Resultados de La Implementación Del Programa de Fortalecimiento de La Cobertura Con Calidad Para El Sector Educativo Rural PER Fase II."

60 C Turbay and A Bacca, "Equidad y Niveles Intermedios de Gobierno En Los Sistemas Educativos. El Caso de Colombia," in Equidad y Niveles Intermedios de Gobierno En Los Sistemas Educativos, ed. Silvina Gvirtz (Buenos Aires: Aique, 2008), 137–83.

61 Miguel Ceballos Arévalo and Gerard Martin, *Participación y Fortalecimiento Institucional a Nivel Local En Colombia* (Bogota: Centro Editorial Javeriano, 2001) 110.

62 "No Hay Presupuesto Para La Educación Rural," Revista Semana Educación, February 2018, No. 29 edition, https://www.semana.com/educacion/articulo/educacion-rural-en-colombia/557157.

63 Ceballos Arévalo and Martin, Participación y Fortalecimiento Institucional a Nivel Local En Colombia.

64 Bautista and González, Docencia Rural En Colombia: Educar Para La Paz En Medio Del Conflicto Armado.

Part V

Legitimacy and democracy

16 Legitimizing and enshrining peace commitments

Inclusivity and constitution-building in the Colombian peace process

Diana Isabel Güiza-Gómez and Rodrigo Uprimny-Yepes

Introduction

The 2016 Colombian Comprehensive Peace Agreement (CPA), signed between the Colombian state and the Revolutionary Armed Forces of Colombia-People's Army (in Spanish, *Fuerzas Armadas Revolucionarias de Colombia—Ejército del Pueblo,* FARC-EP), expressly requires constitutional amendments to guarantee its compliance not only by the signatories but also by the broader society—including economic and regime elites, and the opposition—as well as popular endorsement to assure stable and durable peace. This peace accord is considered groundbreaking as it is aimed at bringing an end to the longest internal armed conflict in the Western Hemisphere. Aside from traditional transitional justice processes, the Colombian peace accord seeks a reparation model harmonized with meaningful political participation, natural resources management, economic development, and social policy.

After a 4-year peace process, the parties reached a peace agreement that was submitted to popular ratification in a plebiscite held on October 2, 2016, whereby the accord was rejected by a narrow margin. Attending to the claims of the leaders of NO-vote, a revisited peace agreement was signed between the warring parties, which was ratified by Congress whose approval triggered a special legislative procedure that allowed the legislative branch to expedite constitutional and legal reforms within a year.

As we explain in detail below, the Colombian case sheds light upon the interactions amongst legitimacy, peacebuilding, and constitution-making in a novel way. Rather than seeking to frame either a new constitution or a comprehensive constitutional reform, the 2016 peace accord adopts an original constitution-drafting design that comprises not only representative democratic mechanisms (e.g., fast track authority to approve constitutional amendments) but also direct democratic measures (e.g., popular endorsement), seeking to secure peace commitments and gain legitimacy among citizens. Due to this hybridity, this case does not fit neatly into the existing theoretical categories on post-conflict constitution-making and, therefore, challenges such explanations, suggesting a novel sequence of peacebuilding and constitution-drafting processes.

After the popular rejection of the peace accord and since constitution-drafting hinged upon popular endorsement, peace implementation has seemingly thwarted adoption of a transformative understanding of peace. Initially, constitution-building and popular ratification were aimed at neutralizing recalcitrant elites that opposed a negotiated settlement to bring an end to the protracted internal armed conflict. However, such innovative design was not accompanied by building up a wide, strong pro-peace coalition in advance. Instead of isolating apparently minor outside spoilers, popular endorsement through direct vote might have broadened elite divisions by reinvigorating the former who not only had remained powerful enough to mobilize voters against the peace accord, but also convinced hesitant supporters to become radical opponents. Once empowered, those minor fractions have threatened to breach the peace agreement by radicalizing politics around the accord and leveraging influence with Congress members and other state officials to prevent peace commitments from being fulfilled.

This chapter is devoted to reflecting upon the constitution-making design adopted in the Colombian peace process from an empirical, theoretical, and comparative perspective. To accomplish this goal, we begin by framing the research puzzle through echoing the metaphor of Ulysses and the sirens, which Elster has applied elsewhere to illustrate the commitment dilemma in constitution-building. Then, we briefly survey the literature on post-conflict constitutionalism and direct citizen involvement, identifying the main questions and arguments posited by scholars in these fields. We then describe how this constitution-making and popular endorsement process was designed and implemented through the ongoing Colombian peace process, by sorting out its strengths and shortcomings, as well as the sequence that peacebuilding and constitution-drafting have followed. Finally, we make a comparative study of the Colombian case and question the extent to which it challenges post-conflict constitutional literature, drawing some conclusions on how this case contributes to exploring wider understandings of constitution-drafting and direct citizen involvement processes in transitional societies.

The research puzzle: Constitution-making, peacebuilding, and legitimacy

In the *Odyssey*, Ulysses and his crew must cross the island of sirens. In order not to get taken away by the bewitched songs of the sirens, Ulysses asks his sailors to cover their ears with wax and tie him to his ship's mast, in a manner that he cannot untie, even if he wanted. Expanding on this metaphor, Elster illustrates how constitutions, arising from a rational act of democracy, are means for "precommitment or self-binding, created by the body politic in order to protect itself against its own predictable tendency to make unwise decisions."[1] It is the so-called *paradox of democracy* which, as Holmes suggests, is reflected in the fact that "without tying their hands, the people would not have hands."[2] This metaphor, thus, is based on the rational actions of people, who self-regulate through constitutional pacts.

However, Ulysses can also be bound to his ship's mast by his crew without having chosen it, in response to the attack of the sirens. In such a context, constraints that benefit the agent may also be externally imposed on herself for the sake of those benefits. In the same way, there would be no rational nor autonomous decision of the people to adhere to a constitution and these are the turbulent conditions in which constitutions are generally written: Right after a revolution, a war or a socio-economic crisis.[3] Under such circumstances, passions take precedence over reason and, therefore, constitutions are agreed upon based on cognitive biases.[4]

Drawing on these divergent metaphorical scenarios, Elster contends that constitutions, as any other rational behavior, emerge from either essential or incidental constraints.[5] The former refers to the initial context where the people, acting as a unitarian entity, impose restraints on themselves to guarantee their survival in the future. The latter, by contrast, applies to the second situation in which constitutions are established to restrict the freedom of action of the people, regardless of why and by whom such constraints were arranged in the first place. In spite of their salient differences, both schemes fall into the prevailing understanding of constitutionalism that relies upon the precommitment or self-binding theory. From this perspective, constitutions are deemed to occur as stationary events that take place after a revolution, war, or socio-economic crisis, thereby encapsulating a previously reached consensus on contentious issues that had sparked conflict and, therefore, are key elements to driving a substantially political change.[6]

Nonetheless, the late 20th and early 21st constitution-drafting processes contest that assumption since many constitutions neither were developed at a fixed episode in the post-conflict era nor did they contain the previous consensus agreed by the majority in a prior period. On the contrary, post-conflict constitutions have derived from peace agreements at the politically unstable first stages following the signing of negotiated settlements and were hammered out after failed, repeated attempts to frame a new constitutional order. Out of the 34 CPAs recorded in the Peace Accord Matrix (PAM),[7] 20 peace agreements expressly required constitutional reform, 3 of them were followed by constitution-building even though it was not established in the accord, and 4 of such accords required adherence to a new constitution that had been adopted shortly before the signing of the peace accord. Only seven agreements were dissociated with constitutional amendments.[8] Hence, constitutions have been envisaged as peacemaking and peacebuilding tools.

Concurrently, constituent support for peace processes has been pursued through popular ratification mechanisms—ranging from referenda to elections—in cases as diverse as Angola (1992), Cambodia (1993), Mozambique (1994), El Salvador (1994), Bosnia and Herzegovina (1996), Liberia (1997), Northern Ireland (1998), Guatemala (1999), and Tajikistan (1999–2000).[9] Not only has citizen involvement sought popular approval, but also has been devoted to regulating political contestation, being elections a key part of most negotiated settlements to end civil wars.[10] In the 1990s, while national peacebuilding endeavors were reaching a tipping point in which a vast majority of conflict-affected states sought to end civil wars through peace agreements, elections were married up with brand-new constitutions to the point that they became pivotal for both state-building efforts and conflict management.[11]

The rise of constitution-drafting and citizen involvement in transitional societies elucidates how legitimacy, peacebuilding, and constitution-making have unfolded hand in hand in recent decades to the point that substantially reforming constitutions and submitting peace processes to popular ratification have become crucial (even mandatory) means to lessen political violence by building a common vision of the future. Moreover, these mechanisms are intended to ensure compliance and sustainability as both post-conflict constitutionalism and popular ratification are deemed to transform the initial peace elite deal into long-lasting normative commitments and a stable broad-based participatory political system.

Despite their potential, constitution-making and direct citizen involvement can also constitute risk to the durability of peace, as they are interwoven in complex ways.[12] Constitutions deriving from peace agreements appear not to be meaningfully inclusive nor to emerge from purely democratic decision-making processes. Given the purported post-conflict constitutionalism' objectives, the framers are bound to a peace agreement that was reached in a process in which they were left aside. Indeed, peace processes are inherently elite scenarios in which only the warring parties are writing down commitments even if the peace table is opened up to hear certain social and political groups' concerns, such as victims. Theoretically speaking, post-conflict constitutions seem to result from incidental constraints, that is, the democratic capacity of the people is reduced by externally imposed constraints.

Furthermore, such constitution-drafting processes are entrenched in highly politically contested contexts in which the previously reached political consensus is threatened to collapse due to the conflictual nature of constitution-making. In turn this revives controversy on contentious issues that were resolved by the peace accord. Direct citizen involvement also runs the risk of heightening political division in transitioning settings, where spoilers retain enough popularity and power to mobilize voters against the peace process.

To put it simply, constitution-making and popular endorsement operate as peacebuilding and compliance means, as they strengthen broadbase popular support for peace, thereby making peace legitimate and endurable.

Despite their potentials, such mechanisms can also risk the durability of peace when spoilers retain enough popularity and power to mobilize voters against the CPA, hampering transformative peace commitments to be fulfilled. This is the research puzzle addressed here.

Prior research on gaining legitimacy and enshrining peace commitments into constitutions

Two main strands of literature are concerned with the puzzle posed above: Legitimate peacebuilding studies and constitutional theory. Drawing on an empirical approach, peace and democracy scholars query how popular endorsement has been employed for allowing peace to triumph. Referenda, elections, and constituent assemblies count as the commonly used means to gain constituent support. Promises notwithstanding, direct citizen involvement exhibits contrasting outcomes: While peace was eventually endured owing to popular approval of the accord in South Africa[13] and Northern Ireland,[14] it was seriously diminished due to the popular rejection of the agreement in Cyprus[15] and Guatemala.[16]

Rather than scrutinizing political forces and conflict dynamics to explain such setbacks, some scholars and peace mediators have warned against entangling peacebuilding efforts with direct citizen involvement in the post-accord era unless the necessary preconditions are in place.[17] However, there is neither consensus nor clarity about what those preconditions are, nor how to assure them, before submitting peace accords to polling stations. Five of the more commonly proposed preconditions that have been put forth concern transitional power sharing governments, demobilization, the granting of amnesty, the release of war prisoners, and third-party guarantees.[18]

Although recent research provides empirical evidence on post-conflict direct citizen involvement timing and preconditions, few studies have been focused on sequencing popular endorsement and peacebuilding endeavors. Indeed, most scholars argue in favor of postponing—and even bypassing—direct citizen involvement in the first stages of peace implementation despite being problematic in philosophical and political terms.[19] Philosophically speaking—as Gargarella highlights elsewhere in this collaborative volume—the more relevant the political matter is, the more citizens should participate directly in decision-making processes. Regardless of which democratic paradigm one stands on, core democratic values demand citizen involvement in discussing and deciding matters of public interest. From a political standpoint—as Saffon Sanín broadly illustrates in this volume—peace agreements are less sustainable if they do not meet strong popular support to overcome hurdles posed by elites who see a loss of economic, political privileges and, therefore, are incentivized to exert power to derail peace implementation.

We concur with these previous studies that direct citizen involvement in peace processes poses risks for peace to flourish, yet we differ with scholars and practitioners advocating for circumventing popular endorsement before or after the signing of agreements. In lieu of discarding citizen participation in peacebuilding, we propose ongoing peace processes face the paradox of peace and democracy: On the one hand, peacemaking and peacebuilding increasingly demand direct citizen involvement through official channels to gain legitimacy and secure peace; on the other hand, such democratic efforts may deter peace by heightening political division and increasing the likelihood for violence to resurge.

Working from a legal perspective, post-conflict constitutional scholars weigh in on legal issues surrounding constitutions enacted after the signing of peace accords. Among other, most recurring questions concern which particular features post-conflict or transitional constitutionalism embodies and differentiates itself from other forms of constitutionalism; whether constitution-making should be connected to peacebuilding at all; why warring parties decide to embark on constitution-building; how constitution-drafting should be addressed in transitional settings; which amendment tools appear to be more suitable to these societies; and which sequencing peace agreements and constitutional arrangements follow within the broader political settlement in transitional settings.[20]

This body of literature mainly assumes that post-conflict constitutionalism faces distinct challenges compared to constitution-drafting in established societies. Suteu, for instance, claims that post-conflict constitution drafting differs from constitutional reform in more peaceful contexts by three distinctive features. Firstly, constitution-building in transitional contexts is more contested, owing to the threat of a return to violence or even the continuance of armed conflict. This results in a short timeframe for constitutional negotiations and high pressure on the constitution to meet ambitious institution-making demands. Secondly, post-conflict constitutions are generally expected to achieve diverse goals, ranging from strengthening the rule of law and shaping institutional frameworks to preventing the resurgence of armed conflict and enshrining the peace elite deal hammered out by the warring parties into a constitutional framework. Thirdly, post-conflict constitutions tend to comprise conflicting institutional designs rather than coherent ones, which may not effectively defuse tension in the long term.[21]

Given the distinctiveness of post-transition constitution-building, Ludsin casts doubt on the necessity of constitution-making processes in post-conflict contexts. Particularly, Ludsin highlights post-conflict constitution-making as differing from peacebuilding in four ways: (i) sequencing, (ii) timeframe, (iii) short- and long-term goals, and (iv) participation in constitution-drafting.

First, constitution-making presupposes certain conditions that are not necessarily assured in transitional settings—such as security and national identity—while post-conflict constitution-making mainly seeks to halt violence and build a common vision for the future. Second, whereas developing a national identity and a shared sense of how society wishes to be governed is a time-consuming process, ending conflicts is an urgent need that should be met in the short-term in order to stabilize transitional societies. Third, trapping the short-term goals of peace agreements in constitutional provisions envisioning long-term compliance may give rise to new battles, which can destabilize the fragile post-conflict political consensus and undermine the peace process. Finally, urgent responses required in the aftermath might prevent constitution-building from achieving inclusivity as questions regarding participation in constitution-drafting—namely who serves as drafters and, therefore, who is excluded—may not be addressed skillfully.

Considering the features of post-conflict constitutionalism, legal scholars assess which amendment measures happen to be politically convenient and technically appropriate to (re)build state frameworks in the aftermath of conflict. Three of the more widely discussed constitutional reform tools relate to interim constitutions, unamendable "eternity clauses" and sunset clauses. While interim constitution-making has been offered as the golden response to post-conflict constitution-building issues—reflected by its widespread use as a conflict resolution tool in cases as diverse as Libya, Nepal, South Sudan, Somalia, and the Central African Republic[22]—eternity and sunset provisions have been recently considered to safeguard hard-fought peace agreements by isolating basic commitments from amendments in transitioning settings, as well as rapidly promote consensus on highly disputed issues in the short-term by postponing a broader discussion for a subsequent moment where broad agreement seems to be more attainable.

Contrary to initial scholars' and practitioners' assumptions about post-conflict constitution-making as a means of peacebuilding, those distinctive processes entail the paradox of peace and constitutionalization. While constitutions are needed to institutionalize a negotiated settlement and reframe the social contract damaged by armed confrontation, they can also jeopardize peace efforts as competing actors seek divergent interests that cannot be reconciled at such democratic forums.

Drawing on these two strands of literature, we explore both paradoxes in the ongoing Colombian peace process, emphasizing on the following contextual factors: The existing constitutional framework and their perceived legitimacy and adequacy; the content of the comprehensive agreement; the constitutional reform devices chosen; and the sequence between popular endorsement and constitution-making.

The Colombian case: Post-conflict constitution-drafting and popular endorsement in the onward peace process

Colombia has undergone one of the most protracted internal armed conflict in the Western Hemisphere since the mid-twentieth century, when the country seemingly achieved a durable peace via a negotiated settlement through which the two predominant political parties—conservatives and liberals—agreed to bring an end to the bipartisan civil conflict known as *La*

Violencia by sharing control over state institution for 16 years.[23] This consociational agreement and its following constitutional reform were popularly approved in a plebiscite held on December 1, 1957, which is broadly remembered not only because of having paved the way to the National Front (*Frente Nacional*) regime but also because of being the first time women voted. In response to this allegedly exclusionary political regime and unequal distribution of wealth—particularly land—three leftist guerrilla movements took up arms against the Colombian state in the sixties: The National Liberation Army (ELN), inspired by the Cuban revolution; the Armed Revolutionary Forces of Colombia (FARC), initially joined by agrarian peasant (*campesinos*) leaders following Marxist ideals; and the Popular Liberation Army (EPL), following Maoist principles.[24]

Claiming to confront violence, the Colombian state issued decrees under prolonged states of emergency periods that not only allowed but also encouraged civilians to create self-defense groups that were broadly supported by the Armed Forces.[25] Other guerrilla movements emerged in the sixties and seventies, who negotiated partial and narrow peace agreements with the Colombian state—such as the 19th of April Movement (M19), *Movimiento Armado Quintín Lame* (MAQL), *Partido Revolucionario de los Trabajadores* (PRT), *Corriente de Renovación Socialista* (CRS).[26]

The 1991 Constitution arose, in part, from the successful peace process with M19 and EPL guerrillas. In the midst of the armed conflict and increased violence by drug lords, the 1991 Constitution was framed to pacify the country,[27] thus giving way to a democratic opening for the Colombian political system and guaranteeing citizens' rights, especially those least favored.[28] Unlike most of Colombia's constitutional history,[29] the 1991 Constitution did not emerge from a victor's peace and, by contrast, it was preceded by a pluralistic and invigorated civic movement.

Whereas the 1991 constitutional framework has assured rights and legal protection for historically disadvantaged groups—such as women, indigenous communities, the peasantry (*campesinado*), Afro-descendants, and LGBTQI[30]—its democratic promises have fallen short due to resurgence of violence[31] as both paramilitary and guerrilla groups expanded throughout the country to the point they operated as actual sovereign entities in peripheral areas. In those areas, the state is barely present and, in not a few cases, colludes with armed actors.[32] Under such circumstances,[33] local political and economic elites have found incentives to align with armed groups and control from-below mobilization.[34]

In 2002, then President Álvaro Uribe Vélez led peace negotiations with the United Self-Defense Forces of Colombia (AUC), which was a unified command organization convening right-wing paramilitary groups. Three years later, AUC began a demobilization process, albeit many paramilitary combatants maintained their weapons and created new armed groups that operate until now. Although it remains debatable whether the negotiated settlement signed by the Uribe administration and AUC entails a peace process, the Colombian Congress approved a legal framework (Law 975 of 2005 also known as the "Justice and Peace Law") for the demobilization and reintegration process, as well as the prosecution of atrocities committed by those paramilitary groups.[35]

The 2016 CPA: Popular ratification and fast track authority

Remarkably, the Colombian state and FARC signed a CPA entitled "Final Agreement to End the Armed Conflict and Build a Stable and Lasting Peace," in November 24, 2016.[36] Here, we refer to the constitution-making process that followed the revisited peace agreement that arose in response to the opposition's demands after the rejection of the first final agreement in the plebiscite held on October 2.

The peace agreement aims not only to satisfy victims' rights but also to resolve the underlying causes to internal armed conflict. Among other purposes, it seeks to (i) to strengthen the presence and effectiveness of the state throughout the territory; (ii) to enhance popular participation at the subnational level whereby citizens are directly involved in matters of development in their municipalities; (iii) to establish a comprehensive system for the protection of victims' rights to justice, truth, reparations, and non-recurrence, which is comprised by the Special Jurisdiction for Peace, a Truth Commission, a Unit for the search of disappeared persons, and an administrative reparations program, established in 2011.

In its sixth chapter, the peace accord includes implementation and verification mechanisms that are intended to assure compliance by the signatories, as well as the Colombian state and broad society. As Jaramillo argues,[37] those mechanisms attempt to tackle the inadequacy of state capacity and political support, which were seen as the main obstacles to fulfill peace commitments. Among other measures, the signatories agreed upon the submission of the peace agreement to popular approval, the establishment of a special legislative procedure—known as fast track authority—for the incorporation of the peace agreement into domestic law and for its regulatory implementation, as well as the peace accord's legal force under international and domestic law.[38]

Popular endorsement

Since the beginning of negotiations, the Colombian government and FARC agreed to submit the final peace accord to popular ratification, albeit not being legally required to do so, as the government enjoyed legal power to enforce a peace agreement and some peace commitments would still require both constitutional and legal reform and hence democratic—yet representative—endorsement. Given increasing opposition from right-wing parties, the formerly warring parties envisaged gaining constituent support crucial for peace to endure owing to normative and political reasons. On the one hand, the peace agreement would touch upon matters of public interest—such as political participation and land policies— that should be discussed in the public sphere if democratic values are taken seriously. On the other hand, the peace agreement was likely to face strong resistance from elites who benefited from armed groups controlling municipalities and preserving the status quo.[39] Therefore, the government's political will seemed to be insufficient to overcome such resistance, reinforce state institutions, deliver social goods, and carry out purported reforms.[40]

However, as no agreement was reached upon which mechanism was to be employed to achieve popular endorsement, a heated debate arose at the negotiation table.[41] FARC and certain leftist groups advocated for a broad-base participatory constituent assembly that would serve as a means to attain popular support and approve required constitutional amendments in parallel.[42] The government negotiators and high-profile practitioners opposed such constituent assembly and, in turn, proposed a referendum or popular consultation for ratification and ordinary legislative procedures to adopt the constitutional reforms mandated by the peace agreement.[43]

In late 2015, the Santos administration presented a bill to Congress, seeking to enable a plebiscite to gain popular endorsement, which initially lacked consensus at the peace table. This unilateral decision triggered tension between the parties to the point where FARC publicly refused to consult Colombians on the question of holding a plebiscite to determine endorsement of the final peace accord. However, once the legal reform enabling the call for a plebiscite had been approved by Congress and was under revision by the Constitutional Court, which finally ruled in its favor,[44] the former guerrilla also welcomed this mechanism.

Fast track authority

Meanwhile, the parties discussed which legislative procedure would expedite the approval of constitutional and legal reforms to guarantee the timely, effective, integral, and faithful implementation of the peace accord. However, such extraordinary mechanisms were controversial as they were considered either unnecessary or a rupture of the 1991 Constitution. Indeed, some scholars claimed that the peace agreement should be implemented through ordinary avenues, following the existing constitutional framework. They further argued that there were neither democratic nor constitutional reasons to lessen the deliberative quality within Congress or to ease procedural requirements for constitutional reform, as fast track intended to do.[45] Moreover, critics claimed that the purported legal force of the peace agreement threatened to suppress the existing constitutional framework.[46]

The Santos administration proposed a constitutional amendment bill before Congress in 2015, which created a special legislative procedure to accelerate the regulatory implementation of the peace accord, known as fast track rule, allocated state budgetary resources for long-term implementation, and granted the President special power to issue decrees with force of law to adopt urgent peace measures.[47] Inspired by the Northern Ireland case, fast track authority would allow to expedite the approval of constitutional and legal reforms by shortening legislative procedures and restricting Congress' ability to introduce changes to the bills presented by the government to implement the peace accord. Hence, Congress could only approve or reject the bill. Moreover, the Constitutional Court would exert automatic judicial review of all constitutional and legal reforms passed via fast track authority. Fast track rule would last 6 months, starting when the peace agreement attained popular endorsement, which would be extended for another 6 months. Additionally, six citizens would hold nonvoting seats in each Congress chamber on behalf of FARC, thereby ensuring that former combatants themselves would not take part in congressional debates, while their representation would remain assured.[48]

In July 2016, Congress enacted this constitutional reform (Legislative Act 1, 2016) and it came into force in December 1 after the revisited peace agreement was submitted to ratification by Congress on November 29 and 30, amidst heated debate as to whether the second peace deal could be implemented without holding a new plebiscite.[49]

Legal force of the peace agreement under international and domestic law

The parties also agreed that the peace agreement itself would acquire a certain legal force both under international and domestic law. At the international level, the peace accord provides that it would be signed as a Special Agreement under common article 3 of the Geneva Conventions and deposited before the Swiss Federal Council in Bern. Then, the President would make a unilateral declaration of the state to the United Nation, requesting to incorporate the peace agreement in a document issued by the United Nations Security Council.[50]

At the national level, initially the peace agreement was deemed to be incorporated in whole into the so called "constitutional block," a legal construct that encompasses not only the constitution but also major parts of human rights law and international humanitarian law (article 4, Legislative Act 1, 2016). This constitutional amendment was fiercely criticized before and after the plebiscite, being one of the major changes made to the first agreement after its popular rejection. Therefore, the revisited peace accord expressly required a constitutional amendment stating that the peace agreement "where it relates to the rules of international humanitarian law or fundamental rights defined in the [1991] Political Constitution and rights related to those rights, shall be an obligatory parameter for interpretation and a point of reference for the implementation and validity of the rules and laws implementing and developing the Final Agreement." The accord would enjoy such constitutional force for three complete presidential terms

Figure 16.1 2016 Popular Ratification by Department.

subsequent to its signature. Moreover, the peace agreement provided that "state institutions and authorities are obliged to comply with [its] provisions in good faith" (p. 289). Then, this new clause was enshrined in the constitution through Legislative Act 2, 2017.

Constitutional amendments expressly required by the peace agreement

The Colombian peace accord explicitly establishes constitutional amendments on matters as diverse as political participation for former combatants and historically marginalized groups, the victims' rights to truth, justice, reparation, and nonrecurrence—by creating the Special Jurisdiction for Peace, the Unit for the search of disappeared persons, and the Truth Commission—the incorporation of the peace accord into domestic law, and the prohibition of promotion, organization, and funding of paramilitary structures. Regarding political participation, a constitutional reform was needed to allocate 10 seats in Congress (five in each one of the chambers) for former combatants contingent upon their demobilization and disarmament, as well as 16 seats in the House of Representatives for peripheral areas that had been neglected from the state: The so-called Special Transitory Electoral Districts for Peace.

The regulatory implementation of the peace agreement (2017–19)

As it is well known, the plebiscite was held on October 2 and the peace accord was rejected by a narrow margin of 0.5%, without participation of 63.6% of authorized voters, compared to the average abstention rates of 51% in presidential elections. The plebiscite's results are explained not only by temporary events—such as Hurricane Matthew battering the Caribbean region that was left isolated from the voting—but also, and mainly, structural factors. Namely the sharp regional divide between rich, central, and less-violent areas tending to vote "NO" and poor, peripheral and violent territories tending to vote "YES" (Figure 16.1).[51] Moreover, popular endorsement seemingly amplified the elite divide between Uribe (the most powerful outside spoiler) and Santos, thereby weakening the already-fragile legitimacy of the peace process.[52]

After the rejection of the first peace agreement, the government and FARC resumed peace negotiations to incorporate most of the main objections raised by the opposition. Despite the significant changes included in the second peace accord, the opposition refused to acknowledge such modifications, referring to them as insubstantial. Worrying that the now groundless ceasefire with FARC would break, the government submitted the peace accord to Congressional approval, seeking to activate fast track authority and other urgently needed measures resulting from the ungrounded ceasefire. Congressional ratification was then backed up by the Constitutional Court that ruled a few days later verifying the parties had delivered to the "NO" mandate by substantively adjusting the first peace agreement, as well as the "YES" mandate for peace by achieving a revisited accord that maintained the core commitments contained in its first version submitted to popular support. Moreover, the Constitutional Court underscored that Congress was the democratic forum par excellence and popular endorsement was regarded as a multi-faceted process, thereby Congressional approval had conferred sufficient legitimacy to the peace accord.[53]

Hence, fast track rule came into force on December 1, 2016 and lasted one year since then, expiring on November 30, 2017. Throughout that period, many Congress members who had joined until then in an apparently solid pro-government coalition began to walk away from the peace process by not supporting and severely delaying diverse constitutional and legal reforms required to fully implement the 2016 peace promises.[54] When fast track authority expired, five constitutional amendments had been approved by Congress regarding the following issues: The creation of the integral system for the protection of victims' rights to justice, truth, reparations, and non-recurrence (Legislative Act 1, 2017); the incorporation of the peace agreement into the domestic law through a temporary constitutional clause requiring its compliance by the three branches of government for three presidential periods (Legislative Act 2, 2017); the creation of FARC's political party and its granting of reserved seats for two electoral periods (Legislative Act 3, 2017); the allocation of budgetary resources for long-term implementation (Legislative Act 4, 2017); and the prohibition of promotion and funding of paramilitary groups (Legislative Act 5, 2017).

The other bills had not obtained the required majority to get approved, as happened with the constitutional amendments to the political system and parties, and with the creation of the Special Transitory Electoral Districts for Peace, which fell one vote short on November 30, when fast track rule ended. This falling has been considered a severe blow to the peace process. Both constitutional amendments are still lacking despite subsequently unsuccessful efforts to enshrine such commitments into the constitution.[55]

Throughout 2017 and 2018, the Constitutional Court has executed prior and automatic judicial review over all constitutional and legal reforms implementing the peace agreement as it was expressly required by the peace accord itself in the following terms: "The laws and legislative acts processed under the Special Legislative Procedure for Peace shall undergo a single and automatic check for constitutionality after they come into effect. The constitutionality of legislative acts shall be checked only in relation to procedural defects in their formation" (p. 289). Overall, the Court has decided approximately 50 judicial rulings, among which 5 pertained to constitutional amendments.

On the political arena and capitalizing on the NO-vote victory, right-wing spoilers consolidated power in the 2018 congressional and presidential elections. Campaigning a minimalist approach to peace, Iván Duque—a young, unknown politician yet backed up by Uribe—successfully ran for presidency with 53.98% of support, altering the existing balance of political power. Such resurgence of right-wing opponents has exponentially diminished the agreement's transformative approach to peace by cornering center-right and -left elites. Furthermore, opponents represented by Duque's administration have endorsed a minimalist understanding of peace that not only discards measures aimed at removing the status quo, but also emphasizes accountability by former guerrilla commanders while diminishing accountability for armed forces, politicians, and other state bureaucrats, who allegedly committed atrocities.[56]

Drawbacks notwithstanding, the agreement's social transformation promises have offered ground for potential beneficiaries to politically mobilize for the implementation of the peace accord. Since those demands significantly threaten national and regional elites, violence against social leaders has dramatically increased, thus making peace seekers more vulnerable to it. After the signing of the peace accord, enforcement mechanisms reopened heated debate over contentious issues, elucidating two contesting approaches to peace that apparently had been reconciled by the peace accord. One the one hand, a transformative understanding that seeks accountability for all perpetrators regardless of their status and profoundly questions existing power and wealth distribution. On the other hand, a minimalist endeavor that only pursues the disintegration of FARC and its rigorous criminal prosecution while offers significant criminal benefits for state perpetrators and excludes any profound political and economic transformation.[57]

A comparative perspective on transitions and constitution-making

Theoretically speaking, the Colombian case also sheds light on distinctive ideal types in the spectrum between law and politics, where peace processes lie on in the last decades. Owing to increasingly enforceable international standards on state obligations regarding victims' rights and the diffusion of democratic values reinforcing legitimate peace processes, peacemaking and building efforts are less likely to fall only either within legal margins or purely political ground. On the contrary, contemporary peace processes are constrained by both politics and law, which interact in complex manners.

Drawing on a provisional categorization we offered elsewhere, here we identify four ideal categories whereby legitimacy, constitution-making, and peacebuilding interrelate.[58] Purely political transitions lie on one pole, which are often crystallized through constitutional reforms that occur once substantial political change took place. An enlightening example is the Spanish transition and its 1978 Constitution. After Franco's death, moderates led by King Juan Carlos reached an accommodation with the Falangist regime's bitterest enemies—mostly the illegal Communist party. By enacting a law for political reform, Communists participated in the first free elections held after the political transition. Relying upon electoral support, moderates pushed for a new branded, democratic constitution that was ultimately approved by the electorate at a referendum.[59]

On the other end of the spectrum, constitutionally normalized transitions happen within the margins of the law. After the enactment of the 1991 Constitution, for example, the Colombian government reached a peace agreement with the guerrilla movement Socialist Renovation Current—in Spanish, *Corriente de Renovación Socialista*—in 1994. Such a peace process was tailored to the existing constitutional framework and did not result in any constitutional amendment to encapsulate the political transition, as did the demobilization of paramilitary groups between 2003 and 2005.

In midway, transitional constitutionalism and perpetual transitions in flexible constitutions emerge on political and legal grounds. The former entails negotiated settlements signed by the formerly warring parties, which is eventually embodied in temporal constitutional reforms—mainly interim constitutions—that lately guide constitution-drafting to assure a permanent, new branded constitution that enshrines main peace commitments. The strikingly successful example is the 1993 South African interim constitution that paved the way to a broadbase participatory constituent assembly some years after the signing of the peace agreement, as framing a new, comprehensive constitution seemed to destabilize the transition at the early stages of peacebuilding. Then, the 1996 permanent constitution embodied the main commitments established by the peace agreement and dealt with other issues—namely disagreements over individual autonomy and property rights, or over race equality and the distribution of wealth—that had been intentionally left unresolved by conflict parties. While the post-conflict constitution laid a set of general principles to tackle those deep divisions, the role of the judiciary was to maintain peace by giving specific content to those principles case by case. Therefore, incremental constitutionalism mainly contributed to removing highly contentious social issues from the realm of ordinary politics thereby enduring peace.

In the fourth ideal type, a peace agreement is hammered out by the warring parties in the political arena—usually, a peace table—and ultimately is encapsulated in major constitutional reforms, seeking not only to institutionalize the peace settlement but also to reframe the social contract. Yet, the existing constitutional framework is not fully replaced after the signing of the peace accord. There is also a certain degree of direct citizen involvement aimed at lending legitimacy to the peace process and justifying constitutional flexibility for peace implementation. Aside from the other categories, this type entails the shielding of peace commitments by granting them certain legal force through their inclusion into domestic law. As the peace agreement retains such normative effect thereby abiding political generations to come, the political transition seems to become permanent.

Hence, two main features single out the fourth type from the other three: Constitutional flexibility and the enforceable nature of the peace agreement.

Colombia exemplifies this theoretical scenario. In sharp difference with preceding sequencing patterns laid out by Bell and Zulueta-Fülscher,[60] the Colombian case has followed a distinctive pathway: A CPA that was deemed to acquire popular support, followed by partial constitutional amendments expressly required by the peace accord, which would be passed by Congress through fast track authority without altering power composition in that representative body, yet allocating six nonvoting seats in Congress for non-combatants to express FARC's standpoints. Such sequencing implied that constitutional reforms could only be proposed before Congress if the peace accord attained popular approval. Thus, popular ratification pursued a threefold purpose: (i) To endow the peace accord with legitimacy and credibility; (ii) to facilitate the regulatory implementation of the peace agreement since fast track rule would only be activated via popular ratification, which would also compensate for the deliberative deficit from fast track; and (iii) to grant stable and durable peace as broadly popular support would prevent future governments from undermining the agreement.[61]

In that manner, the existing constitutional framework was not replaced with a fundamental review of the 1991 constitution nor a new constitution emerged in the post-accord era, albeit constitution-drafting was aimed at serving diverse functions for diverse actors. Whereas the government pursued to reinforce the 1991 constitutional framework by removing structural conditions that had disallowed such democratic promises to come true, grassroots leaders and civil society sought to reshape the mutually bearable future on economic and social issues that had been agreed upon the 1991 Constitution and had not fully satisfy their claims over the redistribution of power and wealth—for example, reinforcing rights to labor unions and community radio stations. Therefore, this case is distinguishable from the vast majority of constitution-making processes in political transitions as constitution-drafting was intended to adjust the existing constitutional framework, thereby concluding incremental constitutionalism that began in 1991 with the establishment of a new constitution to overcome political violence.

Concluding remarks

The Colombian case illustrates both the promises and drawbacks of intertwining peacebuilding, legitimacy, and constitution-drafting goals in transitional settings. On the one hand, marrying constitution-drafting with popular endorsement seemed promissory for peace to last and overcome obstacles from elites incurring some loss of power because of the transformative understanding of peace agreed upon on the 2016 accord. Likewise, as claimed by Nathan regarding general interactions between peacemaking and constitutions, such means might have lessened mistrust, suspicion, and skepticism about the credibility of the opposing party to fulfill its vow after years of killing and zero-sum politics.[62]

On the other hand, acute tensions arose from the interactions between peacebuilding, popular endorsement, and constitution-making in the Colombian peace process. As we have mentioned, the popular rejection of the peace agreement on the 2016 plebiscite deepened political dissensus over the peace process, revealing diverse, opposing understanding of peace that are in permanent tension since then. Thus, popular ratification triggering constitution-making eventually impeded the consolidation of strong political support and, conversely, contributed to strengthening spoilers.

These complex interactions among peacebuilding, constitution-making, and popular endorsement deserve careful attention and visibility among scholars and practitioners concerned with peace, democratization, inclusivity, and the rule of law. Much research is needed to elucidate the potentials and shortcomings of constitution-drafting contingent upon popular support for peace agreements in contexts where the existing constitutional framework is preserved, and preceding political parties' coalitions remain as the main actors being responsible for passing such constitutional amendments to assure durable peace.

Notes

1 Jon Elster, *Ulysses Bound. Studies in Rationality, Precommitment, and Constraints* (New York: Cambridge University Press, 2000) 88.
2 Stephen Holmes, "Precommitment and the Paradox of Democracy," in Jon Elster and Rune Slagstrad (eds), *Constitutionalism and Democracy* (Cambridge: Cambridge University Press, 1988) 232.
3 Jon Elster, *Ulysses and the Sirens: Studies in Rationality and Irrationality* (New York: Cambridge University Press, 1985).
4 Ozan O. Varol, "Temporary Constitutions," *California Law Review,* vol. 102 (2), 2014, pp. 409–64.
5 Elster, *Ulysses Bound.* (2000).
6 Vivien Hart, "Constitution-Making and the Transformation of Conflict," *Peace & Change,* vol. 26 (2), 2001, pp. 153–76.
7 In PAM, CPAs must meet the following criteria to be recorded: (1) They were negotiated in civil wars—for example, conflicts featuring at least 25 battle deaths per year—between 1989 and 2012; (2) the peace negotiations involved the major parties of the conflict; and (3) the peace accord addresses the substantive issues underlying the conflict. Madhav Joshi, Jason Michael Quinn, and Patrick M. Regan, "Annualized Implementation Data on Intrastate Comprehensive Peace Accords 1989-2012," *Journal of Peace Research,* vol. 52 (4), 2015, pp. 551–62.
8 Laurie Nathan, "The Real Deal? The Post-Conflict Constitution as a Peace Agreement," *Third World Quarterly*, vol. 41 (9), 2020.
9 Terrence Lyons, "Post-Conflict Elections and the Process of Demilitarizing Politics: The Role of Electoral Administration," *Democratization,* vol. 11 (3), 2004, pp. 36–62; Marc Mulholland, *The Longest War. Northern Ireland's Troubles History* (Oxford: Oxford University Press, 2002); Enrique Álvarez and Tania Palencia Prado, "Guatemala's Peace Process: Context, Analysis and Evaluation," *Accord Issue*, 2002, http://www.c-r.org/accord/public-participation/guatemala-s-peace-process-context-

analysis-and-evaluation; Rodrigo Uprimny, "La Refrendación o Ratificación Democrática de La Paz: Dilemas y Posibilidades," in *Diálogos de La Habana: Miradas Múltiples Desde La Universidad,* Alejo Vargas (ed.) (Bogotá D.C.: Universidad Nacional de Colombia-Sede Bogotá. Facultad de Derecho, Ciencias Políticas y Sociales, 2013).

10 Carrie Manning, "Elections and Political Change in Post-War Bosnia and Herzegovina," *Democratization,* vol. 11 (2), 2004, pp. 60–86.

11 Vijayashr Sripati, "UN Constitutional Assistance Projects in Comprehensive Peace Missions: An Inventory 1989–2011," *International Peacekeeping,* vol. 19 (1), 2012, pp. 93–113; Jamal Benomar, "Constitution-Making After Conflict: Lessons for Iraq," *Journal of Democracy*, vol. 15 (2), 2004, pp. 81–95; Haider Ala Hamoudi, *Negotiating in Civil Conflict: Constitucional Construction and Imperfect Bargaining in Iraq* (Chicago: University of Chicago Press, 2013); Thomas Edward Flores and Irfan Nooruddin, "The Effect of Elections on Post Conflict Peace and Reconstruction," *Journal of Politics,* vol. 74 (2), 2012, pp. 558–70.

12 Manning, "Elections and Political Change in Post-War Bosnia and Herzegovina." (2004).

13 Neophytos Loizides, "Mandate Referendums and Peace Agreement Ratification," *International Studies Association Annual Convention*, 2011, http://works.bepress.com/neophytos_loizides/21/.

14 Mulholland, *The Longest War*. (2002).

15 Muzaffer Yilmaz, "The Cyprus Conflict and the Annan Plan: Why One More Failure?," *Ege Akademik Bakış,* vol. 5, 2005, pp. 29–39.

16 Enrique Álvarez and Tania Palencia Prado, 2002, http://www.c-r.org/accord/public-participation/guatemala-s-peace-process-context-analysis-and-evaluation; William Stanley and David Holiday, "Broad Participation, Diffuse Responsibility: Peace Implementation in Guatemala," in Stephen John Stedman, Donald Rothchild, and Elisabeth Cousens (eds), *Ending Civil Wars, the Implementation of Peace Agreements* (Boulder, CO: Lynne Rienner Press, 2002).

17 Edward D. Mansfield and Jack L. Snyder, *Electing to Fight* (Cambridge, Massachusetts: MIT Press, 2005); Edward D. Mansfield and Jack L. Snyder, "The Sequencing 'Fallacy,'" *Journal of Democracy,* vol. 18 (3), 2007, pp. 12–27; R. Paris, "Saving Liberal Peacebuilding," *Review of International Studies,* vol. 36 (2), 2010, pp. 337–65; Michael Barnett, "Building a Republican Peace: Stabilizing States after War," *International Security,* vol. 30 (4), 2006, pp. 87–112.

18 Terrence Lyons, "The Role of Postsettlement Elections," in Stephen John Stedman, Donald Rothchild, and Elisabeth Cousens (eds), *Ending Civil Wars: The Implementation of Peace Agreements* (Boulder, CO: Lynne Rienner Press, 2002) 663–71; Stephen John Stedman, "Policy Implications," in *Ending Civil Wars: The Implementation of Peace Agreements*, Stephen John Stedman, Donald Rothchild, and Elisabeth Cousens (eds) (Boulder, CO: Lynne Rienner Press, 2002); Barbara F. Walter, "The Critical Barrier to Civil War Settlement," *International Organization,* vol. 51 (3), 1997, pp. 335–64; Madhav Joshi, Erik Melander, and Jason Michael Quinn, "Sequencing the Peace: How the Order of Peace Agreement Implementation Can Reduce the Destabilizing Effects of Post-Accord Elections," *Journal of Conflict Resolution,* vol. 61 (I), 2017, pp. 4–28.

19 Dawn Brancati and Jack Snyder, "Time to Kill: The Impact of Election Timing on Postconflict Stability," *Journal of Conflict Resolution,* vol.57 (5), 2013, pp. 822–853; Thomas Edward Flores and Irfan Nooruddin, 2012.

20 Andrew Arato, "Redeeming the Still Redeemable: Post Sovereign Constitution Making," *International Journal of Politics, Culture, and Society,* vol. 22, 2009, pp. 427–43; Christine Bell et al., *Interim Constitutions in Post-Conflict Settings: Discussion Report* (Edinburgh: International Institute for Democracy and

Electoral Assistance, 2014); Christine Bell and Kimana Zulueta-Fülscher, *Sequencing Peace Agreements and Constitutions in the Political Settlement Process* (Sweden: International Institute for Democracy and Electoral Assistance, November 2016); Gábor Halmai, "Transitional Justice, Transitional Constitutionalism and Constitutional Culture," in Gary Jacobsohn and Miguel Schor (eds), *Comparative Constitutional Theory* (Cheltenham and Northampton: Edward Elgar Publishing, 2018); Vivien Hart, 2001; Heinz Klug, *Constituting Democracy: Law, Globalism and South Africa's Political Reconstruction* (Cambridge: Cambridge University Press, 2001); Heinz Klug, "South Africa's Experience in Constitution-Building," *University of Wisconsin Legal Studies Research Paper,* vol. 1157, 2011, http://dx.doi.org/10.2139/ssrn.1808168; Hallie Ludsin, "Peacemaking and Constitution-Drafting: A Dysfunctional Marriage," *University of Pennsylvania Journal of International Law,* vol. 33, 2011, p. 239; Charmaine Rodrigues, "Letting off Steam: Interim Constitutions as a Safety Valve to the Pressure-Cooker of Transitions in Conflict-Affected States?," *Global Constitutionalism,* vol. 6 (1), 2017, pp. 33–62; Silvia Suteu, "Eternity Clauses in Post-Conflict and Post-Authoritarian Constitution-Making: Promise and Limits," *Global Constitutionalism,* vol. 6 (1), 2017, pp. 63–100; Ruti Teitel, "Transitional Justice and Transformation of Constitutionalism," *Comparative Constitutional Law,* 57, 2011.

21 Suteu, "Eternity Clauses in Post-Conflict and Post-Authoritarian Constitution-Making." (2017).

22 Arato, "Redeeming the Still Redeemable." (2009).

23 Orlando Fals Borda, Germán Guzmán Campos, and Eduardo Umaña Luna, *La Violencia En Colombia. Estudio de Un Proceso Social* (Bogotá: Ediciones Tercer Mundo, 1962), http://archive.org/details/laviolenciaencol00guzm; Robert A. Karl, *La Paz Olvidada. Políticos, Letrados, Campesinos y El Surgimiento de Las FARC En La Formación de La Colombia Contemporánea* (Bogotá D.C.: Librería Lerner, 2018).

24 Ana María Bejarano and Renata Segura, *El Fortalecimiento Selectivo Del Estado Durante El Frente Nacional* (Bogotá D.C.: CINEP, 1996); Eduardo Pizarro Leongómez, *Insurgencia Sin Revolución: La Guerrilla En Colombia En Una Perspectiva Comparada* (Tercer Mundo S.A., 1996), https://www.academia.edu/35855821/Insurgencia_sin_revoluci%C3%B3n_la_guerrilla_en_Colombia_en_una_perspectiva_comparada; Eduardo Pizarro Leongómez, "Los Origenes Del Movimiento Armado Comunista En Colombia," *Análisis Político*, May 7, 1989, http://biblioteca.clacso.edu.ar/ar/libros/colombia/assets/own/analisis07.pdf; Pizarro Leongómez.

25 Centro Nacional de Memoria Histórica, *Justicia y Paz. Los Silencios y Los Olvidos de La Verdad* (Bogotá D.C.: Centro Nacional de Memoria Histórica, 2012); Mauricio Romero, *Paramilitares y Autodefensas (1982–2003)* (Bogotá D.C.: IEPRI, Editorial Planeta, 2003).

26 Claudia López-Hernández, *Contemporary Subnational State Building through Democratization: Colombia in Comparative Perspective* (Evaston, Illinois: Northwestern University, 2019).

27 Juan Fernando Jaramillo Pérez, "La Constitución de 1991 y La Paz. Un Balance Después de 12 Años de Vigencia," in Mauricio García Villegas et al. (eds), *Constitución, Democracia y Derechos. Textos Escogidos de Juan Fernando Jaramillo Pérez* (Bogotá D.C.: Centro de Estudios de Derecho, Justicia y Sociedad - Dejusticia, 2016) 88–116; Juan Fernando Jaramillo Pérez, "La Constitución de 1991: Un Análisis de Sus Aportes Desde Una Perspectiva Comparada," in *Constitución, Democracia y Derechos. Textos Escogidos de Juan Fernando Jaramillo Pérez* (Bogotá D.C.: Centro de Estudios de Derecho, Justicia y Sociedad - Dejusticia, 2016); Julieta Lemaitre Ripoll, *La Paz En Cuestión. La*

Guerra y La Paz En La Asamblea Constituyente de 1991 (Bogotá D.C.: Universidad de los Andes, 2011).

28 Francisco Gutiérrez, "La Constitución de 1991 Como Pacto de Paz: Discutiendo Las Anomalías," *Estudios Socio-Jurídicos*, 13, 2011. pp. 419–47.

29 In Colombian constitutional history, there abound examples of civil wars that ended with the adoption of a new constitution, arising from the hegemonic victory of one of the contending forces. Melba Luz Calle Meza, *Constitución y Guerra. Una Revisión Del Sistema de Derechos Fundamentales de Colombia Durante El Siglo XX* (Bogotá D.C.: Grupo Editorial Ibáñez, 2014); Hernando Valencia Villa, *Cartas de Batalla. Una Crítica Del Constitucionalismo Colombiano* (Bogotá D.C.: Panamericana Formas e Impresos SA, 2012). In one such example, the 1863 Constitution expressed the domain of liberal radicalism, while the triumphant conservative "Regeneration" adopted the 1886 authoritarian Constitution. These constitutions, imposed by the winning sides, could hardly be considered agreements of coexistence. If the 1886 Constitution managed to achieve longevity, this was due to the 1910 and 1936 key reforms, which moderated its intolerant authoritarianism and gave it a more inclusive and national sense. Moreover, the previous experiences reveal that constitutions were used as malleable political tools that were adjusted to the conjoining necessities of the elites. Mauricio García Villegas (ed), "La Flexibilidad de La Ley," in *Normas de Papel. La Cultura de Incumplimiento de Reglas* (Bogotá D.C.: Siglo del Hombre y Centro de Estudios de Derecho, Justicia y Sociedad (Dejusticia), 2009).

30 Jaramillo Pérez, "La Constitución de 1991: Un Análisis de Sus Aportes Desde Una Perspectiva Comparada," 28–61.

31 Gutiérrez, "La Constitución de 1991 Como Pacto de Paz: Discutiendo Las Anomalías," 423.

32 Measuring the institutional performance at the municipal level, García Villegas & Espinosa R (2013) conclude that the lowest institutional performance was concentrated in "229 municipalities that represented 62% of the national territory (503,426 of the 818,267 square kilometers that were taken into account in the analysis) where 6,686,142 people live, which is almost 14% of the population living in the whole country" (pp. 107–108). Mauricio García Villegas and José Rafael Espinosa R, *El Derecho al Estado. Los Efectos Legales Del Apartheid Institucional En Colombia* (Bogotá D.C.: Centro de Estudios de Derecho, Justicia y Sociedad - Dejusticia, 2013).

33 See Saffon Sanín, this volume, Chapter 5 for a thorough account.

34 Leah Anne Carroll, *Violent Democratization. Social Movements, Elites, and Politics in Colombia's Rural War Zones, 1984-2008* (Indiana: The University of Notre Dame Press, 2011); Gustavo Duncan, *Los Señores de La Guerra. De Paramilitares, Mafiosos y Autodefensas En Colombia* (Bogotá D.C.: Planeta, 2006); Mauricio Romero (2003); Mauricio Romero (ed.), *Parapolítica: La Ruta de La Expansión Paramilitar y Los Acuerdos Políticos* (Bogotá D.C.: CEREC -Corporación Nuevo Arcoiris, 2007); Saffon Sanín, this volume, Chapter 5.

35 María Paula Saffon Sanín and Vivian Tacha, *La Participación En Las Medidas de Justicia Transicional. Un Estudio Comparado* (Bogotá D.C.: Centro de Estudios de Derecho, Justicia y Sociedad - Dejusticia, 2019).

36 An English version of the peace accord can be found at http://especiales.presidencia.gov.co/Documents/20170620-dejacion-armas/acuerdos/acuerdo-final-ingles.pdf.

37 See Jaramillo Caro, this volume, Chapter 2.

38 Andrés Bermúdez Liévano (ed.), *Los Debates de La Habana: Una Mirada Desde Adentro* (Barcelona: Institute for Integrated Transitions, 2018), https://www.ifit-transitions.org/resources/publications/major-publications-briefings/the-colombian-

peace-talks-practical-lessons-for-negotiators-worldwide/los-debates-de-la-habana.pdf/view; Diana Isabel Güiza Gómez and Rodrigo Uprimny Yepes, *Entre Pactos Políticos y Seguros Jurídicos: El Proceso de Paz Colombiano de 2016* (Bogotá D.C.: Centro de Estudios de Derecho, Justicia y Sociedad - Dejusticia, in press).

39 See Saffon Sanín, this volume, Chapter 5.

40 See Jaramillo Caro, this volume, Chapter 2.

41 Bermúdez Liévano, *Los Debates de La Habana*. (2018).

42 Jairo Estrada (ed.), "Diálogos de La Habana y Pertinencia de Una Asamblea Nacional Constituyente," in *Solución Política y Proceso de Paz En Colombia. A Propósito de Los Diálogos Entre El Gobierno y Las FARC-EP* (Bogotá D.C.: Ocean Sur, 2013).

43 Humberto De la Calle, "Humberto de La Calle Le Dice NO a Las Farc. ¿Por Qué?," *Semana*, June 15, 2013, http://www.semana.com/nacion/articulo/de-calle-dice-no-farc-por-que/346491-3

44 C-379 (Corte Constitucional de Colombia July 18, 2016).

45 Fabio Enrique Pulido Ortiz and Geraldine Bustos Zamora, "Momentos Constitucionales y Legitimidad de Los Procedimientos de Reforma," in Julián Andrés Escobar Solano (eds), *Procesos Legislativos y Ordenamiento Constitucional: Abordajes Teóricos* (Bogotá D.C.: Centro de Investigaciones y Altos Estudios Legislativos - CAEL, 2016).

46 Jaime Castro, "¿Golpe de Estado Permanente o Solución Extraconstitucional?," *Ámbito Jurídico*, June 10, 2016, https://www.ambitojuridico.com/noticias/columnista-impreso/constitucional-y-derechos-humanos/golpe-de-estado-permanente-o-solucion; Jaime Castro, "Nuevo Bloque de Constitucionalidad," *Ámbito Jurídico*, July 7, 2016, https://www.ambitojuridico.com/noticias/columnista-impreso/constitucional-y-derechos-humanos/nuevo-bloque-de-constitucionalidad; Juan Manuel Charry Urueña, "Blindaje Jurídico a La Paz," *Ámbito Jurídico*, May 31, 2016, https://www.ambitojuridico.com/noticias/columnista-impreso/constitucional-y-derechos-humanos/blindaje-juridico-la-paz; Juan Manuel Charry Urueña, "Reglas Constitucionales Para El Plebiscito," *Ámbito Jurídico*, September 1, 2016, https://www.ambitojuridico.com/noticias/columnista-impreso/constitucional-y-derechos-humanos/reglas-constitucionales-para-el.

47 Bermúdez Liévano, *Los Debates de La Habana*, 286.

48 Diana Isabel Güiza Gómez and Rodrigo Uprimny Yepes, *Entre Pactos Políticos y Seguros Jurídicos: El Proceso de Paz Colombiano de 2016* (Bogotá D.C.: Centro de Estudios de Derecho, Justicia y Sociedad - Dejusticia, in press).

49 Javier Eduardo Revelo Rebolledo, "Los Riesgos de Una Paz Que Ni Vence Ni Convence," *Razón Pública*, de diciembre de 2016, https://www.razonpublica.com/index.php/conflicto-drogas-y-paz-temas-30/9938-los-riesgos-de-una-paz-que-ni-vence-ni-convence.html.

50 Rodrigo Uprimny Yepes and Diana Isabel Güiza Gómez, "Pacigerancia: El Valor Jurídico de Los Acuerdos de Paz En El Derecho Internacional," *Latin American Research Review*, vol. 3, 2019, pp. 48–77.

51 Leopoldo Fergusson and Carlos Molina, "Un Vistazo a Los Resultados Del Plebiscito," Miscelánea La Paz, *Miscelánea La Paz* (blog), October 4, 2016, https://sites.google.com/site/miscelaneadelapaz/datos.

52 Aila M. Matanock and Miguel García-Sánchez, "The Colombian Paradox: Peace Processes, Elite Divisions & Popular Plebiscites," *Daedalus. Journal of the American Academy of Arts & Sciences,* vol. 146 (4), Fall 2017, pp. 152–66.

53 C-699 (Corte Constitucional de Colombia de diciembre de 2016).

54 María Paula Saffon Sanín and Diana Isabel Güiza Gómez, "Colombia En 2018: Entre El Fracaso de La Paz y El Inicio de La Política Programática," *Revista de Ciencia Política,* vol. 39 (2), 2019, pp. 217–37.

55 Instituto Kroc de Estudios Internacionales de Paz, *Estado Efectivo de Implementación Del Acuerdo de Paz de Colombia 2 Años de Implementación* (Bogotá D.C.: Instituto Kroc de Estudios Internacionales de Paz, 2019), https://kroc.nd.edu/assets/321729/190523_informe_3_final_final.pdf; Secretaría Técnica del Componente de Verificación Internacional CINEP/PPP-CERAC, *Sexto Informe de Verificación de La Implementación Del Acuerdo Final de Paz En Colombia Para Los Verificadores Internacionales Felipe González y José Mujica* (Bogotá D.C., June 2019), https://www.verificacion.cerac.org.co/wp-content/uploads/2019/06/Sexto-informe-trimestral-Secretar%C3%ADa-T%C3%A9cnica.pdf.

56 Saffon Sanín and Güiza Gómez, "Colombia En 2018" (2019).

57 Saffon Sanín and Güiza Gómez, "Colombia En 2018" (2019).

58 Rodrigo Uprimny Yepes, Diana Isabel Güiza-Gómez, and Hobeth Martínez Carrillo, "Domando La Incertidumbre: El Control Constitucional de Actos Legislativos En Tiempos de Transición de La Guerra Hacia La Paz Negociada," in Camilo Eduardo Umaña Hernández (ed.), *La Justicia al Encuentro de La Paz En Contexto de Transición. Reflexiones Actuales Para Desafíos Colombianos* (Bogotá D.C.: Universidad Externado de Colombia, 2018).

59 Bruce Ackerman, *Revolutionary Constitutions. Charismatic Leadership and the Rule of Law* (Boston: Harvard University Press, 2019).

60 Bell and Zulueta-Fülscher, *Sequencing Peace Agreements and Constitutions in the Political Settlement Process.* (2016).

61 Uprimny, "La Refrendación o Ratificación Democrática de La Paz" (2013).

62 Nathan, "The real deal" (2020).

17 The Courts' possible contribution to a dialogic democracy

The case of the Peace Agreements in Colombia

Roberto Gargarella

Introduction

In this work, I want to explore the possible contributions that the judiciary may make to our collective conversation over issues of fundamental public interest. In what follows, I shall first present some principles that may orient the action of judges in this regard, which I believe are in line with the requirements of a deliberative democracy. Then, I shall illustrate the possible implications of those dialogic judicial tasks, by examining one important and recent example, namely the role of judges in the face of popular consultations and plebiscites. In particular, I shall focus my attention on the case of the Final Accord in Colombia, and the role of the Colombian Court in that regard.

Let me then begin by briefly setting the theoretical framework that I shall use. To begin with, I shall say that I define deliberative democracy in agreement with the basic features that I mentioned in previous paragraphs. Accordingly, I will here assume that deliberative democracy is directly linked to the (Habermasian) ideal of an ongoing, permanent discussion on issues of public interest (or public morality) among all those potentially affected.[1] For this definition, a proper democracy, this is to say one that is capable of creating impartial public decisions, has two fundamental characteristics, namely (i) *inclusion* and (ii) *debate*. In other words, public decisions tend to lose impartiality or become unduly biased when certain individuals or groups of people become unjustifiably excluded from the debate (i.e., because of poverty or social marginalization), and also when those decisions are not preceded by a robust, wide-open process of collective discussion (i.e., because of the influence of money in politics and the public life in general). The same reasons that support dialogic democracy (iii) prevent democracy to interfere with issues of *private or self-regarding morality,* this is to say issues where no one else is affected.[2] When third parties are not affected, the matter is about individual autonomy, rather than collective self-government. And democracy has to be reserved to issues of public morality.

The contribution that judges may make to democratic dialog mainly derives from their peculiar institutional position. The judiciary's fundamental institutional mission is that of receiving complaints from all those who consider themselves improperly treated by the majoritarian decision-making process. Judges are obliged to listen and take note of those complaints and give them a justified answer based on public reasons, that is, this is to say reasons that everyone is reasonably capable of understanding and accepting. In this sense, judges are situated in an exceptional position for integrating the views of the wronged, for giving due weight to the interests of those unduly displaced from the democratic arena.[3]

From their particularly relevant institutional place, judges may help improve the democratic system precisely in those aspects where the democratic system is more in need of help. Given the above-mentioned conception of democracy, there are three risks that appear particularly prominent. By helping us to prevent these risks, the judiciary will also be making an enormous contribution to democratic dialog. Let me refer to these different, possible judicial tasks.

Inclusion

The first risk I shall call the problem of *absence of viewpoints*. This problem relates to the first fundamental pillar of a deliberative democracy, namely *political* inclusion: Democratic decisions, as we know, need to be informed by the viewpoints of all those potentially affected. The risk at stake refers to situations where public decisions are not the product of a conversation among equals, but rather the exclusive creation of a few—an elite, a dominant group, the minority of the most powerful. We actually know about numerous cases of contemporary societies where public decisions are in the hands of a few; where the voices of significant parts of society are virtually dismissed or practically unheard; where even majority voices are (perhaps systematically) marginalized from the institutional system. We are in need to prevent those common cases, where the law becomes something strange for large sections of the population, who are therefore unable to understand the language the law speaks.[4]

Frequently, the legislative process is organized in ways that actually exclude relevant viewpoints from the discussion of a norm (i.e., it may happen that directly affected groups have no representation in Congress, or that they are not consulted, even though they are targeted by the norm at stake). In these situations, judges may properly decide to intervene simply in order to ensure respect for the basis of the deliberative process. This is what happened in South Africa in the *Doctors for Life* case. This decision is interesting for different reasons, but particularly because of the centrality that judges attributed to the elements of voice and discussion in the decision-making process. Judges maintained that the intervention of the public in the legislative debates was a necessary part of a process committed to achieving impartiality.

Discussion

The second risk that I want to address concerns the problem of *naked interests*. This risk relates to the second fundamental pillar of a deliberative democracy, namely *public discussion*: Democratic decisions, as we know, need to be the result of open processes of collective deliberation. The risk at stake, then, refers to situations where the law becomes not the product of a process of mutual learning and mutual corrections, but rather the result of the imposition of a particular interest group: The law thus results in the expression of naked interests, rather than of public interests.[5] In these situations, where the conditions of a robust public dialog are not present, what tends to prevail is the situation that James Madison feared the most, namely the situation of factionalized politics, where demagogues gained influence, where passions took the place of reason and political irrationality became to prevail.[6] So, in the face of that possibility, judges could and should help ensure that the democratic procedure is equally open to all, rather than biased in favor of a powerful minority.[7] As a consequence, the Court is authorized to challenge norms that are not supported by a "reasoned analysis."[8] According to this view, Courts may play a significant role in ensuring that legal norms are the product of an exchange of reasons, rather than the mere imposition of one interest group or sector of society upon the rest. These are some possible instances of the judicial contribution to public debate.

Clearing the channels of political change

Courts may make a great contribution to constitutional dialog not only by actively promoting a conversation between political actors, as we shall see below, but also through more "defensive" measures, oriented to safeguard guarding the procedural (pre)conditions of democratic dialog. Scholar John Ely, who popularized this view, argued that the Supreme Court should interpret the Constitution so as to reinforce democratic processes and popular self-government. In order to comply with this mission, judges would be first required to "clear the channels of political change."[9] But, what could this notion of "clearing the channels of political change" actually imply?

According to Ely, his "participation-oriented" or "representation-reinforcing" approach implied, first, a special protection for the rights of speech, press, assembly, petition, and political association, which are central to the functioning of a representative democracy. In other words, judges should examine all restrictions in the area (i.e., limitations imposed upon political discourse) with the highest scrutiny, and presuming that the political decision of the case is contrary to the Constitution. The same goes for voting rights, malapportionment cases—cases of political "gerrymandering" (which basically occurs when voting districts are redrawn to benefit one party over another during elections). This enumeration, of course, is not exhaustive. Below we shall examine other examples, coming from Latin America, where judges properly considered invalid certain reforms that came to restrict the deliberative capacities of the legislative branch.

Arguments, and not force

Similarly, judges may tell politicians that they are not allowed to do what they are about to do, through the mere use of force. They may ask them, for instance, to consider other reasons; or even tell them that they are not allowed to develop certain coercive decisions, without first exploring other—constitutionally required—paths. This can of course be done without telling political authorities what particular content their appropriate policy should have.

The well-known Grootboom case, which was decided in South Africa in 2001, can be seen as a good example in this respect. Through this decision, the Court did not interpret the Constitution as demanding the government to ensure that everyone received shelter, but rather to design an emergency plan for those in need—whatever reasonable plan the government decided to adopt, according to its democratic authority. The Court did not ask political authorities to pass certain specific measures, but rather a "coherent, coordinated program designed to meet" constitutional obligations.

Supervising the deliberative component of the legislative process

Moreover, Courts may require legislators to open the decision-making process to the public, in order to avoid or reduce the influence of interest groups, or require political authorities to call public audiences to supervise crucial aspects of the application of the law. More radically, the Court may scrutinize the legislative process, so as to ensure that the legislative debate is not a mere façade of a legislative debate.

Promoting political dialog

The same South African Court explored another similarly interesting route of dialogic intervention, through what came to be called "meaningful engagement." Thus, in the case *Olivia Road,* the applicants challenged the Municipality of Johannesburg's practice of evicting residents of so-called "bad buildings" for health and safety reasons.[10]

Again, through this decision, the Court showed that it could facilitate the resolution of situations of massive violation of rights, through means that honored the dialogic ideal. Similarly, the Court has been promoting public discussion in other significant cases, usually related to complex cases of "structural litigation." Thus, in order to force political authorities to (i) address violations of rights they were not considering and (ii) do so in dialogical ways, meaning in dialog with (all the) other relevant viewpoints.

The notable series of public audiences called by Argentina's Supreme Court in the Matanza-Riachuelo River Basin case are exemplar, in this respect.

Calling to public hearings in order to enrich the judicial decision-making process

Another instance of the same dialogic principle appears when the Court itself calls a public meeting, in order to enrich its own decision-making process. The Court may thus gain technical knowledge it lacked; recognize and evaluate the content of viewpoints it did not previously consider; balance arguments for and against a certain issue; etc. These procedures may be justified in cases where the required knowledge is fragmented and dispersed; the voices and viewpoints to be considered are numerous; and the risks of making a biased decision are high. Some recent decisions made by the Brazilian, Mexican, and Argentinean Supreme Courts illustrate that the inclinations to call for public audiences are not anymore extravagant exceptions in the region.

Promoting deliberation in the implementation of judicial decision/ through the use of remedies

Courts can also promote deliberation through the means and remedies they choose to implement their decisions. Think, for instance, about decision T-760/8 of the Colombian Constitutional Court, through which the tribunal cooperated in the restructuring of the entire Health System in Colombia.[11]

Constitutional dialog in Colombia and the Peace Agreements

In what follows, I shall examine one example that may help us understand and critically examine the actual life of constitutional dialog, and the participation of the judicial branch in this regard. As anticipated, I shall take as my main example that of Colombia, and I shall focus my attention, particularly, on the way in which the Colombian government in general, and the Constitutional Court, in particular, dealt with the historic Final Accord—I am referring to the peace process between the Colombian government and the Revolutionary Armed Forces of Colombia (FARC) to bring an end to the Colombian conflict.

On plebiscites and their democratic character (or not)

In the examination that follows, I shall pay special attention to the way in which the Colombian Government and the Colombian Constitutional Court responded to the popular consultation that took place during the process. For that reason, I want to begin my analysis by making some general theoretical references concerning the use of plebiscites, and the "democratic pedigree" of such consultations.

Advocates of dialogic constitutionalism may consider the use of plebiscites as an attractive and potential tool for improving our collective conversation on issues of fundamental public interest. However, the problems that we may find in relation to the actual practice of plebiscites and—more particularly for our purposes—the problems that tend to derive from the judicialization of plebiscites seem significant, and call for a more skeptical approach to these kinds of consultations, and also for a different judicial approach to the practice. Let me then begin by saying something more general about the problems generated by plebiscites, according to a dialogical perspective, and then focus more precisely on the problems derived from their judicialization.

From the perspective of dialogic democracy, the use of plebiscites results, in principle, attractive, because it promises to strengthen the participatory or inclusive dimension of the "robust public debate." In the context of exclusive and ill-functioning representative systems, the use of this tool seems extremely important: The problems affecting our political institutions are so damaging that in principle every alternative that helped us to minimize the elitist character of the decision-making process should be welcomed.

In spite of that, the reasons for concern—the risks involved—with plebiscites are numerous, according to a dialogic perspective. On the one hand, from the perspective of "inclusion," it is a problem to have plebiscites in the context of a system of concentrated powers. In those conditions, first, plebiscites may come as "concessions" directed at legitimizing "all the rest," this is to say, a decision-making process where "all other decisions," but one or two, are decided by a few. Second, plebiscites may and have been used in order to mainly strengthen the legitimacy of the person or group in control of power. For instance, Colombian President Juan Manuel Santos assumed that, after an armed conflict that had lasted for decades, most people would simply respond "yes" in the popular consultation concerning the Peace Agreement between the government and the guerrilla. The Final Accord included among its 57 articles numerous clauses that—the President knew—were hardly acceptable for any reasonable person (i.e., clauses regarding pardons to ex guerrilla members, or conferring them privileges that were denied to any other respectable citizen). However, the President assumed that the vast majority of people anxiously wanted the end of the conflict, and that they were therefore willing to put aside any objection to the peace treaty or any of its clauses, in favor of what was their first preference. Unfortunately, the President was wrong. Third, and related to the previous point, in the context of concentrated powers, the risk of having manipulated participatory events seems enormous: The president tends to have, in those conditions, multiple ways and resources available, for guaranteeing the triumph of his/her favorite answer. This is why so many authoritarian leaders, who explicitly repudiated democracy—from Juan Manuel de Rosas to, more recently, Augusto Pinochet or Alberto Fujimori—organized their own plebiscites.

On the other hand, and from the perspective of "deliberation," plebiscites seem particularly objectionable, because the emphasis they put on the value of "participation" tends to contrast with the disinterest or lack of concern with issues about information, transparency, and open discussion. Those who organize them (perhaps, trying to ensure the triumph of their preferred alternative, and thus their own triumph) do not tend to conceive of plebiscites as opportunities for collective reflection; mutual enlightenment; the "laundering" of preferences; and the transformation of initial beliefs. Recent, very noted plebiscites, such as the popular consultation about Brexit, in England, or the one about the ratification of the peace process, in Colombia represent good illustration of what we are saying: None of those events were preceded by serious processes of collective information and discussion. In addition, as we know, popular consultations tend to trivialize and simplify complex issues: They tend to ask people to respond with a "yes" or "no" to extremely intricate and multifaceted issues, such as "abortion" or a peace process. In Colombia's popular consultation about the Final Accord, the people were forced to say "yes" or "no" to a Peace Agreement composed by 297 pages, which were complex and difficult to understand, where some of them looked very attractive while some others looked unacceptable.

In sum, from a dialogic perspective, plebiscites are promising tools, which also carry with them profoundly serious risks, particularly when they are organized and carried out by regimes where political and economic power are concentrated.

An additional concern in this respect relates to the role of courts in the face of plebiscites. Courts should be moved by the principles so far revised, which would require them to (i) ensure the inclusive character of plebiscites, avoiding arbitrary exclusions and strategies directed at undermining the voice of certain groups, and (ii) ensure that proper deliberative conditions are guaranteed, meaning that issues of transparency, information, and debate are adequately protected. In addition, they should supervise these occasional instances of popular participation by taking into account a regulative ideal that says that, in democratic societies, "We the people" should have the "last say" concerning all relevant public issues.[12]

The Peace Agreement in Colombia and the Constitutional Court: Some facts and some initial comments

In what follows, let me focus my attention just on the extraordinary case of the Peace Agreement that was signed in Colombia between official authorities and representatives of the FARC, which came to put an end to more than 52 years of internal armed conflict, which provoked the death of more than 260,000 people (215,000 civilians), and forced the displacement of millions of others.

The Colombian Constitutional Court has had the opportunity to deal with different aspects of the Treaty, which the National Congress tried to constitutionalize and implement, in troublesome political circumstances: Unfortunately, a slight majority of the people (50, 2%) rejected the

Agreement, in the consultation that was carried out in October 2016, regarding the 49, 76% of the electoral roll voted in favor. The electoral abstention was over 62%, the greater in 22 years.[13]

Following the failed consultation process an intense process of negotiations took place between the Agreement political opponents in the plebiscite and the Colombian government in order to reviewing the general Agreement and conclusively trying to achieve a great national pact.

After around ten meetings during 4 weeks, government negotiators received 455 reform proposals that were later discussed with FARC representatives in Cuba. Afterward, a new version of the general Agreement arises.[14]

The Colombian Congress issued many decisions trying to give life and stability to the new version of the Agreement, and the Court has had the opportunity to delve into many of the complex intricacies of those norms. In what follows, I will only make a few observations about two of the Court's decisions in the area.

Let me say something, first, about the Court's decision of May 2017, when it examined the norm allowing the government to fast track laws related to the Agreement (Constitutional Amendment 1, 2016). The government had promoted these laws procedural reforms in order to accelerate the implementation of the Agreement (and particularly the amnesty law that the members of the guerrilla demanded). However, through its May decision, the Tribunal considered (Decision C-332/17) that two basic parts of the "fast-track" mechanism created by Congress were unconstitutional. According to one of the objected clauses, all changes to each of the laws developing different aspects of the Agreement had to be approved by the government before coming to a congressional vote. According to the second objected clause, Congress could only vote to approve or deny the law, implementing the peace process without the possibility of debating and voting each of the articles individually.

The Court's decision followed a petition presented, among many others, by the right-wing Senator and now President of Colombia Iván Duque, a close ally of a very controversial figure, namely the former President of Colombia, Álvaro Uribe, and it was heavily criticized by some of the country's most influential legal analysts.[15] However, if we pay attention to the Court's arguments and to the principles it followed, one could conclude that its decision was, in principle, correct. For the Court, implementing those two clauses would have implied replacing the Constitution by altering the deliberative and decision-making powers of Congress—powers that would have been transferred to the then President Juan Manuel Santos.[16] In the words of the President of the Constitutional Court at that time, Luis Guillermo Guerrero, the ruling was not aimed at undermining the force of the Peace Agreement, but rather to "open up spaces for democratic deliberation."

From a "situated" democratic perspective, which also implied, in this case, taking the failed plebiscite seriously, the concerns exposed by the Court were appropriate. They expressed reasonable worries about the democratic-reinforcing character of the law, and the procedures that it established. Once again, what was here at stake was, perhaps, the destiny of the most important Agreement signed in the country's history, which—regrettably—had received a negative answer by a majority of Colombia's citizenry. All those interested in still implementing the Peace Agreements had to acknowledge both things, which run in the same direction. First, given the singular relevance of what was at stake, decisions in the area required an extraordinary level of democratic legitimacy. Second, given what had already happened in the plebiscite, the official initiatives in the area—trying to revitalize and implement an Agreement that the citizenry had rejected—required an additional, extra effort in the direction of increasing the democratic character/legitimacy of its decision: The government needed to carefully craft the social consensus—the social support it failed to obtain through the popular consultation. As a conclusion, in my view, the Court's strict scrutiny of the "fast-track" law was totally justifiable: The government needed to show that it was doing its very best in order to "build democratic legitimacy," but precisely at that point (!), it showed that it was willing and ready to circumvent the constitutional/procedural requirements of democratic deliberation. The Colombian Constitutional Court reasonably said "no" to the government's ill-fated initiative.

Let us take another example, related to the Court's ruling of October 11, 2017 (Decision C-630/17). In that occasion, the Court upheld a Congress-approved legislation, which established that the Peace Agreement between the government and the FARC could not be amended for the next 12 years (Constitutional Amendment 2, 2017). This is to say that the following three governments would be unable to modify approved parts of the accord. The short-term purpose of the political initiative was obvious: It was directed to shield the Agreement from potential changes to be introduced by the coming government—a coalition led by right-wing candidate Iván Duque who, unsurprisingly, became the President of the country. According to the norm that was upheld by the Court, "institutions and authorities of the state have the obligation to comply with what is established in the final accord in good faith… until the end of three complete presidential periods following the signing." For the Court, that article incorporated a "principle of stability and security that is deferential to the purposes of the Agreement."

Expectedly, advocates of the Peace Agreement within the legal community celebrated the Court's ruling, which was the product of a unanimous vote (9 to 0) within the tribunal. For scholar Gonzalo Ramírez-Cleves, the decision represented a "valuable reminder of the need for the peace process to remain consistent with core constitutional values, and the difficult task Colombia continues to face in balancing peace with other constitutional values."[17] Not surprisingly, too, opponents of Santos' government and the peace treaty, like ex-President Álvaro Uribe, complained about the Court's decision, maintaining that the ruling ignored the will of Colombians, as expressed in the plebiscite. Now, what could we say about the

Court's approach to the matter, from the deliberative perspective that we have adopted in this paper?

Analyzing the Colombian government's response to the plebiscite, from the perspective of a deliberative democracy

In order to begin this analysis, I shall first underline that we are dealing with a historical Peace Agreement, of extraordinary complexity and importance, which received a negative response by the majority of the Colombian citizenry in a recent plebiscite. For that reason, I would claim, if the incumbent government wanted to adopt, develop, and implement the historical Agreement, in spite of the people's negative answer, then the government would have been obliged to carefully build a new consensus, rather than shield the Agreement from politics. A possible step in that direction was, indeed, the decision to support and protect the Agreement through the mechanisms of a constitutional reform. Those mechanisms are interesting as means conducive to the goal of building a broad, new, strong social consensus, but not as excuses directed at replacing it. The (re)construction of an ample collective Agreement is something that requires time and effort, and not something that can be done in a rush. But the Colombian government felt it was in a rush: It reasonably assumed that the coming government would dismantle the Agreement. As a consequence, instead of working for broadening the social support of the Agreement (which was not an impossible task, considering that almost 50% of the population manifested that it was in favor of it), the government hurried to do whatever it could, so as to prevent the future government to undermine the force of the treaty. That was, I believe, a first problem of the official strategy: Santos' government showed (again) that it had no confidence in the Colombian people, and tried to use the law to protect an agreement that required, instead, full and open democratic support.

Secondly, in its "rush against time," the government decided to make things worse, by making it impossible for the next three governments to introduce substantive changes in the Agreement. But, in this way, and through this counter-majoritarian resource, it degraded even more the democratic credentials of the Agreement. Let me be clearer about this point: The democratic force and, finally, the legitimacy of a certain norm do not depend on what we "say" or "do" about it, but on the social Agreement that actually supports it. This was the essence of Bruce Ackerman's great contribution to constitutionalism: The special force of a Constitution or constitutional reform does not derive from any legal formalities or legal tricks, but rather on the "constitutional moment" that we can find behind it.[18] For example, the US 1787 Constitution did not even emerge from a constitutional convention, while the substantive legal reforms introduced by the "New Deal" did not come through a constitutional reform (through Article V of the US Constitution). However, for Ackerman, both cases represent important examples of what a "constitutional moment" would be. Let me quote him at length: "Decisions by the people occur rarely, and under special constitutional conditions. Before gaining the authority to make supreme law in the name of the People, a movement's political partisans must, first, convince an extraordinary number of their fellow citizens to take their proposed initiatives with a seriousness that they do not normally accord to politics; second, they must allow their opponents a fair opportunity to organize their own forces; third, they must convince a majority of their fellow Americans to support their initiative as its merits are discussed, time and again, in the deliberative for a provided for 'higher lawmaking'. It is only then that a political moment earns the enhanced legitimacy the dualist Constitution accords to decisions made by the People."[19]

Of course, we may agree or not with all the details of Ackerman's theory, but its fundamental intuition still seems correct. In the end, the democratic legitimacy of a legal reform does not derive from legal formalities but from substantive social agreements. One cannot gain "the authority to make supreme law in the name of the People," by just calling a certain norm "supreme" or fulfilling a number of legal formalities, without having first "convince[d] an extraordinary number [of citizens] to take [the] proposed initiative [...] with a seriousness that they do not normally accord to politics." This was not the principle that was followed by political and legal actors in Colombia. Rather, Colombian authorities seemed unwilling to assume the educational, social, and democratic costs required by the particular kind of decision that they wanted to affirm. As we have said already, the Colombian government considered it extremely difficult to build or rebuild a broad social consensus in support of the Peace Agreement and, consequently, decided to shield the Agreement not through democratic consensus, but rather through the use of the coercive/legal apparatus of the State.

Moreover, assuming that neither the particular status enjoyed by the Agreement nor the deferential attitude assumed by the Constitutional Court towards the treaty, were enough for ensuring the stability of the accord, the government decided to provide extra-guarantees to it. And it did so by directly preventing the next three governments to amend the Peace Agreement. Instead of trying to strengthen and consolidate the incipient "constitutional moment" already present—fortifying in that way the democratic legitimacy of a "democratically damaged" Agreement—the government decided to promote a new counter-majoritarian reform. But this move seems hardly acceptable for committed democrats: Why should we make it impossible, for tomorrow's democratic majority, to change the Agreement, if it found it necessary?

Let me be clearer about this: Very commonly, in a democracy, and through democratic procedures, we decide to provide special protection to interests that we find particularly valuable, and/or particularly vulnerable, and/or under serious threat. Sometimes, we call certain fundamental interests "rights," so as to express that we want these interests to receive a special protection. Frequently, we incorporate those rights into the Constitution, so as to make our decision even more apparent: We in that way proclaim that "these are the interests we value the most." Moreover, in order to ensure special protection to certain things we value, we say that those things require, in order to be modified, a special majority (i.e., two thirds of the Congressional votes), or a special procedure (we may for instance say that, in order to modify the Constitution, we need to call a special, Constitutional Convention). But it is a different thing to create a mechanism that makes it simply impossible, for the next generation, to revise things that we do not want them to revise. Then, members of the next generation may reasonably comply. They may ask us: "Why shouldn't I enjoy the same degree of freedom that you enjoyed?" "Why do you distrust me so much?" ("Why should I/we instead trust you, given what you are doing to me?"). So, in democratic terms, the choice of the Colombian government was, in the best case very polemical, and in the worst case, directly undemocratic.

The Court's decision from October 2017 was then also problematic: Why did it support, rather than challenge, the government decision? In this respect, for instance, the Court's appeal to a "principle of stability and security" adds nothing relevant to its decision. All our courts should know this: The use of technical terms or a sophisticated legal language does not transform their decision into a sophisticated, legal, democratic, or even valid decision. In the end, the fact that a certain norm is or will be supported by the State's coercive apparatus does not confer legal authority or validity to that norm.

Before concluding this analysis, let me clarify that I am personally in favor of the Peace Agreement like the one signed in La Havana, that I understand the seriousness of the case, and that I am aware of the risks brought by an incoming government that wanted to dismantle the historical pact with the FARC. However, I also think that political and legal authorities, in Colombia, acting in "a rush against time" and distrustful as they were of the Colombian people, proceeded in the wrong way. Instead of working for broadening the democratic support of the Agreement (and they were almost there: half of the population supported it), they resorted to counter-majoritarian strategies so as to isolate the Agreement from politics: The government chose to go in that direction, and the Constitutional Court decided to support that strategy. This was, I believe, an unfortunate strategy, based on an unreasonably and unjustified distrust towards democracy.

Final words

Unfortunately, in my view, our institutional system is not well prepared to foster constitutional dialog. By contrast, our system has been created to contain, restrain, or channel a possible civil war, rather than promote constitutional dialog. In spite of that, if we got—by chance or other unexpected motives—judges—or other public officers—with the good (dialogical) attitudes/dispositions/motivations, or public decisions oriented in the "right" dialogic way, we should, at least in principle, applaud and celebrate them. Lacking the proper institutional incentives and constraints, the Colombian Court has been navigating through the difficult waters of the Final Accord, sometimes in ways that were compatible with the aspirations of a dialogic democracy, and sometimes not. Perhaps, the lesson we can learn from this example is that we should help our tribunals to play a better role in our democracies, by reforming our institutions and providing the different branches with better democratic incentives.

Notes

1 Jürgen Habermas, *Between Facts and Norms* (Cambridge: MIT Press, 1980); Jon Elster, "The Market and the Forum," in Jon Elster and Rune Slagstad (eds), *Foundations of Social Choice Theory* (Cambridge: Cambridge University Press, 1989); Carlos Nino, *The Ethics of Human Rights* (Oxford: Oxford University Press, 1991).

2 Nino, *The Ethics of Human Rights.*

3 Sandra Liebenberg presented a similar, although not identical, approach. For her, "Within a deliberative model of democracy, courts potentially play a valuable role in protecting the vital interests and values which human rights norms seek to protect. In addition, they seek to preserve the conditions for fair and equitable participation in decision-making processes through which human rights are given concrete effect." Sandra Liebenberg, "Engaging the paradoxes of the universal and particular in human rights adjudication: The possibilities and pitfalls of 'meaningful engagement,'" *African Human Rights Law Journal,* vol. 12, 2012, p. 11.

4 For marginalized people, the law would continue to be something foreign to their interests—something to which they would be unable to identify with—even if a translator would decipher the words the law pronounces, and carefully explain their meaning.

5 Cass R. Sunstein, "Interest Groups in American Public Law," *Stanford Law Review,* vol. 38, 1985, p. 1.

6 Of course, many of these risks became aggravated rather than alleviated with the prevalence of a media controlled by private interests and a public sphere dominated by money.

7 Sunstein, "Interest Groups in American Public Law," 49–51.

8 See *Mississippi Univ. for Women v. Hogan,* 458 U.S. 718, 726 (1982).

9 For Ely, the political process is "malfunctioning"—in other words, "the process is undeserving of trust," first, when "the ins are choking off the channels of political change to ensure that they will stay in and the outs will stay out" in *Democracy and Distrust* (Cambridge: Harvard University Press, 1980) 103.

10 Lilian Chenwi, "Democratizing the socio-economic rights enforcement process," in Helena Alviar García, Karl Klare., Lucy Williams (eds), *Social and Economic Rights in Theory and Practice* (London: Routledge, 2015) 185; Liebenberg, "Engaging the paradoxes of the universal and particular in human rights adjudication," p. 14; Sandra Liebenberg, "Toward an equality-promoting interpretation of socio-economic rights in South Africa. Insights from the egalitarian liberal tradition," *The South African Law Journal*, 132, part. 2, 2015, pp. 411–37.

11 Alicia Ely Yamin and Óscar Parra-Vera, "The role of courts in Refining Health policy: The case of the Colombian Court," Manuscript in file with the author,

2009. Let me just say a word about the third risk that I mentioned at the beginning, concerning the problem of moral perfectionism, which in this paper I will not examine in depth. This problem relates to the main fundamental limit of a deliberative democracy, namely individual autonomy: Deliberative democracy concerns issues of collective self-government, rather than individual autonomy. The risk at stake refers to situations where the State uses its coercive powers in order to impose a particular conception of the good. Dialogic courts, in those occasions, have to make clear to political authorities that "neither you, nor I can tell individuals how they should live their own lives (or even less impose upon them a particular conception of the good)." For Carlos Nino, moral perfectionism opposes the principle of individual autonomy, and assumes that "since what is good for individuals does not depend on their preferences or desires, the state may favor, even by coercive means, those ideals of virtue, plans of life, or interests which are objectively better." Nino, *The Ethics of Human Rights,* p. 132. Usually, perfectionism is related to the kind of elitism already explored, which are typical in contexts of inequality and social exclusion. As the philosopher Thomas Scanlon maintained, conservative approaches of the kind have a "strong tendency towards elitism." This is evinced from the fact that they put "a greater emphasis on the needs and interests" of a few, against the needs and interests of others. See Thomas Scanlon, "The Principles of Justice," in Norman Daniels (ed.), *Reading Rawls* (Oxford: Basil Blackwell, 1975) 171. The mission of courts, in this area, is to make sure that individuals are respected in what regards their own private morality—this is to say, with regard to self-regarding behavior. Neither political authorities nor judicial officers can interfere with individual choices that do not affect third parties in a meaningful way.

12 Perhaps the most extreme example in that respect was the one offered by Bolivia's main tribunal, concerning a referendum surprisingly called by President Evo Morales, seeking popular authorization to run for office for a fourth term. This possibility, it should be noted, was prevented by the Constitution that Evo Morales enacted during his mandate. Remarkably, the *Plurinational Constitutional Court*, after a demand set by Morales' Movement to Socialism (MAS) party, on a November 20, 2017 unanimous decision (namely, *TCP Sentencia Constitucional Plurinacional N° 0084/2017*) that limits barring elected authorities from seeking re-election indefinitely, ruled against the American Convention on Human Rights and thus violated human rights. In the words of Macario Lahor Cortez, head of the Plurinational Court, "All people that were limited by the law and the constitution are hereby able to run for office, because it is up to the Bolivian people to decide." According to researcher Sergio Verdugo, the court's decision represented a good illustration of what Professor David Landau calls "abusive constitutionalism," meaning an action that was intended at undermining constitutional democracy using formal constitutional means. Sergio Verdugo, "How the Bolivian Constitutional Court Helped the Morales Regime to Break the Political Insurance of the Bolivian Constitution," *ICONnect,*http://www.iconnectblog.com/2017/12/how-the-bolivian-constitutional-court-helped-the-morales-regime-to-break-the-political-insurance-of-the-bolivian-constitution/. From a dialogic perspective, this was a shameful, offensive decision in its worst form: It challenged a responsible and courageous majoritarian claim in the referendum, which ran in a direction contrary to what those in powers pretended, and at the same time reaffirmed the plain meaning of the Nation's constitutional text.

13 I want to thank Leonardo García Jaramillo for discussions over this issue.

14 Among the changes, the most prominent are (1) the general Peace Agreement is not now part of the Constitution. A provisional article was added conditioning

state authorities and institutions to comply in good faith with mandates prescribed in the Agreement. Actions taken by successive governments must be consistent with the Agreement. This provisional article will be in effect from its incorporation into the Constitution to the end of three presidential terms. (2) The special jurisdiction for peace now shall be limited in time, in principle, to a total maximum of 10 years. Besides, just during the first 2 years it will be possible to receive criminal investigation requests. (3) There shall be no foreign justices at the Tribunal for Peace, just up to ten highly qualified foreign jurists will give specific opinions. (4) In certain cases, the Special Jurisdiction for Peace judgments may be reviewed by the Constitutional Court. (5) The alternative sanctions imposed on those who immediately acknowledge truth and responsibility for their crimes was defined more clearly, particularly the sanction of effective restriction of freedoms and rights, such as the freedom of movement. In each one of the Tribunal for Peace sanctioning judgments must be clearly indicated where the sentence will be served and must include specific details such as the implementation period of restorative sanctions. (6) A provision from the Article 28 of the Rome Statute, regarding the responsibility of commanders, was incorporated. Now a commander shall be criminally responsible for crimes committed by forces under his effective authority where either knew or, owing to the circumstances at the time, should have known that the forces were committing or about to commit crimes. (7) During the surrender of arms process FARC members must declare their goods and assets which will be later used to compensate victims of the armed conflict. (8) The challenge posed by drug trafficking as a crime related to rebellion or with other political crimes was also addressed. Criminal case law rulings already settled by the Supreme Court will be taking into account, enforcing the principle of most favorable legislation. The complex issue here is in what cases this crime, as political, can therefore be made subject of amnesty. Crimes related to political ones will be strictly those aimed at facilitating or financing rebellion, including illegal conducts but excluding crimes against humanity and conducts which have led to a personal enrichment by rebels. (9) Public financing of FARC political party will be reduced in order to establish an equal treatment with the other political parties.

15 See, for instance, César Rodríguez-Garavito, "La Corte y la paz minimalista," https://www.elespectador.com/opinion/la-corte-y-la-paz-minimalista-columna-695478.

16 https://lasillavacia.com/historia/las-dos-caras-del-golpe-al-fast-track-60989.

17 Gonzalo Ramírez-Cleves, "The Colombian Constitutional Court Rules that the Peace Agreement is Mandatory for Three Presidential Terms," http://www.iconnectblog.com/2017/10/the-colombian-constitutional-court-rules-that-the-peace-agreement-is-mandatory-for-three-presidential-terms/.

18 Bruce Ackerman, *We the People. Foundations* (Cambridge: Harvard University Press, 1993).

19 Id., 6.

18 The long road and the promise

Colombia's peace process as an instance of aesthetic justice

Óscar Guardiola-Rivera

Dramatic justice

The origins of the conflict in Colombia lie in the longer history of conflicts over land and the memory of destruction of ties between territorial communities and their surrounding environments; a memory of violent interventions often justified in the name of progress. Buried deep in that narrative is the problem of asymmetrical historical evolution from pre-capitalist to capitalist formations in the Americas. This requires further analysis if we wish to better understand the power dynamics in these conflicts, the nature of socio-political subjects that in their apparent weakness demonstrate the capacity to withstand the most extraordinary onslaughts, and the role they might play in peace-building processes.

Progress and asymmetry being the content of history in general and Colombian history in particular, the question of the specific forms that the resulting conflicts and conflict-resolution efforts might take is our concern. This question is framed all too often in terms of dualistic formalism: Past versus future, fall and failure versus development, good versus evil or a (Hobbesian) state of nature versus the majesty of the state of law. My problem with this kind of dualism is two-fold. First, after Hegel, we should replace such abstract ethics with the presentation of generic content and particular forms in their identity. But despite our claims to be modern, we continue to behave as if violence and conflict were the result of abstract evil, backwardness or inconstancy, and the villainy of individuals or singled-out groups.

Second, after Fanon, neither trauma is metaphysical nor violence an essence of some people's character. Such essentialisms construed under pretenses of "inconstancy" or metaphysical "lack" and buried deep in dualist conceptions of so-called "peripheral" societies (as southern peoples are often represented) leave no room for thinking in terms of temporality. Formalist accounts of progress and essentialist views of trauma, often expounded in supposedly "color-blind" terms, constitute pathologies of freedom. Their history goes back to sixteenth-century frameworks of justification of domination, forced displacement, enslavement, and exploitation. Let's claim that such formalist-essentialism entails, anthropologically, aesthetically, and historically, a failure of imagination.[1]

We fail to see the dramatic, even tragic character of trauma, and conflict as self-division and self-reconciliation. We fail to appreciate how the promise of peaceful alliances—exemplified by archaic oath—sacrifices and modern peace treaties, which subtract men from the circles of killing and rape instead teaching them to see/hear and speak—dramatize violence in ritual formats. This performativity, rhetoric and symbolic, can intensify registers of speech, memory, and gesture. Moreover, the symbolic dimensions and performative forces at play in dramatic ritual processes such as peace negotiations can open up different historical possibilities within given contexts. They even allow cosmopolitical scale jumps beyond context.

This is why when we analyze peace-building processes such as Colombia's it would be a mistake to remain in the world of law represented within the formalist division of sin and punishment and essentialist frameworks misreading symptoms into pathologies of freedom. Such frames date back to the period of Euro-American expansionism but also inform notions of humanitarianism in flux within current development-security and global disaster management networks. Here, a change of standpoint is required: From law's retributive/restorative justice and its essentialism to higher law, clinical critique, and hopeful aesthetic justice.[2]

Let's speak of higher law as what is right from the perspective of the rights of the victims (mostly women in Colombia's war) and their optional claims. Thus, in a similar sense to that which GWF Hegel and Phillis Wheatley before him called "natural right" and its treatment of the tragic. "How well the cry for liberty, and the reverse disposition for the exercise of oppressive power over others agree, I humbly think not require the penetration of a philosopher to determine," said Wheatley. She was speaking of the need to treat reversals as a unity-of-opposites, and to verify their agreement through poetic means if we're to vindicate the "natural rights" of those displaced and dispossessed. Similarly, Hegel interpreted poetic tragedy as presenting the simple identity of particular conflicts and the universality of ethical life, or the cry of liberty to action against oppression. And, therefore, the need to focus on the confrontation between powers grasped on the immanent movement of their agreement in his 1802 *On the Scientific Ways of Treating Natural Right* and the *Phenomenology*. Their point isn't to dismiss conflict (as do those who declare it outside the political, or merely "terrorist") but on the contrary to place it at the heart of a practical notion of negotiations and agreements as transformative oppositions and techniques of freedom.[3]

This paper understands negotiations and agreement in the wake of conflict as a transformative opposition. Let's speak of peace agreement in this sense, not merely in terms of its significance but in terms of its symbolic meaning as orientation. This means to place an emphasis on the communicative and transformational potentialities of peace negotiations, their capacity to fabricate new moral images of the world that in their impatience of oppression call us to transformative action here and now. Both as a critical intervention into the narrative-imaginary constructions of ideologies and history that refuses being stuck in legalistic understandings of rights and justice, and, rhetorically speaking, as protreptic performative actions that shift the perspective of participants towards questioning failed essentialisms thereby rectifying the orientation of processes of institutional injustice that result in continuing relations of oppression, exclusion, and erasure. These critical acts and interventions provide alternative moral world images, principles, and symbolic forms, thereby dramatically intensifying experiential approaches to institutional dialogue.

A clear example of what is meant in this paper by symbolic-narrative justice, aiming at a new understanding of rights and justice as "aesthetic" is the practice of Colombian artist Carlos Motta. His *Six Acts: An Experiment in Narrative Justice* involves a series of dramatic readings of historical speeches by radical political leaders murdered during the bloody civil war in Colombia. Staged in the period leading up to the 2010 presidential elections in Bogotá, these speech "acts" sought to break free from mainstream judicial frameworks and failing institutional forms of reparation. Instead, they focus on effective ways of intervening the representational system that manifests violence, oppression, feminicide, and thus a politics of social justice and activism.

Using documentary forms, fiction, and performance strategies, these experiments try to construct "spaces for social and political interaction based on the memory of violent and traumatic events." Memory may be restorative/re-constitutive of the statu quo ante, or not. If the former, memory nourishes the economy of jouissance (*goce*, in Spanish) that's specific to capitalist discourse. But the artist's memory (like that of negotiators) isn't restorative of given institutions/relations. Rather, adding to Motta's very apt characterization of aesthetic justice practices, they facilitate encounters towards new alliances and alternative futures. Not only a new distribution of surplus value but a mutation in the subject's relation to what Pierre Yoyotte called "the misery of desire."[4]

Whereas critics of peace-building negotiations and agreements often underestimate the political potential of an event of encounter, the efficacy of some of the "acts" in Motta's *Six Acts* demonstrate the exact opposite: the event's powers of activation of a site of conflict, subtracting subjects from the circle of killing and raping. "In colliding a symbolic gesture with the so-called social needs of the public," material as well as symbolic (including ending the symptomatic circularity of psychotic rulers/fetishized rules and the masses' misery of desire), the efficacy of such acts of ritualization of conflict and violence can create a democratic platform of transformative exchange.

Motta's experience is confirmed by a long and rigorous set of studies carried out in a variety of disciplines. From psychoanalysis and neuroscience (where Motta's notion of aesthetic justice originates) to the anthropology of war and peace rituals among Amerindians. Also, theories of ritual performance in classical contexts (such as the well-known "oath by scepter" episode in Book 1 of Homer's *The Iliad*) and the critical theory of the political sense of symbolic forms. Following the work of these artists and researchers, I deploy the question of the fetish/symbol, its symptomatic nature and performative force, and the normative sense of socio-historical formations. I'll ask two questions: "What is the sense of a peace process such as Colombia's?" and "Why today, at every level of our flattened institutional hierarchies, is the place of the ruler (the decider, the exception, the post-*Führer*) the preferred one that enables psychotics to treat their erroneous wandering (*errancia*, in Spanish) by mistreating/sowing hatred of neighbors?" Hopefully, by the end we'll get some answers.[5]

Peacebuilding as ritual

The notion of historical (or "archaic") formations is singularly fit for our purpose. It comes from research focusing on progress as the content of history, and on the meaning of the decay located at the heart of progress which serves as a symptom. The correlation between symptom and decay (*corrupción/contagio*, in Spanish) helps us theorize not only the opposition between forces of progress and reaction, but also the question of what doesn't work in progress and the sense of conflict and negotiations.

Such notions seek to analyze the progressive separation of men and women from the earth, body and land, as their natural laboratory. This process starts with groups and communal forms of relation with the earth, land, and bodies, their rituals, and institutional attitudes. Original communities may undergo dissolution through war, servitude, and then primary allegiance to the rites of the virtual (heroic visuality, our preference for patriarchal glory and death to life and becoming allies with former enemies). Thereafter, individualization: The dividual autonomy of conservative institutions of subjectivation before community and common dwelling. Hence, also, the elevation to the dignity of the transcendental of the various strategies/rules/laws for control over land and time, and the administration of bodies and resources that become established and impose themselves. Ultimately, these tendential developments transform the former community into a de-humanizing mechanism that (although it makes individualization possible) stands outside of and becomes increasingly hostile to individuals and historical groups, making history appear as if it had arrived at its end.[6]

Taking account of these formations, which are as material as they're symbolic, is of crucial importance. Not only to understand the conflict in Colombia and its (for the moment, stalled) resolution, but also the implications for a theory of greater justice and real transformation. This is the case insofar as history, which in the context of persistent conflict and destruction can only appear to most of its agents as bad history (injustice-as-lack being the result of such bad history, rather than some inevitable fate from above), is nevertheless pregnant with possibility and alternatives. In other words, conflicts and negotiations take place because of the other—not some faceless other but seeing/speaking others, other lives, and spacetimes that matter. Put otherwise, the place of language/memory is divided by the subject (or language divides the subject, providing it with imaginings and productive memory, and in doing so constitutes the subject). This division, experienced as a fall in/from history (damnation, in the Fanonian sense), gives rise to a quotient and a residue/remainder, which cannot be symbolized or reduced according to the conventions of linear perspective, contractual laws and property frameworks.

Not all of the real and not all of the time (the Not-Yet) can be represented within such frameworks. Language fails us here, and negotiations must take stock of such failure. A question arises here: Given such failure what is to be done from here onwards? What's to be done in Not-Yet time? How can the stumbling block of our symptom become a token of life? We can explore such questions and implications by taking seriously the role played by what I've called before "formations," both material and symbolic, objective and subjective, in the analysis of social conflicts such as Colombia's and the prospects for peace and transformation.

Real transformation is the most important aim of a peace process, as Navy Pillay has observed. Speaking of the singular-generic sense of the Colombian peace process a few weeks before stepping down as United Nations Human Rights Commissioner, Pillay articulated better than most the relationship between the powers of resistance of "archaic" territorial communities victimized during a conflict that has also affected others and the prospects of real transformation. Pillay stressed the viability of such communal forms: Their capacity to develop together with the rest of the country into a higher form of peaceful co-existence and economy. She spoke of the possibility of a transformation that would involve "a change in the given power dynamics, from victim to survivor and agent of rights and claims" after the conflict's resolution:

> It's important to listen to the victims [both the 6,5 million officially recorded as such during the process, as well as the statistically non-representative group that were present in the Havana exchanges] because they're likely to make representations of and speak to the two mechanisms that weren't felicitously enacted in previous peace processes. The first one has to do with the mechanisms that would make it possible to transform the lives of those most directly affected by the war -in fact the lives of all Colombians-through the production of a wider and more intensive affect or feeling of inclusion. Such [real] transformation, social and individual, is the most important goal, so that the violations of the past can become a catalyst for positive change.[7]

Challenging the periodization proposed by historians and *violentólogos* engaged in the erasure of an image of history from below, and after the conclusions of the II Russell Tribunal and Pillay's comments, let's chronicle the succession of wars in Colombia and elsewhere in the Americas as constitutive and contemporary of a totalizing history of predation. This predatory history would concern the attempts to erase or mask the events of the past and current efforts to crush any hope that, out of the traces of the interrupted projects of the past, alternative worlds and different futures might emerge here and now.

In that respect, Pillay refers to a series of past violations that can become a catalyst for positive change. She speaks of injustices as the result of past history and deems most of that history to be bad if and when seen from below.

The former United Nations High Commissioner for Refugees characterizes so-called "victims" as agents. Not passive, but fully responsible for their apparent weakness and capable not only to withstand the most violent onslaughts but also to engage in a dramatic intensification of their lived experiences of the past, thereby capturing a multiplicity of feelings. Such affects belong to different orders: Axiological, aesthetic even logical. But they're a common presence in the victim's testimonies and interlocutions in dialogical situations taking place during peace negotiations. These statements cannot be judged individually, nor through a set of statements that would supposedly expose the true meaning of the feelings made present. Lured and gathered by ritual images and propositions, these affects can undergo a "dramatic intensification." This is to say that the job of such propositions in peace-building negotiations is to produce an intensification of affects, or to increase the importance of the lived experience and the historical events which these affects or memories are attached to.

In other words, they aim to value. What they value, or increase the value of, is the set of possibilities and other courses of history. They (co)exist in superposition at the heart of every event and history in general. A multiplicity of possible worlds and futures is attached to each act as it plays out. These possible worlds or hopeful *uchronies*, to borrow William James's terminology, aren't mere didactic or heuristic tools. They're conditions of intensification, a life-transforming rise in importance and value. They make re-humanization possible in concrete situations of de-humanization. Conversely, negotiation-propositions aim also to devalue jouissance, the pessimist affect that emerges from situations in which victim-others are at the disposal of some subject.[8]

Pillay refers to the potential of the victim's speculative and hopeful presentations neither in the abstract nor in the pure a priori realm of restorative/retributive morality (the realm of generalized victimhood in which there would be no specific perpetrators but only generic "evil" and exceptional evildoers). Rather, she speaks in the context of Colombia's concrete events in which women and territorial communities came to be at the disposal of warlords and other self-interested parties. Hence, the job of the victim's participation in peace negotiations is to provide their speculative presentations with a concrete milieu that gives them their consistency, as symptomatic of nonrelations (lack) and fullness to come.

This shows two things that have been absent from previous peace processes, as Pillay says. First, it's wrong to assume peace processes result in judgments or decisions for the world. Their institutional make up isn't decisionism. They simply articulate events differently. Put simply, the hopeful action of the victims in a peace process such as Colombia's is principled. Second, the point of peacebuilding is to wonder what it would be like to think of local history and the infinity of hope in terms of the principled elimination of lack and the thirst of lack-in-jouissance of others, and wonder whether we must think of our human societies as in a constant state of war.

Let's understand "principle" very precisely. It indicates, on the one side, the idea of a beginning in all its power or as different beginning. On the other side, the principle is capable of leading that beginning towards the future showing us the direction to follow. A principle makes normative sense in that respect, that is, orienting. Beyond instituting this or that solution as guaranteed destination or a model (for instance, "capitalism" or "communism"), there's a more impatient, urgent necessity: That all are satisfied. That no one should lack more than is necessary, no one should suffer poverty or be marked as damned.

"The people," constituted as such through this act of principled invention, can be sure they won't lack the necessities so long as "the public granaries are full." Some may conceive this movement solely in terms of productive forces and relations of production—as redistribution of wealth. Necessary (or utopian) though this action may be, it wouldn't be sufficient. There's also the matter of small differences: Envy and pessimism invading public space. This small matter of different feelings might make all the difference, as the result of the referendum on the Final Accord between the Colombian Government and the Revolutionary Armed Forces of Colombia (FARC) demonstrated.

This syndrome of small differences and widespread pessimism always gives the advantage to the smoke and mirrors of mass image consumption and capitalist infotainment; to the reality TV presenter and the baby-faced "moral" character of melodrama becoming president-for-life. To avoid such fate, we need not become saints. But more like an association of poets in dialectic relationship with the institution. This means society need not be legalist to be active. Necessary though the law may be, it's only constructive if subjects, like good readers of poetry and keen spectators of drama, know how to mark out its boundaries and take over the stage in order to speak and make the law by themselves. The injunction is this: Learn to live without masters! In Colombia's case, this is "the Spirit of '91" related to the student movement and the constitutional process that in 1991 urged a passage from merely representative to "participatory" democracy. This is also what I've called "the axiom of equality": A hope-principle-of-orientation.

The shift from "solutions" to the generic level of principle is essential. Not only to understand what a peace-building process is really about, but also to read properly any peace accord. That's the stumbling block stalling Colombia's peace process after the Havana negotiations. This stumbling block is our symptom and must become a token of life. The beginning of another association and different institutions. I believe this shift from the particular to the universal did not take place for many Colombians, especially those whose relation to the war tended to happen at the more or less safe distance of spectators well grounded in their city dwellings, looking at the (mostly rural) theaters of the war through the window of their television devices and getting off on such images.

For the most part, these spectators kept reading the Peace Accord in the key of melodrama; that is, looking only for solutions to their current needs and jouissance. They sought to unify participants and parties to the Accord as others, putting them in a box, imagining them as the proverbial villains of soap operas. And the spectators, them themselves, were represented as pure victims. As such, they could impute evil to these others, labeling or representing them in terms of a perverted language ("communists," "gender ideology," etc.). This was the attitude towards the Peace Accord championed by the forces of reaction in Colombia. When called upon to respond yes or no to the Peace Accord in the already reductive horizon of a referendum, these sectors of the Colombian population voted in accordance with their jouissance, indebted to their Father figure. This meant a marginal but crushing victory against the ratification of the Accord. The experience of conflict and of conflict resolution that territorial communities began articulating differently in connection with their archaic historical formations into a transformative narrative and a principle of action became de-intensified. But I also believe that out of this symptomatic experience can emerge a different relationship between the associations and other institutions, such as the Special Jurisdiction for Peace (JEP).

If a peace-building effort can be treated as a ritual, the force of which comes to be symbolized by the written accord or a handshake (such as that between President Juan M. Santos and FARC's Timochenko), then its success or felicity as a ritual invitation or a gift, the gift of time, depends on the acceptance of the addressees or the participation of an audience that lets go of its jouissance. It can turn a momentary (even inconsequential) association into a new institutional relation. What matters is the acceptance of the gift and the addressees' radical investment in the process which thereafter makes them into a "people" (in combat with wannabe kings) where none really existed before.

After evil

The aim of a peaceful settlement is to make the ongoing effects of bad history go away, if not forever at least for a while. Such is the case of the negotiations resulting in the 2016 Peace Accord between the FARC and Colombia's government. It paved the way for the experimental approach to justice which is the principled spirit incarnated in the recently created JEP. The principles of such institutional creativity, its political spirit, resonate with the ideas of optional and aesthetic justice vis-à-vis historical formations presented above.

Theories of aesthetic and optional justice developed by Pascal Gielen, Ian Ayres, Robert Meister, among others—which are analogous to experimental practices in contemporary art and clinical-critical approaches to ritual/symbolic formations—can serve as a welcome counterbalance to mainstream conceptions of transitive and transitional justice.

The latter present the moment of ("democratic") transition as a historically specific end for what used to be known in political economy as "theories of (linear) transition towards socialism." For in accordance with the mainstream conception of transitive/transitional justice, nothing else should follow having done just enough to achieve an additional measure of political stability after conflict. Especially, nothing that might affect the economic advantage of the ongoing beneficiaries of (past) conflict and development. The aim to achieve closure becomes the goal of transitional justice, as in South Africa, Brazil, and Argentina's amnesty laws (though in the latter case such amnesty was reversed, and economic beneficiaries had recently faced the possibility of some other kind of justice).

Closure is also the decisive blind spot of the tradition that started with the Nuremberg trials. Perhaps also the reason why the latter were easily fetishized and assimilated into a pacifying, coercive system for interpreting and managing tragedies, achieving cultural and political catharsis, and self-affirmation (non-negotiation). This system would fit the overarching narrative of a transitional justice project in which closure is closely linked to forgiveness of sin and punishment. In this conception of transitional justice, injustice is seen as an evil cycle of recrimination or mimetic violence to be replaced by a juridical, cathartic, or therapeutic process. The objective is to foreclose the cycle and erase the histories of primitive accumulation and the origins of "white historical capital." The iconic Nuremberg trials came to be treated as an idol. A fetish or totem/taboo addressing the general population rather than the officials (the state military and paramilitary, the politicians, their industrialist national and foreign masters, etc.).

This absolute population, having more or less confessed their collective sin, which in a perverse reversal becomes a claim to generalized victimhood with no structural perpetrators, except for a few evil men, promise that in the future they will steer clear from committing human rights violations. In this way, they not only expect to prevent such violations but also internalize such past future, when violations happened that may happen again, so that they may learn to draw analogies between their feelings about the past and their likely future feelings about the present.

But if a new emergency, a terrorist attack, a pandemic, or a "humanitarian" crisis once again persuades them that there's no time for (historical) justice now, they can then go back to their previous attitude of conformity with the claims of a decider authority. They know if things go awry once again, they can once more feel that in their heart of hearts they would've resisted had they known. This "culture of human rights" anticipates regrets, for it may now and again condone human rights violations out of exceptional deference to an expansive executive authority and "factual" claims that may be proven wrong in hindsight. In such a culture it is always too soon or too late, and, so, the time for refusal or action is never. Being primarily oriented towards the semblance of the interior, catharsis and jouissance, and morally righteous conviction, a normative assessment of the external situation is pushed to the extreme point of complexity without asymmetry: "Be good by being true to yourself. If your 'facts' are proven wrong after the onset of renewed war and intervention, at least be sure you acted out of moral conviction in the name of mankind. You can then go back to respecting human rights and go shopping."

This conduct commits the fallacy of authenticity: "a form of bad faith that turns human beings away from social reality to focus on the self and forms of cultural", imaginary as well as particularistic historical closure." The result of which is "the erasure of human possibility." This conduct is both a semblance of truth and a failure of the imagination. And tends to collapse into self-sustaining moralistic purity. This is so because the search for the genuine article turns into one for the unadulterated, "what is not polluted by the impact of outsiders." This is the ultimate meaning of "be good by being true to yourself": Alienated, insufficient identity with the self and getting off on others. To conduct ourselves as if we lived in a world without others. Politically speaking, a culture that makes it so easy to go back respecting human rights is also one that makes it easy to violate them time and again.[9]

That perspective is neither new nor sophisticated. It's a successor to the conventions on perspective and early stereological viewpoint that helped sixteenth-century speculative jurists–theologians such as Francisco de Vitoria and Luis de Molina frame their considerations about the causes of the differential status of peoples around the world in terms of essential (geo-cultural) characteristics, thereby laying the foundations of imperial juridical doctrine. Especially, doctrines of just war (*ius belli*) and the "free" trade of goods and bodies (*emptio et venditio*). In the wider context of theories of justice, these would help introducing the idea of the unity of all places on the (spherical) surface of the earth and its representation on a bidimensional plane (amenable to numerical/probabilistic calculation and administration) together with correlative concepts of original community, appropriation ("original acquisition" of land title) and will (including the will to jouissance in the supposed lack of the will of others). These helped establish the grounds of property, political authority, and the wealth of nations.

It's well known that the early twentieth century pioneers of "American International Law" in the USA rediscovered this viewpoint in the wake of the Civil War, failed Reconstruction and the emergence of the Manifest Destiny doctrine in the period between the Mexican-American War, the

Spanish-American War and the Great War. At the time, the USA confronted the option to deepen its revolutionary origins or become an empire. Pioneers like James Brown-Scott and Elihu Root reinvented the legacy of baroque speculative geography, linear demarcation and perspective, and "classical" international law, thereby providing an institutional niche for an older morality of fortress and fortitude under the new conditions of white settlerism at home and abroad. That is, in the direction of what Benjamin Allen Coates has termed America's "legalist empire." Less known is the fact that such pioneers applied their theoretical re-interpretations of that tradition to the new situation arising in the wake of the Civil War and external wars. Crucially, white settlers were not merely recipients of land under the 1860s Homestead Acts but also acted as paramilitary agents by turning their weapons against indigenous and black peoples in the West Coast, in Nicaragua, Panama (then part of Colombia) and elsewhere. The demonization of indigenous ways basic to their social tissue was part of that process. Hence, it is not a coincidence that these same pioneers used their legal expertise to invent the "war on drugs" well before the 1961 UN Narcotics Convention, with enduring and disastrous consequences for the prospects of peace and historical compromise in places such as Colombia. The point here is to emphasize the parallelism between white-settler desire for land, paramilitarism, and the war on drugs as an institutional vehicle for land dispossession and cultural genocide before it was applied in 1990s Colombia. Rather than being a minor event in the post-war architecture of modern and contemporary international law and human rights, continued homesteading by paramilitary civilian-deputies of colonialism and the invention of the "war on drugs" to disrupt indigenous and peasant ways of life and their access to resources has been a major precursor of all wars on noun, up to and including the "war on terror," counterinsurgency wars, humanitarian interventionism, and contemporary global disaster management.[10]

Such is the outlook that threatens to drown the spirit of peace-building efforts in Colombia and elsewhere. Combining older elements of neomercantilism and naturalism with Smithian and Lockean liberalism with the more recent faith on the stochastic predictability of uncertain events, it has resulted in an obsession with security and paranoia vis-à-vis virtual "contaminants." This faith is tainted throughout by the hidden trace of justifications of slavery and fallacious claims to original appropriation and authenticity. It's the common thread uniting people as diverse as Karl Rove, Donald Trump, John Bolton, Elliot Abrams, Álvaro Uribe Vélez, and the reactionary forces currently doing their utmost to reduce to size the Peace Accords and Colombia's JEP while exporting the war elsewhere. Their viewpoint reduces time to space and the latter to the (transcendent) form of an empty background within which things and events emerge without dimensionality or rhythmic force. Such a view re-actively forecloses the future in symbolic and informational terms.[11]

The alternative, defended throughout this paper, is to introduce the active reality of time in relation not only to the quest for normative orientation in our theories of justice and the question concerning possibility and progress in history, but also as a way to sharpen, even reinvent, our critical tools and symbolic forms so as to better our analyses of the currency of war ideologies and jouissance in the context of a predatory capture of the subject by capital itself. I refer thus to the zombie mixtures of neo-mercantilism, *kriegsideologie*, masculine jouissance, economic liberalism, and technologies of prediction/foreclosure that predominate among rulers in the 21st century. In asking for (symbolic) forms and principles to abolish the hunger of others (Navy Pillay's "real transformation") and to question whether we must live in societies of unending war, we aim to overcome this situation, retro-futuristically. In the direction of a different beginning.

Symbols and orientations

"How does something become a symbol?" This question is crucial for our understanding of peace-building and human rights, their economic and political dimensions. Let's consider it with the aid of something humbler than the philosopher's thought experiment: An experimental story.

The story in question is old but speaks to the future. A story of ritual alliance and peacemaking involving a shaman seer and a warrior who join forces to denounce the corruption of existing institutions of justice abused by politicians and kingly leaders. Pursuing their own interests, the latter had led their people into a seemingly unending war of pillage and plunder. In the course of that war, women and others came to be at the disposal of these abusers. The story also concerns the origin and content of social obligations, their creation and role in the ritual fabrication of social time, and how they emerge out of seemingly empty ritual forms such as a handshake, a negotiation or an oath. It's the story of the oath by scepter in Book I of *The Iliad*.

Focus on the scepter, or any other such materials that foreground the performance of an oath or compromise in situations of ritual dialogue and communication in negotiation. How does a thing become a symbol of peace? For instance, a piece of wood that becomes a scepter, a textile a text—an inscribed piece of paper—which indexes and points to new times of enduring peace. It undergoes a first death, so to speak. An axe cut it from the tree it belonged to, whose leaves and branches sang as the wind passed through them, resounding nature. Nature and its rhythm are the original force that infuses with its spirit man-made institutions. No longer will it bloom fruit after having been cut and carved by bronze or fire, these elements of destruction acting in the service of creation of human culture.

By its first death, the plant's shoot escapes the logic of nature's entropy, the linear succession of points in time subject to *fortuna*. The wood's piece has escaped the field of chance and randomness to become an artifact in art and culture, a historical or symbolic formation. Both in archaic and modern societies, this phenomenon has been thought about in terms of the sense of ritual communication in drama or tragedy. It has been observed that ritual communication tends to be more restricted in precision and flexibility than so-called ordinary speech. Experts in conflict mediation and peacebuilding often tap into this aspect of dialogical situations by setting the parties involved apart from ordinary spaces, creating around them a scenario that invokes the golden times before divisions took place, projected way back into tradition, the inchoateness of the founders, or some other sense of the sacred.[12]

In turn, the audience-participant to the ritual would tend to project their own understanding upon the ritual intention, which the see/hearing audience may deem to be the intention of an implicit author, "founding fathers" or the ancestors. The inchoateness of the latter allows for the negotiation of meaning by all participants and thus a plural (but limited) variety of interpretations by parties and participant audiences. Meanings and their correspondent signs and signifiers float along the parameters of established paradigms.

Like other acts of communication, the grammar of ritual negotiation involves standard paradigmatic and sequential syntagmatic associations. The interpretation of paradigms by (performer) interlocutors and audience tends to be more restricted in the case of ritual communication due to the relatively invariant shape of the ritual and the tradition that gives rise to it; here, the tendency is to stress equivalence over difference.

Consider the actual case of the negotiations between FARC and the Colombian government that took place through a more discreet channel B set up in San Sebastián, Spain, in which I participated while the main talks were taking place in Havana. Notice, first, that both locations were consciously set apart from ordinary ones. In the case of the temporary channel B set up in the Basque country of Spain, talks concerned the fate of a Colombian Army General retained by FARC that threatened to derail the conversations happening in channel A.

Talks in San Sebastián quickly floated towards the usual rigid stereotypes of rural/urban, order/lawlessness, etc. Our job as performing experts and mediators consisted not only in stressing identity behind such perceived paradigmatic differences, but also, appealing to the more or less direct experience of those involved, maintaining a balance between these very different types of experience while ensuring their relevance for orienting oneself. Yet this capacity also entails an additional job: Assigning trust to the orientation that differentiation may provide, or value intensification. Arguably, we did so by mobilizing floating signifiers of difference along more strict paradigms: It may have been the case that the Army General "retained" by the guerrillas was selling protection services to (illegal) mining operations, while the guerrillas behaved in those areas as if it were the state. This demonstrated the extent to which the persistence of war was having unintended consequences, perhaps against the original intent of their actors. This confirmed the need for the parties involved and the audiences of Colombia's theater of war to shift their perspective and focus on the "counterproductivity" of an "unending" conflict that betrayed original intentions and, moreover, the intent of Colombia's founders (which both parties tend to claim as part of their legitimacy narratives).

Moving closer to and then away from the intentionality of the actors, stressing identity/balance between their different affirmations along a certain paradigm and the possibilities of trust, allowed for a paradigmatic shift. This example goes to show the degree to which dialogical (ritual) performances enjoy a poetic property that results from the projection of the paradigmatic over the syntagmatic axis. To be precise, this poetic property is what rhetoricians refer to as the "protreptic strand" of communication opposed to the "persuasive strand."

While most students of rhetoric and ritual communication tend to overemphasize the weight of paradigmatic patterns by understanding them as near-unchangeable, formal repeatable conventions that "freeze time," as it were, in our practical experience the opposite was the case: The very repeatability of signs/symbols floating along paradigmatic contextual dimensions allows for powerful transformation, trust assigning or value intensification and change beyond the predictions of any conventional system, and the performative hierarchies of standard types and tokens that it organizes. This focus, more attentive to the actual experience of mediators and negotiators in the field, can open the way towards a conception of signs and symbols beyond pure formalism or strict linguistics; one more capable of engaging the field of feigned identity, the vicissitudes of trust, failed recognition, and radical investments that constitute the reality of transhuman/inter-temporal relations. In the latter, the realm of public appearance and presentation, (ritual) communication and negotiation appear as intensely and imaginatively participatory rather than based on some sort of closed textuality and context.[13]

Isn't this precisely—a renewed focus on radical investment and intense/imaginative participation rather than closed textuality—what researchers like Roman Jakobson or Claude Lévi-Strauss and Jacques Lacan observed about poetic and perceptual thought together with their interlocutors? Isn't this also what thinkers and philosophers of the tragic were getting at? If so, what would be the implications for the study and practice of peacebuilding?

For now, let's consider the poets' interpretation of drama, symbolic performance, and tragedy: A potential divided justly and equally, which appears "not in its original strength, but rather, in its weakness." Like a once-living body, or a sacrificial victim facing death and resisting a most violent onslaught coming back to give away its self, becoming a symbol. The symbol in ritual performance, negotiation, and communication lends its force and spirit to give birth to human institutions. We speak thus of an "original thing" in the event of its presentation: The light of life, birth, bodies human and nonhuman giving birth, bodies' labor, which quite properly reveal the weakness of every whole, the contingency of time, or the incompleteness of reality and history.[14]

Anthropologists in dialogue with the original territorial communities of southern Colombia and elsewhere in the Americas have observed in their peace-building ceremonials of vengeance and ritualized violence the appearance of these signs/symbols of orientation, and also in their speculative geographies. They call them "zero-value" or symbolic institutions. They've no intrinsic function other than that of establishing the preconditions for the existence and constitution of the social system to which they belong; devoid of significance (=0) they enable the social system to exist as a whole.[15]

Anthropologists were then confronted with a problem, which their discipline seemingly shares with linguistics and other experimental theories of performance, communication, mind, and action. This problem appears too in the practice of working for peace, in peace studies, and in the history and philosophy of rights, as the fundamental question of "natural rights." Put simply, the issue at stake here is that of the proper relation between nature and art, the fabrication of the social and of different social futures as well as the role played by instituting memory in such fabrications out of conflict situations.

We speak not of a "sociological function of war," dear to social scientists such as Florestan Fernandes or Pierre Clastres who conceived of violence as the constitutive and contemporary element of "archaic" formations. Rather, our aim is humbler: To avoid any such instrumentalist interpretations. They may easily end up justifying war as a functional means towards some purported end: Autonomy, harmony, or the reproduction of society. Such inverted (perverse) means/end logics make no sense in contexts where war has been coextensive with society, whether traditional or contemporary. Like Colombia.

I propose something different: That this problem (of zero-degree institutions/"natural" rights) can be better understood, perhaps even solved, if we follow the example of the anthropologists' interlocutors, the poets, and the philosophers of tragedy. People like Phillis Wheatley and Samson Occom (1774), Friedrich Hölderlin (1798), and Georg Hegel (1803) reflected upon the existential condition of larval subjectivities, which in their weakness could withstand the most violent onslaughts, showing us all a way out of circular violence and into higher forms of relation and co-existence. Importantly, Wheatley was herself an African slave taking a dialogical negotiating position together with Amerindians like Occom, a Mohegan author, before and in combat with the unconditional self-affirmation of their wannabe masters in the context of conflict and revolution in the Americas.

These activists, poets and philosophers of the tragic, to an extent reflecting on and oriented by their own tragic condition, also show the possibility of such higher forms in history. Historical forms such as the ones they speculated about and struggled for in practice. In them, the relation between two parties in conflict, taken as units, could be seen from an entirely different perspective: As a continuous and involuted entity, inward growing and properly interminable. Thus understood, social-political relations could no longer be interpreted simply dualistically, in terms of pre-given unities or binary (non)relations. And the historical memory of such relations couldn't be represented among the usual figures of reminiscence and restoration (*aletheia*, mimesis) or, in terms of the recovery and security of "our" given society and values (Being, or an ontology of the same in history) against the supposedly corrosive assault of allegedly external becomings. It's in these figurations of memory as pure/mimetic practices and their corresponding ontologies of sameness that notions of "cultural identity" and ideological constancy tend to emerge. That is, the "us/them" Manichean logic that writers like Frantz Fanon correctly attributed to the legacy of colonial (non) relations.

Instead, according to the Afro-Amerindian poets and thinkers cited above together with their European interlocutors, the relation between two parties in situations of conflict and peace-building is neither unity nor duality but something almost exactly in between. Something radical, in the most precise and rigorous sense of the term ($=\sqrt{2}$). Brazilian anthropologist Eduardo Viveiros de Castro explains this means we must take all things concerning the foundations of society by the root; beginning with zero-degree symbols and institutions, such as the north-south axis found in Amerindian speculative geography and architecture, or a tree that's no longer just wood but also the foundational seat of a community, or a piece of paper in which the image of a peaceful and interminable relation between formerly warring parties appears, or the handshake that ritualistically seals a peace agreement.[16]

Generally speaking, these constitute the panoply of rhetorical foundations of society and the possibilities of history. As such, they lure our affects and become the underpinnings of our radical investments, acts, and actions.

It's in that sense that we may speak of a peace treaty or an alliance becoming, such as that described in the oath by scepter episode of Book I of *The Iliad* concerning the joining of forces between the prophet Kalchas and warrior Achilles against the corrupt authorities of the Achaeans, as a symbol. Now the victim ($=0$) is no longer dead wood but a scepter, the once living thing coming to be the radical spirit of man-made fabrications and futures ($=\sqrt{2}$): An *underlier, Das Ding*, retrospectively *entrusting* us a share of its own life force to energize our political institutions and stability. Just as the tree's no longer a living tree but *Das Ding*, the dead wood is now a scepter or a textile now an open text, which lend their collective effervescence retrospectively to the entire structure of oaths, agreements, rules, valuations, and institutions that historically evolve and revolve around them. This is how something becomes a symbol.

Now there is an *option* to set the underlying scepter, the symbol, in motion. We could swear by it. Make a promise by it. Throw it into the future or set it off with the wind on its sails as if it were a wooden boat in the sea of time. In other words, we *put* a value on it. In addition, there is another option to *call* upon that value, to make possible a rise in importance.

Symbols in oral rituals, dramatic performances, utopias, or euchronies make possible such rise in trust and importance, or intensification. They're key to unlock the function of speculative thought and practice, without which we would be unable to ascertain the value of historical events.

Philosophers of the tragic refer to the possibilities inherent to each and every event as it plays itself out, which dramatize and therefore intensify what has and has not-yet happened, as the "spirit" of history. Anthropologists and their interlocutors have called it *mana*, *hau*, electricity, or effervescence, a total "social fact." If you prefer, think of it pragmatically as the illocutionary, retro-performative effect of an oath. The point is that such possibilities, existing in real time, energize in ritual communication and dramatic negotiations, the underlying instruments from which the value of events, as well as the speculative propositions about them, can be derived (for options too can be valued).

In other words, this *consideration of symbols as underliers of contingent claims* attached to the possibilities inherent to history allows us to speak of historical justice, of the value of historical events, and therefore to consider justice optional. This is, of course, crucial for the thought and practice of what would be required to do for reasons of historical redress in the case of societies facing times of transition out of conflict. Especially in circumstances such as Colombia's, in which the benefits of past injustice have been cumulative, in which an ever-decreasing number of direct victims survive, and in which individual victims would face obstacles proving losses or direct causation on the scale of the cumulative gains made during the conflict or produced by it.

The basic hypothesis I'm advancing on the basis of the aforementioned conception of symbols and alternative courses of history is that a component of present-day social advantage can be attributed in full or part to a past wrong or injustice and that such component can be valued if we introduce contingent historical circumstances and the possibility of their dramatic intensification. Part of the problem here is that before negotiations, beneficiaries of past injustice tend to undervalue victim's claims to historical reparation, and victimized subjects as well as their successors in interest tend not to understand that their value fluctuates over time or overvalue them.

But a solution to that problem might be found in the fact that the performative aspect of negotiations allows for the fabrication of spatiotemporal milieus that provide consistency to the speculative character of the propositions and signs advanced in the course of negotiations. Therefore, it's not only the case that historical grievances can be conceived as options or contingent claims which can be valued (even priced) based on the volatility of an underlying phenomenon, as demonstrated by currently mainstream legal/economic property and options theory. Also, volatility and effervescence can be understood as phenomena connected to collective performative practices. Indeed, anthropology- and rhetoric-based approaches to performance and communication in dialogical situations and negotiations seem to capture the ways in which values and prices, attached to underlying dramatic events in history, and dramatized by the historical possibilities expressed in speech acts or imagery, can be intensified.[17]

A central point is that justice, when considered an option, can be divorced from its underlying symbolized oath or promise. Now the scepter, no longer wood but a symbol for the promises, oaths and legal dispensations of men, not merely a representative but an option, can itself be valued, bought and sold. If so, can the very symbol incarnating the justice of our institutions can be framed and manipulated, or corrupted? To be precise, this means that socio-institutional and market settings become both the gatekeepers of what justice is and of markets of jouissance (which is also the case for contemporary art). This is to say that what we call justice is produced through clusters of reflexive resonances (Gramsci's "it-thinks"), entirely reliant on the informational framing or second-order observation of the justice symbol. Given that framing is constituted and inscribed into the socio-institutional spacetime domain through information (as words on a piece of paper we call contract, for instance, or verbally swearing by a dead scepter, or numbers) and its circulation, then it can be argued that justice is in very general terms an informational landscape. Like contemporary art according to Arthur Danto, whatever is *seen* as justice *is* justice.

Does this mean that we lose any ultimate grounds for justice and, therefore, justice is whatever some now decide to call justice? Yes and no. Yes, we may have lost the capacity to link up grievance claims to any fully transcendent grounds for justice. Critical theorists and legal scholars have been making this point for some time now, also contemporary artists like Carlos Motta. However, given that the framing of justice and its inscription require circulation, and circulation can and does involve dramatic intensification and radical transformation (at least a "radical" form of dualism, as we've seen), then it can be said that progress towards fuller justice does happen in the real-time dimension. We may conceptualize it in terms of scale jumps, vertical as well as horizontal revolutions happening not only in history but also to history (insofar as the idea of revolution expresses the contingency of every nonrevolutionary moment, or the possibility of generalized intensification). Or, as the view that politics can produce an intensified or effervescent connection between two historical moments: Past wrongs and their rectification in now-time. Put simply, this means that history is incomplete. If so, what is seen as the result of past justice this time, and therefore as just this time, cannot be confused with justice in general. Then, no, justice isn't whatever we may now decide to call justice.

When we deal with serious historical grievances in peace-building efforts, we must take seriously the victims' claim that the (derivative) symbols of what we see and call justice this time may have been stripped of their legitimacy and vitality. This was precisely the effect of Colombia's dominant discourse among its political elites and a considerable sector of the population: To reject and disavow, outside of all fields of the symbolic. As a result of such widespread negativity, the order aligned to the dominant discourse swept to one side "my friends" (and "enemies") along Manichean lines. This is "religious love," in which death becomes love: What unites me and my friends. Or rather, it's transformed into yet another commodity, which would count for something. That is, the annihilation of the other, covering up for the fact that there's no relation, no recognition of the purported enemy.

There is jouissance here, *el goce* of something making up for the counterproductivity and loss brought about by unending war. The end result is a loveless world, with the exception of a religious love for (patriarchal) power and money.

Arguably, such is the point made by prophet Kalchas and Achilles in relation to the fate of the women of Troy victimized by the Achaeans' armies in *The Iliad.* The justice symbol has undergone a new death. Death transformed into a substance through its commodification and that of the institutions. Such counterproductivity (the more triumphant the war the more corrupt its victors become) came to be visible in the objectification and rape of the women of Troy that King Agamemnon wishes to keep for himself. Here, rape becomes the law: Penetration is occupation, displacement, dispossession, and accumulation. A second death, which suffuses with its deadly spirit the entire structure of rules, oaths, and the institutions that surround it. Now the scepter incarnates a rape/death-perpetrating culture.

The scepter's second death, this repeated death, becomes mortifying. For it suffuses not only the given structure of rules/institutions of justice with its death spirit but also the bodies of those who swear by this dead scepter, defend it and the values it incarnates with their very soul by going to war, kill and die for it. In connecting the repeated death of the scepter with the imminent death of those who go to war and those killed or violated by it, we've now extended the cost of the scepter's life, taken to serve human institutions, to human bodies that likewise won't bloom again because of the perversion of justice at the hands of corrupting/alienating forces projected into the image of lesser gods, kingly leaders, and deciders that speak for others on behalf of some non-historical or "developmentally superior" standard.

Hence, the singularity of victims' claims: They refer not only to the intra- and inter-personal dimensions of a given society, but also aim to open an interval in inter-temporal dimension. This is crucial. Especially as we examine the kinds of claims made by victims such as the territorial communities affected by Colombia's long civil war.

This is so because, first of all, this dimension is inherent to any promise or institution and remains in a state of latency. Like a hope principle. And, second, our outdated technologies of (global) judgment and conflict management tend to focus almost exclusively on the intra- and inter-personal dimension. However, it's the case that the challenges our institutions now face belong to a different, inter-temporal dimension. This is something we're becoming increasingly aware of as we confront "the climate of history": Climate change, pandemics, automation, and financial violence in the national and international level such as that which has befallen Colombians.

The promise

Let's conclude taking a second look at the more recent iteration of the conflict in Colombia from our renewed perspective. Ditto, the question concerning the counterproductive impact that such traumatic history has had upon the country's institutions became paramount. This is how the question of the effects of war on Colombia's institutions was identified by Sergio Jaramillo Caro, philosopher, High Commissioner of Peace to the Colombian Government during Juan M. Santos's administration, back in 2006.[18]

Put simply, the more the need for military victory became central to those vying for votes and economic power, the more corrupt the institutions waging war in the name of democracy became: A viciously circular relationship ensued between the armies at war. The circles of fatherly "friends" locked in a fatal embrace with their purportedly absolute "enemies," relaunching ever more deathly cycles of war to the detriment of the lives and love of daughters and sons of mothers all over the country as shown in Manuel Correa's 2019 film *The Shape of Now*.

Also, the question of the efficacy of rituals became crucial. The symbols and ceremonials that may reconnect the longer history of the struggle for natural rights with the currently de-politicized discourse of capitalism and human rights, so as to re-infuse the latter with a different political spirit. Which spirit? One of aesthetic justice and optional ways to do away with historical injustice—patriarchal money/power sundering "good" absolutely from "evil." One in which women, most victimized by war, can opt to create a "room of our own." In such a room, the promised Colombia, men are taught how to speak and act rather than kill or rape. This requires the dissolution of the circular/corrupt institutions set up by "friends" (the founding fathers) and the re-construction of a community acting through dissemination, together with "enemies," rather than viral contagion.

Dissolution means here, simply, subtracting men from the mimetic cycles of killing, absolutization of property, and rape deified as "sacred" by the dominant discourse, thereby making impossible their reintegration in such circles. For instance, by re-directing their activity towards "acts" in the streets, as happened during the late 2019 protests, which, if persistent, may create such a risk to financier patriarchs that the latter would be more amenable to letting go of their stranglehold on the common wealth by paying ever increasing premiums with which to finance projects of grander justice: Universal services first and a universal income. Thus, founding a community that acts through dissemination (universal services and income) or a "universal army" of allies in the streets rather than the vicious circles of friends/enemies in the battlefields of rural Colombia.[19]

To get to peace means, here, to shift: To shed one's own powers or social advantages and re-describe the values attached to them without being forced to renounce the "sacredness" of such values. To re-wire behavior: To get from lack of trust and prejudice, to trust and the transformation of one's own self from the enemy's viewpoint. Such move requires generosity of spirit. It requires us to understand what really works in changing behavior, not theirs but one's own. It requires asking the difficult question: "What are our most sacred values?", and, then, the much more difficult gesture of letting go of the part that might link some such values with the habits, mimetic practices, and jouissance that make war "addictive." It takes greatness, as Luis Velasco, President of the Senate during Santos's administration, pointed out. Arguably, such was the greatness of the student movement of the 1990s. And the spirit of the 1990 Colombian Constitution remains infused with such greatness.

Here we must abandon warrior Achilles and side instead with the Amazon, the She-cannibals of the Amazon basin, the Précieuses, Kleist's Penthesilia or the women of The Penelopiad. But that's another story...

Notes

1 Frantz Fanon, *Peau noire, masques blancs* (Paris: Seuil) 176, citing Günther Anders on "pathologies of freedom." Also, *Pour la révolution africaine, Écrits politiques* (Paris: Maspero, 1964) 13–25, containing a genealogy of racist "color-blind" ideology based on the assumption that every symptom presupposes a lesion or socio-psychological deficiency, and (with R. Lacaton) "Conducts of Confession in North Africa (1)," in *Alienation and Freedom* (London: Bloomsbury, 2018) 409–412, with an argument against the formalist contractual assumptions of medical jurisprudence and legal theory. See Claude Lévi-Strauss, *Tristes Tropiques* (London: Penguin Classics, [1955] 2011) 75, for the genealogy of these psycho-social assumptions. For a decisive and more recent development of these arguments, Nicolás Wey Gómez, *Tropics of Empire* (Cambridge, MA.: The MIT Press, 2008) and Ashley J. Bohrer, "Color-Blind Racism in Early Modernity: Race, Colonization, and Capitalism in the Work of Francisco de Vitoria," *Journal of Speculative Philosophy*, vol. 32,2018, pp. 388–99.

2 Carlos Motta and Niels Van Tomme, "Six Acts, Or an Experimental Approach to Justice," in P. Gielen & N. Van Tomme (eds), *Aesthetic Justice. Intersecting Artistic and Moral Perspectives* (Amsterdam: Valiz, 2015) 247–60, on narrative & aesthetic justice. Also, Kojo Koram, *The Sacrificial International. The War on Drugs and the Imperial Violence of Law*, PhD dissertation, supervised by O. Guardiola-Rivera, Birkbeck College School of Law, University of London, 2017, tracing Francisco de Vitoria's on universalist humanitarianism, international law and the more recent US approach to drug policy including foreign policy. And, on the US foreign policy towards Colombia, Santiago Castro-Gómez and Óscar Guardiola-Rivera, "El Plan Colombia, o de cómo una historia local se convierte en diseño global," *Revista Nueva Sociedad,* 175, Sept–Oct 2001.

3 Phillis Wheatley, "Letter to Samson Occom (1774)," in Lisa L. Moore, Joanna Brooks, and Caroline Wigginton (eds), *Transatlantic Feminisms in the Age of Revolutions* (Oxford: Oxford University Press, 2012) 148–9. Peter Szondi, "Hegel," in *An Essay on the Tragic* (Stanford: Stanford University Press, 2002)

15–22. See also, Drucilla Cornell, "Derrida's Negotiations as Techniques of Liberation," *Discourse. Journal for Theoretical Studies in Media and Culture*, vol. 39 (2), 2017, guest-edited by O. Guardiola-Rivera (Detroit, MI: Wayne University Press) 195–215.

4 Carlos Motta, with Niels Van Tomme, "*Six Acts* or an Experimental Approach to Justice. Niels Van Tomme in Conversation with Carlos Motta," in Pascal Gielen and Niels Van Tomme (eds), *Aesthetic Justice. Intersecting Artistic and Moral Perspectives* (Amsterdam: Valiz/Antennae, 2015) 247–58. Also, Pierre Yoyotte, "Anti-Fascist Significance of Surrealism," in F. Rosemont and R. D. G. Kelley (eds), *Black, Brown & Beige. Surrealist Writings from the Diaspora* (Austin: University of Texas Press, 2009) 42–4.

5 For a glimpse at this extensive literature, see, among others, Ernst Bloch, *Abschied von der Utopie?* (Frankfurt: Suhrkamp Verlag, 1980) and *Natural Law and Human Dignity*, D. J. Schmidt (trans.) (Cambridge and London: The MIT Press, 1996); Drucilla Cornell, *Moral Images of Freedom. A Future for Critical Theory* (Lanham, New York, Toronto, Plymouth: Rowman & Littlefield, 2008); Peter Karavites, *Promise-Giving and Treaty-Making* (Leiden: E. J. Brill, 1992); Margo Kitts, *Sanctified Violence in Homeric Society* (Cambridge: Cambridge University Press, 2005); Michael Taussig, *Law in a Lawless Land. Diary of a Limpieza in Colombia* (Chicago: University of Chicago Press, 2005) and *What Color Is the Sacred?* (Chicago: Chicago University Press, 2009); Manuela Carneiro da Cuhna, *Cultura com aspas e outros ensaios* (São Paulo: Ubu, 2009) 78–101; and Zachary Manfredi, "Sharpening the Vigilance of the World: reconsidering the Russell Tribunal as Ritual", in *Humanity*, Spring 2018, 75–91. Also, Pierre Bruno, *Lacan and Marx. The Invention of the Symptom* (London: Karnac Books, 2020) 2–24, for my understanding of symptom, the circularity of decay at the heart of progress, and the opposition of forces of progress and reaction.

6 Álvaro García Linera, *La potencia plebeya. Acción colectiva e identidades indígenas, obreras y* populares (Buenos Aires: Prometeo Libros/CLACSO, 2008) 24. Eric Hobsbawm, "Introduction," in Karl Marx's *Pre-Capitalist Economic Formations* (New York: International Publishers, [1964] 1975) 9–64, especially 24–27, 36 and 51–2 for historical "archaic formations." Also, for a post- or non-Marxian take on a similar theme, see Eleanor Kaufman, "Do Dual Structures Exist? Deleuze and Lacan in the Wake of Lévi-Strauss," in *Yale French Studies, number 123: Rethinking Claude Lévi-Strauss, 1908–2009* (New Haven: Yale University Press, 2013) 83–99; Ernesto Laclau, "Ethics, Normativity and the Heteronomy of Law," in *The Rhetorical Foundations of Society* (London and New York: Verso, 2014) 127–137; Manuela Carneiro da Cuhna (with E. Viveiros de Castro) *Cultura com aspas e outros ensaios* (São Paulo: Ubu Editora, 2017) 78–101; Pierre Bruno, *Lacan and Marx. The Invention of the Symptom* (London: Karnac Books [2010] 2020) 19–24, 27; and Óscar Guardiola-Rivera, *Cómo construir sociedades. Diez cosas que nunca nos dicen sobre la paz y la guerra* (Bogotá: Editorial Javeriana/Pensar, 2014).

7 Navy Pillay, "Comisionada de Naciones Unidas se refiere al proceso de paz en Colombia", *Revista Semana*, August 15, 2014, available on www.semana.com.

8 William James, *The Place of Affectional Facts in a World of Pure Experience*, n. 18, and his letters in "Correspondence de Charles Renouvier et de William James," published by Ralph Barton Perry in *Revue de Métaphysiqu et de Morale,* 36, 1929, pp. 1–35. For a contemporary take on these themes and the relationship between *uchronie* and *utopia*, which informs some of the ideas in these paragraphs, see Didier Debaise, *Nature as Event. The Lure of the Possible* (Durham and London: Duke University Press, 2017) Ch. 3.

9 Robert Meister, *After Evil. A Politics of Human Rights* (New York: Columbia University Press, 2012) 144–74 and 250–285, offering the example of the state official who in his heart of hearts believed in a danger to the community posed by an element problematic to that community; legitimating a declaration of emergency that would justify suspending the law and reacting in defense of the community and its worldview by imputing evil to others. The community responds accordingly, getting off on the disposal of such others.

10 Kojo Koram, *The Sacrificial International. The War on Drugs and the Imperial Violence of Law*, PhD dissertation, supervised by O. Guardiola-Rivera, Birkbeck College School of Law, University of London, 2017; and Óscar Guardiola-Rivera, "Contingency and The Prescriptive Force of International Law, Chiapas-Valladolid, ca. 1550," and Peter Fitzpatrick, "Latin Roots: The Force of International Law as Event" both in *Events: The Force of International Law*, F. Johns, R. Joyce, and S. Pahuja (eds) with a foreword by M. Koskenniemi (London: Routledge, 2011) 29–42 and 43–54. See, Benjamin Allen Coates, *Legalist Empire: International Law and American Foreign Relations in the Early Twentieth Century* (Oxford: Oxford University Press, 2016). Also, Anthony Anghie, *Imperialism, Sovereignty, and the Making of International Law* (Cambridge: Cambridge University Press, 2005) 20; and Marti Koskenniemi, "Empire and International Law; The Real Spanish Contribution," *University of Toronto Law Journal,* vol. 61, 2011, pp. 11–12. Also, Ashley J. Bohrer (2018).

11 Henrique Joner, "Impressions of Luis de Molina About the Trade of African Slaves," *Patristica et Medievalia,* vol. XXXVI, 2015, pp. 39–50 at 41; David Harvey, "Cosmopolitanism in the Anthropology and Geography," in S. Elden and E. Mendieta (eds), *Reading Kant's Geography* (Albany: State University of New York Press, 2011) 267–84; Edward S. Casey, "Is There Still Room for Freedom?," at 285–289, and Jeffrey Edwards, "The Unity of All Places on the Face of the Earth. Original Community, Acquisition and Universal Will in Kant's Doctrine of Right," at 233–63, both included in *Reading Kant's Geography*, for the tradition underpinning neo-imperialism and self-colonization.

12 Tim Phillips, "The Power of Shared Experience," in T. Phillips, M. Albon, I. Breuer, and D. Taffel (eds), *Beyond Conflict. The Project of Justice in Times of Transition* (New York and Verona: Yolanda Cuomo/Editoriale Bortolazzi, 2013) 13–9, and "In gun control debate, sacred human values often forgotten," in *Global Post*, January 8, 2014. Also, Michelle Boorstein, "How neuroscience is offering hope for a more peaceful world," *The Washington Post*, March 4, 2015. For the classical case study of peace negotiations hinted at here, the Oslo Channel that led to the 1993 Oslo Accords between the OLP and the Israeli government, midwifed by diplomats Mona Juul and Terje Rød-Larsen, see J. T. Rogers, "Introduction" to his play Oslo (London: Nick Hern Books, 2017) ix-xii and 14–15 for the contrast between "totalist" and "gradualist" models of negotiation. See also Maurice Bloch, "Introduction," in *Political Language and Oratory in Traditional Society* (London: Academic Press, 1975) 1–28; Valerio Valeri, *Kingship and Sacrifice* (Chicago: University of Chicago Press, 1985) 342 ff.; and Roy Rappaport, *Ritual and Religion in the Making of Humanity* (Cambridge: Cambridge University Press, 1999).

13 See Ernesto Laclau, *The Rhetorical Foundations of Society* (London and New York: Verso, 2014) especially 79–100 and 139–80; Christian Lundberg, *Lacan in Public. Psychoanalysis and the Science of Rhetoric* (Alabama: The University of Alabama Press, 2012) 1–16 and 178–92 on the prophetic/protreptic strand since Aristotle; and Raoul Moati, *Derrida/Searle. Deconstruction and Ordinary Language* (New York: Columbia University Press, 2014), for some theoretical bases for the claims made in these paragraphs. Also, Alexander Kluge, *Difference*

and Orientation. An Alexander Kluge Reader (Ithaca & London: Cornell University Press, 2019) 10–11, 378–433, observing that the vicissitudes of trust are tied to the increasingly mediated nature of social experience and the metamorphoses of postclassical public spheres, which challenge our powers of differentiation.

14 Friedrich Hölderlin, *Sämtliche Werke: Große Stuutgarter Ausgabe*, F. Beißnew (ed.) (Stuttgart: J. G. Cortasche Buchhandlung, 1943–85) vol. 4, 274; "The Significance of Tragedies," in *Hölderlin: Essays and Letters on Theory*, T. Plausible (trans.) (Albany: State University of New York Press, 1998) 89.

15 Claude Lévi-Strauss, "Do Dual Organizations Exist?," in *Structural Anthropology*, C. Jacobson and B. Grundfest Schoepf (trans.) (New York: Basic Books, 1963) 159, and "Introduction," in *Works of Marcel Mauss,* F. Baker (trans.) (London: Routledge and Kegan Paul, 1987), for the classic treatment of this issue. Also, Marcel Mauss, *The Gift: The Form and Reason of Exchange in Archaic Societies*, W. D. Halls (trans.) (New York, H. H. Horton, 1990); and Jacques Derrida, "The Time of the King," in *Given Time I: Counterfeit Money,* P. Kamuf (trans.) (Chicago: University of Chicago Press, 1992).

16 Eduardo Viveiros de Castro, *Radical Dualism: A Meta-Fantasy on the Square Root of Dual Organizations, or A Savage Homage to Lévi-Strauss* (Kassel and Ostfildern: dOCUMENTA and Hatje Cantz, 2012). Also, Manuela Carneiro da Cuhna (with Eduardo Viveiros de Castro), "Vingança e temporalidade: os Tupinambá," in *Cultura com aspas e outros ensaios* (São Paulo: Ubu editores, 2017) 78–101.

17 For mainstream economic and legal theories of property and options, see Ian Ayres, *Optional Law: The Structure of Legal Entitlements* (Chicago: The University of Chicago Press, 2005, 14–5), and for their application to the specific case of historical grievances in market economies, see Robert Meister, *After Evil: A Politics of Human Rights*, 250–259. See also, Elie Ayache, *The Blank Swan: The End of Probability* (Chichester: Wiley, 2010) and Arjun Appadurai, *Banking on Words. The Failure of Language in the Age of Derivative Finance* (Chicago: The University of Chicago Press, 2016) 83–123, for the connection between financial options theories and phenomena of retro-performativity in ritual situations.

18 Sergio Jaramillo Caro, "La crisis subterránea del ejército," in El Tiempo, 11 June, 2006, available at http://www.eltiempo.com/archivo/documento/MAM-2061221.

19 See Fredric Jameson, *An American Utopia. Dual Power and the Universal Army* (London & New York: Verso, 1–96), for my understanding of "universal army."

Part VI

Concluding remarks

19 Outsider reflections

Future peace?

Nancy C. Doubleday

Introduction

As an academic publication, this volume covers extraordinary territory: It travels from the promise of peace, to disappointments, to lessons learned, to reassessment, then to hope for the possibility of peace. In this complex process in search of an agreement and peace, justice exercises demands—for truth, for victims' rights, for new institutional arrangements, fresh reforms in participation, redistribution of land and resource access, and deeper understandings of political, economic, and social rights, including those of groups experiencing the burden of disproportional violence in the conflict and discrimination in the negotiation of the agreement, and also of those who previously saw violent opposition as their only option.

Contributors include key figures within government, parties to the negotiations, academics who investigate transitional justice, social activists who weigh success in terms of justice, as well as legal theorists and jurists who must give life to the Colombian Peace Process (henceforth, the "CPP"). All who contribute here have sought to find recognizable paths through the complexities of the Colombian conflict, of the multifaceted CPP, and of the intra-jurisdictional challenges of creating and negotiating the CPP interface with the pre-existing legal and social contexts of Colombia, to varying degrees. There is sufficient detail, and diversity of direct experience, perspective and positionality among the papers presented here, to give a vivid sense of the dynamic, complex, and fraught nature of the CPP, from the conflict zones, to the negotiation tables, to the corridors of power, and to the plebiscite.

In this chapter, I take a "high-elevation view," as one at a distance from the conflict, yet well apprised of the difficulties reported in this volume by those deeply embedded in bringing about transformatory change, whether in the establishment of the process, the conduct of the negotiations in Cuba, the management of the creation and acceptance of the Final Agreement, or the analysis of successes, challenges, and gaps that reported elsewhere in this volume.

Here we are concerned with the durability of the CPP as an instance of social learning for *just conflict transformation*. The achievements of the

Colombian people throughout the conflict, the negotiations, and the post-Agreement resolution are indisputable, and remarkable, without question, and we can legitimately ask: "What can we learn about making peace through a system view of the social learning revealed by a close reading of the accounts and experiences reported here?" And "how can this view inform our individual and collective practice?"

Clearly, the lessons learned from the Colombian conflict and its resolution by those of us on the periphery include deeper understanding of, and respect for, the distinctiveness of the subject matter of the conflict and the design of the CPP as unique in hemispheric history and distinctive globally. The diversity and range of the substantive concerns and deep knowledge held by the contributors to this volume concerning the legal, political, and social contexts informing justice and peacebuilding in Colombia provide ample evidence of the dynamic nature of the CPP itself.

What is more subtle, and possibly more significant from the standpoint of transferability, is the essential and iterative nature of social learning necessary to enable transitional justice in conditions of intractable conflict. However, there are challenges that the process still must face, including economic justice, democracy and inclusion, and environmental sustainability. In closing, I flag the relevance of international interests and responsibilities. Just as the parties to the conflict have been called upon to take responsibility for victims and their injuries, so must international actors acknowledge their responsibilities, both for good and for harm. Finally, the cultural transmission of social learning for future peace requires individual engagement.

Lessons and achievements

From the periphery, our understandings are of course colored by our own experiences and expectations, but then we have the opportunity to learn, and to reflect, based on the authoritative accounts given in the chapters presented here. The cumulative effect of these chapters is to lead us to identify patterns of interaction, and to deeper understanding of, and respect for specific factors and features of the CPP, and for the process of social learning which enabled it, including the distinctiveness and diversity of the subject matter of the conflict, and of the multiple forces and interests acting on the design of the CPP; the carefully crafted adaptations of the CCP made when obstacles appeared; and the thoughtful responses to difficulties encountered in the ensuing public processes, extended political legitimacy to the Colombian Peace Agreement. The culmination of these heroic struggles for peace is seen in the judgment that, just as the conflict is seen to be unique in duration and complexity, in hemispheric terms, so must all of the dynamics of the stages of resolution also be acknowledged as unique, in terms of the demands made of all concerned for accommodation and flexibility, and also in geopolitical terms, recognizing the role of the international community at all stages (including contributing to the conflict).

While embedded in the history, culture, and conflict of a particular country over a specific timespan, the acceptance of a very broad range of concerns by the CPP for consideration mobilized, motivated, and empowered the participants. The richness of the insights of the contributors who share their deep knowledge of the legal, political, and social contexts informing progress toward justice and peacebuilding in Colombia point to the value of taking a strategic view—meaning one that is inclusive of all interests, both popular and unpopular—coupled with a willingness to accommodate, and to address all grievances, regardless of the inconvenience or polarization that may result.

The dynamic nature of the CPP itself, bringing peace (and not merely ending hostilities), reveals the subtle influence of diverse actors and multifaceted factors, especially the power of inclusion. Throughout the process of negotiation, because the parties to the negotiation were able to use dialogue and compromise, together, to make "space" for others, for divergent views, and for new ideas about the past and the future, they were able to "hold" the intent for an end to the violence. In terms of resilience in social-ecological systems, the players in the CPP became adaptive in order to transform conflict, but were changed in the process—in short, they became adaptive *in order for conflict to be transformed, but were themselves transformed.* At this point, the peace process becomes alive with an existence greater than the sum of its constituents, and those constituents become actively invested in its outcomes. So we see how respectful inclusiveness actively functioning to create "space" allows for an "open system," for evolution, and for emerging concerns to exercise their voices.

Importantly, the essential and iterative nature of social learning, and indeed of peacemaking, necessary to enable transitional justice in conditions of intractable conflict becomes apparent when the long view of the cycles of engagement, consultation, breakdown, and renewal is taken: The resilience of the people, the process, and in some universal idealist sense, of peace itself, is revealed.

In addition to insights as to process and resilience, the contributors also offer intimate views of the construction of new and particular legal architecture, painstakingly negotiated and designed to rectify injustice, recognize asymmetries of power, build trust, and heal the body politic.[1]

First, the breadth of the CPP initiative is stunning—the political will to address the 50 years of civil strife, civil war, "disappeared persons," and victims of violence—in a negotiation directed to ensuring lasting peace, which is unique in the history of the struggles in Colombia. It is also of global interest: The attainment of peace is all too often aspirational, rather than seen as an essential public good, to be secured urgently, at all costs, for the sake of the People, and the Planet, and for sustainable futures everywhere. Concretely, this process moves conflict resolution into a new global framework, expands expectations of access to negotiations, and privileges new forms of restorative justice, specifically since:

> it represents the first negotiated end to a civil conflict in the world under the new international standards of the 2002 Rome Statutes to hold accountable armed combatants who committed grave human rights abuses. It is also the first peace process to have included victims at the negotiating table. Finally, it is the first end to a civil war that does not rely primarily on amnesty for all sides to the conflict, but instead provides new forms of restorative justice in the actual peace agreement, in a compromise effort to reach peace while also holding perpetrators of human rights crimes accountable.[2]

Without question what happened in the conflict, in the CPP, and what has happened in Colombia since the signing of the Final Agreement is unique: It is a singular encounter with a very complex history and potentially transformative peace-building engagement by opening space, in order to be inclusive.[3]

As well, clear evidence of its impact is given. As previously flagged in Chapter 1, this is measurable in human lives, for example,[4] "the demobilization and disarmament of about 7,000 former *Fuerzas Armadas Revolucionarias de Colombia-Ejército del Pueblo*, Armed Revolutionary Forces of Colombia – People's Army (FARC-EP) combatants, a substantial reduction of one of the world's highest homicide rates (from 81.1 per 100,000 inhabitants in 1991 to 25.9 in 2017), as well as bona fide pacts between the guerrilla groups and their victims."[5]

Indisputably, these are stunning achievements.

Equally important and significant are those elements of the Agreement that actively *enact* the changes described by the Agreement, in its principles, its design of new institutions and formal processes, and its extension of a number of solutions for key elements related to the roots of the conflict, and to previous attempts to resolve it. So, we see in this activity the modification of the frameworks of justice within which the measures for resolution of conflict at the roots are to be positioned and exercised, in order to facilitate the necessary changes throughout the conflict creation and resolution process.

The social-cultural-economic-political innovations involved are also noteworthy. In terms of maximizing the transferability of social learning and the knowledge resulting from the CPP and the design of the Final Agreement, while perhaps not embraced by all participants, deep shifts in relations, in perspectives, and in commitment and practice of recognition and inclusion are enabled by the CCP and embedded in the Agreement, importantly including:

- attention to recognition of political rights of marginalized peoples on all sides of the issues, and the design and adoption of measures to address grievances and asymmetries of power, including (inter alia) respect for

all parties and their views; making space in formal processes for nontraditional participants; and attending to past injustices, and attempting restorative and/or transitional measures to address them (instead of looking for vengeance and imposing punishment);
- willingness to acknowledge the existence of the conflict[6];
- willingness to admit the existence of victims[7];
- willingness to look for measures for social healing, such as exercising inclusivity by applying principles of equality and non-discrimination to the recognition of collective rights of social groups to distinct identities and to practical economic innovations (e.g., to collectively own and occupy land)[8];
- recognition of the experience of groups defined by their collective and distinct identities, particularly women, and gendered marginalization of Lesbian, Gay, Bisexual, Trans-sexual, Intersexual, Queer (LGBTIQ) peoples, by creating the Gender Commission[9];
- acknowledgement of the experience of Afro-Colombians, and recognition of their identity as "peoples" and their civil and political rights (based on the International Labor Organization, in part), through the inclusion of the Ethnic Chapter in the Final Agreement and the establishment of the Ethnic Commission for Peace and Defence of Territorial Right[10]; and
- a recognition of the legitimacy of the demand for "truth," first and foremost, of the rights of those who have been wronged.

All authors speak authoritatively to aspects of the success of the Agreement and of its challenges, for example, calling it "a successful combination of incomplete justice but sustainable peace,[11] while continuing to ask about wider implications—in this case for the International Criminal Court (ICC).

Others are not parties nor participants—but have a deep interest in the process, the outcomes, and the long-term implications of the CPP and Final Agreement. As a result, although they may be slightly less directly involved in specific concerns and the vast array of details that surround them, they have an interest in delineating features of this changing landscape that hold promise for advancing peace.

In this vein, several noteworthy foundational shifts in the peace negotiating paradigm emerge from the accounts presented here the Colombian experience:

- inclusion requires more than bare equality;
- difference in the experience of the application of the law by social groups needs to be addressed; political rights in general need to be expanded in order to further democratic practice;
- punishment-based models demanding vengeance are unable to bring peace to all involved;
- forward-looking responses to ending conflict, to restoring peace and to

achieving social justice and harmony are needed for long-term change to occur; and

- acknowledgement that justice is only made possible by truth.[12]

There are many subtle and significant elements, and it is understood that each reader will draw conclusions and ask questions in their own context. However, for the long game of peace and justice and a sustainable world, the multiple cycles of social learning become crucial, and so it makes sense to recognize a number of key conditions:

- none of the successes would have happened without a leader who recognized the possibility of peace, and who was willing to risk failure and loss, to attempt to end the conflict and build peace.[13,14] the complexity of the situation, due in part to its long history of conflict, and to the intensity, in every moment of negotiation due to the fundamental need to keep the primary combatants at the table, created a limited field of vision - less obvious players, issues and parties had to wait for their opportunity to engage (e.g., women and LGBTIQ and the religious right)[15];
- the dissociation of constitutional development from contemporary Colombian constitutional law and practice was immediately necessary[16];
- a new imaginary is necessary - the old paradigms are empty shells and new relational arrangements, built on transitional justice, are necessary[17]; and in the creation of new options, whether creating territorial space, or designing strategic negotiations that set new patterns, there are logics that are useful but it is necessary to avoid being limited by old assumptions in order to build trust successfully, and to struggle cooperatively for peace.[18]

Visioning is a key component of reinvention of norms, institutions, and practices. For this to be successful, constraints must be minimized or eliminated, and sources of inspiration, courage, and creativity need to be encouraged and liberated. Not everyone will immediately be at ease with the ferment of ideas that is necessary, but social learning can help by positioning the new and untried imaginaries as subjects of inquiry and learning (rather than as terminal win/lose outcomes of conventional power struggles). By engaging with the unfamiliar, even in simulated contexts, people can begin to employ their own capacities for visioning, bringing their own dreams to the foreground. Equally important is the fundamental property of social capital—trust building—that is released. We saw good examples in the process of the early negotiations in Cuba. Now the challenge is to expand the trust building and visioning to all of Colombian society, and I would argue to the larger non-Colombian world as well.

Continuing challenges

These are not new. Elements of each appear in diverse accounts of the conflict and its origins, but they are important, and so, we take note of them here. There are three main points.

The first one is Economic Justice and Access to Employment and Livelihoods. There are continuing concerns about economic conditions and the transition required to provide access to lands and resources, particularly employment for youth. Experience points to a generational shift in the guerillas potentially favoring greed and the big money of the drug trade,[19] and a recent BBC production shows that for some 16-year-olds, although they want to participate in the formal economy, there are no jobs in the remote areas—only coca. There are other issues that stem from the lack of legitimate economic opportunities, particularly in borderlands and in the "Deep Colombia," notably the destructive illegal mining activities that interface with recognized corporate activities to bring their production to world markets. These small-scale miners destroy watersheds and fisheries resources in the process of alluvial mining (especially gold extraction using cyanide) and impact environmental potential, injure livelihoods, and impair sustainability. This challenge—legitimate and rewarding—livelihoods for youth, women, ethnically diverse groups, and demobilized FARC members—is recognized as a root cause of the 50 years of conflict. If this does not change, some see a serious risk of a return to the violence.[20]

The second is further development of democracy and diversification of recognition of peoples. The recognition, after some three years of negotiations, that distinctive groups of people who had been disproportionately impacted by the conflict, were not represented, and had no voice is telling. It speaks to the negotiation process as a learning process. While carefully designed (three days on and one day off, parties as equals and all to be respected, and so forth) and committed to inclusiveness, the absence of women, Indigenous Peoples, (particularly noteworthy in light of the parallel development of the United Nations Declaration on the Rights of Indigenous Peoples [UNDRIP] in other fora) and other subaltern and marginalized peoples at the outset indicates that power aligned with privilege remains a barrier to advancing conceptions of democracy beyond that of the status quo.

It is a tribute to the wisdom of those who were present at the initial rounds of negotiations, and to their capacity to enter into new relationships, and to build new paradigms, that the process evolved to include many of these distinctive voices, *including the adoption of the important innovation of the "differential approach" to justice.* This is a strong example of negotiations as fostering adaptive capacity through the process of social learning and trust building.

Further evidence of the capacity of the process itself and of the will to reach a Final Agreement is found in the inclusion of the Ethnic Chapter, and the mandated "Ethnic Commission for Peace and Territorial Rights."

Significantly, in systems terms, here we see that spaces have opened for a "differentiated approach,"[21] through creation of institutions such as the Ethnic Commission for Peace and Defence of Territorial Right. This is an extraordinary advance in thinking about equality, *inter alia.*

The role of the Truth Commission in cooperation with the National Space for Afro-Colombian Consultation, in consultation with Afro-Colombian Communities, established important guidelines for future interactions, including methodology of the ethnically differential approach against racism, racial discrimination, and related forms of intolerance; and the Protocol for relations with the authorities and victims belonging to Indigenous, Black, Afro-Colombian, Raizales, and Palenqueras communities, and Rom people for a three-year term.[22,23]

Finally, the third challenge concerns truth. We are left wondering—Does a term of three years allow enough time for the serious work of determinations of truth by the Truth Commission, given the lack of progress on questions of lands and resources in some areas, for example? The Final Agreement included an entire chapter dedicated to the creation of a Comprehensive System of Truth, Justice, Reparation and Non-Repetition. Learning from previous experiences, the system includes judicial and extrajudicial mechanisms to protect the right to the truth. Learning from the South African experience makes special criminal justice treatment conditional on the verified contribution to the clarification of the truth. The system also includes the creation of a Truth Commission that promotes the participation of marginalized minorities and peripheral regions usually neglected in the Colombian political arena. However, the Colombian Truth Commission has a challenge that other commissions did not face: The increasing emergence of mass media and fake news used to discredit its work and obscure the process of finding the truth. The truth has always been a site of contestation in conflicts generally, and Colombia is not an exception. In Chapter 11, we learn of the continuing attacks on truth, by the government in power:

> This government's desire to modify and control the historic reconstruction of the internal conflict is one of the biggest challenges of Final Agreement. Instead of creating a healthy distrust toward public institutions, this approach helps to consolidate institutions that have systematically violated human rights in Colombia, and silences extra-official voices and spaces required for the right to the truth be able to fulfil its purpose.

So, this development was one of the irritants in the conflict. And truth, about the conflict itself, may be among its greatest casualties, as official—and unofficial—voices mount a chorus of implausible denials and subterfuge. This concern is not restricted to Colombia, as we see in contemporary global news coverage of our "post-truth, fake-news world," as it is sometimes described.

Local peace, global peace

As the grief and death in the Mediterranean as refugees flee shocked the world, so the migrants fleeing drought in Honduras and violence in Guatemala and Mexico make clear, peace operates inside a complex interconnected world, and so I think of understanding and creating peace as innately requiring a complex systems approach. And so it is also in Colombia, further complicated by a 50-year long civil war and millions of affected people. The symptoms are also similar, in terms of outmigration, unequal economic development, and the influence of criminal activity on conflict and violence, and taking up space where civil society has left gaps.

In the detailed accounts in this volume, we have learned that the non-Colombian world impacted the CPP both positively and negatively, helping to create and sustain the conflict, and helping to support the building of sustainable approaches to peace. For example, Cuba hosted the negotiations, Norway, the USA, and Spain helped to advise and facilitate, international organizations played important roles, such as the International Red Cross in brokering FARC-EP participation, and the National University of Colombia was important for its role in identifying representatives of underrepresented groups. Some countries also assisted with funding for the CPP, and later for implementation: Canada, for example, has funded the process.[24] So, in a sense, the CPP and the Final Agreement can be thought of as international efforts. However, there are other sides to external influence, as well. We also heard concern expressed for the potential impacts of the Colombian Peace Agreement on the world, in part through impacts on international institutions, such as the ICC.[25]

Most importantly, we have seen former opponents learn to collaborate and to cooperate for the sake of mutual gain, for peace. And in this social learning, we find hope, because social learning empowers people to make change peaceably. While commentators typically note favorably that support of the international community was critical for the success of CPP, the internal community has seldom recognized the role international players have in the process. Many of the dynamics of Colombian conflict are partly derived from international actors: For example, a number of contributors have observed that Colombian drug and criminal policy is significantly influenced by the US "War on Drugs" and threats of extradition of Colombian nationals.

Distinctive to the CPP, supporting countries had clearly established roles, and they were fundamental at critical moments (e.g., the international community was critical for the release of Brigadier General, Rubén Darío Alzate, kidnapped by FARC, and which led to the only suspension in the complete negotiation).

However, in other cases, the relationship seems less direct. Consider, for example, the Canadian role in the Hidroituango Dam Case, in which national media in Canada questioned Canada's role in funding the

Hidroituango Dam, on grounds of violations of human rights, and environmental, and anti-corruption measures in a series of extensive reports in 2019, following a disastrous failure of the then underconstruction dam project.

Above ground, a Canadian NGO has documented Colombian perspectives, and expressed concerns about Canadian complicity in providing funding to a project with massive environmental consequences without any form of environmental review.

As Nolan writes, in the Globe and Mail,[26] an independent Colombian expert evaluated the failure of the project and the catastrophic release of water and found a litany of engineering design errors as well as evidence of construction malfeasance: Shoddy designs that were changed frequently, and failures to follow design and precautionary measures in building the project. Even though the report was commissioned by the Colombian authorities, they rejected the report and demanded changes. In the background are massive multinational corporate fraud issues.

The outcome: A botched construction process, people driven from their homes, and absolutely no benefits to Canada from this "tied-aid" contribution to an environmental and engineering disaster. The project is now subject to three investigations by the Attorney General in Colombia.

How does this relate to the Colombian Peace Agreement? The dam in question is located in Northern Antioquia, an area of contestation in the Conflict, and the dam project was opposed by guerrillas operating there, on the grounds of environmental destruction, and in opposition to the imperialism of capitalist development.

Further, there are serious allegations of mass graves in the area of the reservoir and the much larger region of impact, stemming from decades of murders of the "disappeared" prior to the construction.[27] Indigenous peoples have also experienced brutality, including assassinations here. And Canada was one of the funders.

In this way, we see another link between the Colombian Peace Agreement and the world—we are all connected and need to be mindful as to the nature of the connections made on our behalf by our governments. International development needs to assist peace, not generate conflicts.

There are reasons both for optimism and caution. Some reasons for optimism: We see openings filled with the promise of more "space"—democratic space—in economic, political, and social terms, for the participation of more peoples within Colombia.

The path to a durable peace may require us to consider emergent approaches in law, both as exemplified by the Final Agreement and others that are emerging elsewhere: specifically the thoughtful consideration of the role of complexity of social-cultural-ecological systems, the implementation of UNDRIP and indigenous rights within human rights doctrine and institutions, and the reframing of agency in ecocentric governance under new rules for peaceful co-existence that call on international actors, as well as the parties to the conflict, to respond ethically with responsible measures supportive of Colombian self-governance and of democratically driven peace.

However, there are also reasons for caution. Each generation must learn the value of resolving conflict, of making accommodations, and of adaptation to allow for the needs of others to be met for the sake of peace. Until the value of durable peace is taught to children everywhere, together with the skills and lessons of the negotiation table, and peace acquires a value privileging it over conflict, of course the risk of violence remains.

However, if fear is the real enemy of peace as some of us believe,[28] then peace values and negotiation skills alone will not be enough. To overcome fear, we need strong bonds of community, belonging, and care. A currency based on "remembering our humanity,"[29] and not on "disappearing" those with whom we have political disagreements; on love, and not hate; and on recognizing that we all want a living, sustainable, just, and peaceful world for our children, and that in order to have this, some important questions remain.

First, a question for the Colombian people and their political leaders—If justice is the price of peace, and the pursuit of political power is lethal to peace, what next steps in political development—in Colombia and internationally—could contribute to further development of a transitional justice architecture capable of bringing justice into the fundamental design of partisan government in order to further enable Colombian democracy?

In the first instance, the question above obviously relates directly to the CPP and to Colombia.

But—in the grand view—from the periphery of a world that still tolerates war—this question has meaning for those outside Colombia too.

The final question is for us all: *Do we have the resilience, adaptive capacity and goodwill necessary to teach our children, by our own examples, to accommodate others, and to envision and build a respectful civil society that privileges "future peace," at all levels of organization and enterprise?*

Clearly, in advancing the paradigm of social learning, the answers of the Colombian people have contributed to significant innovation, extending well beyond Colombia, in international peace building.

For future peace, in Colombia, and globally, we see that answers from the periphery can also impact prospects for peace across international borders. More importantly, we have learned from Colombia that with good will, and struggle, and learning, peace can become "a possibility."

Notes

1 See Chapter 11.
2 From Chapter 6.
3 Chapter 2.
4 As is noted in several places above, including the Introduction.
5 Chapter 11.
6 See Chapters 2 and 3.
7 Chapters 2, 5, and 6.

8 Chapter 14.
9 Chapter 13.
10 Chapter 14.
11 Chapter 6.
12 See Chapter 11.
13 See Chapter 2.
14 See Chapter 3.
15 See Chapter 13.
16 This point is made clear in the Chapters 2, 3, and 13.
17 As argued in Chapter 19.
18 As argued in Chapter 2.
19 Elster and many others have also made this point.
20 A connection here has been observed with security: Defectors from the peace process often lack formal economic opportunities, so they return to drug trafficking, illegal mining, and ordinary criminality, to earn their living. See also associations with land in Chapter 4.
21 See Chapter 14 of this volume: "In Colombia, the notion of a differentiated approach emanates from the principle of equality and non-discrimination. This notion recognizes that, even though individuals are equal under the law, the law can affect people differently depending on aspects such as class, gender, ethnic group, age, physical or mental health, and sexual orientation. In this sense, State authorities are thus required to adopt positive measures to render equality effective by taking into account such differences."
22 See Chapter 14.
23 As a result of that process of consultation, in December 2018, the National Space for Afro-Colombian Consultation and the Commission agreed on a methodology with an ethnic perspective, a protocol for the interaction between the authorities and victims, and mechanisms for participation throughout the Commission's three-year mandate. The Truth Commission is connected—through the Ethnic provisions—to land questions, although indirectly, and has much work to do.
24 https://www.international.gc.ca/gac-amc/publications/odaaa-lrmado/colombia-colombie.aspx?lang=eng Results around the world—Colombia.
25 See Chapter 5 of this volume: "The government must also satisfy its international constituents—namely the ICC and the Inter-American Human Rights Court—due to its legal obligations as signatories to the 2002 Rome Statutes and the 1979 American Convention on Human Rights."
26 Nolan Stephanie, "Despite warning signs, Canada's EDC helped build this Colombian dam. Then disaster struck," *The Globe & Mail*, Wednesday, July 3, 2019, pp. 8–9. *The Globe & Mail* is a prominent Canadian national newspaper.
27 This case is actually under investigation by JEP: "La JEP busca la verdad sobre desaparecidos en zona de Hidroituango," *Revista Semana,* October 8, 2019, https://www.semana.com/nacion/articulo/la-jep-busca-la-verdad-sobre-desaparecidos-en-zona-de-hidroituango/635170 Antioquia is a big region with more than 60,000 km^2, and not all the region has suffered from violence. Northern Antioquia was not only particularly violent but also was a space where the paramilitary violence was extremely violent.
28 Nancy Doubleday, "Canadian Peace Processes from the Inside Out: Making Peace from Below," Conference presentation. *Global Perspectives on Peace: The Colombian Peace Process with FARC: A Colombo-Canadian Dialogue*. McMaster University, May 9, 2017.
29 The Russell-Einstein Peace Manifesto, July 11, 1955. https://www.theguardian.com/world/2016/jul/11/russell-einstein-peace-manifesto-archive-1955

Index

Note: Page numbers in *italic* refer to Figures

FSC
www.fsc.org
MIX
Papier | Fördert gute Waldnutzung
FSC® C083411

Kolibri 360 GmbH
Ferdinand-Jühlke-Straße 7
99095 Erfurt, Deutschland
produktsicherheit@kolibri360.de